THE REAL T

EDDY HAMPTON ARMANI

BLAKE

First published in Great Britain in hardback by
Blake Publishing Ltd
3 Bramber Court
2 Bramber Road
London W14 9PB

A CIP catalogue for this book
is available from the British Library

ISBN 185782 183 1

Typeset in Great Britain by BCP

Printed and bound in Great Britain by
Creative Print and Design (Wales), Ebbw Vale, Gwent

The publishers wish to make clear that this book
is not authorised by Miss Turner.

Every effort has been made to contact the relevant
picture copyright holders, but some were unobtainable.
We would be grateful if the appropriate owners would contact us.

This book "I" dedicate to Pain

ACKNOWLEDGEMENTS

Thank God for dreams.

Tina, I thank you for you, your music and your friendship.
By the way, 'Love Has Everything To Do With It'. Love always, Ed.

Love is family, and mine started at home.
I can fly because of your endless, devoted support and guidance.
To my mother, Inez; my father (Morris Ray), my sister, Glenda; my brother, Robert;
my nieces (my girls), Brandy and Melissa (MISSY). Love, Eddy.

Maria Raymond, thank you for your help in putting this project together. I appreciate all you have done and thank you from the bottom of my heart. Love always, Eddy.

Cheyenne, thanks for sharing your mother with me. Love, Muther #2.
Nick Davies, a true English gentleman, you made this deal a reality. You took the time, I'm ever so thankful. Love, Eddy.
John Blake, for giving me this opportunity, I am truly grateful. Thank you, Eddy Armani.
Adam Parfitt, you are a special talent; you worked terribly hard; as a musician you kept us all on the beat. By the way, you give a good edit — thanks, mate. Eddy.
Sadie Mayne, I thank you for overseeing this project, your smile kept the production running smoothly.
David Blake, an executive player in the book game. Major thanks, Eddy Armani.
Blake team, I want to thank you all — Rosie, Graeme, Charly, Anne Marie and everybody at Blake. Love, Eddy (a.k.a. the Royal Pain).

I have been BLESSED with a special kind of Love. YOU: Linda Kraus, Beverly Dawson, Jeannie Cunningham, Allen Zentz, Mars Bonfire, Ed Saunders, Nic Cooper, Susi Landford, Baby Ella, Julie Pratt, Rupert Anderson, Maya Djajakusuma, Joe Simon, Marchella Mah, Jean Trimble, Duchess Edna Sims, Ann Thomas, Juanita and Vanessa Carter, Helena Springs, Sinitta, Marilyn, David Elliot, Kurt, Andreas, Sam, John, Roxy Moon, and Glen Powers; the boys in the band, Glen Matlock, James Stevenson, Dave McIntosh, James Hallawell, Gianni Luca, Dean Ross, Julian Standen, Andy Barnett, Andy Wright, Frank Ziener, Gary Barnacle, Kookie, John Sinfield, Jürgen Marcus, Steven Partridge, Ike Turner Jr., Steve Stein, Eric Robinson, Ray Low.

A C K N O W L E D G E M E N T S

London Christian Life Centre, a place of prayer and worship, Pastor Gerard and Sue Keehan, Pastor Steve and Karina, Maile, Rachel Wright, Robert and the family of worshippers, personally I want to thank you for your prayer, faith, guidance and loving support. CLC London is my Church home. I love you all. God Bless. Love, Eddy Armani.

LIFE IS DRAMA! I want to thank you for being a major part: Sheva Waite hair, London, Dr Mark Nourmand, Beverly Hills, Martin Greene Ravden, Accountants and Business Advisers, London, Stephen Daniel and Sunil Chopra, Julie Pratt, London, PA. Dr Russell Clayton LA, Barrie and Jenny Marshall, London, Clive Black, London, Far-Out Productions LA, Steve Gold, Marilyn Mikos, Dusty, Signe Johnson, WAR, Richard Aaron, Epic Records, Alley Cat, Hell Cat, and XL Rated music around the globe. London's under- and over-ground music scene — the clubs, the pubs and all the people who booked me, came to see me, and supported me throughout my musical career in Europe.
From the film *Bad Influence* — Lisa Beach, Steve Tish, Curtis Hanson, James Spader and Rob Lowe.
Ike Turner, the Turner boys, Ike Jr., Craig, Michael and Ronnie. Alline and the Bullock family. All the musicians who played with the Ike and Tina Turner Revue, Soko Richardson, Warren Dawson, Jean Brown, Claudia Lennear, Lejeune Richardson, Ester, Marcy Thomas, you know who you are. I thank you for bringing music to my ears.

Would one dare leave the stage without mention of your name? You would never forgive me. Chip and Kathy Lightman, Angela Barton, Elaine Swayenson, Marion Ramsey, Jenny Bellstar, Stephen Mar, Eric Mills, Nancy and Lee Chapman, Martin and Sue, Terry, Miss Anne (London), David Rogan, Fred Mays, Debbie and Adrian, Peter Kaye, Howard Rottenberg, Peter and Fiona, Steve Hinchfeld, David Worth, Jerome Turner, Rava Daley, Simon and Kate Edwards, Kookie and Linda Reiss family, Laura Sinfeild, Boy George, Kevin O'Dowd, Rudy Calivo, Jake Scott, Shane McRoe, Mark Armstrong, Patrick, Adam and Brooke, Tony Broccoli and Maggie Ryder.

Everyone connected in a family way, the Armanis, Baldwins, Foleys, Hamptons, Caldwells, Hughes, Sims, XOXO.

In my travels I've had the pleasure of meeting my idols, incredible talents, stars who will forever shine bright in my eyes: Shirley Bassey, David Bowie, Iman, Mick Jagger, Keith Richards and the rest of the Rolling Stones, Rod Stewart, Chaka Khan, Diana Ross, Bryan Adams, Steve Forbet, Bob Dylan, Bette Midler, Cher, Eric Clapton, Elton John, Joan Collins, Patti LaBelle, Ann Margret, Martha Reeves, Tom Jones, Tracy Chapman, Vitas Gerulaitis, Björn Borg, Gladys Knight, Naomi Campbell, Rudolf Nureyev.

In loving memory GUARD ME ANGELS, Mommie, Aunt Hattie, Pee Wee, Aunt Pearl, Kenny Moore, Steven Partridge, Kevin Hamilton, Lester Wilson, Roland Lewis, Curtis, Tom Thurston, Niles Gaye, we will meet again.

PROLOGUE

The light from Tina's bedroom spilled through the vast sliding glass doors, shedding a bold beam on to the garden of her dream home. She paused for a moment, enjoying the stunning moonlit view of the tree-filled terra cotta pot garden in bloom. Satisfied, she took a few deep breaths and composed herself before rejoining Bernadette, Lejeune and me in her dressing area

Tina glared disapprovingly at Bernadette, the gorgeous mixed race girl she had always wished was her own daughter, chastising her with her angry eyes as she repositioned herself in front of her large make-up mirror.

Tina was fed up with Bernadette, and made no effort to hide her disappointment while making her feelings clear to the girl who was once her son's fiancée. To make her point, Tina lifted her index finger and wagged it furiously, her trademark red nails glistening as she spoke.

'Bernadette, I don't know why you keep messing with these guys. And after all the things you've seen and all the things I've told you.'

Lejeune and I continued with the two-day job of reweaving human hair into Tina's newly prepared braids. As soon as we saw Tina wag her finger, we knew she meant business and knew to stay silent. Bernadette quietly wept and mopped the tears from the corners of her eyes while Tina delivered a stern lecture.

'So why did you bother with him in the first place? Because he's Michael Jackson's brother? That doesn't mean anything. That Randy Jackson's no good. He's like any other man getting their kicks scaring their women. And you put up with him running his mouth all over town saying you and me are lesbian lovers. Who does he think he is?'

Although furious, Tina remained in total control, moving only her eyes and lips while Lejeune tightened the edges of the basket weave braids which would leave her scalp aching for days. Tina's hand reached for a glass of white wine. She took a large sip and pursed her angry lips. 'And you gave him my phone number and address ... How *dare* he keep pressing my intercom. If he presses that intercom one more time, I'll call the police. He better get off my property.'

She rolled her eyes in despair. No one ever showed up uninvited. Tina had gone through the ritual of informing everyone we were going out of town so we could be left in peace while reweaving her hair. But with Bernadette showing up unannounced, followed by lovesick calls from Randy Jackson before his uninvited arrival, Tina's house suddenly seemed as busy as a bus terminal. And it had really thrown her off balance.

I left the dressing area, passed through the large opened partition and walked across Tina's bedroom to the adjoining bathroom to check on the hair I had just coloured and washed. Alone, I listened to Tina as she continued delivering the motherly lecture to Bernadette, nodding my head in agreement.

'Bernadette, let me tell you something ... you've got yourself an Ike Turner there. You'd better get rid of him. I know you're scared. Aaagh.' Tina threw her hands up in disgust. 'I know what it's like, Bernadette. It's best you stay here tonight. Just make sure you get rid of that Randy Jackson first thing tomorrow.'

But no sooner had Tina spoken, than the noisy shuffling of footsteps could be heard outside. I paused and watched her from across the bedroom. The worry on her face was unmistakable. Bernadette had already scared the daylights out of us with horrifying stories of Randy's violence. Lejeune and Tina remained still and silent as the intrusive sounds outside continued. There was a momentary eeriness, and then, without warning, one of Tina's huge, treasured terra cotta pots burst through the glass doors, exploding on impact.

Shards of razor-sharp glass sprayed like darts throughout the bedroom. There was soil and terra cotta everywhere.

Everything else that followed seemed to happen so quickly.

Randy Jackson leapt through the broken window and paused for a moment, breathing and sweating heavily. Then, as he moved, glass fragments on Tina's plush cream carpet could be heard crunching beneath his hard, determined steps. He seemed possessed and his wild eyes rapidly scanned the bedroom. It only took a split second to focus on what he had come for. Like an animal stalking prey, he walked towards Bernadette, muttering like a crazy man about how much he loved and needed her.

In all the years I had spent with Tina, she had drilled me over and over on certain safety procedures should an intruder gain entry into her home. We had always thought if it happened, it would be her ex-husband Ike. On this particular day, we were wrong. Worse still, everyone froze in shock, forgetting Tina's meticulous safety drill.

The only one to spring into action was Tina herself.

She calmly and purposefully walked into the bedroom, where her eyes immediately darted to the framed pictures on her bedside table where she hid her loaded handgun. Without looking away from the table, her hand whipped out with shocking speed and grabbed a second gun — a shotgun —

from behind the freestanding oval antique mirror just next to her. She cocked the weapon, then turned and aimed the loaded barrel at Randy Jackson's head. Her body stiff and her aim steady, she said with true determination, 'Freeze, or I'll blow your brains out.'

Randy did stop, but only for a split second. Locking eyes with Tina, he ignored her warning and lunged for Bernadette.

Tina, still several feet away from Randy, raised the gun and blew a hole in her own ceiling. Randy, his face a mask of brutality, charged straight at Tina like a raging bull.

Still in total control, Tina moved the barrel slightly to the side and fired towards the doorway. She pointed the gun at Randy.

Randy, suddenly terrified, leapt through the broken window, fleeing for his life.

There was a silence as we all stood, shocked by the scene we had just witnessed. Then Bernadette snapped out of her trance and raced in hot pursuit of her lover. Tina, Lejeune and I stood in stark amazement listening to the voices in the distance. Bernadette's voice was breathless and tearful as she professed her love and loyalty to Randy. Only then did Tina's body start shaking, and although in shock, she had the presence of mind to press the panic button beside her bed. Like a robot, I handed Tina a white towel which she numbly wrapped around her half-finished head of hair. Lejeune, whom I had rarely seen touch any form of alcohol over the many years I had known her, uncharacteristically swigged straight from the bottle of wine.

Over the next few minutes, none of our eyes met. We couldn't believe what had just happened. Like zombies, we stepped over the debris of the elegant bedroom which now looked as if a bomb had hit it.

Barely able to breathe, we all sat on the bed, completely stunned. It wasn't until we heard the police sirens in the distance that we snapped back to reality. Tina, still slightly dazed, nervously ran her sweating palms down her thighs, smoothing the fabric of her designer knit sweat suit. She glanced at herself in the mirror and took several deep breaths, calming herself.

Then she held her head high and adjusted the towel tightly wrapped over her hair in readiness to deal with the uniformed officers.

I couldn't help but think that when I prayed Tina Turner into my life as my best friend, I had no idea it would be like this ...

1

often recall with fondness the first time I saw Tina. It was the summer of '64, a warm, sunny day at the house of my cousin Vanessa, in Seattle, Washington. Vanessa and I had four things in common: we were both eight years old, we had a younger brother and sister each, we lived a few doors apart and we both loved rock 'n' roll.

We lived in a low rent community called the 'Projects', and we would turn her garden into a musical showcase. We passed our spare time by singing and dancing for hours on end with only the surrounding flowers and greenery as our audience.

On this hot summer day, Vanessa dragged me into her house by my shirtsleeve and while breathlessly tugging me along the corridor, she said, 'Eddy, hurry, that Wild Woman I told you about, she's on the TV!'

I could hear this powerful voice booming from the television, and the hallway was filled with a foot-stomping rhythm. My little heart started racing and I was suddenly desperate to see who owned this astonishing voice.

I stood at the doorway of the living room, my eyes glued to the television, watching dumbfounded as this beautiful lady with the biggest vocal chords on earth screamed her way into my life.

Her fingers were wrapped tightly around the microphone, and her lips seemed almost to snarl. At the time, the biggest compliment we could pay somebody was to call them a 'low down, dirty dog'. And this was the most low down, dirty thing I'd *ever* seen. Her legs shook, her hair swung ... her whole body gyrated!

And behind her, this raw, powerful band led by a sharp little guy on guitar; and three backing singers mesmerising the audience with their skimpy costumes and hot steps.

The camera panned in on her face and her deep, dark eyes stared straight into the camera lens, and I felt she was staring straight at me! Then she abandoned the mike and leapt into a frenzied dance routine.

I barely heard my cousin Vanessa whisper, 'Well ... do you like her?'

I couldn't take my eyes off the television. I had to know who the Wild

Woman was. Dick Clark, the host of the chart show *American Bandstand* announced, 'That was Ike and Tina Turner performing their new song, "I Can't Believe What You Say".'

As an eight-year-old, I thought Ikantina was one word. And I thought her surname was Turner. I was mesmerised by this vibrant woman with the funny name Ikantina Turner.

Those words echoed over and over in my mind: Ikantina Turner ... Ikantina Turner. And from that moment on, she became an integral part of my daily life.

When my mother arrived home that night, I told her about this amazing woman called Ikantina Turner. My mother was astonished, as well as concerned — I suppose because I was suddenly into an act that was so sexy, and not really meant for eight-year-olds! But she did correct my mistake and explained that the wild singer's name was Tina Turner and Ike was her husband.

For the next four months leading up to Christmas, I drove my mother crazy. I asked several times a day for Ike and Tina records and a record player. She would return home exhausted each evening after standing eight hours on her feet and I would further wear her out with Ike and Tina.

I worked my butt off for that Christmas present.

It's not that I carried on any differently. It was the same routine but I would always try to do something extra that wasn't expected of me. I would wake up every morning, get my little brother and sister dressed, make their breakfasts, then I would drop my brother at the baby-sitter and walk with my sister and my cousins to school. After school, I'd collect the younger two, take them home, prepare sandwiches for them and make them change into play clothes. I'd send them to the back yard to play, then go through a list of daily chores that my mother would leave out — all of which had to be completed by the time she got home. After dinner, while my mother put the younger kids to bed, I'd stay up clearing away the dinner table.

I knew that asking for a record player was asking for a lot. My mother was the only provider, working day and night as a registered nurse since my dad had left us years before. I took the role as the man of the house, and although I was close to my mother, my sister and I always called her by her first name, Inez, and some people found it a bit over-familiar. I didn't bother my mother, because she knew I always respected her. I took my duties seriously and felt proud that I was of some help to my overburdened mother who vigilantly kept us warm and fed.

I had never let my mother down and, although she was a strict, no-nonsense woman, I was certain my Christmas dreams would come true that year.

Early December I reorganised all the closets in the house. When I cleaned out my mother's huge closet, I found a hoard of toys, obviously for Christmas. There was no sign of a record player.

Later that evening while slicing potatoes, I asked my mother if I was good enough.

'Good enough for what?' she asked.

I told her I feared I wouldn't get my Christmas wish.

She exploded. 'What's wrong with you boy? If you talk about that Ike and Tina one more time, you definitely won't be getting anything for Christmas. You're starting to wear it out, and me with it!'

I knew at that point not to mention Ike and Tina to my mother again. I drove the rest of my family crazy instead. On Christmas day my brother, sister and I raced to the tree at 5 a.m., tearing through all the presents. I picked through my gifts, tossing them to the side in search of a heavy box. There was nothing. My mother came down the hallway to the living room and I gazed at her through a haze of tears, whimpering, 'Mom ... there's no record player.'

A sweet smile crept over her face and she stepped past me, gently pushing the Christmas tree to the side. There it was — a box with a big bow on it. My mom's eyes sparkled as she whispered, 'Merry Christmas, darling. You have been the best boy in the world. This is for you.'

I was so overwhelmed with emotion that I couldn't get the bow off the box. My mother, understanding, carried out the task for me. I had been searching for a huge box, thinking record players were big things. But this was small and beautiful, very compact with a bright red lid on it. I undid the latch on both sides and lifted the lid to see a 45 rpm Ike and Tina Turner record nestled in its rightful place.

Over the following two years I scoured record shops twice a week asking if there were any new Ike and Tina releases and if I couldn't afford a record, I would stay in the shop asking the assistant to play new tunes over and over again. I grew up attending church every Sunday, always singing in the choir. Once I had my record player, my vocal style took on a new twist. I belted out hymns like Tina Turner, letting out a raspy scream in the middle of a traditional holy song. The priest and flock didn't know what to do with me.

Every day, after school, I danced in front of the mirror like Tina, then, thirty minutes before my mother was due home, I'd sling the house into order. I'd hurriedly sit at the table with homework spread everywhere as if I'd been at it for hours but, naturally, my grades started slipping which resulted in Ike and Tina Turner being relegated to the deep recesses of my mother's closet. I felt like my life and light had been taken away. I couldn't eat, sleep or think straight but my stern mother wouldn't give in.

I finally resorted to deception. I found a way to reach the high, deep area in the closet where the record player was hidden and religiously played Tina songs until thirty minutes before my mother was due home. But this time round I was wise enough to keep my grades up and every night I said my prayers, begging forgiveness for deceiving my mother, and always finishing with a special wish: I begged the Lord to make Tina Turner my best friend.

When I was ten, my little sister was sent off to spend the summer with our father. My brother was still being sent to a baby-sitter, leaving me free to attend summer camp, a popular American ritual where parents unload their children during the long summer break. I went to Mount Ranier, one of the most beautiful areas of Seattle. There, youngsters learned to survive in the wild, living in tents, bathing in rivers and cooking over open fires. We would end the evenings with a sing along, using pots and pans to make music and rhythm.

Everyone was into James Brown at the time and they would always ask me to sing a tune. I'd start off with a James Brown number which would inevitably turn into an Ike and Tina tune by the end of the song. My camping mates and I entered a local talent contest as Eddy and his Third Beach Rhythm Band — why we called ourselves that I'll never know. My rhythm section sat on the floor with pots and pans between their knees, two guys sang backing vocals and I sang lead. I held the microphone, which had a very short lead, and belted out a tune we wrote called 'Sambo'. I presented it like a cross between James Brown and Tina Turner, dancing so wildly that I snapped the microphone cord in half — but even so, broken microphone and all, we won the contest and the audience roared with approval. Feeling that thunder of applause and the smiles on people's faces, that feeling rushing through my body made me realise that music was the life for me.

I had stars in my eyes as I returned home from camp. But I was returning to the biggest blow of my life: my mother was getting married and we were moving to Los Angeles, California. I wasn't ready for that change, and had no desire to leave my settled Seattle life.

Still, there was nothing I could do to change my mother's mind — she wasn't prepared to split up the family and leave me with my aunt or my grandmother — so I consoled myself with one thought: at least in California, I stood a good chance of meeting Tina Turner.

My new stepfather, Morris Ray Caldwell, was the wealthy owner of a trucking company. Although I had little in common with him, he was a kind, good man to all of us. My mother no longer needed to work and we had a maid which resulted in me, not yet eleven years old, being made redundant. I was no longer needed for daily chores, baby-sitting or cooking. I was put into very early retirement and felt I didn't fit in any more.

My mother had always related to me as a person with responsibilities and when that went I felt as though something had been lost. My brother and sister, both younger than me, had a chance to develop a proper parent–child relationship with my mother. My time had passed.

We settled in a wealthy area in LA, populated by well-to-do black families. We lived in a mini-mansion with all the trappings, and I was pleased my mother didn't have to work any more. There was only one drawback. I had never been to a black school before and I didn't make friends easily. The black kids couldn't stand me because I was well-spoken. Back in Seattle, nearly all the students at my school were white, and so were most of my neighbours. Consequently, I didn't grow up speaking heavy street lingo. If I ever used any black slang as a child, my mother would react as if I had just cursed. The black guys in my LA school were not amused and beat me up at least once a week.

Without friends and with nothing to do, I further projected my thoughts on Ike and Tina Turner. Being an ardent fan gave me sense of purpose. Once, I even thought I could hail an LA cab and ask the driver to take me to Tina's house. Of course, life doesn't work that way. But I wasn't to be put off easily. I found the local record shop and now, with plenty of money to spend, I snapped up everything by Ike and Tina, parting with one US dollar for each single.

My bedroom walls were covered in pictures of Ike and Tina that I vigilantly cut out from newspapers and magazines. I had to use the ceiling because I ran out of space on my walls.

One day I lay back in bed reading the cover of the latest recording I had bought and noticed an address for Bolic Sound Recording Studios, 1310 N. La Brea, Inglewood, California. Inglewood was an area where affluent black people lived, not far from my home. I wondered if the studio could help me find Tina. I called information for the number and froze in amazement when they gave it to me. That day I rang the studio number several times, putting the phone down each time it was answered. I didn't know what to say. Finally, sweating with nerves, I dialled and asked for Tina Turner.

'Sorry, Tina isn't in right now. Can I take a message?'

I didn't leave a message, but said I would call back. And I did for two solid weeks.

The patient lady who answered the phone clearly wanting to know the nature of my call, enquired as to why I was ringing so often. I was too shy to reply but continued phoning for a further two weeks. Finally the lady introduced herself as Linda Kraus, Ike and Tina's secretary. I told her I was Ike and Tina's biggest fan and I was 12 years old.

Linda Kraus and I developed a wonderful phone relationship over the following few months.

Sometimes I would hear a voice in the background bark out, 'Just put the phone down on him!'

'Call me back tomorrow!' she would whisper. And, of course, I would.

Before I had even met Tina, I knew everything about her thanks to my new phone friend Linda.

Just before my 13th birthday, my mother took my sister and me to a swish department store in Inglewood, to kit us out in new school gear. I was on my knees tugging at a pair of Levis on a bottom shelf when I heard a voice I knew so well.

I forgot about the jeans and peered over the top of the display to see Tina Turner. She was nattering away to a stunning mixed-race woman who, as gorgeous as she was, couldn't make me tear my eyes off Tina. She was a knockout. She wore a black 'apple cap' — a New York cabby's style hat which was trendy in the sixties, and the very one that she wore on the cover of her album *'Nuff Said.*

I studied her every movement. She seemed to me to be an impatient woman that day. Her natural, unpainted lips quivered before she snapped at her friend, 'No, no, Mez. That isn't Craig's size. Look at the list!'

I got off the floor, my knees unsteady, took one step forward and gushed, 'My God, you're Tina Turner!'

'No I'm not,' Tina replied firmly, before abruptly turning her back on me. I stood mesmerised as she announced, 'Come on, Mez. Put that thing down. Uh-uh, you *know* Craig's bigger than that shirt!

'I know you're Tina Turner,' I squealed. 'I know your voice. It's you!'

Tina glared at me, lifted her index finger, and shook it menacingly. 'Now look little boy, if you don't leave me alone, I'll call security.'

I didn't care. I ran and grabbed my sister, dragging her to where Tina stood. Before dropping the garments in her hands, Tina turned to see me gaining on her. The look on her face was unmistakable, saying, as clear as words, 'Oh no, he's bringing another little pest.' Tina grabbed her friend by the arm and bolted for the exit. I ran after her, dragging my sister along, telling her, 'Tina's got a white Jaguar. Her secretary told me that Sammy Davis Jr. gave it to her.'

Sure enough, Tina did climb into a white Jaguar, and as the car pulled away, she craned her head, shooting a final look of annoyance my way.

I had to wait another year to see Tina again. I would still phone Linda Kraus, sometimes twice a day.

And then, one day, Linda said something which would affect my life forever.

Her words were simple and clear. 'Eddy, I have a surprise for you. You can meet Tina very soon if you wish.'

I was numb. How I took in the remainder of the conversation I still can't remember. Linda explained that Ike Turner owned Bolic Sound Recording Studios and, although it had been up and running for over a year, he was having an official grand opening which would be attended by the media and press. She said, 'You're the only child fan we know of. I thought it would be a nice idea to invite you. It's under one very strict condition. Tina said she'll trust my judgement, but made it clear that you better not bug her or get in the way.'

My stepdad bought me new clothes and shoes for the event. I got my little afro hairstyle trimmed and barely slept a wink during the week leading up to the big evening. My mother made me go to school that day, and it was the longest school day of my life. I didn't hear a single lesson — my eyes were fixed on the large clock, begging the minutes to pass.

My mother and my aunt Pearl drove me to Bolic Studio that evening, and when I spotted the studio I nearly leapt out of the moving car, resulting in a firm ticking off from my mother. My Aunt Pearl, who had a mouth like a sailor, said, 'Boy, if you don't sit yo' ass still ...' She took a long drag on her cigarette and slowly rolled her eyes. I was so impatient that everything seemed to take forever. My mother didn't move any faster or slower than she normally did, but I felt as if she took her sweet time getting out of the driving seat. It was pure torture for me. I just wanted to get in there to meet Tina.

As we walked to the entrance, I could see steel letters and digits, '1310 La Brea'. I couldn't believe it. We were really there! We pushed the heavy, unlocked wooden doors open and entered a party in full swing.

All the guests were dressed beautifully, each and every one of them looking more glamorous than anything I'd ever seen in my thirteen years. Cameras flashed constantly and the champagne was flowing like water. We were greeted by Linda Kraus who assured my mother I would be well looked after.

This was the first time I had met Linda, whom I had known for the past year only as a friendly voice on the phone. She was Canadian with the whitest teeth I had ever seen and had a full head of blazing red hair. I had never seen a person with that colour hair before and I found her totally fascinating. Her beautiful face fit her personality perfectly, and although she was much taller than I imagined, I felt I already knew her.

My mother glanced at her watch. It was 6 p.m. Linda promised to get me home at a reasonable hour. As for me, well, I was wearing a huge, silly grin across my face; my eyes wandered everywhere, and everything seemed larger than life.

To my immediate left was a large office. It was Ike Turner's private office, lavishly decorated like something out of Caesar's Palace. At the time, I thought Ike's office was elegant and grand. In reality it was downright tacky.

My eyes eagerly scanned the crowd for Tina. I searched for her through a forest of legs, champagne glasses, glittering jewels, cigarettes and well dressed bodies. But there was no sign of her.

I grabbed Linda's hand and asked if Tina arrived yet. She pointed down a long, arched corridor, and told me I could find Tina in one of the recording studios at the end. Then she gave me a look of encouragement as I wandered along the hallway.

I made slow progress, pausing every now and then to muster up some courage.

I stopped in front of a panelled wall decorated with a large clock. It would be nearly a year before I discovered that it was a secret entrance to a flight of stairs leading to Ike's private apartment, one of the numerous harem 'get laid rooms' he enjoyed so much. I quickened my pace until I came upon the room I was looking for.

Pausing just outside the door, I could hear a song featuring Tina that I hadn't yet heard on the radio. I shyly entered and when I looked up, there she was — Tina Turner. She was sitting behind a control desk listening to the new song, and I walked slowly around the small studio, patiently waiting for the right opportunity to approach her, and I wished everyone would move out of the way so that I could walk up to her. I knew she had already spotted me, but she made every effort to pretend she hadn't — I was afraid she recognised me from the last time — so I marched straight up to Tina, blurting out 'Hi Tina, I'm Eddy. I'm your biggest fan ... and ... I love you so much.'

Dazzled by her presence, I stared at every eyelash and every single strand of hair on her head. I studied her beautiful red lips, her long nails, the ring on her little finger and her diamonds. She shifted position and I noticed how easily her body moved under her long black crepe evening dress. I sighed and thought, 'So, this is what it's like to be in love.'

Tina smiled sweetly and she forced a laugh. 'Oh, my biggest fan! That's nice.'

I immediately launched into a detailed description of how I owned every single one of her recordings, how I'd kept everything ever published about her, and how I'd squeezed myself to the front of the stage at a few of her live performances. I waffled on about how much I liked her new dance routines, her inventive costumes and her trendy make-up. Tina fluttered her eyelashes in amazement. While she made every effort to be polite, I could sense she was uncomfortable with me, this over-excited, talking-a-mile-a-minute kid. I felt sorry for her. She suddenly looked like a woman who needed rescuing.

When I finally paused for a quick intake of breath, Tina seized the opportunity to end the conversation. 'Well, it's so nice to meet you,' she said. 'I've heard so much about you. I'm glad you're a fan. Now you run along and have a wonderful time. Enjoy the party, OK?'

I was glued to the spot.

After a brief, uncomfortable silence I could see that if I wasn't going to hit the road, Tina would — and so she did, by politely excusing herself.

I guess Tina didn't realise that I knew her inside out. I knew what her favourite colour was, the way she walked and talked; I knew her hand gestures and her body language; I knew her mother's name, her sister's name; I even knew what food she liked. I knew everything about her, right down to her bedtime rituals.

I ran down the corridor to the main party and started networking. I introduced myself to the Ikettes, Tina's beautiful backing singers, and I felt a sense of pride when they said that they knew who I was. They had noticed me pressed against the front of the stage during a few of their performances. One dancer said, 'Honey, we couldn't help but notice you. We don't normally see kids in the audience.'

I guess I did stand out from the adult crowd.

As the crowd started thinning out I followed the remaining revellers into Ike's office. I moved near Tina and heard her introducing her friend Ann as her sister. But she wasn't her sister. I knew from Linda Kraus and from magazine articles that Tina only had one sister, called Alline. I watched Tina and Ann carry on like schoolgirls, giggling and exchanging knowing looks with each other, and I recognised her as the beautiful woman from the department store a year earlier. But I couldn't understand why Tina introduced Ann as her sister. They looked like sisters, but I knew they weren't.

At that moment, a beautiful black woman in a china cut wig approached me. She seemed curious about my knowledge of Ike and Tina. We got along brilliantly and she immediately treated me as an equal. Her name was Beverly Dawson, and she was the wife of Ike's bass player Warren.

I knew I would be able to learn more about Tina through Beverly. I played naïve and said, 'Isn't Tina's sister Ann beautiful?'

Beverly rolled her eyes and leaned in to whisper. 'That's *not* Tina's sister, honey. Tina's sister ain't here. No, dear. That woman there is Ann Thomas. Ann is Ike's mistress. 'Course, Tina knows about it ... everyone knows but it is not discussed.'

There was no stopping Beverly, as she gave me all the dirt on who was sleeping with who. Beverly, bless her, loved to gossip. I realised straight away that if I wanted to know anything, I'd only have to ask a musician's wife.

Soon, everyone was approaching me and I absorbed every bit of information humanly possible. But as the evening wore on, I noticed a woman glaring at me from across the room. I learned it was Rhonda Graam, Ike and Tina's road manager. She was very young but wore a hard, bitter look on her face, like a young, angry school mistress. Being white, she stood out in the crowd, and she prowled around like a cat. She leered at me distrustfully. Even though I was only a young teenager, she seemed to think I was a threat.

But the evening was over. Ike and Tina made their way to the foyer to say goodnight to their guests as Linda arranged for a car to take me home. I stood patiently waiting to thank the host and hostess for the wonderful evening. Just as I was about to speak to them, a member of the press raced over and asked if I was Ike and Tina's son. Tina laughed and explained that I was not her son, but certainly I was their biggest fan.

Ike turned to the journalist and said, 'Ah gotta job fo' this kid. Seein' how he's our biggest fan, he can sort out our big stack of fan mail.'

'I'll start a fan club for you! Yes! You need a fan club!' I squealed.

'Good thinkin', kid,' said Ike. 'You can start Monday right after school.' Ike and Tina laughed with the journalist while I was escorted to the car by Linda.

I was dazed. I was going to work for Ike and Tina Turner and I was only thirteen years old! I phoned on Monday to see what time I should start work. Linda replied, '*Work*? Uh, Eddy, I'd better phone you back.'

Linda discussed it with Ike, who barked, 'It was a joke, man. Did you see the way that kid gawked at Ann all night? Ann would be uncomfortable with that kid hangin' round. *Shit*! That kid'll drive us crazy. Hell, no.'

Ike always referred to Tina by her real name, Anna Mae — Ann for short

—except when in the presence of the press or business people. Only then would he refer to his wife as Tina. But I wasn't taking no for an answer. I had already told everybody that I was going to work for Ike and Tina. It was my dream come true, and no one was going to take it away from me.

I asked Linda to point out to Ike that not a single letter that I had sent in four years had been replied to. All that mail tossed to one side. That's not right! Ike was unfazed. And so I spent a further year bombarding Bolic Sound Recording Studios with calls, pontificating about how much they needed a fan club. Ike would often have messages relayed back to me, one of which I'll never forget: 'Tell that kid that if he don't stop pesterin' me, I'll sew his damn lips closed.' Finally I sent a letter to Ike. I waited four days then asked Linda to ask Ike to reply, please, to my letter.

I could hear Ike in the background. 'What fuckin' letter? I ain't got no letter from that little fucka.'

I asked Linda to let Ike know he had just proven my point. 'Please tell Ike I sent him a letter. He just never got it. Point out to him that there could be many pieces of important personal post lying unopened.'

Ike caved in. He told Linda I could come in once every two weeks, but the cost of the fan club would have to come out of my own pocket. Ike hired me by saying, 'I ain't payin' fo' shit. I ain't payin' you neither. And stay outa' me and Ann's way.'

On my first day, Linda laid down the rules as spoken by the man himself:

1) I was Linda's responsibility;
2) I wasn't to approach Ike or Tina at any time;
3) I was not to strike up conversation with Ike or Tina, even to say good morning, unless Ike or Tina spoke to me first.

I heard out the rules and thought, 'No problem.' A corner of the secretarial office was allocated to me. It was a room immediately to the right of the entrance of the studios with a large window separating the small pool of secretaries from the foyer. I was given a license to go through everything: files, photographs — the lot. There was so much work to do that I showed up ready and willing once every two weeks, and remained as busy as a bee and perfectly obedient. Everyone seemed comfortable and let me get on with my ideas.

I found loads of interesting photographs of Ike and Tina that fans had never seen. I carefully chose a few pictures and had them reproduced in huge quantities to send out with the newsletters. Since my mother remarried, I had a weekly allowance which I put to good use. I had a logo professionally designed for the fan club and ordered special, high-quality tinted stationery on which the logo was printed. My name was in pride of place on the letterhead as President of the Ike and Tina Turner Fan Club.

The secretaries had sanctioned everything by confirming my position to the necessary companies, but I'm sure they had no idea how much I was actually spending, far more than my allowance. When the letterhead, the stationery and the huge batch of reproduced photos arrived, it came with a whacking great invoice for a couple of hundred dollars.

Ike hit the roof. He looked as if he was about to explode as he stuttered, 'Who the fuck ordered this shit?'

The secretaries buried their heads and typed for their lives. All equally horrified by the invoice, none dared look up. An amused in-house accountant calmly wrote out a check for Ike to sign and stuck it under his nose. As Ike scribbled his signature in the appropriate place, he grumbled, 'Muthafucka. I knew I shouldn't have let him in here.'

I reached into my pocket, pulling out nearly $20 of my pocket money and I offered it to Ike to put towards the bill. Ike stared at the notes and coins in bewilderment. 'Keep yo fuckin' money, boy,' he barked, and breathing heavily in my face, carefully stared at me for what seemed an eternity. Little beads of perspiration formed above his brows as he squinted one eye, glaring at me as if I was some kind of devil. Then without saying another word, he stormed off to the refuge of his own personal studio.

I was still too naïve to be frightened of Ike. He had mistaken my naïvety for balls of steel. My youthful innocence had saved my neck as well as my job. Over the following months, I would witness first hand exactly how dangerous a man Ike Turner really was.

2

ke Turner, actual name Izear Luster Turner, was born November 15, 1931 in Clarksdale, Mississippi. His father was a preacher and his mother a seamstress. Ike was the baby of the family with one sister ten years his senior.

Although he was still young enough to be in his mother's arms, Ike never forgot the terrifying day when his father was attacked by a gang of white men. The front door of the family home was forced open and a group of thugs beat his father so badly, it led to his slow, agonising death.

'Mama was tryin' to hold on to daddy and me an' they pushed her to the floor,' Ike recalled. 'It was a long way for a kid to fall, ya know? Daddy had holes in his stomach. They kicked holes in his stomach. The white hospital wouldn't take daddy so the health service set up a little tent outside our house. Daddy died there.'

The fatal beating of Reverend Turner was a revenge attack. The preacher stood accused of having a fling with a white woman, a crime unheard of and unacceptable in 1930s America. Whether it greatly influenced the road to fame and fortune for the Reverend's son is something only Ike would know for certain. But soon, no one would dare think of kicking Ike Turner's ass.

At the age of six, Ike would chop wood for an old lady next door in exchange for the use of her piano. His mother finally bought him a piano of his own, on which he developed remarkable musical skills, skills equalled only by his astounding streak for survival.

Ike Turner knew how to hustle a dollar. His home town was segregated, the blacks warned strictly to stay on the East side of the track. If a white person chose to walk through the black area, the blacks were warned always to look to the ground and never stare at a white person. Being restricted in territory didn't stop Ike from earning a living, however, and while still a boy, he hustled coins by leading a blind man around town. When he found that the blind man's wife played guitar, he enticed her to teach him.

Ike was influenced by the blues, which was the style popular in his segregated area. He was also influenced by the style of music broadcast over the wireless at the time, good old country, foot-thumping classics.

Blues was formed by using a basic set pattern of harmonies. Simple but strict, three lines of poetry would be set to twelve bars of music, over which the performer could set his own variations.

Country music was sung in a southern accent, emphasising the hillbilly twang, utilising foot-stomping instruments like banjos and fiddles.

Ike would sneak out of his home at night to peek in on local jam sessions, then when his mother enquired as to his musical progress, he would knock out bits of a tune he had picked up from the session the night before. Mother, not realising where he was collecting his skills, was more than pleased with her darling son's progress.

Ike always had to take things a step further. He had a keen ear and started experimenting with cocktails of music, mixing blues with country, resulting in a fascinating new sound. He wasn't even nine at the time. By the age of ten Ike was spinning discs at the local radio station during the DJ's break. In time, Ike would have his own show at the very same radio station.

At the age of 17, Ike joined a swing band, playing for anyone who would have them, and a year later, Ike and six friends formed their own band calling themselves The Kings of Rhythm, who started gigging regularly for the next three years.

One evening The Kings of Rhythm travelled to Memphis to see recording artist B. B. King play live. After the gig, Ike and his clan played a few tunes for King, who was so impressed he suggested Ike should record. He consequently arranged a session with his own record producer.

While there, Ike and his band penned a tune called 'Rocket 88', the title inspired by the latest vehicle produced by Oldsmobile.

'Rocket 88' became a huge hit, selling half a million records. It made a great deal of money yet Ike Turner didn't earn more than $20 from the song. 'Rocket 88' was acclaimed as the very first rock 'n' roll record, but Ike Turner wouldn't be credited with that achievement. Years later, Elvis Presley, as handsome as he was white, would be the first sung hero of rock 'n' roll — but Ike knew The King when he was an unknown truckdriver, and it was Ike who claimed to have invented rock 'n' roll.

Ike's original band eventually fell apart at the seams, but Ike always held fast to his dreams of bigger and better things. He would drift back to Memphis on occasion, sometimes making the hundred-mile round trip by bike, in search of his dreams. On one occasion while in Memphis, Ike sat in on a recording session that just wasn't working out. He took it upon himself to sit behind the piano and play his version of what he thought the band was trying to achieve. The white producer and co-owner of Modern RPM records, Joe Bihari, hired Ike on the spot to complete the recording session and paid him handsomely for his services — nearly twice the amount earned for 'Rocket 88'.

Joe asked Ike to introduce him to more people like himself and between both of them, they scouted for and recorded numerous acts, such as Bobby

Bland and Howlin' Wolf. Again, Joe paid Ike handsomely for his services, a staggering $300 a week.

Ike's first encounter with 'real money' was through a white man, and he would utilise this fact later in life. 'The only way to get anywhere is surround yo'self with powerful white people. White people have the power. White people is the way to make money. Shit. They done made enough off the black man.'

By the mid '50s, Ike had been married twice. He moved to St Louis, Missouri, taking his newly re-formed Kings of Rhythm with him. Once there, the work never stopped. The East side of St. Louis was a tough area littered with gangland violence. Ike and his band all carried guns. Ike once said, 'We carried 'em cause we needed 'em.'

One friend of Ike's was sliced to pieces and left to die. Ike was determined that he would never meet the same fate, doing anything to stay alive. One of Ike's co-musicians walked out the front door of one the clubs they were gigging at and got riddled with bullets. Ike said, 'Yo' couldn't see his meat, man, fo' all the holes.'

But Ike survived well and became immensely popular, attracting fans who gladly travelled from far away towns to experience his musical style and brilliance. When Ike realised how well he could draw the crowds, he started running hard bargains with anyone who wanted his services. If anyone dared argue about Ike's worth, he'd settle it by cracking them over the head with the handle of his gun.

Ike was a man of few words who knew his personal value. Nothing irritated him more than a white person trying to take advantage of him. People were so drawn by his talents that those in the music industry would turn a blind eye to his unorthodox negotiating habits.

Less than two years after his arrival in St. Louis, Ike would encounter Annie Mae Bullock, a shapeless, pencil-thin waif of a girl with lungs of iron. She would later adopt the name Tina Turner.

Anna Mae Bullock was born November 26, 1939 in Brownsville, Tennessee, near to her hometown, Nut Bush. She was the last child born to Zelma and Richard Bullock, a couple whose marriage was suffering.

Anna Mae had an older sister, Alline, and a half sister, Evelyn, (the result of Zelma's fooling around as a teenager), both of whom seemed to benefit from parental affection — something Anna Mae longed for but would not experience during her developing years. Forty years later Tina would tell me, 'I don't know what real love is. I never had it. No one ever really loved me.'

As a child, Anna Mae grew up feeling alienated within her own household. She had come along just when her parents were on the verge of splitting up, definitely neither wanted nor welcomed. Her mother didn't seem interested and her father pretended she didn't exist.

Anna loved the great outdoors, sports and picnics, but most of all she loved her sister Alline, who looked after her the best she could. Her parents moved to Knoxville when Anna Mae was three, leaving their two daughters with different relatives. Alline and Anna Mae finally joined their parents two years later, staying in Knoxville for two months. Both girls got an insight into what a bigger town was all about. They also realised there was another world beyond the Nut Bush city limits. But after their two-month stay, Anna Mae and Alline returned to the care of assorted relatives.

Not surprisingly, the fact that she was an outcast within her own family always played on her mind. She was never a victim of poverty. Her family and relatives always had a roof over their head and good, healthy food on the table.

But she did have to put up with the rumours that always went about amongst her relatives. The rumours were fuelled by the fact that Anna Mae fair skin, nowhere near as dark as that of her parents or sister Alline.

She came to accept this as the reason why the majority of her adult relatives rejected her.

Come what may, the little girl simply loved her mother and hoped day after day that her mother might love her back, too. She waited ... and waited ... But during the brief years she did live with her parents, the only emotions that ran rife in the household were bitterness, resentment and anger. Her memories of her parents became dominated by their constant arguments. They were never affectionate, not to Anna Mae, not even to one another.

During this very lonely time in her life, Anna Mae had noticed that other couples who lived in her town were warm and affectionate to one another. She thought that the tenderness and love the other families openly displayed towards each other and towards their children was the most beautiful thing she had ever seen.

By the time Anna Mae was ten, her parents moved back and her family once again lived under the same roof, having resettled in a town called Flagg Grove. On the odd weekend, she would be allowed to go to the cinema, and it was through the silver screen that she realised there was a world full of glamour, and she yearned for the life she saw in the movies. She had joined the local church choir, the only kid amongst teenagers. Her voice was so strong that she would often lead the choir in song. Her life became more settled, but just as she started to feel happy in her new life, her mother walked out. Anna Mae thought she would never stop waiting. Decades later she had said she waited and waited, hoping she would come back but it didn't do any good.

And in all the years I spent with her, even through the most horrific, trying periods of her life, I only saw her cry a few times. And she always managed to stop the tears as quickly as they started.

Within a year of her mother's departure, her father remarried and relocated to a city called Ripley, taking his daughters, his new wife and stepdaughter with him, but within a year his marriage was over. Anna Mae was thirteen when, without warning, her father left home. Now without a father or a mother, she moved with her sister Alline to the house of Ella Vera, her cousin.

Her mother had not made contact since she left; her father sent money on occasion, but that soon stopped, and Anna Mae had to become independent.

She started working for a young white couple, looking after their child and cleaning their house after school. Soon, she was pretty much living with them. They introduced Anna Mae to art and culture, broadening her mind and her world.

They taught her to be thorough and meticulous, and treated her as if she was part of the family. Anna Mae started to do well at school and got involved in numerous activities, including cheerleading and eventually joining the basketball team. Her teachers were fond of her and found her to be somewhat more cultivated than the rest of the kids. Anna Mae put it down to the influence of the white family she had been living with.

And then she fell in love with a boy named Harry, and lost her virginity to him. But he broke her heart by suddenly marrying someone else. It was at this time, though, that her mother reappeared, coming to Tennessee for the funeral of a relative. She suggested that Anna Mae move back with her to St. Louis, pointing out that Alline had already done so. Anna Mae felt her mother had only invited her home because she had outstayed her welcome elsewhere, but when she arrived in St. Louis she was amazed. Alline had become remarkably glamorous and had turned into a real woman — she wore pretty dresses, high heeled shoes, stockings and make-up; she worked in a high-class bar and dated well-to-do professional men who collected her in shiny new cars and took her to fancy restaurants.

Anna Mae idolised her stunning sister. Alline knew all about the jumping night life in St. Louis, and had told her about this fantastic group called the Kings of Rhythm — and the leader of the band was hot, too! His name was Ike Turner. Late '56, while out one night with Alline, Anna Mae clapped eyes on Ike Turner for the very first time. She was sixteen years old.

Two thousand miles away, in Seattle, Washington, my mother was preparing for my imminent birth. She would christen me Eddy Hampton. Two decades later, Tina Turner, formerly Anna Mae Bullock, would tell me, 'My psychic was right, Ed. We were fated.'

During an intermission at the nightclub, Anna Mae, skinny little Anna Mae, grabbed a microphone and started singing while Ike relaxed on stage. Stunned by her voice, Ike muttered, 'That girl can really sing!'

Over the next few years, Anna Mae became an integral part of Ike Turner's show; eventually he changed the name of his group to The Kings of Rhythm featuring Little Anna Mae. Ike and Anna Mae developed a firm brother–sister relationship in the beginning, and Ike was very protective of her. Meantime, Anna Mae had baby boy by one of Ike's bandmembers. She named him Craig.

Soon afterwards, though, Ike and Anna Mae would start a relationship of their own.

In 1960, Ike announced to Anna Mae that she would be called by a new name, a more marketable name. Anna Mae would be known from that moment on as Tina Turner. Changing her name was a bold move by Ike in preparation for a song they were about to record called 'A Fool in Love'. It became a successful R & B hit and soon crept into the national charts, eventually becoming Ike and Tina's first million-selling single.

They were invited to perform live on the hugely popular national music show, *American Bandstand*. A staggering number of people tuned in, and their appearance on the show left an indelible mark on the record-buying public. Through *American Bandstand*, Ike and Tina were introduced to the lucrative white market. Nothing could stop Ike and Tina after that show.

Following the success of 'A Fool in Love', Ike made drastic changes. He dropped the bandname Kings of Rhythm in favour of The Ike and Tina Turner Revue. Soon after that was put into effect, he and Tina married in Mexico.

Ike and Tina had one son, Ronnie. With Craig, Ronnie and two sons Ike had from a previous relationship, Ike Jr. and Michael, Ike and Tina were the parents of four boys. But the boys were left behind in St. Louis while Ike and Tina moved on to California where they hoped to settle and find a home. Once in Los Angeles, Ike started paving his way to making a fortune. He and Tina were dubbed as the hardest-working act in showbusiness, and Ike Turner began to get seriously rich. He bought a three-bedroom house in View Park Hills, an area largely populated by white families, but where successful black artists such as Ray Charles and Nancy Wilson also had homes. Eventually, Ike and Tina's four sons arrived in LA to be looked after by housekeepers while their parents toured the United States incessantly, raking in money. Ike, while still creating hits like 'Idolize You' and 'It's Gonna Work Out Fine', continued to pull in the cash by leasing out his famous backing singers and dancers, the Ikettes. This kept Ike in the style to which he had become accustomed.

Early '66, enter Phil Spector. It was a time when people were breaking boundaries in music. The Beatles were conceiving their acid-rigged masterpiece *Revolver*, and Dylan, no stranger to the mind-bending effects of LSD, was creating his crazy, disturbed, brilliant kaleidoscope *Blonde on Blonde*. And in America, Spector was king of the crop, producing sounds in people's heads more immense than they'd ever experienced.

Spector was blown away by the power of Tina's voice, and he knew he had to produce her. But it was Tina he wanted, not Ike, not the Revue — so he paid Ike $20,000 for the right to produce Tina, and Tina alone.

'I wanted a tender song,' Spector said, 'about a chick who loved somebody very much ... so we came up with a rag doll, and "I'm going to cuddle you like a little puppy." ' And the result? Spector had found a match for his wall of sound. He'd never been more wild, his sound never more huge, and Tina followed him every inch of the way, her voice like a perfect scream over the apocalypse of Spector's swirling instrumentation.

And we'd never heard anything like it before. Spector spent more on the song than anyone would have thought to spend on the average album. But it bombed in the States — who knows why? Maybe nobody was ready for it. Still, it made number 3 in the UK charts, and so Ike and Tina went to England as the opening act for the hottest live band at the time: the Rolling Stones.

The Stones had caught their act while in the US, and had become huge fans of the Turners.

Opening for such a major group's tour was a turning point in their careers. It was an introduction to yet another lucrative market, Britain, who absolutely loved and embraced Ike and Tina. Touring with the Stones gave Ike and Tina a taste for the big time. They believed huge success would immediately follow but it simply didn't. This left Ike Turner angry, and Tina sad and depressed.

Three years after touring with the Stones, Ike and Tina failed to have another hit record, yet they remained one of the hottest live acts in the business. They were one of those rare acts that could pull in audiences year after year without having a hit record on the market.

1969 was a turning point for Ike and Tina. They charted with a cover of an Otis Redding tune called 'I've Been Loving You Too Long'. Immediately after that, the Stones came to the States to promote their new album, *Let It Bleed*. It was announced that the Stones' opening acts would be B. B. King and Ike and Tina Turner. It was then that Tina would be dubbed by the hottest music magazines as 'the most sensational female performer on stage'.

Straight after the Stones tour, Ike and Tina charted three times in a row with a cover of the Stones' song 'Honky Tonk Women', then Sly Stone's tune 'I Want To Take You Higher' and the Beatles' 'Come Together'. Along with their success came Bolic Sound Recording Studios. It was Ike's dream to have his own recording studios, and it was a long time in the making. And it was there, as a young teenager, that I embarked upon the task of creating the Ike and Tina Turner Fan Club.

3

Putting Ike and Tina's first newsletter together was easy. Being their biggest fan, I already knew every detail about their career and I made good use of all the knowledge I'd acquired. In my own little designated space in the secretarial office of Bolic Sound Studios, I created the Ike and Tina Turner Fan Club.

Initially, I kept to Ike's main rule of not pestering him or Tina, but every moment I spent in the studio was with the firm wish that I would see a lot of Tina. During my first month, she popped in and out and was always very polite. She would say 'Hello', and I would respond. As much as I wanted to, I was careful never to spark up conversation or invade her space. Finally, I passed the 'leave Ike and Tina alone' test and they became comfortable with my presence. Even Ike cooled down after seeing the results of my extravagance with the stationery. They were genuinely stunned by the first newsletter.

The newsletter informed fans of Ike and Tina's forthcoming releases, their touring schedule for the next three months and a few items of interest about the band and the Ikettes. There was a competition fans could enter, asking them to send in their favourite recipes because Tina loved cooking in her spare time. Within two months the fan club was a success, and Ike was impressed, I guess, because by informing fans of upcoming events and releases, the newsletter would encourage record sales.

I could see they couldn't quite work me out. I was young, but without a kid's mentality, yet I wasn't an adult either. Over the following months, I got to know the place like the back of my hand. Ike had his own personal studio, Studio A, which he would never book out to other bands. He also had his own office on ground level, just near the entrance, and an apartment on an upper level, where entry was gained through a secret passage in the hallway.

I would spend weekdays at the studio and weekends at Linda Kraus' house or visiting some of the other girls. All the Ikettes and band members' wives became close friends of mine. And the gossip was rife. I was totally bewildered as to why Craig and Ike Jr. were the same age. All the press I had ever read about Ike and Tina referred to the boys as Tina's sons. Of course, I found out that Ike was not Craig's father, but I had to be careful to never say anything because Craig, who was two years younger than me, had no idea. Ronnie was the only kid Ike and Tina had together — Ike Jr. and Michael being the sons of a previous partner of Ike, Lorraine Taylor. Still, Tina was mother to all four.

Over the following few months I worked out another way to get closer to Tina — by developing a relationship with her kids. Two guys in my neighbourhood, brothers Armando and Mark Williams, told me they hung out with Tina's sons and played football with them at least once every two weeks. I volunteered to join the team, and before I knew it I was hanging out at Tina's house and had become firm buddies with Ike Jr. Soon enough, I'd wait until a game was well under way, then I'd sneak off to have a look through the windows of Tina's house.

Up to this point, the housekeeper Liz would prepare lunch for us boys, and we would always be served by the pool. I befriended Liz, and before long she would invite me to eat lunch indoors where I could subtly pump her for information. One day, while she was preparing lunch, I had a little wander around Tina's house. I found an amazing bar, the actual walls of which were made out of custom built fish tanks.

I had a look at the boys' rooms. Ike Jr. and Craig shared one room and Ronnie and Michael shared the other. The four boys were all as different as night and day. Ike Jr. was remarkably confident and got along brilliantly with Michael and Ronnie. Craig was the outcast. I learned that Ike would criticise every little thing that Craig did, and disapproved of Tina giving the boy any sympathy whatsoever. It didn't make sense to Craig, but it made sense to me. Craig wasn't Ike's son — but he didn't know that.

One day while at the house, Tina's sister Alline popped over. She only lived three minutes away, and would drop in to make sure everything was alright while Tina and Ike were touring. I instantly adored funny, witty Alline. She was very pretty and petite, like Tina. She was loving, affectionate and tactile with the boys and they always looked forward to her visits. Alline chain-smoked and loved to talk. Everything she said was amusing. She had a deep, southern accent and once she started talking, there was no stopping her. Naturally, whenever Alline came around, I would abandon the boys and listen to her wonderful stories.

One particular day, Liz went to clean Ike and Tina's bedroom, a room which was always kept locked. I was dying to see what it looked like so I crept to the door and popped my head in. Liz firmly snapped, 'Eddy, now this is off limits. No one is allowed in the Turners' bedroom, not even the kids.'

I didn't have to be told twice. I apologised and quickly went outdoors to play but not before I had had a quick look at the bedroom. I saw a huge, round bed elevated on a platform. There were bedside tables with mini, matching chandeliers hanging above each one. The rest of the furnishings were an antique white with decorative trimmings finished in gold. It seemed terribly grand at the time but really it was just gaudy.

Through working at the studio, I was always aware of Ike and Tina's movements. I'd never go to Tina's house when she was in residence, and, at that point, I didn't even know if she was aware that I hung out with her kids. The boys told me that they had to play elsewhere when their parents came home. Tina was often so drained after a tour that she would spend two days resting in her bedroom, sometimes not coming out at all. If Ike was home, the kids had literally to tiptoe through the house or he would explode. The entire household walked on eggshells when Ike was there and Tina would have to stay with him in the bedroom for the duration of his entire visit. She could only get out of bed to go to the bathroom, and then it was back to the clutches of Ike.

For the first time, I realised that Tina actually feared Ike. I had heard rumours at the studio but I was beginning to see the reality. It began making sense as to why she would show up at the studio, sometimes bruised, or hiding a black eye behind large sunglasses. I thought of how often a cloud of uncertainty would engulf the studio, everyone's behaviour being dictated by Ike's mood.

My curiosity involving anything to do with Tina was unquenchable. One day, I wandered out of Bolic Sound Studio and went around the corner to the rehearsal hall, which was also Ike's property. By this point I had taken advantage of complimentary tickets to see numerous Ike and Tina performances, rarely missing a show when they were local. I was desperate to see the background work that their energetic performances involved. I stood quietly in the doorway of the rehearsal studio, not realising that I'd been noticed and felt myself blush when Tina, still dancing and singing with the Ikettes, beckoned me over.

She was dressed in a dance body leotard and ballet slippers. While keeping in step with the Ikettes, she broke off from singing to ask me to run an errand for her.

'Ed, go to Rhonda and ask her to give you a tampon. Bring it to me. And hurry!' Then she continued singing as if she had never stopped.

I had no idea what a tampon was — but whatever it was, I could sense through Tina's anxious voice that it was something she needed with urgency. I ran as if my shoes were on fire. Having reached Rhonda's office, I paced back and forth while impatiently waiting for her to finish a phone call. She finally put the person on hold and snapped, 'What do you want? Can't you see I'm on the phone?'

I told her in an apologetic kind of voice that Tina wanted a tampon right away. Rhonda pushed her chair back, reached in a drawer and slipped something into an envelope. I ran out of her office clutching the envelope and once outside the building, I paused to have a peek at this mystifying item. I couldn't work out what purpose the item served. It was just a long tube wrapped in thin white paper, and my mind boggled as to what a person might do with this thing! Still, whatever its use was, Tina needed it, so I scurried along. I burst into the rehearsal studio, ran breathless to the end of the large room and handed Tina the envelope.

She looked at me as if I had just saved her life, then disappeared for a few minutes and, upon her return, she danced like mad and kicked her legs in the air as if she were a new woman.

Whatever that tampon was, it was good stuff.

Later that night I asked my mother what a tampon was used for. She was speechless, then asked why I needed this information. I told her the story, and my mother explained that it was something a woman used monthly. I thought it might be some sort of vitamin pack. I had a feeling my mother wasn't telling me everything. I was more confused though when my mother expressed concern over the tampon incident and worried about the company I was keeping at the studio. After dwelling on it for a while, mother finally said, 'Maybe I'm over-reacting. It can't be too bad. At least you have a hobby and you're not hanging around with the wrong crowd.'

The next day I asked Linda Kraus what a tampon was and got a proper explanation.

That incident marked the start of a slow, developing relationship between Tina and me. Ike and Tina had been invited to perform a live radio-link broadcast from Ike's studios. Back then, this live radio link-up was a bit like sending a man to the moon.

The families of the band members came for this unique occasion, and there was technical equipment and tons of electrical cable spread all over recording studio B. I sat on the floor facing the band, and when Tina started singing for the live broadcast she perspired like Niagara Falls. Her white top became transparent and her nipples stood out. Tina noticed what had happened and, rather than being embarrassed, she played it up for her private audience knowing that the radio listeners couldn't see. The radio station took a commercial break and Tina beckoned me over to fetch her a cola drink. I handed it to her and after she took a sip, she sang the words 'Things go better with Coke' and the tiny audience burst out laughing.

It was mesmerising watching Tina sing, joke around and put her small audience at ease. Then as soon as she was signalled that they were back on air, she snapped straight back into professional mode. I remained cross-legged on the floor right in front of Tina. I was shocked when, while still performing, she winked at me and raised her eyebrows as if to ask, 'You like it?'

'Yes!' I mouthed back. She looked satisfied that her biggest fan approved.

At one point, Tina asked me to nip into the game room where the record executives were and listen to the actual broadcast coming over the radio. She wanted me to report right back to her. After listening for a few minutes, I went straight back and told Tina it sounded great. I realised she was taking me seriously and valued my opinion. After the broadcast was over and all the technical equipment had been cleared away, Ike returned to his personal studio to broadcast the show, which he had taped, so the entire building could hear the taped playback.

Ike had all the rooms in the studio piped with speakers, and Ikette Jean Brown and I stayed in Studio B to listen to it. As the playback filtered through the speakers, I started mimicking Tina, and Jean Brown mimicked Ike. I belted out the songs just like Tina did during her performance — I had the whole act down to a fine art, doing her facial expressions and body movements and her favourite 'shake a tail feather' dance routine.

What I didn't know was that Ike had taped us.

He used secret video equipment he had installed all over the studio. Ike could hear and see what was going on everywhere and no one realised it. I later learned that Ike had ordered someone to fetch Tina, and had made her sit and watch my impromptu performance. Tina didn't say a word before walking out.

A few nights later, Norris Williams, who used to look after Tina's kids, took me and the boys to the movies. He went to drop them home after the film and invited me in by saying, 'It's cool. Ike ain't in, only Tina.'

I'd never been in the house when Tina was in residence. I suddenly felt very shy. I walked in and saw Tina dressed in a casual, light tan suede button-up shirt, suede hot pants, brown socks that came halfway up her thighs and dark, flat-heeled knee-high boots. She wore her trademark apple cap, which covered her natural hair as she wasn't wearing her wig. The boys greeted her, calling her 'mother', then she immediately sent them to wash and prepare themselves for dinner. She moved in the kitchen with the same grace and energy that she used in her stage performances.

Once the boys left the kitchen, Tina casually turned to me and said, 'Ed, tell me, how did you learn to dance like that?'

Beaming with pride, I told her it came from watching her and the Ikettes for years. Tina busied herself preparing the boys' meal and replied, 'I know which dance steps were mine. I'm talking about those steps that I've never seen before.'

This was the first time Tina and I engaged in proper conversation. I told her I was now a regular dancer on *Soul Train*, a black orientated nationwide chart show which competed with *American Bandstand*. Anyone who wanted their moment of fame would give their right leg to be seen on *Soul Train*. I sat down and explained to Tina that every Saturday was cutthroat day. Kids would do anything to get on that show. Her eyes widened in amazement when I told her how some of the kids got on *Soul Train*. They would beg, borrow or steal other's names that were on the call-up list to appear on the programme. Then the genuine person would arrive only to be turned away because their name had already been crossed off the list. I told Tina I would never stoop that low. Every week, I would simply climb over the fence and sneak into the studio unnoticed, appearing on the show regularly as a dancer, happy to dance eight hours a day with only a box of Kentucky Fried Chicken as my pay.

Tina stopped what she was doing and laughed before saying, 'So Ed, that's what you get up to in your spare time.'

Then, almost nonchalantly, she added, 'I'll tell you what, Ed. The Ikettes and I are rehearsing on Friday. Why don't you come down and show us a few of those new dance steps?'

I immediately accepted the invitation, feeling as if I had just been knighted by a queen. When I walked into the rehearsal, one of the bandmembers said, 'Goooo on little Eddy. You done got Tina dooowwwn.'

Tina silently stared at me. During my first year at the studio, she didn't really know what to make of me or how to treat me. Now I watched as the corners of her lips raised into a soft grin and I suddenly realised that Tina viewed me as a person who was no longer a child. She could communicate with me and she knew I was thoroughly focused on her. Already being tight friends with the Ikettes and the band, I was very comfortable at the rehearsal. An Ikette suddenly said, 'Come on Mr Soul Train. Show us your stuff. Go on boy. Move that body!'

Tina watched in silence. Then she stood and threw her coat over a chair and stepped out of her trousers, revealing a daring body leotard underneath. Very business-like, she said, 'Okay Ed. I'm ready. Show me those steps again and tell me what they're called.'

She stood back while I took the Ikettes through a dance routine. Tina directed the whole thing, sometimes saying, 'Okay Ed. Do that step again but slowly. I want to get a grip on what's going on.'

I went wild with the Ikettes, but when it came to dancing with Tina, I perspired and tripped over my own feet.

It was easy with the Ikettes because I liked them but I didn't idolise or love them like Tina. She understood what I was going through and eased my tension by joking with me. Only then could I perform with her. That first rehearsal resulted in an open invitation to join Tina any time she rehearsed.

Both Ike and Tina's attitudes towards me changed. They realised I was their number one fan and loved any minute of being around them. We developed an easy relationship. At the studio, everyone sensed I had become an equal and made little effort to hide anything from me. I continued dancing on *Soul Train* and was immensely proud when Ike and

Tina were invited on the show as special guests. I was the envy of all the teenagers because Ike and Tina treated me as a friend. During rehearsals, Tina would talk to me from the stage, and invited me back to her dressing room before the actual taping.

Tina had a way of emphasising a point by striking a certain pose. She would stand back and tilt her chin up with authority. It would make her appear much taller than she actually was. One day, she struck her famous pose, wagged her index finger, and said, 'Ed, we are broadening our stage act and bringing on two more dancers. You will be one dancer and we will audition for the other.'

I nearly fainted — I was only fifteen years old!

4

Cocaine is a devilish drug.

Over the recent months, Ike had been sniffing a great deal, wiping his nose with tissues and constantly rubbing his nostrils between his fingers. Sometimes he'd inhale through his nose, as if he was desperate to keep what most people would want to blow out. He stuttered more than usual and his eyes were wilder than they had ever been. Most disturbing of all, however, was his increasing bad temper. Ike would explode over anything, although thankfully he never directed his tantrums at me.

The studio had become a madhouse by night. It wasn't unusual for bands to book the studio for the evening, but the place was constantly packed with people from the music industry, whether they were paying customers or not, most of them just drugged-up hangers-on. Musicians would arrive at the studio in the evening with assorted groupies in tow and next morning they'd still be there, clearly having been up all night and sometimes longer. The spotty teenage groupies who always dressed beyond their years would look like old, abused women by the next morning, ravaged by too much cocaine and booze. The stench of their cheap perfume would have disappeared, replaced by the familiar smell of sex that often filled the corridors.

Assorted zombies would drift around the studio for days — we'd never see them again; we wouldn't even know their names.

Ike would still be awake from the day before, and on those occasions, his temper was vile. Fortunately, he had taken to spending long periods of time in Studio A, writing, creating or recording songs, most of which would never see the light of day. One day he spotted me and dragged me to his studio. He talked at high speed and seemed more hyper than normal. 'Yo, Ed! Quick! Yo just gotta hear this. Man — wait 'till yo hear this! I wanna know what you think ... what you think ... wait 'till yo hear this. This shit is good ...'

As soon as we got into Studio A, Ike pressed play on the 24 tack tape machine, turning the volume up full blast. It was a new tune called 'Golden Empire'. It pulsated with a funky beat and Tina's voice was extraordinary —

almost as if she were in love. I felt privileged that Ike wanted my opinion on a song he hadn't yet released, and just as the tune was ending, he asked, 'Whadya think? Whadya think, boy, whadya think?'

'Tina's voice is amazing!' I replied.

The blood vessels swelled on his forehead as he snapped, 'No, no, man, no. I ain't asked yo nothin' 'bout Ann. Whadya think of the whole fuckin' song? Yo know, the whole fuckin' thing?'

At that moment, some unfortunate soul wandered into the room and Ike ranted, 'This muthafucka don't think 'bout nothin' else but Ann. The only thing he hears in this muthafuckin' song is Ann's voice. He ain't knowin' no other shit but Ann ...'

I mumbled that I had to go — tearing out of the room before Ike could answer, and leaving him yelling at the poor innocent guy who had just walked in. It didn't take much to set Ike off.

It was soon after that that Tina contracted tuberculosis. Ike never told the staff when Tina was in hospital — we would always have to discover it through other sources. I found out through Gerhard Augustine of United Artists Records, who used to give me promo recordings of Bobby Womack, Ike and Tina, Shirley Bassey and others before they even hit the shop shelves. I was at his office when Gerhard said, 'Isn't it terrible ... poor Tina in hospital.'

I fled out of the building straight to a phone box and rang Tina's sister Alline, who told me what was happening. 'Now calm down, boy. Ann's strong as a horse. She got tuberculosis again. Ain't life-threatinin'. Ike's just gonna have to give Ann some time for restin'.'

In the early 70s, white roses were next to impossible to find, and Tina had once said how much she loved them. So after scouring every florist in Los Angeles, I collected a beautiful bunch of white roses and had them sent to Tina's room in Midway Hospital. A few days after being discharged, Tina phoned to thank me for all the trouble I had gone to find her favourite blooms. Referring to her illness, she simply said: 'Ed, this is my life. I had it before and I'll get it again.'

She had a way of accepting certain things so easily.

Back at the studios, Ike was fuming. He had to cancel gigs because of Tina's illness, and acted as if she had contracted tuberculosis in order to make his life miserable. He was also agitated because he had been caught in a good mood by a journalist who convinced him to let her be an Ikette for a night for an article to be published in *Esquire* magazine.

'Shit, man,' he stormed. 'Them muthufucka's go send a milk-white, no-dancin' muthafuckin' bitch to be an Ikette. An' they don't want the bitch to stay white. They done want the bitch to be black! How the fuck they expect a white girl to be black? ... Bitch can't dance ... Sheeez gonna fuck up my show.'

Ike thought the journalist's job would take one evening, but it stretched to a month. The journalist had been hanging out day after day at the studio which made Ike uncomfortable.

He was concerned that her daily presence would increase the likelihood of her seeing things she shouldn't. Every time he spotted the journalist he hid, avoiding her for two solid weeks. His face was a swollen mess, something he didn't want the journalist to see. The cocaine Ike had been doing was eating through his sinuses, causing huge inflammations around his nose and eyes. Ike wasn't concerned, acting as if the cocaine damage was the least of his worries. He fobbed off his decaying face by saying, 'It's good shit man ... burnin' a hole in my face and all ... good shit!'

Meantime the real Ikettes, Marcy, Yolanda and Esther, were at their wits end with the journalist. It was their job to keep her busy so she 'don't see nuthin'.' They kept the journalist's nose out of Ike's business by trying to teach her a stage routine. Tired of Ike and irritable about baby-sitting the journalist, Marcy and Yolanda ended up in a full-blown fist fight, scratching and pulling the wigs and hair off one another's heads. The journalist was delighted. Now she really had something to write about. Ike, who had been eavesdropping on the journalist, dashed into Studio B to break up the fight.

Everyone in the office cringed. Esther and Marcy were at it big time, tearing at each other with their nails, one yelling, 'You black bubble-ass bitch,' the other screamed, 'You wide-ass, wide-nose coon ...' It was a low-down cat fight — so bad that Ike sustained battle wounds separating the girls.

He was livid. Ike had ordered the girls to portray a real 'family' atmosphere for the journalist, because *Esquire* was a serious, powerful publication. The Ikettes were just following their orders, really, because that's what the atmosphere was like in those days, with Ike's hideous mood swings rubbing off on everyone. Tina was forced to act the 'mother' and try to put things right with the journalist.

While trying to mend the damage by convincing the journalist that each of her staff loved each other like family, she nearly lost her voice pontificating about how well everyone got along, lecturing the journalist for a good half hour. 'I will have to fine the girls for this. It's like taking a kid's pocket money away. It's the only way the girls will learn. I fine them because they represent me and must remember that at all times. We are a solid and a tight-knit family ...'

The journalist interrupted, telling her that Ike claimed he hired the musicians and Ikettes according to their horoscope signs. Tina stiffened and rubbed her forehead and, battling to keep her voice even, she picked up where she left off. 'I'll slap a fine on these girls if a boob slips out of their costume or if their wig isn't on tight enough. There is no room for sloppiness or unprofessionalism.'

As soon as Tina disappeared, however, Ikette Esther snapped at the journalist, 'That's bullshit. Yeh, we get fines. But we ain't had a tight-knit group in five years. The Ikettes ... man ... we all hate each other. *Damn.* They been through two hundred Ikettes in the last twelve years ...'

Meantime, Ike ended up in hospital with an eye infection and had to have his pupil lanced. He returned to the studio angrier than ever, having had to cancel a couple of gigs because of his inflamed eye. He was nervous over his lack of income. He and Tina spent money faster than they made it and it was essential to get back on the road and to work. The atmosphere in the studio was tense and everyone tried to avoid Ike. Some of the girls feared breathing too loud, worried Ike might notice their presence and curse them over some issue that had personaly upset him. Ike was further annoyed when he had to cancel a tour because Tina ended up in hospital with a bad case of bleeding haemorrhoids. The affected area was beyond treatment and had to be cut away.

At this point, no one at the studio knew where Tina had disappeared to, and no one asked. Most of the girls assumed that Ike had punched her lights out and she was recovering at home. I discovered Tina's whereabouts when I overheard Ike storming at Rhonda Graam. 'Fuckin' Ann. Bleedin' outa her asshole. She's fuckin' up, runnin' up doctor's bills ... and that journalist is still hangin' round ...'

Scared and worried, I phoned Alline and she told me what hospital Tina was in.

Again, I ran all over town looking for white roses but this time I found something completely new and different. It was a beautiful terrarium with assorted plants landscaped and enclosed in glass. It had just come on the market and I had it sent straight around to Tina's hospital room. When she was due out of hospital, I baked her one of my famous butter cakes and brought it around to her house. I knew she was in a lot of pain and didn't want to disturb her. Having planned to leave the cake with housekeeper Liz, I suddenly heard Tina's weak voice filtering through. 'Liz, who's at the door?'

Liz replied, 'It's Eddy.'

'Oh, it's okay, Liz, let him in.'

Tina seemed so fragile and vulnerable and was clearly in agony. My voice shook almost as much as the cake in my hands. 'Look, Tina, I know you're not feeling well. I just wanted you to know I was thinking of you so, here, I baked your favourite. I'll leave it here so you can get some rest.'

Tina's eyes seemed moist but she managed an affectionate smile. 'No, no, Ed. Why don't you come in?'

After accepting her invitation, I took a seat at a round kitchen table. Tina asked Liz to prepare tea for us then turned to me and said, 'I can't wait. I have to have a piece of that cake right now!'

I watched Tina gently lower herself into a chair. She looked so soft and beautiful. She wore a tasteful, floral silk lounging suit by a top designer of the time called Vera. Tina cut the cake like a little girl with a sweet tooth who couldn't wait for that first bite. She nibbled a crumb on the end of her finger and appeared to be lost in her own thoughts. 'You know Ed, I just love that terrarium. I've never seen anything like it. You always do such nice things for me. You always bake my favourite cakes and they're waiting for me at home when I get back from tours. I sometimes think of those cakes when I'm heading home ... and you go to so much trouble to find my favourite flowers.' She blinked rapidly and looked down at her napkin, her voice slightly vibrating with emotion. 'You see Ed ... no one ever does things like that for me. No one. Only you. Thank you, Ed.'

Realising her eyes had reddened with tears, I looked to the floor to save her any embarrassment. She suddenly looked up, playfully searching the kitchen with her eyes as if I had hidden something. 'Ed! Only one cake?'

I knew what Tina's joke was about. Everyone in Tina's household always swarmed on my fresh home-made butter cakes. It had reached the point where my cakes were so popular that I would bake one for the boys and one just for Tina. When Alline once popped over and saw me dropping off cakes, she had said: 'Boy, you go bakin' all these cakes fo' Ann and when you come to my house you ain't baked me no cake. Shiiiit. You better bake me a cake, you hear boy? You know you gotta bake me one 'cause Ann ain't sharin' none of hers. And if she does give in, the slice is so damn thin, shit!'

Tina and I shared a laugh over her sister Alline, whose words were always laced with affection and humour. While helping herself to another slice of cake, Tina's eyes darkened and her mood became heavy.

She stared at her slice of cake and her face became cold and rigid. As she spoke, each word seemed tainted with irony. 'You know, Ed, the good thing about this operation is that I can finally get some rest. The doctor ordered three to four weeks of bed rest. All the pain is worth it just so I can get a break.'

It was a sad statement about her life, but at that point of our friendship, I felt it would be misguided to pry or cross certain personal borders. Feeling deeply sad for her, I said my goodbyes and promised to phone in a couple of days. One week later, while gassing with Tina on the phone, it sounded as if she had a party in full swing. She had to raise her voice to be heard. 'No Ed, I'm not having a party. Just the opposite.'

There was a long pause while she turned down the music, then Tina sighed, 'Ike isn't having it. Ike's not letting me rest. He'll end up killing me first.'

Then I could hear Tina inhaling deeply, as if suddenly distressed. 'Ed ... Ed, I'm going back on the road.'

I objected, reminding Tina of the doctor's orders, but my words fell on deaf ears. She had resigned herself to the fact that she was returning to work. 'What can I say, Ed? This is my life. Anyway, the girls are here rehearsing. Why don't you come over?'

I was there within twenty minutes. The Ikettes were gathered in Tina's bedroom swaying to a Ringo Starr song that was blaring at full volume. Ikettes Marcy and Yolanda were both trying to tell Tina about the journalist from *Esquire* having two left feet. Marcy shrieked while telling Tina about the goings on at the studio. 'Tina, you be glad girl, be glaaaaad that ya'll stitched up. Shit. If ya saw that white girl tryin' to dance it woulda made ya'll sick any old way. We been teachin' that journalist to dance for three solid weeks and she just ain't got the rhythm. Damn. We told the girl to just think like a black man but it ain't done her no good. She still ain't got no soul.'

Tina battled not to laugh. Every time a laugh escaped her, she had to grip her lower abdomen and backside to relieve the ensuing daggers of pain. When Tina was with the girls, she would mimic a deep southern lingo. 'Come on now Ed. Ya ain't holdin' out on me, are you boy? Give us a look at some new steps from *Soul Train*.'

Tina flicked her index finger towards the centre of her bedroom, her freshly-manicured nail gleaming. 'Git on over there, boy. Stop holdin' out on us. Get them feet pumpin'.'

Tina sat like a director, playing music and clapping to the beat. 'Stop Ed. What's that called? Darn. I like that step. Let's see it again.'

The dance was called the robot — a new craze involving well-timed robotic movements, with the head, torso and arms stiffly moving to the beat. The Ikettes jumped up to try it and we all laughed at the comical trial and error involved with getting the steps right. Tina got up with a broad smile on her face, ticking off the Ikettes as if they were children. 'No, no girls. Ed didn't do it like that. Oh, no. I'm in all this pain and I still have to show you girls how to do things right.'

Tina went through the moves while saying, 'See, jerk your head and body like this ... like this ... like this ... got it?'

She proudly trooped on with one hand tightly pressed to her bottom and the other hand gripping her stomach, but that huge smile never left her face. Tina showed Ike the new dance routine and, while out of his head on cocaine, he made her do it continuously, until finally, four hours later, she started bleeding. It didn't matter. Ike had lined up a gig for the following night and expected Tina to perform. The journalist from *Esquire* came to the house for a costume fitting. Tina loaned the journalist her own gold, plastic platform shoes, a gold chain bra top and mini skirt as well as dancing briefs and tights, all of which she wanted returned. The journalist later muttered, 'Tina wants me to return used underwear and tights? This is what she calls a class act?'

Everyone became uncomfortable, harbouring a terrible suspicion that the article would be written with a poisoned pen. The only joy anyone got out of the journalist was when she had a hideous allergic reaction to the wig Tina insisted she wear. Ike had booked the gig at a tiny venue, a backstreet in comparison to their normal showcases. The venue was called Baceda's Nightclub, a smokey spaghetti and beer-serving restaurant with two small stages. The dressing rooms were dire. There were no mirrors and a single, dirty lightbulb hung from the center of the ceiling. There were remnants of burgers, ketchup and squashed french fries spread across the filthy floor.

The Ikettes quickly applied tanning make-up on the journalist, making her look black. She was squashed into Tina's tiny shimmering gold outfit, and even wore a pair of Tina's shoes, which were too small. Her flesh could be seen painfully bulging out between the ankle straps. Finally, a booming voice introduced the Ikettes, and the girls leapt to the stage and started their hectic dance routine.

But as soon as the journalist swung her head, her wig nearly did a full turn. Blinded, the journalist nearly trod on Tina who, while singing Ringo Starr's 'Oh My My', bumped the journalist out of the way with a single hip swing. The journalist stumbled onto a curtain and before returning to her performance, paused to wipe her allergy riddled eyes and nose on the stage curtain fabric.

She quickly adjusted her wig and returned to her dance position, only for her ankle to give way, which sent her tumbling to her knees. Tina, the band and the Ikettes carried on singing 'Oh My My' while the journalist crawled off the stage on one knee with her arms splayed everywhere.

Later, back in the dressing room, Tina was as sweet as she could be, telling the journalist, 'You did just fine, as good as any Ikette on the first night.'

The journalist turned for Ike's approval. He scraped the filthy linoleum floor with the heel of his shoe and said, 'It don't mean shit.'

Ike's eyes were bulging and the journalist looked more than a little scared. She couldn't get out of there fast enough. She ran back to the girls' dressing room, peeled off the stage outfit and disappeared out of Ike and Tina's life forever.

Later that evening, Ike complained endlessly about the show and fined the Ikettes a quarter of their salary for not looking happy enough on stage. He then made Tina do a punishing dance routine over and over until she finally burst her stitches. She ended up right back in hospital.

This time round, the doctors confronted Ike and gave him a firm warning that Tina was not to work until they give her the all clear. Ike even seemed a little humiliated over the way he had treated Tina. The doctors, by now, knew Tina well. She had become a familiar patient, always arriving battered and sometimes with broken ribs. The doctors hated Ike and they let him know it. Sadly, back in those days, men weren't pulled up for wife battering. The doctors' hands were tied, but they made it clear they knew what sort of bastard Ike was. His shame turned to outright fury, and he angrily complained about Tina's operation, stuttering abuse to anyone who would listen. 'Ain't nuthin' wrong with Ann. Bitch just actin'. Muthafucka ain't sick. That bitch just lazy ... actin' and shit. She should just tell a nigga when she wants a vacation. See how sick she feels when I don't give her no money. No money. Then she really be sick.'

Everyone was sick — sick of Ike Turner, a tiny man who knew how to raise almighty hell. During his outburst, everyone stopped what they were doing and the ringing phones went unanswered as we stared at him in silence. Ike was uncomfortable with all eyes on him, and he scowled at the secretaries, searching for a victim on whom to vent his anger. It had become common for Ike to choose an unlucky member of staff to abuse which always made him feel a lot better. With Tina off ill, someone else was certainly marked for a beating. I stood defiant. Ike never picked on me but he would stare me down once in a while. He did eye me that day but I was too upset over Tina to make an effort to hide the disappointment on my face.

Before disappearing into Studio A, Ike took a deep drag on his cigarette and complained, 'I ain't done shit to her. Bitch just wanna lay in bed all fuckin' day and night. Shiiiiiiiit.'

Once Ike had left us in peace, we all started breathing once again, counting the days to Tina's recovery.

After Tina's convalescence, it was more important than ever for the Ike and Tina Turner Revue to get back on the road. They had missed over a month of cash income. Ike and Tina wanted to headline the top Las Vegas entertainment circuit where their earnings would easily treble. The likes of Cher and old favourites such as Frank Sinatra and Elvis Presley raked in fortunes playing Vegas. Their Las Vegas acts were very stylish, glitzy and almost bordering on the theatrical. In order to achieve that standard of showmanship, Ike and Tina knew they would have to revise their show completely. It called for their entire act to be scrapped and replaced by a bigger, better, more glamorous one.

Tina had already befriended Ann Margret, the lead actress in the classic rock film *Tommy*. Ann was one of the hottest properties in Vegas. Tina noticed how she had hired choreographers, the best personal costume designers, stage technicians, the lot.

She came to realise that with a little extra input from people in the know, she could turn a good show into a great one. By now she had started styling herself a bit on Ann Margret and she wanted all the pampering that went with it. Tina had already told me that she would have two new dancers, and I would be one of them. They would audition the second dancer. I arrived for rehearsals and heard the chroeographer directing the dancers, 'Awright. Now. Kick — two, three ... Turn, two, three ...'

For the life of me, I simply couldn't follow his direction. I'd never been exposed to that level of professional dance direction and I was completely out of step. He excused me from the show by saying: ' 'Ere ... uh, you mate, wot's your name? You 'ave to do better than that. Oi, you. Tha' just won't do, willit mate?'

It was clear to everyone, as well as myself, that I wasn't up to scratch. Tina immediately called me over for a private chat, gently breaking the inevitable news that I was scratched from the show. 'Ed, I really want you to come to Vegas with us but you won't be able to. Jack says you need more professional training. I'm sorry.'

I understood. I gathered my belongings and left the studio, bursting into tears in the refuge of a public phone box. Tina had given me a magic opportunity and I blew it. Feeling too embarrassed, I didn't return to the studio straight away.

Ike and Tina left on a long tour to win over Las Vegas, while I got on with my life as a normal teenager. I had told everyone I was off to Vegas, a dancer in the Ike and Tina stage show. I was so upset I could hardly face these people.

By this point, attitudes at school had changed and I had become very popular. I was rich, stylish and went to all the best pop concerts and managed to sneak pretty successfully into a few clubs. I still spent one day a week at the studio, doing odd jobs related to closing down the club and keeping on top of the latest gossip. Ike and Tina's new live stage act was a great success and they won over the audiences in Vegas. They decided to stick to the new formula of glitz and glamour and take the show on the road, inviting me to fly to San Fransicso with them to see the new act. It was in San Fransisco that Ike realised the audiences were not packing out the houses to see the Ike and Tina Turner Revue. The seats were filled with fans who wanted to see Tina Turner. The look on his face said it all — Tina Turner would pay dearly for that.

On the flight home from San Fransisco, Tina was buzzing. She knew something had changed. She had become a star in her own right and she glowed with this knowledge. During the flight, Tina, as always, sat on one side of Ike, and his mistress, Ann Thomas, sat on the other side. Once the plane was airborne, Ike laid his head on Tina's lap with his legs stretched over his mistress' lap. It was a disgusting sight. Tina, who had never cheated on Ike, was forced to be a part of Ike's perverse, public displays. The stewardesses and other passengers would glare at the scene, staring from the mistress to Tina. Passengers could be overheard making comments about Tina, saying things like, 'She must be sick in the head. Look how he's spread across both of them. They all must be sleeping in the same bed.'

I wanted to get up and scream that they didn't know Tina Turner at all. I wanted the world to know that Ike made Tina give in to his twisted demands. I was desperate to defend her but knew to keep my mouth shut. If I were to say anything, Ike wouldn't touch me but he would certainly punch Tina's lights out. The only comfort was a newfound strength that was suddenly filling Tina. She knew, really knew, that she had a chance of surviving without Ike. She held her head high and smiled as if she didn't have a care in the world. Every now and then she would look down at Ike snoring on her lap and a grin would creep across her face. It was a strong grin, like she knew something he didn't.

Ike's days with her were numbered. There was suddenly an aura around Tina as if it had already happened — as if she were already a free woman. During the short flight, Tina lost herself in a void of bizarre contentment. She knew at that moment she would spread her wings and fly away from Ike forever. When? Soon. It was just a question of how. She needed to be cool, to take control.

Tina knew she would liberate herself. She had no idea she would nearly die doing it.

5

Tina's hysterical screams could be heard filling the hallway of Bolic Sound Studios. Items crashing and glass breaking mingled with the choking noises coming from somewhere deep in Tina's throat.

Ike had just thrown boiling hot coffee over her face and neck and not satisfied with burning her, proceeded to strangle her as well.

Groupies, druggies and layabouts shook with fear and one by one made themselves scarce. Ike had been up on cocaine for days. In one of his many twisted, unreasonable states, he had taken his madness and frustration out on Tina. Not caring whether everyone had gone or not, Ike embarked on one of his most brutal attacks ever.

A frightened druggy pushed past a few nameless faces, desperately clawing her way to the ladies room before throwing up on the floor out of fear. Another girl covered her ears with her hands and shut her eyes tightly, not wanting to see or hear Ike's brutality. She shook her head from side to side in a vain effort to block out the horrid sounds reaching her ears.

Tina wept hysterically, pathetically begging Ike, 'Noooo, noooo ...' while he landed one body punch after another. Suddenly, there was an eerie, almost peaceful silence. Ike clutched Tina around her neck with his strong hands, squeezing hard until she could barely breathe. There was no more screaming, only gurgling noises rising from Tina's strangled throat.

That was just the way things were. If anyone was stupid enough to interfere, Ike would attack the brave, stupid girl and subject her to the same treatment or worse. Tina had a motto. No point in two people suffering. Just let Ike get on with it. And everyone did just that.

The kids, by this point, were accustomed to seeing Tina arrive home from the studio with a bruised or bloodied face or the odd broken bone. They had grown to accept this as a normal way of life.

When Tina came home battered, they would causally look up from whatever they were doing and make comments like, 'Oh, look, Father's split Mother's eye this time,' or, 'Mother's broken a rib again.'

Tina had never fussed over her beatings in the past and the kids grew to learn never to fuss over them either. More importantly, Tina firmly told her sons never, ever to interfere. But the coffee incident changed their attitudes for ever. Craig, who was around 16, went crazy when he saw the injuries to Tina's neck. He actually cried when he heard how Ike had choked Tina, twisting at the raw, burnt skin on her neck until it ripped away from her flesh. 'Why is he doing this to you? Why is he doing this to us?'

Completely hysterical, he stumbled towards the door of his home vowing to go to the studio to avenge his mother. He swore he'd do whatever was necessary to protect Tina, but she wouldn't hear of it. She firmly ordered Craig not to interfere. 'Darling, stay here. Going to the studio will only make things worse. I want you to promise me you won't say anything. Trust me, Craig. Just stay away from Ike. There's no point in both of us getting hurt. It'll be OK.'

It was hard to know what Tina was made of. She could recover from brutal incidents with Ike, sometimes within hours, and act as if nothing had happened.

Everyone was tiring of Ike. There were very few old faces left at the studio, employees often leaving after being attacked by him — some wise enough to walk out before their turn came, some being fired after their boss had been on a long drink and drugs binge. This particular attack on Tina would cost Ike dearly, though. Ike and Tina found themselves performing at a prestigious LA venue, the Beverly Hills Hilton, in front of a star studded audience dotted with familiar faces like Bill Cosby and Chaka Khan. It was a Hollywood show with a glitzy, Vegas-type setting, the focal point being a magnificent stage that had been specially erected for Ike and Tina's glamourous new act.

Under the new running order, the band warmed up, then the Ikettes were introduced, working their way through two numbers before Tina's grand introduction. Following her cue, she stormed on stage like a lightning bolt and the audience gasped as she energetically demanded, 'Do you like good music? Sweet soul music?'

She stood like a goddess until the audience roared and begged Tina to start singing. She was so mesmerising that the audience failed to notice the bizarre accessory around her neck, a scarf, totally uncharacteristic of Tina Turner. The band started playing and Tina's body automatically moved to the beat, her performance electrifying as she hit notes I'd never heard her reach before. Then I noticed that the perspiration dripping down Tina's chest had suddenly deepened in colour, finally becoming as red as a rose. She wiped at the wetness, noticing the blood on her hand while still singing; she finished the entire song then excused herself before leaving the stage, returning a few minutes later wearing a fresh scarf around her neck.

The audience sat stone silent, staring straight at Tina, creating an atmosphere that demanded an explanation. Understanding this, Tina clutched the microphone, her voice even and calm as she spoke. 'You see ... Ike and I were playing around and he ... well, he accidentally spilled hot coffee on my neck.'

Ike shot daggers at Tina — she was becoming strong, letting the audience know that the injury was induced by Ike, yet being diplomatic enough not to say that he had deliberately burned her. Ike seemed genuinely embarrassed. His reputation was becoming known and he could see the star studded audience glaring at him in disgust. The bulk of the audience, especially those from the showbiz world, knew straight away that Tina's injuries were not accidental. They coldly stared Ike down.

They fidgeted uncomfortably, seeming repulsed by Ike and when they turned their attention to Tina, their eyes filled with pity and compassion. Tina was a true professional and pretended not to notice the crowd's reaction. For her, it was on with the show and even though injured, she would not deliver anything short of her best. She did a raunchy, sexy number called 'I've Been Loving You Too Long'. It was very erotic, with Tina simultaneously singing and clutching her mike suggestively, finally finishing the song as if she had just climaxed. Burnt neck and all, she performed the song while totally transfixed on Ike, singing to him as if he was the only man on earth — but this time the innocence was lost. Tina was mad. The audience loved Tina and respected her all the more, knowing how hard it must have been for her to perform that number at a time when she probably loathed Ike. They screamed in adulation.

Ike had never experienced anything like this before and did the only sensible thing he could think of. He cancelled the remainder of their tour so that no other audience would see Tina's bloodied neck.

After Tina came off stage, I raced to her hotel suite, which was given to her as a dressing room. On the way up, I had been stopped by Chaka Khan and Bill Cosby who were concerned over Tina's well-being. Chaka kept asking if I knew what had really happened to Tina, but I pretended to be none the wiser. By the time I reached Tina's suite, she had already made herself comfortable having changed from her sexy costume into a designer knit lounge suit and soft ballet slippers. The scarf she wore on her neck during her performance had been replaced by a proper gauze bandage, the gossamer fabric unable to hide the rawness on Tina's neck. Nearly on the verge of tears, I went to console her. Tina took one step back and firmly said, 'Ed, just stop. No sympathy. No tears. I'm not having it.'

She carried on as if nothing had happened and started chatting idly.

Her eyes warned me not to say a word about her neck and I was wise enough not to intrude on her moment of strength. There would be no tears from Tina and none from anyone else. She refused to fuss or feel sorry for herself and she wasn't prepared for anyone else to, either. When Tina saw that I had slipped into the role she needed at that moment, she held her head high and said: 'You know something, Ed. I nearly scared Ike to death. When he wrapped his hands around my neck and started choking me, I didn't move an inch. I just let him choke away and I relaxed myself like a rag doll. The skin pulled away from my neck where he'd thrown coffee at me. Since I didn't react, he was worried about me being able to perform with such a wound, and was shocked at my reaction. He got scared — terrified. It was spooky.

'My eyes were cold. Ike freaked out. He let go and backed away. He was scared. Real scared.' A smile crept across her face.

Once everyone had returned to the studio, Ike, for the very first time, tried to justify himself to others. 'Ann does this to me. She made me pour that hot shit on her. She knows how to do it to me. She made me hurt her.'

No one believed him and no one was listening.

Tina went to the hospital to have her burns treated and returned somewhat distressed. The doctors had made it clear to Tina that she would be left badly scarred. Tina was beginning to display the permanent scars of Ike's brutality; but it was at this point that Rick Kellis, Ike and Tina's horn player, became instrumental in changing the direction of her life. Rick was a white, peace loving hippy — a flower child who wore kaftans and John Lennon glasses. He was obsessed by the mysteries of the spiritual world, tarot cards and chanting. All his personal friends shared his interests. On the very day Tina learned she would carry a scar on her neck for the rest of her life, Rick brought a woman to the studio, a nameless, slightly spooky, beaded flower child who, Tina claimed, walked straight up and placed her hands over the bandages on her neck. Tina didn't even ask the woman what she was doing — she sensed she was safe and allowed this complete stranger to touch her. And the scars on her neck healed up. The doctors were astounded and baffled when they saw what had happened. Tina was convinced it was a miracle.

At that moment, Tina deeply believed that these amazing, spiritual people were sent to her by God to give her strength and lead her to a better life. She took it as a clear message that certain beliefs were as powerful as they were real. These new beliefs would set Tina free. She threw herself into setting the groundwork for the day she would exit from her sham marriage. She no longer relied on Ike on stage and her personal performance went from great to astounding, so much so that the audiences no longer referred to 'Ike and Tina' — they simply came out to see Tina and no one else. As coked up as Ike was, he still noticed this and he knew he had to take drastic steps to keep hold of Tina. One thing he came to realise was that, slowly, Tina was learning not to fear him. He would have to embark on a new psychology as means of keeping control over her.

Meantime, a woman called Valerie Bishop came into Tina's life. Ike paraded home with Valerie one day, introducing her to Tina as his new secretary. Tina, at this point needed something to focus on, something to believe in. Not surprisingly, Valerie caught Tina's interest with stories of Buddhism and chanting. Tina started sneaking off with Valerie, spending many secret hours learning all she could about the power of Buddhism, and learning how to chant.

Tina had Valerie secretly purchase a small altar where you would burn incense, place offerings such as fresh fruit, water or items that represent life.

This is done as a measure of respect and the idea is that these items help you to focus, enabling you to attract goodness into your life. You chant in front of the altar, and this puts you in the right frame of mind to achieve and receive the things you need. In other words, you're in rhythm with the universe.

Tina set the altar up in a secret area of her house. One day Ike came home unexpectedly and caught Tina in front of the altar chanting. He became demented. 'Git that witchcraft shit outa' the house.'

Ike was terrified of things he didn't understand. He was an atheist, his only god being money and the things he could buy with it. If Ike couldn't see it, touch it or understand it, he would freak. He had a genuine fear of certain things and the harmless little altar terrified one of the most feared men in LA. But Tina did not dispense with the altar. She simply hid it more carefully and was discreet about using it. She also knew that she could chant by facing the East or the West.

She hated being a prisoner and chanting helped her to see with clarity. After one particular session, she devised a way of avoiding Ike's confrontations and beatings, the new concept coming to her like a flash. If she was unhappy about something, she would simply write a letter to Ike, the strategy being that if he didn't like what he read, he had time to cool down before confronting Tina.

The letters worked a treat. Ike would find a letter Tina had left in the studio, read it and have an almighty fit. But by the time Tina arrived at the studio, his wrath had cooled down. The letters also helped Ike to rationalise a bit more. He had time and space to filter what Tina had said in the letters and by doing so, he became a bit more sensitive or aware of her pleas. In one letter, Tina wrote, 'I do everything you ask me to do. I do the shows the way you want. I put up with your women, your low-life friends and your drugs. I do everything you ask. I sing your songs the best I can, Ike. But the one thing I can't take any more is your beatings. Beating me is a sign that you really don't care about me. After you poured hot coffee on me, you had to choke me too. I'm tired, Ike. I'm weak. I'm not in the best health. I am on your side. You just don't care about me.'

The letters had an astonishing effect. Ike started treating Tina as if she were one of his mistresses, showering her with cash, jewels and expensive gifts. He knew when he had to pamper Tina. It was Ike's way of admitting he had been an asshole, and although he still gave Tina the odd slap or beating, it was nothing in comparison to the past. He simply beat the living daylights out of his mistress Ann Thomas instead. But he wasn't to remain so laid back for long.

On Tina's 34th birthday, Ike threw a party for her. I was about 18, and it was around the time that Tina was putting in a stunning performance as The Acid Queen in the film version of The Who's *Tommy*.

Mike Stewart, head of United Artists Records was present at the event. In the middle of the glittering celebration, Ike instructed the guests to gather in the driveway, where he made a great show of presenting Tina with a stunning, second-hand classic silver Bentley, an English model with the steering column on the right-hand-side of the car. Topped with a huge birthday bow, the car was a beautiful sight. Tina, a bit surprised by the choice of gift, graciously told Ike how happy she was. She was baffled. When Ike had asked her what she wanted for her birthday, she had told him she wanted a brand new convertible Rolls Royce. She was genuinely pleased with the Bentley, yet a little disappointed at the same time. Ike protectively wrapped his arm around Tina, and they both smiled, pretending, as they always did in public, to be the happiest couple on earth.

But then Ike made another announcement, telling Mike Stewart that he had a gift for him, too. Under the moonlight, in front of all the puzzled guests, Ike bellowed, 'I have one more surprise. Mike, man, yo' bin' good ta' us. Real good, know what I mean? So ah got a little gift fo' you too. A little sumthin' fo' you 'cause we owe everythin' to you.'

He signalled to the other end of his drive where one of his cronies had been patiently waiting. The man disappeared and within seconds, gently drove Mike's gift up to where he stood. There, glistening like a diamond, was a brand new Rolls Royce Silver Shadow, elegant and dark in colour, just like the one Tina had wanted. Shocked, Tina's knees nearly gave way. She held on to Ike's arm with the broadest, most bewildered smile stretched across her face. In Ike's drug ravaged mind, he felt he had made a shrewd move. He hadn't had a hit record for a while and believed the gift would secure the renewal of a contract. However, everyone else knew that Tina had just been deeply humiliated. The whole crowd felt acutely embarrassed for her, none more so than Mike Stewart.

Sensing his discomfort and embarrassment, Tina stepped in to rescue the innocent man. 'Mike ... you've given us a great deal of guidance and support over the past few years. You've been instrumental in carefully guiding our careers. We both want to say thank you for all you've done for us.'

When Tina emphasised the word 'both', Mike stopped perspiring and graciously accepted the gift. By rescuing him, Tina had unwittingly stolen Ike's thunder. Ike stood staring at Tina, anger gnawing away at him while his face twisted with fury.

Tina was on a roll. Mellowed by her chanting, and inspired by the psychic readers she had begun to consult, her calm strength became noticeable. Her performances became more and more exciting and erotic; and the release of *Tommy* brought her rave reviews, stating that she had stolen the shown, that *Tommy was* Tina Turner. She cropped up in practically every publication in America, and she appeared on chat shows by the dozen.

On one programme, Tina was asked what the difference was between her white and black audiences. She made the innocent mistake of suggesting there was a difference between the two audiences.

Ike was livid. Don't yo' know how to think befoe' yo' talk? Them blacks buy our records and spend on us ... now how the fuck we gonna make a livin' without them?'

Ike devised a way to crawl back into the black audiences good books. A black militant group had organised a special fund-raising benefit show in San Fransisco. Ike jumped at the opportunity, and they shared top billing with Sly and the Family Stone.

Back then, bands were always paid in cash. They would receive half the money on booking and the other half just before they went on stage. Often, this would result in Ike easily having over $40,000 cash on him at a time. As usual, Ike was paid a vast amount of cash in his dressing room just before he was due to go on stage. But something was making him edgy, so he ordered Rhonda Graam to get the car and park it right outside the exit. Then he ordered Ann Thomas to gather his and Tina's personal belongings and take it along with the money to the car, lock the vehicle doors and stay put. Rhonda and Ann were told to wait in the car for him and Tina and not, under any circumstance, to set foot back into the building. While Ike and Tina were on stage, their dressing room was broken into and turned upside down. The culprits didn't find what they were looking for and, within minutes, militant members invaded the stage during the performance. Tina had her back to the band and didn't realise a brawl had started. Suddenly, the music stopped and the audience gasped.

Just as Tina turned to look at her band, a militant grabbed her by the hair and threw her to the floor. She landed hard and fell to the corner of the stage — her wig landing somewhere nearby.

She scrambled on her hands and knees to grab the wig and coiled in a corner while trying to place it back on her head. She was more terrified of the audience seeing her without her wig than she was of getting her lights punched out. Ike suddenly grabbed Tina and pulled her to her feet, dragging her through the backstage corridor to the exit and safety of the waiting car. Tina, Ike, Ann Thomas and Rhonda Graam took off at high speed and never slowed down until they reached the airport, and the armed security guards had escorted them safely to their seats.

Ike and Tina were badly shaken over the incident and the rest of the band arrived soon after, bruised but safe. Ike said, 'I knew I shouldn't have done the gig but I had to win back our black audience. Shit. I'm gonna listen to ma feelin' in the future. I'm gonna listen, man.'

It was one day in March, 1976 that Ike fired Rhonda Graam, but not before slicing her face open first.

Rhonda was amongst the very first whites hired to work for the Turners and, because of her colour, she would open many doors that would have otherwise remained closed. She represented two milestones in Ike's life. She was the first white woman to run his organisation and the first white woman Ike had ever slept with. He had set himself up like a king. He would leave Tina's bed, nip a few minutes down the road and hop into Rhonda's bed, then leave her to hop in the sack with Ann Thomas. When he fired her, it was a sign to us all that he was losing it.

Tina asked me to send the most beautiful girls I could find from *Soul*

Train to audition as Ikettes. I found a devastating beauty called Tahise, a stunning model and great dancer but who couldn't sing even if her life depended on it. Tahise was of mixed blood and was tantalisingly exotic. Tina was impressed with the look of her. She instructed Tahise to follow her dance steps.

Tina had nothing. There wasn't a single thing accumulated during her marriage, apart from clothes and jewellery, that she could call her own. She longed for her own house, somewhere she could decorate to her own taste, and constantly badgered Ike to buy her one. She thought Tahise, with whom Ike was already infatuated, might be the key. But as beautiful as Tahise was, she wasn't enough to earn Tina that house.

Ike's relationship with Tahise got a bit messy. He fell madly in love with her. Tahise became a permanent fixture at the studio and Ike could focus on little else. This threw Tina off balance. She loved her husband, but she didn't like him. She wanted to leave him but seeing him actually in love with another woman threw all Tina's ideas and perceptions out the window. No one was going to steal her man. Tina finally admitted later that she never stood a chance against Tahise. 'It's stupid, Ed. I didn't care who he beat as long as it wasn't me any more. But I didn't expect this.'

But the relationship wasn't to last. In the middle of a marathon coke and booze session, Tahise was stolen from right under Ike's nose by none other than Sly Stone. Tahise gave me all the dirt.

'Eddy, guess what! Sly Stone is my new man! Ike sent me off in the early hours to get coffee for him and Sly. Well, Sly slipped something into my hand and whispered, "Don't say a word, just phone me." After I left the building, I looked at the paper and it was his phone number. I waited a few hours after he left and called him. he offered to beat Ike's offer and take me all the way!'

Tahise went home, packed her bags and moved in with Sly. She loved all the clothes, furs and jewellery Ike gave her, but she wasn't very fond of what went with it. Ike was history.

No one had ever seen Ike suffer the way he did over the loss of Tahise. As each day passed, it became apparent how deeply in love he was with her. Strangely enough, no matter how much we despised Ike at times, it was actually heartbreaking to see how much he suffered over the loss of Tahise. He was going down fast, losing all control. But he was soon to lose much, much more.

The band had prepared for an important show. They were booked to kick off the Independence Day celebrations in Dallas, Texas to mark America's 200th birthday.

On the day they were due to leave, Ike was still awake from a five day coke binge, not having slept a wink.

Tina arrived at the studio in a white Yves St. Laurent suit, and was ready to leave for the airport with Ann Thomas and the rest of the band, but every two hours she had to cancel the flights and re-book later ones because Ike was in a dreadful state and could barely stand, let alone get on a plane.

Tina kept glancing at her watch, noting each passing hour, knowing how important this particular performance was. Although impatient, she had an air of peacefulness — almost as if she knew something no one else did. She seemed to be reminiscing, her eyes glazing over as she slowly turned the pages of an old photo album filled with pictures of her and Ike. She stopped and stared carefully at each and every picture in the album, which was a catalogue of their life together. She suddenly slapped the album closed and looked up, her face remorseful as if she had just lost her best friend.

Finally, after waiting and waiting, Ann Thomas asked Tina to lay out some clothes while she put Ike into the shower. Tina looked at Ike in disgust and snapped, 'For goodness sake Ike, the band needs to do soundcheck and you're not even on the plane yet. I have to dress you like you're some sort of invalid.'

Although out of his head, Ike was shocked by Tina's words. She had never spoken to him like that before. The date was July 4, 1976 — and as Tina mumbled a hasty goodbye to me before leaving for the airport with her deranged husband, I had no idea it would be the very last time I would see them as a couple. Independence Day had come early for Tina. By the time the rest of the nation was celebrating the 4th of July, Tina was in hiding, barely hanging on to the threads of her life. Independence, for Tina Turner, was barbaric.

6

During the journey to the airport, Ike snuggled up like a teddy bear, positioning himself comfortably, with his mistress and Tina on either side of his aching body. Ann Thomas and Tina exchanged looks of relief, hoping Ike would sleep during the short journey.

Tina stared silently at the passengers in the limousine, realising how much of a fool she was to be sitting there amongst them. She looked over at Ann Thomas, then she turned her attention to the petite, pretty white girl sitting opposite her. She wasn't even sure of the girl's name, but Ike had introduced her as his new woman from Canada. And there sat Tina, with two of her husband's lovers travelling to Texas with her.

Ike stirred, and Ann Thomas nearly jumped out of her skin when Ike's bloodshot eyes suddenly sprung open. Looking disorientated, Ike stared at her for a long time as if he was trying to focus, before slowly demanding, 'Ann, ya got ma chocolate? I need somethin' sweet.'

She scrambled through her bag and nervously pawed at the wrapper, removing the foil so Ike could eat the large bar straight away.

Still suffering the effects of staying awake on cocaine for five solid days, he bit into the chocolate but was too weak to chew. The chunk rested in his mouth as he started to doze off while Tina and Ann exchanged looks of disgust.

Suddenly Ike snapped to consciousness and shoved the melting bar of chocolate Tina's way. 'Have some. This shit is good, Ann.'

The Los Angeles heat was intense and Tina stared at the chocolate, which was now softly melting down Ike's fingers. 'No, Ike, I don't want any.'

'I said eat it, muthafucka.'

'Ike, get that away from me. It's melting. I'm wearing all white. It's going to ruin my outfit. Can't you see I got all white on, Ike?' Then Tina did something she had never done before. She forcefully shoved Ike's soiled hand away from her beautiful, white Yves St. Laurent suit. Ike, totally shocked, stared at Tina as if she was an alien before cracking her hard on the side of her head with his fist. Tina struggled, holding his arms so he couldn't strike her again, while Ann Thomas recoiled against the car door. Ike smacked Tina but, still weak from his coke binge, didn't land as many blows as he could have. Tina fought Ike with all her strength but he was still much stronger than her.

The car pulled up to the airport and Tina managed to shove Ike once more before the vehicle reached the kerb. Barely waiting for the car to come to a full stop, Tina leapt out and raced into the LAX building ahead of Ike. Ike, confused, mumbled to Ann Thomas, 'What the fuck's gotten into her tryin' to hit me and shit, I'll kill that bitch.'

Tina had never raised a hand to Ike before.

Ike caught up with her and grabbed her by the arm, digging his fingers deep into her flesh with his fingers. 'Damn, woman. Look at yo' face. Go fix yo' face.'

Tina, her face in disarray from being struck, simply grinned defiantly at Ike and carried on with the process of checking in and boarding the plane. This time she made no effort to hide what he had done to her and for once, Tina didn't care what she looked like, nor did she care who saw her. This made Ike sweat. He glared around nervously when people took a double look at Tina, focusing on her reddened cheek.

Once on the plane, Ike and Tina continued to poke at each other until the aircraft ascended and the seat belt sign went off. He finally said, 'Fuck this shit', before undoing his belt and stretching across the laps of both his mistress and Tina. But Tina was too wound up. She had had enough of Ike Turner and wasn't prepared to make the journey to their 4th of July gig in Texas one of comfort for her offensive husband. It only took moments for him to doze off before Tina was able to make an attempt at getting back at him. Tina shoved his head off her lap, telling him: 'Nuh uh, Ike, I'm not having this.'

Ike raised his body and sent an almighty kick right into Tina's shin then furiously stared her down, his eyes defying her to challenge him again.

But every time Ike got comfortable Tina would nudge him with her elbow, making it impossible for him to sleep. Ike was angry as hell but knew better than to keep striking Tina on an aircraft full of witnesses; yet his eyes made it clear that he wouldn't let it rest after the two-hour flight.

The plane finally landed in Dallas Fort Worth, Texas, and on the way to the waiting limo, Ike glared threateningly at Tina, trying to instill fear in her. Knowing she was marked for a beating, she no longer cared what he did or said and stared straight back at him as if he were beneath contempt.

Ike's car door wasn't even closed yet when he raised his hand and struck Tina across her face. Tina snapped and went for Ike, her small hands striking out with the speed of a terrified cat, becoming more like a panther. Someone reached over and closed Ike's door and Tina struggled, desperately trying to hurt her husband for all his years of abuse. Cursing him — something she never did — she shouted, 'Fuck you! Yeah, I know, I'm really gonna get it, huh?'

Ike didn't like this Tina and decided there was only one way to put her back in her place. He took his shoe off and beat Tina over her head, striking time and time again with the large solid heel.

Tina was badly injured and seriously dazed by the blows to her face and head. Despite this, she lashed out with determination. She thought she would probably die this time — but she would go with dignity. Tina wasn't going to let Ike get away with it without a struggle and she fought him with every ounce of strength left in her bruised body.

When the car drew up to the hotel Tina balled her fist and hit Ike with all her might, dazing him for long enough to leave her free to leap out of the car. But Ike was tough and, shoe still in hand, he caught up to her within seconds. He twisted Tina's body around and whacked her hard across the side of her head, sending her wig flying to the ground. He stood panting hard while slipping his foot back into his shoe and barking orders. 'Muthafucka, pick yo' fuckin' hair an' put it on yo' head.'

Tina, her lip sliced open and one eye bloodied and swollen shut, swayed with dizziness while trying to focus on Ike. She stared at him with her one good eye and bubbles of blood spilled out of her mouth as she uttered a painful 'No.'

Ike reached out and grabbed Tina by her collar, shoving her in the direction of the wig. 'Put your wig on.'

Tina regained her balance and stood for a moment before she stumbled to where her wig lay. The corner of her mouth twitched defiantly as she looked down the front of her own body, taking in the irony of the situation. Ike was worried someone might see Tina without her wig, yet he wasn't concerned about the rest of the mess. Tina's white suit was now stained red with her blood; she was bruised, bleeding from her face, ear and head, and all Ike was worried about was whether she had her wig on. She slowly bent down, the movement racking her body with pain and she held the tangled wig in her hand for a while. Then she turned towards Ike and plopped the wig on her head, letting it rest any way it landed. It teetered on the side of her head like a Frenchman's cap. It was pointless for Tina to try to stretch it over her head because one side of her skull had swollen out like a melon.

She walked, each step painful, into the foyer of the Hilton Hotel. Ike raced in stuttering that they had been in an accident and the staff wasted no time directing them straight to their room. Everybody in the limo was in a total state of shock. They had just witnessed Tina getting the beating of her life.

Ike was tired, far too tired to fight any more, and fell straight on to the bed as soon as he entered the suite. Tina, well trained from years of abuse, suddenly acted as if nothing had happened. She forced words out of her cut and battered mouth, asking Ike if he was hungry and if there was anything he needed. But Ike had fallen into an instant deep sleep, and Tina massaged him for a moment to make sure he wasn't really awake. Then she tiptoed through the room, throwing a scarf over her head and a cape over her bloodied suit, and silently picked up her toiletry case before quietly letting herself out of the room.

Using stairways and a rear exit, Tina bolted out of the hotel unseen by the rest of Ike's entourage. She ran down the alley, crouching and hiding herself between trash cans, and stayed still and silent until she was certain she hadn't been seen or followed.

When night fell, Tina ran for her life, dodging speeding cars as she crossed a busy freeway. On the other side was a Ramada Inn and Tina ran straight in there, seeking safety and refuge. She had 36 cents in her pocket and a Mobil gas card, and swore to the manager that if he gave her a room, she would pay him back. She tried to offer him the jewellery she wore, but he wouldn't hear of it and put her in the best suite he had. He offered her food, but her mouth was too damaged to eat most of the items on the menu. The kind man ordered her soup and posted hotel security guards at Tina's door, ensuring she would be able to rest without worry.

Tina hand-washed her suit and laid it out to dry, all the time wondering who she could turn to for help.

She phoned Mel Johnson, a Cadillac car dealer, then realised she had made a terrible mistake. Mel was good friends with Ike and she shook with worry, realising he would phone her husband. She then phoned Nate Tabor, Ike's attorney, who was familiar with Ike's violence and had always been sympathetic towards Tina. He arranged for an older white couple he knew in Texas to collect her the following morning, give her cash and take her to the airport where there was a ticket back to LA waiting for her. Over the fourth of July weekend, Tina hid in the safety of Nate Tabor's LA home, with his family offering her advice and comfort.

Meanwhile, back at the studio, everyone was sweating buckets. The morning after they flew to Texas, we heard that Tina had run out on Ike. Ike spent the following two days phoning from Dallas, pretending he was bewildered by Tina's absence. He failed to tell us that he had beaten her to a pulp.

Linda Kraus nearly gnawed her lip raw with worry. Tina was far too professional simply to 'walk out' when there was a booking. Something horrible must have happened. At one point, we reached such a state of paranoia that we thought Ike might have murdered Tina and hidden her body. When Ike flew back to LA, he marched straight into the studio and locked himself away. It was Ann Thomas who told us what had really happened. After she finished the story, everything fell into place and made perfect sense.

Tina had not contacted a single member of her family, not even her children. Ike had underground connections, and she knew one wrong call and it would be over. We were deeply concerned about her safety.

Ike, anxious and desperate, kept phoning Tina's mother, swearing he wouldn't hurt Tina again. 'Muh' couldn't help Ike — she genuinely had no idea where her daughter was. Feeling someone had to know of her whereabouts, Ike became suspicious of everyone who worked for him. He prowled the streets all night into the next morning, showing up as his staff's addresses, intimidating them and demanding they tell him where Tina was hidden. Then, frantic, he resorted to the 'nice' approach, but he couldn't hide the ugly, threatening tone in his voice. 'Yo' know ... me and Ann gotta sort this thing out. This thing be between me and Ann. She gotta get in touch with me ... she just gotta.'

Ike exhausted every avenue trying to locate Tina. His judgement was terribly misguided when he reached the conclusion that I was the only one who actually knew her whereabouts. Sweating, he would stare hard at me through one eye and say things like, 'Boy, you tell me where Ann is ...'

He would walk off ashamed after seeing the hopelessness on my face.

At the studio, we were under strict orders that if anything occurred indicating Tina's location, he was to be told instantly. On the Friday, exactly one week after Tina left, I took a call at the studio from a doctor. He was very restrained, and told me that he wanted to speak to a Mr Ike Turner. I kept buzzing through to Ike but he wouldn't respond. Ike's private studio was soundproof so it was pointless banging on his door, which was always bolted.

Finally the doctor told me to tell Mr Turner that he had examined Mrs Tina Turner and it was impossible for her to carry on working for the foreseeable future. He refused to leave his name or number and said Mr Turner would be receiving a letter on Monday. With that he said thank you, and hung up.

I told Linda Kraus about the call and she used her key to gain access into Ike's private studio. Within a minute of being informed of the call, Ike was standing over me, sweating with fury. 'Boy, yo' gimme that docta's name.'

I told him the doctor said Tina couldn't work and a letter would arrive on Monday, but that wasn't what Ike wanted to hear. His fist whizzed past me and dented the wall behind my head. It must have hurt him but he didn't even wince while he pointed a finger in my face and threatened me. 'Boy, yo' hidin' sumthin' from me.'

He then paced back and forth, his face contorting with anger. Then he bolted towards me, his hot, furious breath licking at my skin while he spoke. 'Let me tell yo' sumthin', boy ... yo' gonna get hurt. Real bad. This be between me and Ann.' Then I could feel his lips on my ear as he screamed at the top of his voice, 'NOW THINK!'

I was a nervous wreck, wondering why I had the misfortune to pick up the phone when the doctor called. Ike spent the next three hours interrogating me. He made me repeat the story over and over and over, hoping it would differ in some way and he'd catch me out. Menacingly, Ike made his feelings clear. 'Boy, I think yo' betta come up with that phone number. Yo' mem'ry betta come back fast, boy ... real fast.' He returned to his private studio and left me shaking — after hearing what had happened in Dallas, I was scared shitless of him.

Ike ordered Linda Kraus to continue pumping me for information but I had none to offer. Five hours later Ike was up in his private apartment and I could hear his voice in the background when his mistress Ann Thomas buzzed for me. She sheepishly said, 'Eddy, please give Ike what he wants. *Please*, if you can remember *anything*.'

Thirty minutes later I buzzed through to Ann Thomas and asked her to come downstairs. I knew Ike had been listening to me through his secret system, monitoring my calls, hoping I'd make one to Tina or the doctor. And I knew he was listening when Ann Thomas came downstairs. I didn't say a word. I simply handed Ann Thomas my set of studio keys, and she suddenly blurted out, 'Eddy, I don't think this is a very good idea.'

I didn't wait for Ike to come barrelling down the stairs. I fled to my new Corvette and took off at high speed, hoping never to see Ike Turner again.

On the Monday that followed, Ike received a letter from the doctor just as I said he would. Linda Kraus phoned me and said that Ike realised I had been telling the truth. I didn't care. I had no intentions of returning to the studio.

The doctor's letter was followed by a call from Nate Tabor, Ike's lawyer who had been hiding Tina. He informed Ike that Tina wanted a divorce. Ike responded by threatening the lawyer and his entire family. Tina didn't want Nate's family put in danger because of her, and so she went back to the refuge of an old friend of hers, Maria Booker. But Ike had hassled Maria Booker in the past and Tina feared he would do it again. She didn't want her friend put in that position so Maria asked her sister, Anna Maria Shorter, if Tina could stay with her.

Anna Maria was married to saxophonist Wayne Shorter. Wayne was travelling with Weather Report at the time, so Anna Maria, a high society white woman with an uppercrust Portuguese accent, welcomed the company. 'You tell Tina to come stay with me. I am not afraid of this horrible Ike Turner.'

And so, stony broke, Tina moved into Anna Maria's house with her other house guest Tina Bannon.

Anna Maria's guest Tina Bannon was as wild as wild could be, very dramatic, utilising her deep, sexy accent and voice to attract any man she wanted.

Wayne and Anna Maria were as different as night and day. Wayne, although one of the world's greatest jazz musicians, was shy and seemed to be a bit of an introvert, whereas Anna Maria was the extrovert. When Wayne was touring, Tina Bannon and Tina would paint the town red; Anna Maria was guilty by association.

Tina had never experienced the Hollywood nightlife until she befriended Tina Bannon. Ike was a stiff when it came to things like that and he was socially unsure of himself. Now, Tina started experiencing all the things she had missed in life. If Tina seemed negative about the evening's plans, Tina Bannon would sway her by saying, 'Oh Tina, you must do this. It is good for you to come out with me.'

In one single evening, Tina Bannon changed Tina's life. 'Tina. Come in the den, darling. We will drink some wine before we go out. Yes?'

'Uh ... no thanks Tina ... I don't really drink.'

'Oh, Tina! What is it you are saying? This is not possible! You must drink. I cannot sit here and drink by myself.'

This is when Tina became a social drinker. Tipsy after leaving the den, Tina and Tina Bannon painted the town red. They revealed a great deal to each other that evening, and Tina Bannon was astounded to discover that Tina had never had a lover while with Ike. Tina Bannon made it clear to Tina that she had to solve the 'man problem'. 'You can take your pick. Tina, you're in the Beverly Hills circle now.'

Through Tina Bannon's guidance, Tina learned how to flirt and, if that didn't work, she would use Tina Bannon's brazen approach of telling a man exactly what was on her mind. Tina Bannon had explained, 'What is there to lose? If you want it, tell him. If he doesn't want it, there are many, many more men to choose from in a single evening!'

Through Tina Bannon, Tina became a popular face on the nightlife circuit of LA.

Soon, though, Ike found out that Tina had been staying with Anna Maria, and he dumped all four kids at her door, leaving only $1,000 to rent a house for herself and the kids. It was a good strategy, knowing Tina would get herself into debt, and thinking she would return to him. It was a sunny, late August day when Tina finally contacted me by phone. 'Hi Ed. It's me, Tina. Listen. I'm okay, I'm fine in fact, but I'm broke. I haven't got a dime.'

My heart leapt all over the place while she gave me her address and phone number. 'Now listen Ed. It's Craig's birthday in two days and I can't even afford a cake for my son. Would you bake one of your amazing butter cakes for him, only this time frost it and decorate it?'

Knowing she didn't need a confirmation as to whether I'd carry out the task, Tina added, 'By the way, Ed, don't forget the candles! I'll tell you everything when I see you — we'll have a long chat.'

She had rented a house just off Hollywood Boulevard in Laurel Canyon. I arrived a couple of days later at the small, white house, and marvelled at all the greenery surrounding it. Tina wasn't home and the boys told me I was to wait for her. I put the cake away, wished Craig a happy birthday and left them to party with their friends while I had a good look around.

The front door opened straight into the living room which had a long sofa and other essential furnishings all leased from a place called Abbey Rents. The wooden tables and soft fabric covered seats resembled top-grade hotel furniture. It was not elaborate and bore no resemblance to Ike's surroundings.

On the far end was a mirror panelled wall leading to the dining room furnished by a simple wooden table with matching chairs. Another opening led to a sunken den, furnished with modern sofa sections which could be separated into single chairs or joined to form a length of wall seats. A modern chrome lamp tilted over the furniture. Large glass doors led to the rear garden, and the view was leafy and green for as far as the eye could see. I knew that, although it was a rented house and wasn't at all grand, it was the family home Tina had long yearned for.

The boys joined me and we played games for a couple of hours. When I realised it was nearing midnight, I asked what was keeping Tina. Ronnie wrinkled his nose and said, 'Mother's gone to see a play called "A Chorus Line" with some new white guy called Wim.'

'Tina's on a date?!?' I screeched.

The name Wim was familiar, and I searched my memory until I realised he was a guy in the record business who had popped into Bolic Sound Studio in the years gone past. Whenever he went to the studio, Tina and Ann Thomas used to sit in a corner, sizing him up and whispering about how gorgeous he was.

Just after midnight, I could hear footsteps out the front, so I peered through the window for a couple of minutes then leapt on the couch and picked up a magazine, waiting for Tina to stroll in.

The last time I saw Tina was the fateful day she flew to Dallas when her mood was unbalanced and harassed. When she strolled through the door, I saw a new woman, radiant, fresh and soft. Tina was a little tipsy and her eyes sparkled while her laughter filled the sitting room. She apologised for being so late, then ordered the boys to go wait for her in the den. With the boys out of the way, Tina gave me a hug then dragged me off to the kitchen. She put a doily on a silver tray while I placed the candles on the cake. In a bright, buoyant mood, she spontaneously gave me a warm hug as I struggled to light the candles. We carried the cake to the den while singing 'Happy Birthday' to Craig, who dutifully made a wish and blew the candles out. He turned to Tina and said, 'Mother, it's about time you got home. We been dying for a piece of cake and Eddy's been hiding it from us all night, 'cos we were ready to, like, *dig in*!'

After the cake ceremony, Tina sent the boys back to the den to hang out with their friends, affording us time on our own. Tina looked absolutely amazing. She was wearing her hair shorter, and she looked like a different woman. She was wearing an Yves St. Laurent black tuxedo, and full-length trousers with a black satin strip down the side. She offset this with a black sheer knit blouse. She reeked of elegance with her black silk stockings and her satin stilettos.

With the kids out of the way, Tina suddenly seemed a little tired. Sitting down, she ran her fingers over her knees and shook her head. 'Oh, Ed. I tell you. It's been too much. I know what you're like and I know you have a million questions to ask me ... anyway, what do you think of the house?'

'Tina, it's ... uh ... very *family*. Different to the one you shared with Ike.'

'Oh please, Ed. That house *was* Ike. Nothing there had anything to do with my style. I know what you're like, you must have had a good old look around. Have you been upstairs yet?'

'Nuh uh.'

'Well come on, let me give you the grand tour!'

The upstairs area was compact, with the boys' rooms set back to back, Ike Jr. and Craig sharing one with Ronnie and Michael sharing the other.

Tina's room was not too large but cosy with a skylight directly over her bed. To the left was her personal bathroom fitted with exquisite wall and floor tiles. There were magnified mirrors which lit up when pulled out on their extending arms. The shower was made of clear glass and Tina had all her lotions, potions, shampoos and body gels tastefully laid out in view. She didn't like keeping things in their original packaging and rebottled everything in ornamental glass decanters.

Tina showed me to her walk in closet which was bulging with designer clothes. All of them were on good wardrobe hangers with her accessories and shoes all meticulously laid out in an organised fashion. We both flopped on her bed and Tina rolled over and laughed like a naughty schoolgirl. Her eyes sparkled mischievously as she said, 'Ed, I have to tell you about Wim. Aaahh ... he's fantastic ... tall and gorgeous ...'

'Oh, that's who dropped you off?'

She sat bolt upright and screeched, 'Ed! Were you spying on us? Were you watching us kissing?'

'Tina, I tried not to. I mean, well I heard a noise outside and looked out the window and when I saw you two in each other's arms I ran back to the couch and ...'

Tina cut in, 'And pretended you were reading a magazine!' Then we rolled all over the bed in fits of laughter. Tina sat up with a start and excitedly said, 'Anyway, let me tell you about Wim! He's Dutch and I'm crazy over his blonde hair covering his whole body. And I love his accent!' Then Tina stopped and curled her lip, biting it gently while choosing her following words carefully. Looking as if she was caught doing something she shouldn't, she said, 'Wim is, well, he's kind of married. Him and his wife aren't getting along and he's not cut out for a family. That's what he told me anyway.'

'Did you decide that, or did he?'

Then Tina grabbed me by my arm and said, 'Do you remember seeing him at the studio years ago? Ann Thomas and I used to pinch each other when he came in. He was so hot! I never thought I'd be dating him one day! Wait 'till I tell you how it all happened.'

It was Tina Bannon who had masterminded the whole affair. When Tina revealed she hadn't been with another man since Ike, Tina Bannon asked if there was anyone she was attracted to. Tina told her about Wim, adding that she didn't have a clue as to his whereabouts. But that was all Tina Bannon needed to know. 'Tina, think. What record company did Wim work for? I'll phone the company and they'll give me his number.'

Within minutes, Tina Bannon had Wim's number and while dialling it, she said to Tina, 'When Wim comes to the phone, you tell him he must meet you for a drink.'

Running away from the phone, Tina said, 'I can't do that!'

So Tina Bannon sprung into action when Wim answered. 'Hello, is this Wim? Ah, good. My name is Tina Bannon. You don't know me but I am a friend of Tina Turner's. I am having a dinner party and Tina is guest of honour. It would be nice if you could join us. If you don't mind, the invitation is only for one person but I'm sure you will make many friends at the party.'

On the night of the dinner party, Tina acted surprised to see Wim there. They were immediately attracted to each other and embarked on a heady affair.

Tina and I rolled on the bed in fits of laughter while she told me of the wild nights she spent with Tina Bannon, adding, 'You know Ed, Tina was God-sent. I've been hanging out at Le Dome on Sunset Boulevard and The Daisy in Beverly Hills. I've been hanging out with all the beautiful people. And you know something? I'm a bit of a celebrity. I never really realised that until we'd walk in restaurants and get the best tables because I'm Tina Turner!'

I studied Tina carefully. She looked great and I told her so. She looked towards her closet and said, 'I'm grateful for all the clothes I got. Bernadette managed to sneak most of them out of Olympia Drive for me. '

Bernadette was Craig's high school sweetheart, a truly beautiful mixed-race girl and the daughter of a founder member of The Platters. Tina and Bernadette grew to love each other, Tina viewing her as the daughter she never had, and trusting her with her deepest feelings.

'Remember all the fantastic stuff I'd buy and never wear? I knew it would all come in useful one day. I don't have a dime in my pocket but that don't stop me from lookin' like a million dollars. Hmmm. I remember all the times Ann Thomas and me would spend fortunes on clothes then we'd go back to my hotel suite and try everything on for each other. I knew I'd never wear any of it when I was with Ike. He never took me anywhere! Now that I'm friends with Tina Bannon, I know I'll put it all to good use. Ed, I want to change and put on something comfortable. Go downstairs and get a bottle of wine and some glasses. You'll find the wine hidden under the vegetables at the back of the fridge. I have to hide it from the boys, you know. They're at that age, wanting to drink. If I don't hide the alcohol, there won't be anything left!'

After fetching the goods from the kitchen, I returned to Tina's room and pawed through her clothes while she changed and removed her jewellery. With Tina in white silk pyjamas and ballet slippers, we jumped back onto the bed like kids having a slumber party. We had a lot of catching up to do and talked for a few hours. It was wonderful watching the new Tina. At the age of 37, she started living. She was like a new person, mysteriously youthful, dating, going to parties and meeting new people.

'Ed, I got my own friends now. No one can tell me who I can or can't see. Most of my friends are from the showbiz world and they're all practicing Buddhists and into chanting. But record companies are staying away from me. They all think I'll end up going back to Ike and his name is mud now. Ike is taboo. He's been hearing about me hitting the town with my new friends. Everyone knows, and Ike knows, I'm not going back to him. When we kept having to cancel flights that day because Ike was all screwed up on cocaine, I knew I was walking out on him then. I just knew. Come hell or high water, I was out of there.

'Then we sat in the limo and I looked at Ann Thomas and the new girl Ike'd flown in from Canada and it made me feel dirty. Then when we were on the plane and we were sitting in economy with Ike's sweaty body spread over me and Ann Thomas, I felt real cheap. Ike always made a display of his women and I was embarrassed, downright humiliated. It always looked like there was a threesome or something ugly going on.

'Ike thought he was rock and roll, you know, like the Rolling Stones. But we weren't the Rolling Stones and I am not a rock chick, you know, free love and all that stuff. With the way he carried on, Ike had people thinking I was sleeping with him *and* his women. Ike didn't have style like Mick Jagger or Keith Richards or Rod Stewart. Ike always got it wrong, looking more like a pimp instead of like one of them rock boys. Ha! Poor old Ike. Well, Ed, I sat on that plane getting madder and madder. I wasn't going to let him sleep. I was out of there — leaving — I was gone. I was getting out of his life but I didn't know it was going to be like that. I thought, "I'm going. Even if it kills me," and it damn near did.

Tina's face stiffened as she continued, 'Ike freaked because I hit him. He took his shoe off and whacked me around the head. While he was beating me, my wig went flying and he stopped out of shock. My wig never budged when I worked on stage but that's how hard he was hitting me — that wig took off like it had wings. I mean, you know what I'm like about my hair Ed. Believe it or not, I didn't care who saw me looking like a nappy rabbit that day. Ike was shocked. He yelled all sorts of profanities at me. He was saying stuff like, 'Pick up yo' fuckin' wig, bitch. Put yo' muthafuckin' hair on.' Ed, I took my sweet old time picking that wig up. I just plopped it on top of my swollen head and stared him down. I marched in that hotel not caring who saw me. Ike got worried. Really worried. Ike and me — we're history.'

Tina took a large sip of wine and pursed her lips before continuing. 'I thought a few weeks would pass and he'd leave me alone. But he's got people keeping tabs on me. Everytime I change my phone number he gets it at the drop of a dime. And you know, he took me out planning to kill me recently. He called out of the blue and said, 'Hi Ann, it's me.' He wanted to have a talk – a *talk*, like we're on good terms or something – and I thought to myself, I'm not that little Ann from Nut Bush anymore. I'll have a talk with him, but only in a public place. It was the same old Ike talking. He drove me somewhere for a coffee and we didn't have much to say to each other. He drove me home and before I got out of the car, he said, 'Ann, I really love you. I'm gonna change.' I told him it was over. I saw his hands flinch and the corner of his face twitched. Then he leaned forward and I don't know what got into me ... some inner voice said "don't go moving too fast". I quietly reached for the door handle and as soon as my foot touched the ground, I ran, really fast, and locked myself in the house. He phoned Muh later and told her he was three seconds from blowing my head apart but I ran before he could reach the pistol he had hidden under his seat. Imagine telling my mother that. "I was three seconds from killing your daughter, Muh!" '

Tina nearly dozed off while talking then she looked at me and said, 'Ike thinks I won't be anything without him. You wait Ed. Everyone will see. I can do it.'

I watched Tina as she slept, her breathing so gentle. I checked on the boys and made sure the house was secure before letting myself out. As I drove home, I couldn't help but dwell on Tina's last words. I knew she could survive without Ike. She was a superstar and she knew it. In time, the rest of the world would realise it, too.

7

Nothing was as it seemed. Although Tina swanned around town draped in sparkling jewels and wildly expensive designer clothes, she was actually penniless and living on government handouts. I'd try to make light of it by saying she was the best dressed woman on food stamps. As an easily recognisable face, Tina found it impossible to stand in a checkout line with her food trolley and listen to people whisper 'Isn't that Tina Turner?' then reach inside her designer handbag and pull out food stamps. In order to save Tina the embarrassment, her sister Alline, who was not proud at all, carried out this task on a regular basis.

Tina held on to her last thread of sanity by reasoning that, although left with the most monstrous debts imaginable, at least she was free of Ike. As it was Tina who had walked out on Ike, she was technically responsible for any cancelled dates that ensued. Now she had two major hurdles to overcome — how to earn a living while, at the same time, paying back the tour promoters who were suing her over the six-months' worth of cancelled bookings — a lot of money. In the latter part of 1976, Tina knew she was in danger of disappearing from the music industry's memory without a trace and desperately needed to return to the showbiz circuit. It was just a question of how to go about it.

Tina was a performer — end of story. During her twenty year career, she had never handled bookings, money or anything technical that went with her live performances apart from rehearsing and doing the show on the night. In short, she didn't know how or where to begin. And to make things worse, nearly everyone she knew of in a position to lend a helping hand still had links with Ike Turner. The only person she could think of to help was Rhonda Graam. Rhonda, who had walked out on Ike three months before Tina, needed no persuasion, and soon leapt into action. Before we could blink, Tina was booked on to all sorts of TV shows — entertainment programmes, celebrity slots — anything that could rake in the coins.

Rhonda was not the most pleasant person in the world but she knew her business. Within a short space of time, thanks to Rhonda's skills, Tina started making money to pay the rent and clothe the boys. After she started helping Tina on the road to recovery, her home was twice set on fire. One evening, after returning from Tina's, Rhonda found the windows in her home had been blown out with a shotgun; soon afterwards, her car met the same fate. There were no prizes for guessing who was responsible, but with no witnesses there was little the police could do.

Tina developed safety drills which she would practice regularly with her children and Rhonda. Tina taught them all to hit the floor and crawl under hard furnishings should anything 'unusual' happen. But soon after Rhonda's car was shot up, detectives from the homicide squad arrived to inform Tina that the word on the street was that Ike Turner had put a hit out on her. Craig, who is very sensitive, listened to what the police had to say, and nearly cracked up. Tina put on a brave face but knew that if a hit man wanted to get her, he would probably succeed. The police warned Tina to be on her guard, but in the same breath made it clear that they couldn't offer her protection because of lack of evidence. Depressed, worried and fearing for her life, Tina went into hiding in Germany. Staying with acquaintances, she never left the house, fearing word of her whereabouts would get back to Ike. Not even Tina's sons, mother or sister knew her exact location. Tina left without telling the boys where she was going and she didn't make contact while away, leaving her sister Alline to look after them. Tina was aware of her children's welfare through her trusted housekeeper and close friend Bernadette.

Alline was going crazy juggling her own personal life while caring for Tina's four boys. I phoned Tina's house to ask her how she was coping and she sounded like a woman condemned. 'Oh, Eddy, shit, Ah can't talk right now. Things are too crazy here. The boys have no clothes, Ah gotta do some laundry, fix up some food and go back to my own place and look after my own kid. An' in the mornin', Ah gotta git ma Jackie to school, then Ah gotta come here an' feed an git this lot on the road, an' oh yeh, somehow Ah gotta git to work on time after all that shit. Ah'm gonna have to talk to you later, Eddy. Bye!'

I put the phone down and rang Alline back two minutes later, offering to lighten her load. She asked, 'Boy, ain't you got no school?'

I was in college by then and wouldn't have any trouble making up for lost time. I could hear the boys in the background arguing and tugging at Alline. 'Aunt Alline, where's all the underpants? Aunt Alline, I can't find my teeshirt. I'm hungry. Aunt Alline, Ronnie won't get outa' the bathroom ...'

Alline was clearly overloaded so I jumped in my Corvette and arrived at Tina's house thirty minutes later. When I walked in Alline looked frazzled and the house was in disarray. The boys, all in their teens, had always been accustomed to maids and household help. They didn't know how to cook, or use a washing machine, and the chaos they caused was driving Alline mad. In the midst of folding towels while trying to cook dinner, Alline realised she had forgotten to collect her daughter Jackie from school. I told her to go and look after her kid and that I would take over. While I continued with cooking a meal, Ike Jr. and Craig grilled me as to the whereabouts of their mother. They were deeply distressed over her disappearing without saying a word to them. Thrown totally off balance by Tina's silent exit, Ronnie and Michael both gave me a bastard of a time, certain that their mother had been in contact with me. Tina had no choice; she feared for her safety if she contacted her family.

The kids were well and truly spoilt. They weren't the first to fall victim to a parental parting of ways and I felt they had a lot to be grateful for. Fed up with their tiresome behaviour, I served dinner then ordered them into the den. I tidied the dishes and embarked on the monumental task of tidying up the house. The house gleamed by the time I fell into bed, exhausted. My last thought before retiring was 'tomorrow will be a better day'. I was wrong.

The following morning, turmoil reigned supreme. When I went to wake the boys for school, they retaliated with a chorus of abuse. 'You're not my mother, so I don't have to listen to you. Don't try to tell me what to do. Who do you think you are? You're only a year older than us so you can't boss us around. I'm not going to school and you can't make me. Get out of my room. Get *out!*'

I dragged them out of bed by their teeshirts and terrified them into washing and getting dressed. After feeding the lot, I forced them to my car only to realise that the four boys would never fit into my two-seater Corvette. I ran back into the house and found the keys to the white Jaguar that Sammy Davis Jr. had given to Tina. Once I piled the boys into the car, the most horrible row ensued, giving me an insight into how badly they were affected by Ike and Tina's split. Ronnie suddenly snapped, 'Let me out of this car. You're not my mother and if it wasn't for her I wouldn't be in this mess.'

Then Michael piped up, 'Yeh. Look how we have to suffer just 'cause Mother decides to have some sort of long vacation in Europe. She won't even phone us or tell us where she is. All this is her fault.'

Ike Jr. had a bit of complaining to do, and the only one who stayed silent was Craig. I let the boys voice their anger, feeling it would do them some margin of good to make their feelings known. None the less, I remained strict. It wasn't always easy, man, but we got there. I also insisted they take responsibility for any mess they created and taught them how to have enough consideration to pick up after themselves. I made it perfectly clear I was not their maid. It took a full five days to get the house and garden back to Tina's meticulous standard and during that time, the boys learned to accept me and their situation a little more.

We settled in well together, but boys will be boys. Two weeks after my arrival, Ronnie and Michael had a horrific fight, resulting in Ronnie ringing his father. When Ike discovered I was there, he insisted I come to the phone. 'Boy, what the fuck you doin' there?'

'I'm helping out looking after the boys, Ike.'

'What you mean, boy? This thing be a family thing. Boy, git yo' stuff and go home. This be between me and Ann. Now git yo' shit and go.'

Ike slammed the phone down and I called Alline. After telling her that Ike ordered me out of the house, she said, 'Don't you go packin' no bags, Eddy. Ya ain't movin' a muscle outa that house. No. I'll just phone Ike Turner and put things right ...' As she continued to speak, I could tell she was in no mood for Ike Turner. By the time she put the phone down, she was ready to give Ike a good old fashioned telling-off. 'Ah mean, you be helpin' me an Ann out. That Ike Turner can keep his useless ass down in Inglewood, thank you very much.'

Having hyped herself into a frenzy, Alline said, 'Ah'm callin' him. Ah'm tellin' him where he can take his orders, and where to put them.' Click.

Alline was great. She didn't stand for any man's crap. She held on to her ground, and had no bones telling a man where to go.

Five minutes later, Alline rang me back, saying, 'Don't be scared. You ain't gonna hear from that skinny little fucka again. No sir. I'll kick that little muthafucka's ass ...'

Tina decided she couldn't hide away from Ike or so-called hitmen for ever, so after a month or so she decided it was time to come home to work, pay bills and face an uncertain future. She asked for the white Jaguar to be brought to the Beverly Hills Jaguar dealership for a tune-up so it would be ready for her arrival. I drove the Jaguar to a garage, with Alline following behind. I turned into Beverly Hills and pressed the brakes but the car wouldn't come to a stop until I ploughed straight into a Volkswagen Beetle. Incredibly, the Volkswagen survived but I put a good dent in the Jaguar. I thought Tina would freak. The night before Tina was due back, I returned home with my tail between my legs. Worried about the car, I thought it best not to phone Tina until she phoned me.

A couple of days later she called, saying, 'Ed, before you say a single word, I want you to know that I'm not upset over the car. It was my fault, anyway. The brakes been acting up and I should have seen to it sooner. Now, I don't want to hear any apologies at all.

'I'm phoning to thank you for looking after the boys and the house. You've been a real friend. Alline and the boys told me how wonderful you've been and I don't know how we would've coped without you. As soon as I settle back in, I want you to come over for dinner.'

Two weeks later I arrived at Tina's for the promised meal. When I laid eyes on her, my mouth nearly fell open. She had changed. She had lost her confidence and seemed like a tiny, frightened, insecure woman. Tina had lost her vibrancy and I was gutted to see what she had been reduced to.

In her absence, the boys had also undergone changes. Still angry over Tina disappearing without a word, they seemed determined to punish her and behaved like monsters.

Tina looked at me and I could see the shimmer in eyes had long since gone. 'Tina, what's the matter?'

'I'll tell you Ed. I've never been so scared in my whole life. Would you believe I considered going back to Ike purely out of fear? Then I thought, nah, I'd rather be dead.'

'It's going to be okay, Tina.'

'I don't know, Ed. Everytime I find some sort of peace or happiness, Ike comes a long and puts a big dent in it. I thought, after a while, he'd just go away and find someone else to abuse. But I know, now, this Ike situation ... it's far from over.'

Having both lost our appetites, we spent the evening pushing our food around our plates. 'And the boys, Ed ... they're like a bunch of animals. I don't know what's gotten into them. It's like ... they're mad at me or something.'

I didn't want to further depress Tina by spelling out the boys' problems. But it wasn't long before the inevitable happened.

One night, Tina and I werre sitting in her bedroom talking, when she suddenly blurted out, 'Oh, Ed. My boy Michael has been acting real strange, like he's deeply disturbed. I took him to a doctor and found out the kid is having a nervous breakdown. Ed, The kid's not seventeen yet. Anyway, I have to send him for psychiatric treatment.'

I covered Tina with a blanket then went downstairs and gathered all the boys in the den to have a heart to heart with them.

Michael explained that his mother, Tina, had agreed to pay for his treatment. I looked at the boy and could see how lost he was. It was pitiful and heartbreaking. He was a fragile, sensitive teenager. He told me, 'You know, umm, my real mom moved to town. Her name's Lorraine. I want to live with my father or my real Mom.'

I discovered Ike had made things worse by trying to use Michael to get at Tina. I left wondering whatever would become of them all.

8

Tina realised the time had come for to sink or swim. She made a valiant effort to pull her life together with the aid of her old friend, Mike Stewart. She had ever-increasing financial commitments, as she had just moved into a larger, more comfortable house. Mike organised finance, making available $150,000 to put a new band and show together. He also hired lawyers and accountants, who would carefully monitor the expenses to make sure the money would last long enough to get Tina's career back on the road.

Tina held auditions and chose her new band along with two male and two female singer-dancers. Her new costumes were designed by Bob Mackie, designer of stage clothes for superstars like Cher and Ann Margret. She had the entire band and dancers kitted out in fabulous new costumes and to make the money last, Tina held some of the singing and dancing rehearsals in her own home rather than hiring a studio. I would sit through the rehearsals, nodding my head towards Tina with approval if the act looked good.

Tina was always motivated by something and organising the new show kept her energetic for weeks. Once she was satisfied with the act, she had to find a new challenge to stimulate her, and this usually came in the form of work or romance.

It was at this time that Tina met Henry Weinberg, Elizabeth Taylor's ex-lover. Tina was fascinated with Henry, and he enjoyed a reputation of being the most well endowed man in Beverly Hills. Henry was wonderfully knowledgeable about everything from fine restaurants to antiques and, at this point of Tina's life, she was a willing student to anyone who could bring up her standards. I don't recall exactly how the two met, but Henry eased his way into Tina's life — the irony of the union being that Tina thought Henry was wealthy and Henry thought Tina was wealthy. In reality, they were both nearly skint but neither would realise this until some time later. At least they were both masters of appearing to be affluent.

Tina had a hopeless addiction to living beyond her means which drove

Mike Stewart and the accountants around the twist. Mike would bombard Tina with phone calls warning her to stop spending. When the accountants refused to forward her any more money, she would simply go to all the swish Beverly Hills shops and have them bill the accountants. Once a bill arrived, the accountants were forced to pay up rather than sully their client's name. When it came to money, Tina was crazed, irresponsible and, worst of all, unstoppable. One day I popped by and Tina whisked me off to town to 'pick up a couple of things'. Thirty minutes later, she had parted with $5,000 and did this without a penny in her pocket. She bought fresh flowers for the house, then saw a few garments she wanted, then a few other small items and within half an hour, had spent the thousands. She still didn't have the house completely decorated and furnished, but at least her spirits were up.

With Henry Weinberg on the scene, Tina's financial irresponsibility escalated. She went on wild sprees, lavishly spending money she didn't have. Henry was not a great looking man. He had a big nose, full head of hair and dressed very Beverly Hills conservative. He wore custom made suits, Gucci loafers, Cartier rings and all the accessories and labels that were in keeping with Beverly Hills high society. Henry was terribly knowledgeable about what you should wear, where you should be seen, how your home should be decorated , and he was very well read on antiques. He had a way of making Tina feel secure. The fact that he wasn't married helped — her relationship with Wim had faded because of his family obligations, and she was ready for a new man.

When Henry was with Tina, he looked more like a father with his adopted daughter, and she loved being linked with him. Very excited over their relationship, Tina said, 'Ed, tongues are wagging all over town. I could actually hear people whispering sometimes, saying stuff like Tina Turner and Henry Weinberg are an item! Now I know his reputation as a playboy but it doesn't matter to me. I feel just like one of them Beverly Hills high society women when I'm with him.'

Wild Tina Bannon played a part in encouraging the relationship by telling her, 'Oh Tina ... you know what they say about Henry. He is meant to be very well equipped! Go with him so you can tell me if it is true!'

Tina was nervous about dating Henry, but she had a gift for recovering from insecurities as fast as lightning. 'What am I saying? I don't have time to think about things like that. I'm just going to have a good time!'

Henry kept his own apartment but moved in with Tina, introducing her to a totally different lifestyle, a higher level of society and the finer things life could offer. Although Tina had been introduced by Anna Maria and Tina Bannon to a fun bunch of people, Henry's friends were the ultimate in class. With her new home still not completely furnished, Henry made certain suggestions to Tina. 'You know, Tina, you should get into antiques. They are great investments and leave visitors with a good impression. Antiques are so ... should we say ... classy.'

Tina and Henry spent entire weekends scouring antique markets and shops. Henry, like a skilled advisor, chose almost everything Tina invested in at the time. He educated Tina on fine glass, crystal, cutlery and other good household accessories. Henry enjoyed spending Tina's money as much as she did. Sadly, while doing so, he would sometimes be condescending and would belittle Tina for her lack of knowledge. I found this terribly offensive but Tina did not. 'Okay Ed. So what if Henry is snobbish over my lack of social knowledge. I'm not bothered. I don't care because I'm learning. Mark my words. You'll see the day when no one will have a reason to look down at me or criticise me again.'

Meanwhile, much to the horror of the accountants, Tina went from living just beyond her means to living ten times beyond her means. They constantly phoned Tina pleading with her not to write out any more cheques or have things billed to them. But Tina was in the school of Henry Weinberg and was more than happy to pay the price.

Over the space of a couple of months, however, Henry had taken too much for granted and had become over-generous with Tina's finances, playing the big man and drinking too much. It took a while for Tina to notice that on all their shopping sprees and flashy dinners at top restaurants, Henry never put his hand in his own pocket. Tina realised she had been paying for absolutely everything, from their own dinners to evenings of Henry entertaining his friends. Tina cringed and complained, 'The guy is in a good business, dealing used cars and stuff. But I've been paying everything, Ed, I mean everything. I even pay for the presents he buys me. Since I met him I can't remember Henry ever pulling out his own wallet. And you know something else? He doesn't even have the decency to look embarrassed when I pay the bills at restaurants. Thinking about it, Henry acts as if I should be proud or honoured to be seen with him.'

Tina had Rhonda Graam to manage her business life; but with trying to get her career back on the road *and* look after four kids, she needed someone else to help out at home. That someone else was another relic from the Ike days, a woman called Ann Cain, whom Ike had met in an LA record shop in 1963. He was impressed with her intelligence, style, musical knowledge and good looks. Ann Cain was impressed with Ike Turner because he was Ike Turner — so she jumped at the chance when he offered her employment within his own household.

Ike had just lost another housekeeper who couldn't put up with his unruly, messy children and feeling they needed strict discipline, he enlisted Catholic school educated Ann Cain. Hoping she could perform some sort of miracle, Ike and Tina gave her free rein with the children who were thoroughly disrespectful and ill mannered. Ann Cain regarded the four boys as a challenge — they destroyed their own property, couldn't tell the time, didn't wash their bodies properly or brush their teeth and on the whole, behaved like a pack of untrained animals. Within a couple of months, Ann

Cain had taught them impeccable table manners, etiquette, good hygiene and she sat over them every day like a school mistress helping them with their homework. She transformed their lives. She was strict and often resorted to taking out the belt, but it took drastic measures to break the children of their unruly habits. The kids hated her, but in later years, they all admitted to me, at one time or another, that they respected her.

Living with Ike and Tina, Ann Cain took over every aspect of the Turner household, including Tina's husband. Tina flipped and threw her out when she returned home one day to find Ann Cain on her knees performing oral sex on Ike. But throwing Ann Cain out of the house did not serve to remove her from Ike's life. Ike got her an apartment nearby and showed her the ropes of the music industry. Ann Cain became Ike and Tina's business manager, working in that capacity for nearly five years.

Ann Cain, the same age as Tina, travelled with the couple on all their tours, looking after every fine detail of business while bedding Ike. But she soon tired of touring with Ike, his wife and all the other women he was bedding apart from herself. Unwilling to share Ike, she left his employment.

Tina had reason to hate Ann Cain with a passion, but eleven years later, she phoned her and urged her to return to her employment. With Rhonda and new recruit Ann Cain, there were now two of Ike's former lovers working for Tina.

It was late 1977 when Ann Cain, as her first duty, found the perfect house for Tina to lease. When Tina clapped eyes on the house, she was determined to have although it was way out of her budget. Rhonda Graam came up with an idea to raise the extra money needed to secure the home. Rhonda cleverly went to BMI, a company that collects royalties for records that have air play. Without Ike knowing, Rhonda arranged for the payments to be re-routed to Tina. It was above board because Tina was listed as the songwriter on several of their records, and Ike never noticed that the payments stopped coming to him.

With the extra income, Tina had joyously moved into her new home just off Laurel Canyon. The house was approached by a long driveway leading to the entrance. Tina loved it because it was surrounded by so much greenery that you couldn't see or hear your neighbours. The house was unpainted, the stained wood giving the exterior a natural charm. Entering the house was like walking into a Chinese garden. The floor was uncarpeted and Tina returned all her rental furniture to the shop and enthusiastically started from scratch.

Soon after moving into the house, Tina became totally disillusioned with Henry Weinberg and whinged endlessly about him, almost as if she was searching for faults and finding reasons to dislike him. 'Ed, I've been thinking. I've been looking at Henry real carefully. His clothes are smart, okay, but they are old, really old and threadbare. His clothes are nearly as worn out as he is. His trousers are frayed at the bottom and his shoes must have been heeled a hundred times. I don't see the point of having him laying around my house the whole time, sponging off me. Anyway, I have to go to Vegas and do an engagement for a couple of weeks. If that guy doesn't pull his socks up soon he'll be high-tailing his way back to his messy little apartment.'

While Tina was away, Henry lounged around Tina's house as if he was a king. He had a boyish charm about him, was very likable and hard to get annoyed with. He had been boozing so much of late, that he hardly noticed the signs that Tina was due home. Ann Cain had completely filled the house with fresh flowers and dusted and polished everything. She always did that when Tina was on her way home from a tour.

Tina walked in, tired from her journey, and the first thing she saw was Henry, drunkenly slouched in an armchair with a full glass of spirits in one hand. He leered at Tina and slurred, 'Helloooo, darling.'

Tina studied Henry with distaste before saying, 'Just look at you. I come home mid-afternoon and you're already drunk.'

She marched purposefully to her room, ordering Ann Cain to follow. She threw her things onto the bed and turned to Ann, saying, 'We've got a problem, Ann. I'm not happy with what I see. I'm not in the mood. It's time for Henry to go home.'

Ann Cain was a skilled bearer of bad news, and Tina conveyed all her bad news through other people. She would always have Ann, Rhonda or myself reprimand others on her behalf, and she would try to listen in while we carried out her instructions.

Ann left Tina's room, walked straight up to Henry who was slouched on the couch and said, 'Henry, it's time for you to be leaving now. Tina has decided that you are to take all your belongings and go. Right now. If you aren't capable of doing it yourself, I will gladly pack for you.'

Henry slurred, 'I ain't fucking going nowhere. I'll do what I want, when I want. I'm not going anywhere.'

Ann Cain walked straight up to him and firmly replied, 'We don't want an ugly scene, Henry. If you insist on getting ugly, I will get help. Now I will put a pot of coffee on so you can sober up and, while you do that, I'll pack for you.'

Ann returned to Tina's room and Tina eagerly asked, 'How did he take it?'

Ann calmly replied, 'The problem has been dealt with. Henry Weinberg will shortly be on his way.' Then she excused herself and packed all of Henry's belongings.

9

Tina rolled across her bed and grabbed the phone, eager to tell Anna Maria about the demise of Henry Weinberg. 'Hello, Anna Maria? It's Tina. Guess what? Henry Weinberg is history. Ann Cain just helped him move out. I got fed up with the guy — I mean, listen to this. Henry and me were flying on trips, eating at the best restaurants and the guy never had any money. I paid his tickets, food, drink, everything! The guy was shabby. I should've known the first time I went to his apartment. It was a mess. Really untidy. Now you know I can't stand filth.'

Tina came up for air and continued, 'Anyway, you know the two weeks I just spent working in Vegas — well I met a great guy. His name is Axel and he's gorgeous!'

Anna Maria's strong Portuguese accent could be heard booming through the receiver. 'Teeena! Darleeeng! This calls for a celebration! I will organise a big party for you and this Axel. We will do Portuguese food. We will order from caterers!'

Tina chewed on her bottom lip and slowly said, 'Well ...'

Anna Maria cut her short, saying, 'Teeena, you know what you're like. You are so slow with these love things. You will take too long to organise a party. It will take me only a second to do it. I will take care of everything.'

Tina, still dazed from her trip, replied, 'I don't know. Anna, you're moving a bit too fast for me. I haven't got that far with Axel yet. I haven't made plans for him to come here. I haven't invited him.'

Anna Maria passed the telephone over to Tina Bannon, who had an answer for everything. Firmly replied, 'Why do you wait? You call him now. Say you are not working for a week — make it two weeks. You tell him to come over. You tell him there is a ticket waiting for him at the airport. This is how to do things. Now don't be a silly girl. You phone him right now.' Click.

Tina phoned Axel, invited him to LA and, as Tina Bannon suggested, arranged for a ticket to be waiting for him at Las Vegas airport. The couple of weeks leading up to Axel's arrival were busy ones. Rhonda Graam assisted on the road, and while Tina earned money, Ann Cain busied herself spending it. And by God, that girl could burn through money.

When the accountants phoned Tina to chastise her for spending so much, they were stunned to learn that it was, in fact, Ann who was making the extravagant purchases all over Hollywood and Beverly Hills — and with Tina's full consent! Tina set up charge accounts at the finest stores, which Ann could sign for. She used Tina's money to surround her employer with the most beautiful items imaginable. Thanks to her, Tina now had breakfast dishes and lunch dishes as well as formal and informal dinnerware. She bought the best cutlery from around the world, silver trays, silver pots, crystal glasses, vases, ornaments — you name it. All the items on display sparkled with class.

Around this time, Tina once made a small noise to Ann that perhaps she had bought enough for the house. Ann replied, 'Well. That's fine, Tina. If you want to have your breakfast off the same plates you ate your dinner on, that's fine with me. You are receiving proper people as guests now, as well as cultured boyfriends. If you don't wish to leave an impression on them ... well ... that's entirely up to you.'

Tina never complained about Ann Cain's spending again. Ann was a woman of impeccable taste and she shopped for assorted items for the home that she felt Tina needed. Silk sheets, beautiful vases and linen table cloths and napkins were amongst the essential items. With Ann's help, the house really started to take shape. One evening, following an out-of-town gig, Tina came home and inspected the changes in the house, thoroughly approving of all Ann's purchases. She moved on to the living room and found Craig and his lovely girlfriend, Bernadette, enjoying a quiet evening. Tina commented on Bernadette's cute sportscar which was parked in the drive — a gift her parents had given her for her eighteenth birthday — and then, tired from travelling, she retired to bed, leaving Craig and Bernadette sitting in front of the television.

Just as she was settled under her cosy duvets, the sound of gunshots was heard outside. Craig went to the window to investigate and suddenly yelled, 'Mother ... mother!'

Bernadette's new car was surrounded by a ring of fire, the flames crackling like tiny, bursting pellets. The tyres of the car caught alight and Tina ordered Craig to move the vehicle for fear of the tank exploding. He bravely did so by putting the car in neutral and pushing it way beyond the flames before extinguishing the blazing wheels. Upon further investigation, they found the back window of Tina's car had been blown out by a shotgun, and the house had been fired at as well.

Distressed, Craig said: 'It's Father ... I know it's him. It's Father, again!'

Totally fed up, Tina replied, 'I should have known it. As soon as I get comfortable, there's Ike again. Just when I think everything is fine, he comes along trying to ruin it all for me.'

Tina paced while staring out of the window, then her nostrils flared with anger as she added, 'It's him alright. I just can't prove it. What the heck does he want from me now?'

The SWAT team arrived, removed pellet samples which were deeply embedded in the house and warned Tina to tread carefully. There was little else they could do.

Finally, Ike Jr. told me what was going on. 'Eddy, all this has to do with the divorce. Mother's lawyer wants her to get what she is entitled to but Father doesn't want to play fair. Father isn't gonna give mother nothin'. He still thinks there's a chance she'll go back to him. Father has properties all over the place, and Mother wants the one near Disneyland. She wants to sell it to finish paying off all the promoters who want their cancellation money back. She's working — officially, Father isn't. So the promoters are still going after Mother.

'Father thinks he'll either scare her or starve her into going back to him. She ain't going back. We all know that by now. Well, everyone but Father knows it.'

After the incident with Bernadette's car, Tina gave up and decided she didn't want anything. She effectively bought her way out of her marriage. She told the judge that she only wanted to keep her stage name — Tina Turner — without having to give Ike a percentage of her earnings. After all the millions they had amassed over the years, Tina walked away with only two cars and her name. Although the judge felt Tina deserved much more, he had no choice but to agree to her wishes. Her marriage to Ike Turner was over, and Tina was free.

Unbeknown to others, Tina did manage to snatch a few crumbs for herself. Without Ike realising it, Tina went to storage and removed her tremendous collection of furs. She had also given Bernadette the combination numbers for the safes in her former home, and Bernadette managed to sneak out personal possessions from there. All Tina's jewels and diamonds that were in the safes at Bolic Sound Studio were never returned to her. It didn't make a blind difference to Tina. She got what she really wanted: her freedom.

Tina ran around town preparing for Axel's arrival, taking her new companion with her — a trained Doberman guard dog. Tina hired the dog from a specialist company and it was trained to follow Tina out of the house and stay by her side at all times. From the moment Tina opened her front door, the Doberman stuck to her like glue, and she kept the dog employed for nearly a year.

She also applied to keep a gun, but was told she had first to take a course on a shooting range. When she completed the course and earned her certificate, she proudly framed the paper body she shot full of holes. 'Ed, look at it. Those holes earned me my certificate. I shot it perfectly. The instructor said I showed real skill. I'm hangin' this up as a warning to Ike and his low-life chums.'

Meantime, Ann Cain ran Tina's household like an army drill sergeant, whipping the boys into shape. When they didn't toe the line, she would chuck the offending teenager out to live with Ike; inevitably he would crawl back to Tina's.

It wasn't always smooth sailing however. Ronnie got involved with a bad crowd and started messing with drugs. Ike Jr. suddenly got fed up of Ann Cain's strict ways and made a career out of trying to get the upper hand over her. One morning, all the boys united and hurled obscenities at her. She found foul language the lowest form of filth and showed the boys the door. The boys complained to Ike, who turned around and whacked the boys about their heads saying, 'Yo' little fuckers probably deserved it!' Incredibly, Ike approved of Ann Cain.

The final climax with the boys came when Ike Jr. gave Ann such a hard time she packed both him and Michael off to their real mother, Lorraine. Ike Jr. and Michael felt uncomfortable around Lorraine because she was well and truly poor, but at least they got to know her. Ronnie, whose drugs exploits were rapidly escalating, got packed off to boarding school by Ann Cain. With Ronnie in boarding school and Ike Jr. and Michael floating between the homes of Lorraine or their father, the house was relatively peaceful. Craig, who was an angel and deeply in love with Bernadette, remained at home.

Tina's busy working lifestyle, and increasing successful career meant she saw her children less and less. Craig was the only one who had occasional, direct contact with her, and that was only when she was in residence. It was difficult for her children to contact her when she was on the road as she moved city so frequently. Ann Cain relayed any messages between mother and sons and, inevitably, they drifted apart.

This left Tina time to concentrate on her career. Meantime, Axel's arrival caused a flurry of excitement. As an outsider looking in, I viewed him as a heart-breaker. He still enjoyed a sexual relationship with his daughter's mother, Sherry, but Tina wasn't to know that at the time. Madly in love, she told me, 'When I first laid eyes on him, he took my breath away. The moment I saw Axel, I stopped in my tracks. I couldn't look at him because he was so fine — just so good-looking. And I'll tell you what else Ed, it's a small world. There I was in Vegas and you know Linda Kraus? I bumped into her. You know she's living there now. Well, she's only Axel's ex-wife's best friend. Can you believe it?'

I contacted Linda and rekindled our friendship in order to get information on Axel and his ex, Sherry. Linda told me that their relationship was always torrid and volatile, so finally they split. Linda told me they still saw each other, but I wasn't about to burst Tina's bubble. I thought that in time, she would make Axel well and truly hers. Axel was a suave handsome playboy. He was around 6' 2" with light hair and a sexy moustache. He was well mannered, well spoken and had a regal aura about him. Things couldn't have been better for Tina. She was glowing over her new love mission and steeled herself to win Axel's heart.

Tina had everything she wanted at that moment, and was spending a great deal of time with her dancer Rava Daly. Rava was a tiny, sexy Jewish girl who had an astonishing body and attracted men like bees to honey. She had shoulder-length brown curly hair, a tiny waist and fabulous legs. Tina said, 'I love hanging out with Rava. The men just come in swarms when she's around. They go crazy over her. She's so much fun that it's like having a girlfriend at home, and it's good to have someone on the road that's intelligent and classy. Rava does not mess around, and honey, she knows how to work men. That's why I like her. The girl keeps me on my toes.'

Tina's ploy was always to get a guy to move into her home straight away so she could keep an eye on him and train him to suit her needs and lifestyle. This didn't quite happen with Axel because he flitted back and forth to Vegas, using his daughter Dominique as an excuse for going off for weeks on end. As a way of seeing more of him, Tina would often invite Dominique to LA when her dad visited. She always wanted a baby girl. It was her lifelong dream. When Tina took Dominique out on shopping sprees, she pretended Dominique was hers. She spent hundreds of dollars at a time on the cute little girl and, eventually, got to know her mother Sherry.

Meantime, Tina remained mystified over Axel's movements and income. No one had a clue as to what he did for a living. He definitely had an income but from what, we never knew. Nonetheless, when with Tina, Axel never had to put his hand in his pocket. This would become a trait of Tina's.

She always paid for everything from flights to hotels. She felt it would be unfair for her lovers to have to spend their own money to visit her in LA or when she was on tour. Moreover, she would shower her boyfriends with expensive gifts — clothes and accessories — and redesign them to suit her taste! Still, try hard as she did, she never found out how Axel made his income. He was secretive, and this played on Tina's mind.

It was around this time that Tina decided to have a breast enhancement. Mike Stewart's wife, Gabriella, found the perfect surgeon. Tina had a six week tour coming up, but she told everyone she would be gone eight weeks. She would use the spare two weeks to get her breasts done. Dr. Larry Sieford carried out the operation, and he warned Tina to take an entire fortnight to convalesce, keeping the bandages tightly wrapped around her breasts and not doing anything strenuous with her arms. His final warning was that Tina mustn't go out partying or dancing. Did she follow his advice? Did she hell.

I phoned to see how Tina was doing and Ann Cain very formally told me, 'Tina is not receiving calls right now.'

I was miffed. I told Ann, 'Tell her Royal Highness that when she is quite finished with her rest, perhaps Her Majesty will have enough strength to use her little Royal finger and dial my number.'

Ann calmly informed me, 'I will pass on your message.'

Two minutes later my phone rang. 'Excuse me, what's this message Ann just gave me?'

I replied, 'Tina, I want you to know that I am curtseying as I speak. Clearly

I have now to book an appointment, and I know I should be deeply honoured that you made this call. Did you do it by yourself or did you have your lady-in-waiting dial on your behalf?'

Tina, amused that I was so annoyed, said, 'Yes, those were my instructions to Ann. I'm recovering from surgery, you know.' Girlishly she added, 'I need to use X amount of muscles to dial a number ... I mustn't strain myself ... doctor's orders, you know.'

Bored from staying indoors convalescing, it didn't take much for Tina Bannon to talk Tina into a night on the town. When Tina explained none of her clothes would look right over the tight boob bandages, Tina Bannon replied, 'Tina, you must. There is a wonderful party and you must go. Just hide the bandages under a gorgeous dress. Come on, with your designer wardrobe! Please.'

Tina objected to putting a dress over the bandages so Tina Bannon took charge. 'I tell you what, Tina. Put the bandages to the side for now.' Pulling out a beautiful bra from Tina's undie drawer, she added, 'Here, just put this on and the dress will look good. Now do this and we must.'

Off Tina waltzed, partying the night away with Tina Bannon and in the midst of it all, a stitch burst where the incision had been made under the breast. Like a schoolgirl caught doing something naughty, Tina confided, 'Dr. Larry was so mad. There I was havin' a good time and suddenly I felt something wet. I had to phone him immediately and he said he'd come straight to the house. I shot out of that party with blood seepin' out from under my breast and when he got to the house, he wasn't very amused.'

Tina clutched the area under her breast and her eyes widened as she said, 'I had to fib to Dr. Larry. I told him I had to go to an industry party. He didn't want to hear it. He said this is a serious thing and I must do as he tells me.' Then, suddenly annoyed at herself, she added, 'Honestly, that Tina Bannon. Why do I let her talk me into these things? I should have stayed at home.'

At that time, incisions under the breast were considered serious. Tina could have had her breasts lifted and implanted from around the nipple area, but many women had complained that they lost sensitivity, so Tina took the other option. She retreated back to her bed for the remainder of the convalescence period.

Incredibly, Tina was wonderfully naïve about sex and would ask me about how gay guys performed. Tina's girlfriend, Rava, never short of tips on seduction, once said, 'This is what you gotta do. Just sit on a chair, any chair, and casually lift one leg up — like this, straight up — and gently stroke your calves and thighs while talking to him. Stare like a sex goddess straight into his eyes and tell him you want him to make love to you there and then.'

Tina looked at Rava like she was a crazy woman and said, 'Come on now, Rava. You know I can't do none of that with my leg. I can't get it up in the air like that. Tell me something I can do. Don't go giving me no more of that rubber band stuff. I'm not made of elastic, you know.'

Tina loved her girlfriends, and the naughtier they were, the better. Having been surrounded by women her whole life, she far preferred girls as friends instead of men. Tina desperately wanted an education into how gay guys performed because there was so much she didn't know about sex. It was amazing looking at Tina as a raunchy stage performer who oozed sex appeal when, in reality, there was so much more for her to discover. I reminded her that life began at forty and she was at the ripe age to make all these wonderful new discoveries.

Tina adored her lovers. She sighed, 'Know what I love best about sleeping with men? Looking at them when they fall asleep after sex. I love looking at their beautiful skin and hair. I love stroking their face and hair while they're sleeping.' Then she smiled, as if overwhelmed by some sort of inner peace, and said, 'I can be the woman I want to be now.'

10

Although Tina was still living beyond her means — at one point, she had to sell off all the gaudy jewellery Ike had given her to clear debts of nearly $150,000 — she was truly enjoying life. The same could not be said of her family.

'Muh', as Tina's mother was known, had lived in Ike's house in St Louis. But because of Tina's separation, it became unsuitable for Muh to continue living there. Tina phoned her sister. 'Alline, it's me, Ann. We got a problem. Muh has nowhere to live. Find a place in the building where you are and I'll pay for it.'

Then she phoned Muh and told her, 'Muh. It's me. I'll pay the rent on an apartment for you and help you out the best I can. Alline is finding a place for you in the building she's living in.'

Tina entered a nervous time once Muh moved to LA. She didn't really know her mother at all. Tina and Alline helped Muh to find a job in the beauty salon of the very swish Bonwitt Teller department store in Beverly Hills. Muh, missing her friends from St. Louis, enjoyed the job because it gave her a chance to meet lots of new, rich people. In the salon where she worked, she served coffee and tea to wealthy clients and enjoyed the prestige of being Tina Turner's mother. Bonwitt Teller often hired older women and mothers of known celebrities or wealthy people. A lot of those women didn't have to work, but they genuinely enjoyed having a reason to wake up each morning, to gossip with their peers and the society women that frequented the salon. Muh, who must have been near 60 at the time, was in her element, and when she returned home in the evenings, Alline's daughter Jackie would nip to her apartment and spend several hours with her. Things couldn't be better for Muh.

Way back, at that first party at Bolic Studios, I was told that Tina was embarrassed by her sister. This was not true. In fact, she loved Alline dearly, even though Alline would stand for nobody's nonsense. Never living in her sister's pocket, Alline made ends meet by doing any odd job going, and when Tina was on the road, she started to work as her assistant. She didn't mind working hard for her living. Always referring to Tina by her real name Ann, Alline told me, 'Shit Eddy. If Ah be lettin' Ann pay ma' way, she be tellin' me how to run ma' life. Ain't nobody gonna be tellin' me what to do. Nuh uh. Nobody.'

During that time, Tina had a brilliant drummer called Ron Silico, who had a bit of a drinking problem. While on the road, Tina became totally distraught when Alline suddenly announced she was marrying Ron. Neither excited nor happy about the impending union, Tina made it perfectly clear she did not approve. Like Ron Silico, Alline also loved booze. It was only a matter of time before Alline and Ron would engage in fierce, drunken arguments while travelling with Tina's band. This agitated Tina to no end.

Another thing that annoyed Tina was that Alline would always call her by her real name in the presence of media or business people. Alline didn't care. If Tina complained, Alline would say, 'Well shit girl. You be changin' so much you done forgot your own name. Your name be Ann and I'm gonna call you Ann.' Then Tina, always embarrassed by Alline's display of her roots, would gently try to urge Alline to speak properly. Alline would say, 'Nuh uh. Fo'get that. Ah ain't white so Ah ain't havin' to talk like a white person. Shit, Ann, you be so white now you done forgot that you're black.' Tina would bristle, and shake her head as if Alline was a pitiful, lost cause.

But I loved Alline and her down-to-earth ways, and she always seemed fond of me. Once, I went down to Vegas to catch one of Tina's shows. I was at the bar, with Rava and Tina's keyboard player Kenny Moore, when I spotted Alline and called her over to join me. She marched up and, in her strong Nut Bush accent, said, 'Damn boy, there was me in the wings while Ann was performin' an all Ah could see was your big ol' white teeth flashin' in the audience at Ann. Ah still got lotsa' things Ah gotta do. Come on backstage with me an' keep me some company.'

On the way to the dressing room, Alline never stopped talking, barely breaking for breath as she told me what it was like to look after Tina. 'Shiiiit. Ann got ma' ass workin' from here to kingdom come. That girl thinks she the queen.'

I couldn't restrain myself from pawing through Tina's amazing stage costumes while Alline packed, cleaned and talked away. 'Ann don't gimme a break. If it ain't one thang, it's anotha' thang. Ya know what Ann's like. Everythin's gotta be perfect. Ah dunno how much longer Ah can take this.'

I'd have done anything to trade places with Alline and told her so. 'Oh my God Alline. I'd love to be in your shoes. I'd love to do all this!'

Alline looked at me as if I was crazy. She put her hands on her hips and rocked her body and head with each word, emphasising her statement. 'Well shit, boy. When Ah git tired, Ah certainly will refer you. Hell. Ah'm ready to git outa this work anyway ... all this travellin' an bein' away from ma' daughter and shit. Ah can't have a life with this job.' Then she chuckled and shook her head, almost pitying me, adding, 'You be sorry ... real sorry if you find your ass doin' all this for Ann.'

At this point, Tina lived her life as if she was ten people rolled into one, accomplishing more in a single day than most people would in a week. She was still making improvements to her home, she was still being courted by elegant old Hotel Henry, a man she occasionally dated while she was in Vegas, and still had Axel flying back and forth. And on top of that, Mike Stewart had arranged for her to record in London, and had put together a mini European tour to help cover the costs. When she arrived to play Italy she met a man called Adrianno, the Italian promoter of that leg of her tour.

Adrianno was a small man with a great sense of humour, wildly entertaining and full of fun. He fell madly in love with Tina and did everything he could think of to make her visit memorable. He showered her with flowers and gifts and took her to the most expensive restaurants in and out of town. While she enjoyed being treated like a superstar, Tina pretended she didn't realise Adrianno was crazy about her.

One day, they were driving along the motorway in Adrianno's convertible when he made a bizarre request. 'My love, let me see that shoe you are wearing.'

Utterly astonished, Tina peered at Adrianno over the rim of her sunglasses and asked, 'Why do you want to see my shoe?'

Her mouth fell open when Adrianno said, 'My love, I adore women's feet. I just want to take a look at your shoe.'

The sun beat down on the open-top car and the breeze licked around their heads while Tina fiercely objected to the request. Adrianno pleaded, 'One little shoe — just one!'

Unable to resist Adrianno's carefree, boyish charm, Tina giggled nervously and removed her expensive new Maud Frizon shoe. She cautiously handed it to Adrianno who promptly chucked the shoe out of the open top car and watched in the rear view mirror as it rolled across the motorway.

Tina twisted to look at the shoe as it tumbled across the tarmac, watching helplessly as it disappeared, a shrinking dot in the distance. 'Adrianno! How could you?'

Holding the remaining shoe in her hand, Tina yelled, 'These are ... no ... they *were* my favourite shoes. What am I going to do with just one shoe?'

Grabbing the shoe, Adrianno said, 'Give it to me, my love!' While speeding along, he took it and threw it on to the motorway.

Tina was astounded. 'Damn it Adrianno. I can't believe you just did that.'

Adrianno, the picture of innocence, said, 'I love it when you are angry. You are beautiful when you are mad at me. I like this!'

Before Tina could say a word, he bellowed, 'My love, we go now and I buy you twenty pairs of the same shoe!'

Tina couldn't help but laugh at his boyish charm. Adrianno drove into an area lined with top designer shops. 'Adrianno, this is pointless. You won't find Maud Frizon in that colour here. This colour was specially made for me, and ordered by Donald Piner at that specialist company, The Right Bank

Clothing and Shoe Co. He's the Beverly Hills guy that caters for the needs of people like me, you know, entertainers. Those shoes weren't stock colour. They were a one-off ... made for me!'

Adrianno spoke in a carefree tone. 'It is not a problem, my love. As soon as we get back to the hotel I will personally phone this Donald and order the shoes in every colour! But right now, I take you shopping.' He parked in front of a jewellers and from the car Tina could see a Rolex watch, a design she had always yearned for but felt she couldn't afford. She stared wide eyed at the watch and Adrianno noticed her interest. He left her in the car while he nipped off to buy her a pair of shoes. Tina stared at the shoes for a moment, and, as she slipped them onto her feet, she glared at Adrianno and announced, 'Okay big shot. I want that Rolex.'

He took her by her hand and marched her straight into the jewellers. Adrianno, with a great deal of colour and flair, announced to the staff, 'That Rolex in the window. I want it for this beautiful lady. Do you know who this lady is? She is my love! And my love can have whatever she wishes!'

Tina, thoroughly embarrassed, whispered, 'Please Adrianno, stop it!'

Adrianno, amused by his blushing date, became more vocal. 'But my love, I am proud of you. You are the most beautiful woman I know. I want everyone to know this watch is a tribute to your beauty!' He put the watch on Tina's wrist and she melted. She had wanted that very design for the longest time. Tina once tore a photo of the watch out of *European Vogue* magazine and put it in a portfolio. She told me at the time, 'Ed, anything you really want, put a picture of it in a portfolio. Make a dream book of the things you want and you will attract those items into your life.'

Tina was always putting things in her dream book. I told her at the time, 'Tina, girl, you better become rich. An Arab Sheikh couldn't afford half the stuff in your dream book!'

But she had astounding confidence in her beliefs. 'Ed, I'll have everything that's in that book someday. And soon, Ed. Really soon. I don't know how but it's coming.'

So the watch in Tina's dream book finally arrived — via Adrianno. And he didn't stop there. He whisked Tina through the swish shopping precinct and bought her more shoes and beautiful, expensive clothes before returning her to her hotel. While dropping her off, he said, 'My love, I have another surprise for you. I want you to dress in all your beautiful new things and I will collect you in four hours to take you to Italy's finest restaurant.'

When Adrianno collected Tina, who looked stunning in the beautiful dress he had bought her, he took her to a candlelit dinner where he played footsy under the table. Tina later told me, 'I suddenly thought, "Uh oh, he's starting to get familiar." Then we got back to the hotel and you'll never believe what he said to me. He said, "My love, I got another surprise for you now." Well, Ed. There we were in my suite laughing, having a good time sipping brandy and coffee then suddenly, Adrianno just leapt on me! I mean, he was all over me like a little rabbit, showering me with lots of little kisses. I said, "Slow down ... slow down Adrianno ... you're going to ruin my new dress." Well, I burst out laughing when he said, "Don't worry my love, I'll buy you many new dresses in many, many colours!" '

Tina chuckled a bit then continued, 'Ed, well ... Adrianno was just so sweet and funny and magical, would you believe that suddenly I was really in the mood to make love! I genuinely wanted to do it. Well, I started doing a little striptease, just like Alline taught me, and when I thought about my coaching, I burst out laughing in the middle of it all. And there was Adrianno going, "Oh yes, Tina, yes, Tina ... and I just looked at him and told him to shut up so I could finish my striptease.'

Tina had a huge smile on her face and her skin glowed and her teeth flashed as she continued, 'Adrianno was ready to burst out of his pants.' She cracked up laughing and had to compose herself before she added, 'Guess what number I sang and stripped to? Shirley Bassey's "Hey Big Spender".'

At this point, we were both holding our ribs and after a fit of uncontrollable laughter, Tina dabbed the corners of her eyes and said, 'Well ... there I was singing "Hey Big Spender" while peeling off my dress, then I kicked a shoe off and the heel nearly stuck in the wall. Poor Adrianno ... he couldn't take any more. Honey, he just grabbed me and threw me on the bed and jumped right on me.'

After a long period of silence, Tina suddenly snapped out of it and inhaled deeply through her nose before concluding, 'You know, it didn't matter in the end that, physically, Adrianno wasn't my type. I became really fond of him for the person he is. He made me laugh and really knows how to enjoy life. Yeah, I like him. I like Adrianno.'

11

David Bowie is a man who doesn't need to try too hard — when he wants something, he gets it. After all, he's David Bowie. And when he caught Tina's show in Switzerland shortly after her signing to Ariola Records, he decided that what he wanted was Tina Turner.

Tina was fairly naïve when it came to stars and celebrities. We would have to tell her who was in the audience then explain what songs the famous artist was known for. If the star wanted to go backstage to meet Tina, she would be able to act as if she knew who they were. In reality, stars meant nothing to Tina. At that point, she barely listened to radio or played music. For a person in the business, she was remarkably out of touch. But David Bowie was one of the rare stars that Tina didn't need to be heavily briefed on. Prior to his arrival, Tina proudly announced, 'I'm sure I know who David Bowie is — he's the strange one, isn't he?'

Rava raced breathlessly into Tina's dressing room and said, 'Oh my God, Tina, you'd never believe who's here!'

Tina very casually replied, 'Yeh, I know, David Bowie, and he wants to see me.'

Rava, on the verge of fainting, nervously stuttered, 'Ohhh, Tina ... I always wanted to meet him. Teeeenaaaaa ...'

'Well then, Rava, if you want to meet the White Duke, I guess you'd better stick around.'

Tina savoured every moment of Rava's anticipation. While on the road, at this point, Rava was the only person Tina really socialised with because she was naughty, witty and, on a girly level, loads of fun. Tina, fully aware of her actions, wound Rava up even more, making the tiny dancer as nervous as a bird in the clutches of a tiger.

As soon as David walked in and laid eyes on Tina, he became very familiar with her and flirted mercilessly.

Rava stood poised, in true dancer style, before seductively strolling over to David's side. You could spot from a million miles away that Rava was a dancer from the way she walked and carried herself. She had an aura about her that attracted the wealthiest of men. All she had to do was stand in the middle of the room and they would gravitate towards her. Tina introduced Rava to David and he looked over and said, 'The show was very good and so were the dancers. Lovely show.' Then he immediately returned his attention to Tina.

Other people started drifting into Tina's room, including the very talented keyboard player, Kenny Moore. Kenny, very soulful, found it easy to speak with David. Rava, who would have gladly traded everything to have one chance in bed with David, flirted as if her life depended on it. David was not at all interested in Rava, and this confused her to no end. No man had ever turned her down. She oozed sex appeal, and always got every single man she wanted. She was, therefore, speechless when David blatantly ignored her and made an obvious play for Tina. Tina, though, was not attracted to David and pretended she didn't realise he fancied her.

David excused himself and headed towards the door to use the communal gents. Tina said, 'No, no David. Don't go there. Use mine.' He gratefully headed towards the bathroom which was attached to her dressing room.

As soon as David stepped away, Tina and Rava launched straight in. Rava gushed, 'Oh, my God Tina. He's so sexy!'

Tina wrinkled her nose at the opinion, replying, 'Eeewww. I don't think he's good looking at all. I'll tell you what Rava, this one you can have — OK?'

Rava, unable to believe her ears, replied, 'Tina, are you sure?'

'Rava, honey, I'll even set it up for you.'

David was in the toilet for quite a while and when he emerged, Tina thought he seemed a little different, his eyes a little wider. Touching Tina at any opportunity, David tried every tactic imaginable and called on all his powers of persuasion to entice her over to his place. 'Tina, I want to take you in my limousine. I have a limousine waiting outside. I want you to come with me for a ride — I have a beautiful house here. I want to show you my house.'

'No. No. No, that's okay. But, uhmmm, Rava would love to go.'

Rava piped up, 'Oh, yes, I'd love to go!'

David looked at Rava then at Tina. Referring to Rava, he said, 'I've had that type before. I'm not interested.'

Any other woman would have been floored by the insult, but not Rava. As far as she was concerned, David's rejection made him more appealing. It only fuelled her determination to jump on him that night. Tina, a little fed up, said, 'David, the only way I'll go is if Rava comes with me. I'm not going to your house by myself.'

'Why, are you afraid of being alone with me?'

'No David,' Tina patiently replied, 'I'm not afraid of you at all. It's just that, well, you are a bit frisky!'

David reluctantly backed down, and the two of them went back to his house. After a couple of drinks, David had his driver return them to Tina's hotel. Tina always stayed in a good hotel while the band stayed in a mediocre one. This particular night, Tina was feeling a bit devilish and invited Rava back to her room. 'Rava, don't bother going to your hotel right now. Come up to my room for a drink and chat.'

Tina, feeling totally confident over all the attention she received that evening, was on top of the world. Meantime, Rava smarted and licked her wounds over David Bowie's rejection.

While in the elevator, Tina causally asked, 'So Rava, what do you think of your White Duke?'

'Fuck off.'

Tina purred with contentment when she saw how pissed off Rava was. 'Ravaaaa, I'm sure I saw a glimmer in David's eye for you ...'

Before Tina could finish what she was saying, Rava had worked herself into a tantrum. 'Look, Tina, if you're going to tease me about David all night, I'm not gonna come to your room. I'm not gonna have a drink with you if you're gonna be this way. I know what you're like when you get like this. If you're gonna be bitchy you can have your drink by yourself!'

Tina lips stretched into a mile-wide smile. 'Noooooo, Rava. What do you mean? I can't believe how rude David was to look you right in your face and say he wasn't interested because he had your type before. How insulting ...'

'Tina, you're starting!'

'What's wrong with you, Rava? You run into my dressing room all excited because Bowie is coming backstage and when he gets there, you're all over him like a cheap suit. Now, all of a sudden, you're not interested in talking about him. What's with you?'

Rava, in a rage, barked, 'Well how would you feel if a man turned around in front of a room full of people and said "Oh, I've had that before"? I mean how the hell would you feel? I felt like a dish he ordered and tried a long time ago and couldn't be bothered tasting it any more. Know what I mean? Bowie was rude, rude, rude. To me! I thought you said he was well mannered. He was horrible to me! I know why he's after you, Tina. My skin is just the wrong colour or he would have been all over me like the rest of the men. He only went for you because you're black.'

Tina smirked. She'd had her fun with Rava and allowed the petite dancer to find any excuse she wanted to make sense out of David's rejection.

After recording her album, Tina flew straight into Los Angeles Airport, and while working her way to the exit, she spotted Lionel Richie and his wife Brenda. Tina had never met Lionel before, and at that time he was the hottest solo recording artist in the world, topping global charts with slow melodies and romantic tunes. With absolutely nothing to lose, Tina marched straight up to him and introduced herself. 'Hello? Lionel? I'm Tina Turner. I know we've never met before but I have to let you know that I love these ballads you're writing, particularly "Still". I use it in my new show. I know how busy you are, but I'd love for you to write something for me!'

Tina was dumbfounded by Lionel and Brenda's reaction. 'Oh, Tina! I'm so pleased to meet you. My wife and I are big fans of yours ...!'

Cutting Lionel off, Brenda excitedly piped in, 'I just love your music. We have all your recordings ...'

Between Lionel and Brenda, Tina suddenly felt as if she had introduced herself to two star-struck fans. Lionel and his wife were the sweetest people on earth and weren't shy about letting Tina know how much they idolised her.

Tina could never understand why people liked her music so much. In a naïve way, at that point in her life, she genuinely couldn't see what they saw.

Lionel didn't let Tina go without exchanging phone numbers and he told her he would love to write a special song for her. This was the best thing that could have happened to Tina, and she left the airport on a wonderful high. Over the past few months, Tina had been desperately searching for original material and inspiration. Bursting with new-found energy and hope, she gushed, 'Imagine that, Ed. I've been searching for new stuff and it came straight to me! You can't get much better than Lionel Richie!'

During this phase, Tina was thoroughly addicted to psychic readers. As soon as she arrived back in America, she went straight to her favourite psychic, Carol Dryer.

Carol told Tina, 'What I'm seeing is that you must concentrate on work. You've got to make some drastic changes. I see you amongst the greatest of stars ... you are one of them! But you must go through a lot of changes before you get there. Your present man is not what you think him to be. You must build on your own reputation and name and you still have a lot of baggage to get rid of.'

Tina was happy with what she heard.

Having just recorded an album and then bumping into Lionel Richie, she was more focused on her career at that moment than anything else.

Much later in the evening, Tina suddenly brought up Axel. 'Ed, I've been trying to get hold of Axel for weeks and I couldn't track him down anywhere. I think I'll try his ex, Sherry.'

After making small talk with Sherry, Tina asked if she knew where Axel was. Tina was shocked rigid when Sherry casually said, 'He's right here. I'll put him on the phone!'

Whilst chatting with Axel, Tina became visibly uncomfortable. She was getting the same feeling that used to grip her in the past when Ike had slept with yet another woman. Axel said, 'Now that you are home, shall I fly over for the weekend?'

Tina, somewhat confused, replied, 'Well ... uh ... I'll tell you what. I haven't worked out what my schedule is ... yet ... now that I'm back. So, ummm, why don't you call me in a couple of days and by then I'll know what I'm doing with myself.'

Tina placed the receiver back in it's cradle and held it down hard while she stared at the wall.

'Ed, something's not right. I've got that feeling. I feel sick. Axel's involved with someone else ... I just know it. What is wrong with me when it comes to men? I mean, in the past three years I've had Wim and Henry Weinberg and Adrianno ... sweet Adrianno. But there's always something not quite right.'

She looked as if she was on the verge of tears. 'I'm nearing my mid-40s. I want a proper relationship. What have I done so wrong?

'Ed, I want someone serious. Not just a one night stand. Not a long distance lover. Something proper. Someone who'll come on the road with me. Someone who's here when I get home. Someone who's here for me ...'

She turned to Bernadette for advice. Bernadette came around and spent the evening listening to Tina pour her heart out over her misgivings concerning Axel. Bernadette told her, 'Axel is real good lookin'. Real fine. When a man is that fine, you gotta be a bit wary of him. If Craig was that fine I'd be scared of all the cat around. Axel is suave, but there's mystery surrounding him, he's always in Vegas with his ex. I couldn't swear it would be easy for someone like him to resist all the cat that must be rubbing up against his leg all the time.'

Tina listened carefully to what Bernadette said and rubbed her lips while deep in thought. 'You know what, Bernadette? You might be right.'

That's all Bernadette had to hear. She advised Tina, 'Phone him. Go on. Tell him you went through your schedule and you're free this weekend. Have tickets waiting for him at the airport. Have a nice time with him. Get him relaxed then ask him straight out for the truth. One way or another, because he's here right in front of you, you'll know what's really going on. But you won't be able to suss him out over the phone. Go on. Invite him.'

Tina did just that.

When Axel arrived he was terribly sunburnt and he winced in pain when Tina went to hug him. He claimed he had fallen asleep in the sun and Tina made no mention of his tender skin during their romantic dinner. She had gone all out to create a charming atmosphere. Should her worse fears be realised, she wanted Axel always to remember with clarity what he had thrown away. Everything was perfect, especially the bedroom which was carefully prepared for an exquisite, gentle seduction. Her wooden bed, which was built to look like a ship, was beautifully fitted with lace and silk sheets. One wall was all glass, overlooking the hillside which was full of trees. There was an end table which supported a lamp, topped by a crystal shade engraved with cherubs. The dim light of the lamp completed the setting.

Once in the bedroom, Axel removed his shirt to reveal horrific patches on his back. Tina recoiled at the sight, wincing as if she could feel the pain herself. She laid a cotton sheet over her silk bed-coverings and a large fluffy towel over the lot. She told Axel to lay on his tummy while she gently treated his sore back with extract of the Aloe Vera plant, a tried and tested remedy for burnt skin. Originally, her ideas were of a romantic nature but she ended up playing nurse, instead. Wanting Axel to realise just what he would be missing if he messed her about, Tina made every effort to treat him like a king. He was far too burnt to make love that weekend but they spent all their time in bed, being served day and night by Ann Cain.

Tina knew it was impossible for Axel to make love but she still sensed something was amiss. She stared at him while he relaxed in her large bed and she suddenly remembered what the psychic reader had said — that her present partner was not the ideal man Tina imagined him to be. She stared for a moment longer, then asked Axel, right out of the blue, if he was still sleeping with his ex, Sherry. Axel casually replied, 'Well, she is the mother of my daughter!'

Tina was stung but tried not to show it. She knew it would never work with Axel and after that weekend, despite the numerous calls he placed to her, Tina barely spoke to him again.

Despite all the work she was doing, Tina was still not a wealthy woman, and she was distraught when she was informed that the lease on the house she had been renting, and on which she had spent tens of thousands of dollars, would not be renewed.

She held a meeting with her manager, Mike Stewart, and her accountants and explained the situation. Tina said she didn't want to rent again. She wanted to buy a home of her own. She was over forty years old and with all the money she had generated in her lifetime, she had never personally owned her own property. The accountants were firm in their reply. They told her that, at that point, she couldn't possibly afford a house and that she had to be patient and wait. Tina argued, 'I'm paying someone else's mortgage. I pay a lot in rent and I want a house. I have never owned a piece of property with my name on it. If I'm going to go out there and work hard doing two shows a night then I want something to call my own.'

Mike Stewart reasoned with her. 'Fine, Tina. You want a property? Where are you going to raise the down payment?'

'Well, Mike, how much do I need for a down payment?'

'You'd have to find a house first, then the down payment would be a percentage of the overall fee, say something like ten percent. Right now you can go out and buy ten percent of nothing. Because you've got nothing. You have spent it all. You have spent more than that. You are in the red. You cannot afford it. Understand?'

Tina held her head up high and said, 'Right. First things first. I'll find a house.'

She immediately rang Ann Cain and said, 'Ann, we don't have much time. You know I been given three months' notice to move out of that house. We have to find somewhere else — fast. Go on. Go find something. You know the sort of thing I'll like.'

Ann Cain was on the case. Within days she saw the most stunning piece of property in an affluent area called Sherman Oaks, just near Encino where many of the rich and famous live. The house was on a street called Royal Woods Drive, and was of Asian–Oriental influence, with plenty of bedrooms and loads and loads of living space. Ann Cain phoned Tina to announce, 'I've found your new house.'

There was only one small problem. Tina had told Ann to look for something in the region of $300,000 and the house Ann had found was around $150,000 more than expected.

'Come on now, Ann. Don't even think of showing me anything in that region.'

'But Tina, this is your house. This is the house you want. Just have a little look at it.'

Tina made arrangements through the estate agent to view the property which was approximately fifteen minutes away from where she was currently living. As she approached the house along the drive, she saw that it was lined with bamboo bushes which also surrounded the entire structure. The entrance to the drive could easily be missed, and it was impossible to imagine the stunning property that lay beyond the simple entrance. It was a wooden structure, with dark stained beams supporting a great deal of glass. One whole side of the house was made up of huge panels of glass. The outer grounds were planted with shrubs, trees and pure greenery for as far as the eye could see.

Once you neared the house, the driveway suddenly sloped down and under the house, where cars could be nestled under the property. Tina immediately warmed to the safety aspect of it. When she broke the news to the accountants that she had found a home, they told her that under no circumstances could she buy it. But telling Tina she couldn't have something was like holding a red rag to a bull. Come hell or high water, she was going to have that property no matter what they said, and when she asked the estate agent about the down payment, she didn't flinch. Where she was going to find the $50,000 down payment was anyone's guess, but this did not bother Tina. She would find a way.

Tina phoned her agent, saying, 'Book me. I don't care, just book me for any gig, day and night. I need to raise a lot of money fast. Take anything going.'

After she put the phone down, her mind went in overdrive. She suddenly decided she didn't need the bejewelled Liz Taylor lifestyle any more and told me, 'Ed, I'm selling every piece of jewellery I own ... well, nearly every piece.'

And so she did, but the money she raised was nowhere near enough for the down payment and redecoration. More than a month had passed and Ann Cain continually called the owner of the house begging her not to sell to anyone else but Tina.

Tina had two more months before the lease ran out on the house she was living in and this is when panic set in. Tina was at a crisis point and had to get a result, fast. And so she did what she always did in these situations.

She chanted what she needed right into her life.

Following one of her marathon chanting sessions, her phone rang. 'Hello, Tina, my love? Is that you?'

Tina was thrilled to hear the carefree Italian voice on the line. She warmly replied, 'Adrianno! How are you? I haven't heard from you in a long time!'

'Ah, you may not have heard from me, my love, but I am always thinking about you. I am coming to America next week, Los Angeles! I am staying at a wonderful hotel and I must see you.'

Tina paused for a moment and said, 'Adrianno ... why don't you come stay with me? It would be lovely. Come stay with me and we'll have a great time!'

'Are you sure?' Adrianno replied. In slightly broken English, he added, 'I tell you what, my love, I check into a hotel first. Then I will call you and we will get together.'

Tina put the phone down, snapped her fingers and announced, 'Adrianno is coming to town. He's coming to see me! Now listen to me, Ann. This house has to be in tip-top shape. Next week I'm having a dinner party. I want this house to sparkle. I want everything to be absolutely perfect.' She wanted to introduce Adrianno to all her friends and show him a great time. Tina invited Mike and Gabriella Stewart and some other influential and entertaining people to welcome Adrianno.

The dinner party went beautifully and Tina was on form, being a fabulous, entertaining hostess until finally, one by one, people started leaving. When Tina bade goodnight to the last guest, Adrianno swept her into his arms, saying, 'My love, you know how to give a wonderful party! Now, my love, I have something for you.'

Adrianno presented Tina with a large velvet box. 'Tina, my love, I wanted to give you something special. You yourself can design jewellery to have these set into. Have beautiful things made that you really want!'

Tina opened the box and gasped as she was confronted with a stunning array of beautiful precious stones. Dazzled, she stammered, 'Adrianno ... are these ... are these *real*?'

Adrianno was so thoughtful and romantic that Tina melted. Although, physically, not to Tina's taste, she still couldn't resist Adrianno. He was so caring, and as such, more beautiful than any obviously handsome man. Her head went into instant overdrive. She felt this was the way she deserved to be treated. She later told me, 'Ed, I decided on the spot. I want to be with Adrianno for a while. He makes me feel good about myself. He arrives with gifts. The Rolex I wear is from him. I have loads of beautiful new clothes and shoes — all Adrianno. He makes me feel like I'm special. And he's special for making me feel that way. To heck with other men. I'm going to be with Adrianno for a while. I'm going to enjoy being treated like a queen. Why not?'

Adrianno checked out of his hotel and moved into Tina's house, just as she had planned well before his arrival. Ann Cain was on the case and had really feathered a comfortable nest for him. Between Ann Cain and Tina, Adrianno felt like a king. One morning he announced: 'My love, I will take you to The Daisy this evening for dinner.'

Tina dressed beautifully and they ate, drank, danced and had a fabulous time. They were on cloud nine when they left, with Tina tipsy and

Adrianno driving while adoringly playing games and acting the fool for fun. The great thing about Adrianno was his ability to make Tina laugh. When in his company, Tina was often reduced to stitches, needing to hold her stomach with laughter. With Adrianno, Tina had the chance to be herself and act wild.

That evening, Tina sat in the passenger seat, kicking her legs in the air and flirting away. She finally propped her feet up on the dashboard and smiled seductively as the warm breeze daringly licked around her thighs, sending the hem of her dress flying in all directions. Adrianno was well and truly wrapped in Tina's delicious web. The next morning, rather than announcing she would show Adrianno another great day, Tina said, 'Oh, Adrianno, I'm sorry. I've got some business matters I have to look after urgently. I have to finish trying to raise some money I need for a house. I haven't raised enough for a down payment and redecoration. You see, the woman who owns this house has decided, now that I've spent a fortune improving it, to move back in. That leaves me homeless if I don't sort this out quickly. I found a house I want to buy, but it's painted turquoise and I'll have to redecorate. I'm not getting myself in a rent situation again so some landlord can take advantage of me.'

Adrianno sympathetically said, 'My love ...'

He enquired if Tina had consulted her accountants and when she confirmed that she had, he said, 'My love, I will help you! I will give you the money you need to redecorate your home! I will not have you live in a turquoise house. We'll find a way. Now, my love, how much do you need?'

Tina told him. Adrianno protectively said, 'My love, I leave in a couple of days and when I get back to Italy, I have my bank immediately send you the money.'

Tina said, 'No, Adrianno. I won't let you give me the money. It has to be a loan. That's the only way I will accept it. I'll only take it if you promise to allow me to pay you back when I can. With interest, or I can't accept the money.'

'Whenever you can, my love. You need to get this house. Then, my love, it shall be redecorated.'

Adrianno returned to Italy and, true to his word, a few days later the money Tina needed to create her new dream home arrived. Tina was ecstatic. This would be the very first house she had ever owned. No one else's name would be on the contract. It was hers — all hers, and she was delirious over this achievement. Finally! — a home to call her own!

12

Tina busied herself preparing to embark on another small tour while Bernadette, now Craig's fiancée, all but moved in. Bernadette and Tina had become so close that Craig often sat on his own while the two women spent time together. Craig would sometimes sit back and watch Tina hug or stroke Bernadette's hair. She would never mother him but she devoted herself to mothering his fiancée. Tina had always wanted a daughter, and Bernadette seemed to fill that role.

Craig was deeply in love with Bernadette, but he had no direction, no ambition and, over a period of time, had simply become bone idle. Thoroughly unmotivated and not knowing what to do with his life, Craig turned to Tina for advice.

With appalling timing, considering Tina was not in the best of moods, Craig said, 'Mother, can I have a word?'

Tina replied, 'Yes Craig? What is it?'

Rocking from foot to foot, Craig began, 'Mother, well, you know, Bernadette and I have been having some problems. I don't know what to do. We want to get married and I haven't got a career and we're going to need a home of our own ...'

Tina didn't even let Craig finish the sentence. She said, 'Well you know, Craig, you can't afford to get married. You need to try to do something with your life. Taking on another person at this time is premature, when you can't take care of yourself. I thought you wanted to go to college.'

This was not the reaction Craig had expected. He had hoped that Tina would approve because she loved Bernadette so much. But Tina had no time for Craig's self-inflicted dilemmas, seeing as the answer was simple — get a job. Craig knew his mother well, and had always had jobs since he was small. She had just put her foot down and that was it — he would have to do something.

Like his brothers, Craig had not benefited from good guidance during his developing years, and work was hard to come by. He had little experience, hadn't gone to college yet and soon realised he was wrong in thinking that just because he was Tina's son, doors would open for him. They wouldn't. But a guy working for a valet company in Beverly Hills told Craig there was a job going parking cars, if he was interested. Tina knew how to survive and believed a person should take on any job, no matter what, as long as it kept you warm and fed. When Craig forlornly announced that after searching and searching he was forced to take the only job on offer, parking cars, Tina was delighted. His mother said, 'Good darling! That's real good! I'm proud of you. When do you start?'

Craig took the job, and although he had a good time with the people he worked with, he became downcast and depressed when at home. This did not gel well with Bernadette. In confidence, she told Tina, 'I don't know what to do with him. He's not motivated, he's always moping around. I mean, he's just not *fun* any more. When we were in high school, he was different. Nowadays he's like an old man.'

One day, when Craig was away, Tina was going through all her jewellery to see what else she could sell. Bernadette knocked on her bedroom door and sheepishly asked, 'Tina, do you have a few minutes?'

Tina smiled at the beautiful young girl. 'Of course, darling. What is it?'

'Tina, I gotta talk to you. I gotta talk to somebody.'

Tina patted her bed and gestured to Bernadette to sit down. 'What is it? Come on Berni, tell me, spit it out.'

Bernadette batted her lashes then stared at Tina with her huge eyes before blurting the words, 'I met someone else. I met this guy, a football player, real successful, famous ... and rich! His name is Len Swann. I only met him a couple of times and I gave him my phone number at my mother's house. He only went and sent over gifts and jewellery and flowers. He took me out and sent a limousine to pick me up and take me home. I feel so bad about goin' out behind Craig's back, but we don't have fun any more.'

Bernadette was genuinely tortured over the idea of hurting Craig and could barely face the idea of the pain it would cause him if she left him. She was riddled with concern and guilt.

Over the prior two years, Tina had taken Bernadette out on numerous social evenings, introducing her to stars and celebrities. Tina was close friends with Bernadette and she was like the daughter Tina never had. Tina saw how men and women both stared in wonder at Bernadette's ravishing face and figure. That's how beautiful Bernadette was, and Tina was trying to get her into modelling.

Tina, meantime, went on the road, and while away she received a call from Ann Cain. 'Tina. Congratulations. The paperwork's gone through. You are a home owner.' Tina screamed with delight. There was one major condition linked to the purchase of the house. Tina promised Mike Stewart and the accountants that she would not complain, she would stay on the road and work, work, work to cover her debts and foreseeable outgoings. Tina promised to go slow on decorating and only do what she could afford to over whatever space of time it took. She agreed to everything but even while she vowed to be a good girl, she knew it would be impossible. Tina never did anything slowly, and she knew that she was financially irresponsible.

Still on the road, Tina instructed Ann Cain to start furnishing the place. One of the largest outgoings at the time was a phone bill of outrageous proportions. Tina would phone Ann Cain at the new house and ask her to move the furniture all around and tell her how it looked. Ann Cain, being very sensible, suggested she moved the items and phone Tina back in an hour when everything was finished. Tina wouldn't hear of it. She said she would hold on the line while pieces of furniture were lugged all over the place. At one point, Ann Cain kept totting up the mounting bills and reminded Tina that the accountants would flip. 'Tina, these removal guys are expensive, not to mention the monstrous phone bill you're going to have. You can't do things this way.'

No one tells Tina what she can or can not do. Ann Cain's statement got her claws out. 'Ann, the last time I checked, the accountants were working for *me*. I won't ever remind you again that I pay all of you. Now get moving and stop wasting time.'

Tina returned from her tour like an excited little girl, unable to wait a moment longer to see the changes in the new home.

Although a lovely house, it was in need of repair. There was a wooden sundeck, surrounded with chicken wire, which would have to be removed. A lot of the wood needed re-staining and some pieces had rotted and needed replacing. The garden was neglected and was begging for attention. Tina decided she had better things to spend money on and didn't want to pay for professional help. Between a few friends and herself, she would get the job done. She popped on an old pair of jeans, a pair of gloves and a big straw hat and tackled the jobs that needed doing.

Physically, Tina is a very strong woman and she utilised her strength to knock down fences and pull down chicken wire all by herself. Tina would never ask anyone to do something she wouldn't dirty her hands on herself. If Tina asked someone to do something and they were too slow, she would say, 'That's okay. Forget it. I'll do it myself but thanks anyway.' It was too draining to have to explain herself twice and she had no tolerance for foolish behaviour.

A few days after she got back, I phoned Tina to see how she was getting on and she barked, 'What do you mean? Where have you been?'

I explained I had left several messages with the office, and when days passed without me hearing from her, I decided I should leave her alone for a few more days.

'You what? But no one said you phoned. I never had any message from you.'

There was a problem brewing in Tina's camp. It became apparent to her that she hadn't been getting all her messages, and she claimed that people were making decisions without consulting her.

Tina said staff had taken it upon themselves to vet Tina's friends, deciding who would and who wouldn't be allowed to talk to her. In short, they would only pass on messages they chose to pass on and Tina said this made her extremely uncomfortable.

The long silence on the phone suddenly ended when Tina snapped, 'Get over here, Ed.' Click.

I was there twenty minutes later with one of my famous cakes in hand. I rang the front bell and I heard someone yelling from the garden, 'Come to the back.'

I walked to the rear of the house and stopped in my tracks. Someone was painting, someone else was hammering away and there was Tina, ripping apart some wood like she was the Incredible Hulk. There were no hellos. Tina marched over like an army sergeant, gentle beads of perspiration trickling down her forehead and neck as she said, 'Okay Ed, I'll take that cake. No one gets any cake, hear? We got work to do.'

With the cake now safely in one of Tina's gloved hands, she stood back and scrutinised me from head to toe before saying, 'Uh, excuse me. You didn't come to help out, did you?'

'Well, uh ... yes!' I fibbed.

'Well, just look at you. This ain't no fashion show. Now go to the closet and find something suitable to wear. I don't think Armani designed your duds with this kind of work in mind.' Then she laughed while holding the cake up to the sunshine and added, 'Boy, when you come back down you better look like you're ready to work!'

I was deeply involved with dismantling a loose fence when Tina wandered over and squatted next to me for a discreet chat. I carefully pulled at the wood while Tina, bent at the knee, glanced around before whispering in my ear, 'Ed, listen. Don't say anything...' Then she paused and rapidly scanned the space around us, ensuring she couldn't be overheard before continuing, 'I been thinkin' about you ... a lot. Keep this between you and me. I've been havin problems with someone working for me. Things aren't working out. In the future, soon, there's going to be some work for you.'

'What?'

Tina sternly looked at me and raised her index finger to her lips. 'Shhh! I don't know how I'm going to work you in but somehow I will. Now this is between you and me. I'll have to find some way to see if you can handle this job ...'

At this point, my heart stopped. When Tina saw me freeze and light up like a beam of sunlight, she poked me and said, 'Not a word to a soul. Understand?'

My head spun and my hands shook while I endeavoured to finish what I had started.

The last straw came when promoters complained about a member of staff's attitude to them and the ticket-paying fans. Tina was very good with fans, taking time out for them when she possibly could. I have never seen her act nasty to a fan or cut them off short. Tina always said she couldn't meet or say hello to everyone but added, 'I do the best I can do.'

There was one particular, handicapped fan for whom Tina took time when she knew he was in the audience. Tina always made sure she said hello to him after the show or took a photograph with him. When Tina was last on the road, the man asked staff to let her know he was there and, if she had time, he'd love to say hello to her. His message was not passed on. When Tina discovered this had happened, she went off her rocker. She blew up and was merciless over the incident, telling her staff, 'I'm tired of you and tired of you making decisions for me. I'm tired of you selecting who I will speak to or who I will socialise with. This isn't Ike's show anymore where I'm meant to be hidden from the world once I'm offstage. Times have changed and you better change too. This is my life and I am to be consulted about everything. Understand? You don't respect me on that level and it's making me mad.'

But it was a while before I hit the road with Tina as her employee. I'd have to prove my worth first.

13

ke had been phoning persistently, always trying to persuade Tina to do a reunion tour with him. He had burnt through his amazing fortune, and hadn't had a real chart success in years. Knowing how Ike's dangerous temper could be set off at the drop of a pin, Tina chose her words of refusal very carefully. 'Ike, I checked and I'm totally booked up for a year. It's just impossible. I can't afford to cancel any dates. I wouldn't be able to pay off the promoters.'

Tina then told me, 'I think I've worked out how to handle Ike now. I just have to be patient, no matter what he says, and I have to think hard how to word my replies without setting him off.'

Tina felt uncomfortable and unsafe when she was at home. She couldn't afford automatic security gates and felt totally exposed everytime she walked out her front door and every time she returned. Deep inside, she feared Ike would be waiting one day.

'I'm going back on the road,' she decided. 'I'm gonna stay on the road as long as possible. I feel safer. It's crazy, all of this. I'm too scared to be in the house I always dreamt of.'

So she embarked on engagements that would keep her away from LA, while I got a telemarketing job selling office supplies. I started six every morning, and soon began raking in serious money through commissions. But I had moved away from home, and with as much money as I made, I still had to sell my precious Corvette to cover the cost of living on my own. Having had a privileged upbringing, I found it totally depressing, and in the end the only thing that brightened my dark moods was the odd friendly phone call from Tina while she was on the road.

During this time, LA suffered one of the worst rain storms in its history. There were mud slides with entire houses literally slipping down hills, resulting in a state of emergency. It was abysmal — electricity cuts were rife and LA was in a state of complete chaos. Like many others, my phone hadn't worked for days, so I was completely shocked when it rang in the middle of the night, and equally stunned to find Tina on the other end of the line. 'Hi,

Ed, it's Tina. I hope you're okay.' Without waiting for a reply, she fired on, 'Ed, it's a mess. My house has been hit hard by the rain storm. Now I know you got a job at the moment but can you take a couple of days off work and do me a big favour?'

'Sure, Tina.'

'Good, Ed. Now listen. Apparently my house is a disaster. The roof is leaking with buckets of water pouring in from everywhere. At least the house is still standing, though. Ann Cain is away, so the accountants hired me a girl called Andrea Farber. Andrea is safe, she worked for Stevie Nicks, Fleetwood Mac, The Eagles and all them sort of people. She looks after their houses but the only problem is that she comes at a high price — $200 a day. She seems to be as good as gold but I really can't afford her.'

'Don't worry, Tina. Just tell me what you need.'

'Ed, you know my house really well. I need you to go in and tell me exactly what shape it's in and how bad the rain damage is. You know where all my clothes are. See if they're wet and, if they are, hang them to dry. Please don't let any of my personal stuff mildew if it can be avoided. Now, I've already told the accountants to take you to the house and let you in. They have keys for you. Would you do this first thing in the morning? Please, please, please?'

After putting the phone down, I couldn't help but smile. Tina knew I could never refuse her. She had already arranged for the accountants to meet me at her house before she'd even spoke to me. I'd always drop anything for Tina and she knew it. I arrived at the house and collected my set of keys. Tina's dream property was in a real state. Rain had seeped down the inside of the house right into the fittings. Everything from kitchen cupboards to the comfortable den was soaked. Imagine heavy rain seeping down the outside of a window. Well that's what happened to Tina's house except that, with the house being made of glass, the rain seeped down the inside. Incredibly, the one room Tina was most concerned about — her bedroom — was the least damaged. I pulled all of Tina's shoes out of the closet and opened her drawers to air everything out. I placed her favourite angora sweaters out so they wouldn't attract any of the high moisture that was soaked into the woodwork. Tina rang within a half hour of my arrival. 'Thank goodness you're there, Ed. What's it like? Is it bad?'

'Tina, it's a mess.'

'Oh,' she replied in a small voice. After a deep sigh, she said, 'Well, Andrea will be back tomorrow, but I can only afford her for a couple more days. I'll phone you back and we'll have to sort out money.'

'Don't worry about that right now. I'm on the phone with you while I should be rescuing the house. Let me get on with things and I'll phone you back later.'

I washed down all the walls and windows so they wouldn't mildew and scrubbed everything that mould could possibly attach itself to. I emptied all the cupboards and closets and dried them out completely. Over the following three weeks, Tina kept in constant contact and I promised her I wouldn't be leaving until the sun shone on her house once again. When Tina arrived home, Andrea, house saviour to megastars, told her, 'I couldn't believe it. I was gone for two days and when I returned, your friend here, Ed, had transformed the house. Tina, you may think your house is hideously damaged now but I assure you, it was a lot worse than this. The interior damage would have been extensive if it hadn't been for Ed.'

Tina looked at me and then said to Andrea, 'Well, Ed is a chip off the old block. Ed and me are from the same seed. He's been a good friend for years.'

She then turned to me and asked, 'Would you like dinner? Don't bother going home. Stay here tonight.'

I told her I hadn't been home for three weeks and had been using spare clothes from the guest bedroom. Tina and I could share certain shirts and jeans. There was one other problem. I hadn't been back to work for three weeks and I told Tina that if I didn't return the following day, there probably wouldn't be a job waiting for me. Tina smiled warmly and said, 'Ed, don't go home and don't bother returning to that job. I'm hiring you as my personal assistant at home, and Ann Cain can pop in now and then to give everything her personal touch.'

I didn't even try to conceal my delight. She didn't have to ask me if I wanted the job, she already knew I'd never refuse. Amid my squeals of joy, Tina added, 'And I'll pay you for the time you spent here so far.'

'Noooo, Tina. You don't have to pay me for helping you out. I was glad I *could* help.'

'Well,' she smiled, 'you've rescued me again, Ed. You're always there for me.'

After seeing Andrea to the door, Tina said, 'Okay, Ed. Make a list of food that you like and I'll make a list of food that I like. You can do the shopping and cook us a nice dinner tonight.'

I was on the case like a rocket. After we joined our lists together, I was relieved to see we liked a lot of the same things. Tina told me, 'Now remember this Ed. I like fish, chicken and spicy foods and make sure there is always Haagen Dazs and Pepsi in the fridge.'

I was stunned when Tina handed me the keys to her precious Mercedes. I raced out and did all the shopping, phoning her before I returned to see if there was anything else she might have thought of.

I returned loaded down with shopping and immediately put everything in it's rightful place without having to ask her to show me where the goods belonged.

At that point, I didn't realise Tina was testing me just as she tested everyone. She wanted to see how capable I was and if I was sharp enough to go on the road with her. My new job was that of a housekeeper, laundryman, personal assistant, plus cook. And I looked after her dry cleaning which deserved a job description category of its own. It was a monumental, detailed task. Tina never wanted creases pressed into her trousers, and I'd have to count and list all her garments, ensuring that everything that left the house came back. Tina only wore clothes once and then they were immediately dispatched to the cleaners. Once they had been returned, I'd remove them from the wire hangers and place them on plastic ones.

Walking into Tina's closet was like walking into a fabulous store in Beverly Hills. Starting from white, all her shirts were colour coordinated, brand coordinated and ordered by season. All her leather was in one place, the silk in another. The Armani was separated from the Yves St Laurent and so forth. Her shoe area started with summer items (which would also be colour coordinated) leading into winter shoes and boots. If Tina said, 'Ed, get me my white Maud Frizon open toe shoes with the cone heel', I'd find the exact item in a split second without having to search through her vast collection of footwear.

This is how my day would pan out. I would stay the night in the guest bedroom, and as soon as I got up in the morning, I'd switch off the alarms and open the windows to let fresh air in. Next, I'd put on a pot of fresh coffee. Tina was a coffee fanatic and a true connoisseur of blends. She had to drink only the best.

There was a golden rule. Whatever my own personal routine was, no matter how long it took, I had to do it all before my workday started for Tina. I had to be dressed and very well groomed by the time she opened her eyes. She told me, 'Ed, once you get started for me, you won't have time to run off and brush your teeth. I am the priority. You are not. Understand?'

So, while the coffee brewed, I'd jump in the shower, brush my hair and teeth then get dressed for Tina, usually in jeans but very, very stylish. Like Tina, for comfort I'd wear dance shoes when in the house. Tina insisted I must always be of smart appearance from the moment she woke, in case I had to run to the shops with or without her at the spur of the moment. All I would have to do was pop on a pair of cowboy boots and a smart jacket and I'd be ready to go in seconds. Tina felt that because I worked for her, I also represented her and that I must always look smart.

Before Tina woke, I'd buzz around the entire house plucking dead leaves and buds off her flower arrangements. Tina loved a house filled with fresh flowers, but all dead leaves or dried pieces had to be discarded on sight.

After that, I'd prepare Tina's breakfast tray. I would place a beautiful, decorative cloth on the silver platter then put a small bud vase with a couple of fresh flowers on the cloth. She always insisted that her breakfast be served on very expensive white bone china dishes. She explained, 'Ed, I always want to be served at home as if I'm being served in my room at a good hotel.' And so she was.

Having laid out the silver service platter, I would wait for her to buzz me over the kitchen intercom and drowsily say, 'Good morning, Ed. I'll be ready for breakfast in a few minutes.'

This could be any time of the morning because Tina loved her sleep. I would be ready to serve from the crack of dawn, just in case she woke up early, but the average was around 10 a.m.

As soon as Tina buzzed, I would start preparing brown toast and eggs exactly to her taste. Tina liked her egg broken, and as soon as it fell in the pan, she would want it turned over so the egg was fried on both sides but not cooked to death. She always took a piece of fresh fruit as well, bananas being her favourite. I would spread the banana on the toast, just as she liked it. I would then pour the freshly brewed coffee into a silver coffee pot with a matching small pot of powder creamer on the side. Tina didn't take fresh milk or cream in her coffee because it brought down the temperature of the brew. Finally, I would place a silver bowl filled with brown sugar on the side and go on up to her room. Before taking the tray in, I would gently ask her if she was ready for me. Her tiny morning voice would filter through, saying the single word, 'Yes'.

I perfected all Tina's needs because I really was still just her number one fan. All in all, Tina assessed that I had adjusted to her needs so easily because we were like two peas in a pod. I was eager, full of energy and never tired. Like Tina, I could do five things at one time and she loved that. We realised at this point of our lives that we had a great deal in common. Tina said, 'Ed, you coming into my life. It wasn't a coincidence. We were *meant* to be in each other's lives.'

Tina would always inform me of her agenda for the day and I would write down everything in detail with a pen and pad that I always kept on my person. 'Ed, today I want you to go to the dry cleaners. Then go to Maxfields and pick up two gowns I had put on hold. And go by the bank and cash a cheque for petty cash. You know what ... I think I'd like chicken tonight. Make sure we have a fresh chicken.'

Five months rolled by and I had long since passed Tina's efficiency test. We got along like a house on fire, and she never had to tell me the same thing twice. Over a glass of wine, she informed me I was on the verge of much bigger things and she would now prepare me to go on the road. Alline, Tina's sister, was still working as her personal assistant on the road. Tina said, 'Ed, when I return from being away, I want you to unpack for me — not Alline. I don't want Alline unpacking for me any more. And, oh yes, the next time I go on the road, I want you to do the packing, not Alline. You understand clothes, if you know what I mean. Alline really doesn't.'

It took a very organised person four hours to unpack for Tina. Next time she returned home I did it in two. She was wildly impressed and said: 'Ed, you're not good at this, you're great!'

When I packed to prepare her for a two day stint, I placed all the shoes in shoe bags, colour coordinated her blouses and trousers, and did everything as it was in her own closet. She was delighted.

At this point, Tina became curious over my own interests, my tastes, my likes and dislikes. I seized the opportunity to get Tina into listening to music.

Incredibly, she never listened to music at home — the house was always silent. She never played anything on the stereo and didn't have a clue as to who was in the charts. At that time, if you mentioned the current number 1, she had no idea as to who they were or what their songs were. I always kept a radio switched on no matter what corner of the house I was working in. She slowly became accustomed to hearing music in the house. I never played it loud, just soft enough so I could hear it, but the sound would filter through to her. Tina started asking me the names of certain songs and who was performing. Then, after a while, I would hear her humming a current tune. Popular music slowly started influencing her and it was like a breath of fresh air for Tina. If I went to turn it down, she would say, 'You don't have to, Ed. I really like this! What's it called?'

Tina and I started staying up late at nights, sitting in her bed while I fielded all these detailed personal questions she'd throw at me 'Ed, are you seeing someone right now?' If I said 'Yes' to any of her questions, she would have to know every single detail about our emotional relationship. In that sense, she was a great deal of fun. We started enjoying each other's company so much that she would sometimes stop me from carrying out my duties and I would have to give her a gentle ticking-off for it.

Meantime, Rhonda Graam, still on the scene, seemed uncomfortable with our closeness and friendship. Tina and Rhonda were going to the movies one day, and while patting her handbag to see if she had her wallet with her, Tina piped up, 'Ed, why don't you come with us?'

Rhonda looked at me, saying, 'Ed, have you seen Tina's wallet, and by the way, is that Rolex real?' It was gold and gorgeous but it wasn't real. I told her it was. Rhonda asked, 'How can you afford a Rolex? And by the way, Tina, Ed can't come to the movies with us because we only have two tickets.'

Tina glared at her and snapped, 'Rhonda, I didn't ask you. Now Ed, would you like to come with us?'

I agreed to go then Tina stared at my watch and said, 'My God, Ed, it's beautiful!'

I turned to Rhonda and said, 'As far as my watch is concerned, my great uncle died and left it to me.'

Tina enjoyed the rivalry and loved people clawing for her attention. She was brilliant at adding fuel to a fire and enjoyed the harmless fun of winding people up. We climbed into the back of her car and she asked Rhonda to drive us to the movies, while Tina and I huddled together whispering and laughing. Tina knew how much it wound Rhonda up and it was her way of letting her know that her position wasn't as secure as she may have imagined.

I lived with Tina five days a week, returning to my flat on weekends. I never left without preparing entire three course meals for Tina for each day I wouldn't be there. We became so close that no sooner than I would arrive at my apartment for the weekend, after spending 24 hours a day with Tina, then she would ring and we would stay on the phone for a good three hours at a time. Then one Saturday she phoned to tell me she had a problem. In a very steady, even voice, Tina said, 'Ed, when I was living in the last house, Adrianno gave me some stones. They are precious and very valuable. I had hidden them and now they seem to have disappeared. The only people with keys to my house are you and Rhonda. Now I'm not accusing you, Ed. I'm going to ask you first. I told you when you got the job that I would not tolerate a liar or a thief. If I find out you've lied to me or stolen from me, you are out. Now I'm asking, did you take those jewels?'

I was stunned to near silence. After I recovered from the shock, I replied, 'Tina, I want you to know I would never take anything from you. Never, never, never.'

I heard Tina sigh deeply before she said, 'OK, Ed. I just want you to know I'm uncomfortable now.' Then she put the phone down without another word.

I felt horrible and my head spun with the agony of knowing that Tina doubted me. I could hear it in her voice. Tina had never doubted Rhonda for a moment, mildly asking her, 'Did you see my stones? Do you know where they are?'

Rhonda honestly replied, 'Duh Duh, you know I wouldn't touch your stones.' Duh Duh was the name the Ikettes had given Tina years ago, and if one thing annoyed her above all others, it was Rhonda calling her by that name.

Tina said, 'It must be Ed. Now I have to find someone else ... again! I've got Ed trained perfectly. Just when I think someone is right or special in my life, something like this happens. And Rhonda ... if I told you once, I told you a million times, stop calling me Duh Duh.'

Tina then phoned Alline and asked her if she thought I was capable of stealing her jewels. Alline, calling Tina by her real name, replied, 'Oh please, Ann. The two of you are just alike. Shiiiit. You two deserve each other. The good Lord knows he's taken a lot of the workload off me. I'm glad Ed's around. And I'm glad you got someone in your life. If Ed told you he didn't take them stones, then I don't know what to say. It's hard to imagine.'

And then Tina phoned Zettie. Zettie was an old Southern black lady, a friend of the family who gave psychic readings. Zettie was different. She was as bossy as she was supernatural and because she dabbled in the occult, no one dared question her. Right into old age, she was renowned for predicting the future. Word of Zettie spread far and wide and people would travel from afar to hear her predictions.

Tina, at that moment, had to know what Zettie could mystically see and tell her about her missing jewels. She phoned her and said, 'Zettie, it's me. Tina. I really need you.'

Zettie, in her Southern drawl, replied, 'Awwwwrat Taynaa, bat ya kna', ya' live so far.'

'Zettie, this is really important. I really need to see you.'

'Waaaail, awwrat Tayna. Ya know it's ganna take me a waayal ta git at there, you livin' there with all them white folk.'

'Zettie. Just get here. I'll pay you.'

Tina should have said that in the first place because after those words, old Zettie arrived at Tina's in record time. As soon as she stepped through the front door, Tina got down to business straight away. 'Zettie, I need you to concentrate on something. I had some jewels — precious stones that were given to me — and I had them here in the house. I had them and now they're missing. I need you to concentrate on these stones. They're missing and there's only been a couple of people in my house — Rhonda and Ed. Apart from me, they're the only two people with access. I need you to concentrate on the stones.'

Zettie went through her ritual, throwing tea leaves and laying cards on the table, then she broke the calm by booming, 'Tayna. Ahma tell ya. That boy dunn stoled yo' stones.' She rose out of the chair like a preacher woman and ranted, 'Dang-it, Tayna, that boy dunn gotya stones. Ahm tellin' ya, that boy dunn stoled ya' stones.'

Tina was devastated. Heartbroken, she phoned me and said, 'Ed, uhm … I have no choice. I'm going to have to let you go. You can work out next week so you'll get two weeks' pay, but I can't keep you on any longer. You broke my trust.'

I burst out crying on the phone. 'Tina, you can't … I didn't steal anything … I didn't take anything from you …'

'Ed, I called a reader. The reader told me it was actually you. You took the stones. When you come in tomorrow, leave your keys and I'll let you in until the end of the week, then you have to go.'

I tried to reason with Tina and begged her to see sense. We volleyed words but there was nothing I could say to convince her. Tina trusted her readers and I could understand how she saw things. It could only have been me or Rhonda, and Rhonda was around years before Tina noticed me. I could understand, after exhausting every avenue from asking her sister's opinion to consulting a psychic, why she came to that final conclusion. I had to respect that she consulted everything and everyone she trusted in an effort to vindicate me from the situation. Still, I lost, a fact that was made very clear to me.

That very same night when Tina retired to bed, she was too upset to fall asleep. She had a deep gut feeling that I didn't do it. Tina was very close to her instincts and feelings and, at the end of the day, would always listen to her inner voice. She sat up in bed and decided she would have one last look — a thorough one, because she never did anything by half measures.

As she got out of bed, her eyes landed on a set of drawers. She stared at the drawers for a moment and had a flashback — there was one hiding place she had completely forgotten about.

Tina had a drawer of sweaters that she wasn't using and deep in the back was the hiding place she had overlooked. Tina opened the drawer and gently opened the perfectly folded sweater. There, nestled in the centre, was the packet of stones. She stared at the large packet and it was exactly as she had wrapped it many months before. Tina put the stones on her bedside table before climbing under her blankets to settle into a deep sleep.

As per normal, I arrived at Tina's on Monday morning to let myself in. I felt like a condemned man as I carried out the rest of my routine. As I went to open the shades, I picked up the scent of fine, freshly brewed coffee wafting in from the kitchen. Tina never got up to make coffee, and, feeling slightly alarmed, I went straight to the kitchen to see who was there. There in her dressing gown, sat Tina. Placed neatly in front of her on the table were two coffee cups, sugar, powdered creamer and a pot of fresh coffee.

'Morning, Ed. Sit down.'

I was still highly emotional and wanted to tell her once more that I didn't take anything from her, but I felt it was futile. As I sat in the chair opposite, I noticed a paper nest filled with beautiful jewels. My eyes darted straight at Tina and before I could say a word, she calmly said, 'Ed, I owe you an apology. The first thing I want you to know is that this wasn't some sort of test. It was very real.' She fidgeted for a moment and continued, 'Ed, I asked you something and you answered me honestly. I wasn't sure and I doubted you. I asked Rhonda what she thought, and she agreed with me that you might have taken it. I asked my sister, and she couldn't imagine it. Then I phoned Zettie and she said her reading indicated you definitely took the stones. Somewhere deep inside I couldn't accept you really did it. I went to bed then decided to have one more look. You see, I couldn't let it rest because I didn't want it to be true ... we have so much fun together and I was so happy to have a friend in my life. I didn't want that to end.'

Tina poured me a cup of coffee and said, 'Ed, last night I leapt out of bed and my eyes landed on a hiding place I had completely forgotten about. Anyway, in one of my fluffy sweaters were the stones, wrapped in paper exactly as I had left them a long time ago.' She looked slightly emotional and tried to steady her voice as she added, 'I feel really good with you Ed, and I couldn't let this thing rest. I couldn't sleep. That's why I kept looking. I made a terrible mistake I'm sorry I put you through all this.'

I burst out crying. Tina immediately reacted by saying, 'Oh, Ed. Please don't cry. I feel bad enough now so don't go crying. Stop Ed, I'm sorry. I know, I know, I know, I got all upset too. Oh, now stop it ...'

Not knowing what to do with herself, tears formed in her eyes as she said, 'Oh, Ed ... what can I do to make it up to you? It's alright now, Ed ... it's alright ...' Then she suddenly piped up, 'I know Ed! You just sit here and calm down, and I'll make us a nice breakfast. Now you just pull yourself together while I cook.'

I froze and a single word fell from my mouth, 'Whuut?' Then I leapt out of my chair objecting, 'No, no way, don't do that Tina. No way!'

We stared at each other, then we both fell into fits of laughter. It was a long standing joke between Tina and me that she could whip up a few good meals, but breakfast definitely wasn't one of them.

14

As strong as Tina was, there were demons that had been chipping away at her armour for years. Finally, the angry demons surfaced for a final battle — a war that Tina had no intention of losing. 'Ed, there's been a lot on my mind — things that I can't shake. I can't carry this garbage any more. I want a better life, and I can't have it if I'm anchored with things I don't understand. I've been told I should have a past life regression. If I don't break these chains I won't ever get ahead. There's a lady that does regressions — she's about an hour, maybe two hours drive away. Will you drive me, Ed?'

Following the directions I was given, I drove to a desert-like area surrounded by hills. I pulled into an opening leading to a long dirt drive which would bring Tina and me to the regressor's home. I'd never seen Tina so nervous, but she was determined to cleanse herself from her past and progress with a new life.

When Tina was greeted at the door, she held my arm to lead me in but the regressor carefully explained that this was something that was best left for Tina to do alone. Tina flashed me an apologetic look and before she could say anything, I cheerfully said, 'Oh, that's fine. It's a beautiful day and I'm happy to sit out here and enjoy the sunshine.'

Tina seemed relieved that I wasn't offended and I could hear her take a long, deep breath as she was led away. As the door closed behind her, I pushed all worrying thoughts to the back of my mind and smiled supportively, firmly trying to send positive, strong vibes Tina's way. The sun was scorching and I passed the time by reading magazines and finally, two hours later, the front door of the house slowly opened.

The Tina that emerged from the house was a very different person to the Tina that went in. I leapt off the hood of the car when I saw her. She was being helped out of the house as if she were disabled. She was weak, in a state of distress and her eyes were tender and red, as if she had been crying. She seemed so vulnerable and small as I protectively took her into my arms. I barely heard the regressor's words as I led Tina into the car. The lady, who had obviously seen people in this state before, spoke in a calm voice as if everything was normal. 'Eddy, don't try to talk to Tina or draw her into conversation. She's been through a lot. Let her, in her own time, do all the talking.'

I helped Tina into the passenger seat and headed straight for her home. We drove in silence for nearly an hour when Tina suddenly got the jitters and kept wrapping her arms across herself as if she were freezing cold. Out of the blue, she burst out crying and mumbled for a while. I struggled to understand what she was saying, but her speech was incoherent — she was making whining noises as if she was hurting somewhere deep inside.

Very softly, I urged, 'Tina, let's wait. We'll be home soon. Wait until we get home, where you can relax.'

I could tell her past life regression had revealed a great deal. Whatever happened had helped Tina to face a lot of the issues she hadn't dealt with in the past. After unlocking the door to Tina's house and switching off the alarms, I helped her to her bed, took off her shoes and made her comfortable. I ran downstairs to make a pot of tea and by the time I reached the foot of the stairs, I felt Tina's presence. I turned to see her standing on the stairs, looking almost ghostly. 'Tina! What are you doing?'

'Ed, I need to talk to you right now.' While still standing on the stairs, she began, 'In my former life I was Egyptian ... and so was Ike. We did something wrong, real wrong. We were brother and sister and we slept together. I was cursed with that horrid karma and I carried it on to my new life — this life.'

The memory of the regression came flooding back and Tina's eyes flickered like lamps as she spoke. 'Ed, I knew when I met Ike he was like a brother and he told me he felt the same weird thing too, like I was his sister. That's why he looked after me for all that time when I first met him but never tried to sleep with me. We finally did sleep with each other and it felt horrible. He felt it, too. We both felt sick and strange — like we had slept with our own blood relation. From that moment everything changed. Life with Ike became awful. It was the curse we carried into this life. All that awful karma ...'

She paused and looked long and hard at me. She looked so sad as she added, 'We blew it. Me and Ike blew it. We repeated the same mistake again. We had a chance to put it right in this life and not sleep with each other but we fucked it up. We blew it. That's why my life was so horrible with him. I was paying for doing it again.' Tina began weeping as she ran to the base of the stairs. She grabbed me the arm and tugged me towards the living room. 'Ed, so much makes sense now.'

Pausing in front of assorted pictures on the wall, she said, 'Ed, one time Ike and I were waiting for a plane and we went to the shops in the airport. I saw this book — a beautiful book — and I really wanted it. No, it was more like I *had* to have it. It was a huge coffee table book with beautiful pictures of Egyptian gods and goddesses. I begged Ike to buy me the book and when he saw it, he looked like he was scared. The same spooky look he gets when people talk about witchcraft. He refused, real firm, that no way was he buying that book.'

By now, Tina had her arms crossed in front of her and she looked lost in her memories. 'You know me, Ed. I had to have that book so I phoned someone to go to the airport to buy it. I had to hide it — God forbid Ike knew I had the book, he would have killed me. I hid it for years. When Bernadette went to the house to sneak things out for me, I told her where the book was.

'And here it is, Ed. On the wall. All these pictures are from the book. I cut out the pages and had them framed.

'Now it makes sense, Ed, why I felt this need to surround myself with Egyptian things. When I think about it, Ike, Ronnie and I all have very Egyptian looking profiles. We've got that bone structure.'

Tina walked around the sitting room, talking and telling me stories and, while doing so, brought herself into a calm, peaceful, frame of mind. Now that the pieces of the puzzle were falling into place for Tina, she seemed to glow. 'Ed, I know what I have to do. I have to deal with the issues involving my mother and father. This regression focused on family matters.'

Tina called her accountant and had a stone put on her father's grave. With that out of the way, there was one other problem to deal with. Tina needed to speak to her mother and know the truth about her childhood. 'Ed, I'm going to need a proper heart to heart with my mother, but first I have to cleanse out my body. Go to the health food store and pick up some things for us. We are going on a three-day fast.' The fact that Tina used the words 'us' and 'we' did not escape me!

This would be the first time I realised that if Tina fasted, everyone fasted. If Tina dieted, everyone dieted. As it stood at that moment, I was going to fast for three days — something I had never done before. I was keen to fast because I would do anything for Tina — as long as it made her happy or made her feel better.

'Tina, this isn't gonna be easy.'

'Well, Ed, we will have to stick to the rules, starting on Friday.'

For me, the thought alone of not eating for three days brought on an instant dizzy spell. Tina continued, 'Ed, you'll have to pick up Aloe Vera gel from the health food store. I'll use it to clean all the toxins out of my body so I'll have a pure body and mind. I already started unloading a lot of past garbage and I have to get rid of any residue of the past. It's good for the spirit. Clean body — clean soul.'

This would be the first of many three day fasts I would have with Tina. We prepared by emptying all the food from the fridge. Tina wisely insisted on getting all temptation out of the way. On the first day, the only thing we could consume was Aloe Vera chased by water. The Aloe Vera gel came in a big bottle. It was like a thick, green shampoo. The bottle had to be shaken well to dislodge and mix the sticky, green slime which had settled at the base of the container. We poured a small amount into our glasses and drank it slowly. It was the most vile thing I ever tasted, and we needed to chase it with two glasses of pure mineral water to take away the nasty aftertaste. The first day was the hardest. Our stomachs felt cramped and we could hear each other's bellies gurgling which only added to the misery. We were grateful for each other's company. Considering how much Tina and I adored our food, fasting was an awful exercise.

On the second day, following our glass of Aloe and water, we were allowed a bit more to consume in the form of half a glass of cranberry juice diluted with water. Halfway through the second day, we were allowed half a banana each. I had to hand it to Tina — she never complained. For me, every hour was harder and harder and I wondered how this form of self-inflicted torture could possibly benefit the body or soul. By the evening of the second day, it was virtually impossible to sleep and we found ourselves tossing and turning during the night. I couldn't bear it a moment longer and I snuck into the kitchen to find some scrap of food that I could put down my throat. I tiptoed from my bedroom along the level path that led to the kitchen. Very quietly I opened every cupboard desperately looking for a morsel. Anything would do, even a single potato chip. Tina, anticipating that I might weaken, had hidden absolutely everything. I opened another cupboard when, horror of horrors, I heard familiar, tiny footsteps.

Tina hadn't reached the kitchen yet and she was already preaching. 'Ed, I know what you're going through. I'm going through the same thing, too.' She reached the kitchen and stood in the doorway, staring at my shamed face. Her voice was laced with strength and understanding as she added, 'You have to be strong, Ed. It's as simple as that. Do not eat anything. You can't cheat.'

I pleaded with her, ' But Teeena, I'm dying! I'm sooo hungry.' I was on the verge of tears. I looked at her but she was unwavering. Finally, we both returned to our respective bedrooms. Knowing Tina's radar was in perfect working order, I didn't risk returning to the kitchen. No matter what else crumbled, her sense of hearing remained undamaged by the fast!

On the third day, we carried out the same routine, Aloe Vera followed by water, followed by diluted cranberry juice. Thankfully, we were allowed a treat — dry toast and a piece of fruit. We spread a banana on toast and at that point I was so hungry, all I could think about was tucking into a sirloin steak.

On the fourth day, when we woke, the fast was officially over. Sadly, we had to wean ourselves back on to ordinary foods. We could not jump straight into a juicy hamburger smothered in raw onion, pickle and ketchup as we would have preferred. It would only have made us ill. We had to start off with very light foods like thin soup and leafy salad.

On the fifth day, Tina and I were eating like animals and while doing so, we admired each other's healthy glow. We had cleansed ourselves of toxins and our skin looked amazingly healthy. While stuffing food into our mouths, we noticed there was a difference in each other, and we both agreed it was very hard going but we did ourselves the world of good.

That Saturday we collected Muh from work to bring her to Tina's where she would spend the weekend. Tina was on a mission to sort things out, once and for all, with her mother. They lived only forty minutes away from each other, but Muh treated the occasion as if she'd been invited on an exotic vacation. Tina prepared for the visit by stocking the house with all the things she thought we might need. As an afterthought, we picked up a couple of videos we wanted to watch — two Bette Davis and Joan Crawford movies.

Tina's diet was basically light foods and Asian foods, whereas Muh liked good old-fashioned, solid food. Tina asked me to prepare a dinner that Muh would enjoy. I cooked a gorgeous meal made up of roast chicken, gratin potatoes and assorted vegetables. For dessert, I prepared one of my famous home made cakes which we would top with Tina's favourite Häagen Dazs ice cream. While busy in the kitchen preparing the lot, I could hear Tina making Muh comfortable in the den. They then had a heart to heart discussion which was emotional, but liberating for both of them.

Tina systematically dealt with every issue the regressor had suggested she should with both Muh and Alline. There were no skeletons in Alline's closet and for that reason, Tina did not have a problem with her. Alline was always very good to Tina, but they were as different as night and day. Alline never told Tina what she wanted to hear, she would tell Tina the truth. If Tina didn't like her honest answers, she would tell her: 'Well shit, Ann, you asked me … I didn't ask you. What the hell yo' go askin' me fo', if yo' ain't wantin' the truth?'

Nobody bossed Alline around. As far as being protective over Tina and looking after her, Alline told me, 'Of course Ah took care of Ann, shiiit, no one else was gonna. Maaan, she mah kid sister, mah little Ann …'

Men adored Alline. They'd look at her and know that if she went out with them, they'd have the time of their lives. She was not timid and really kept her men in check. If a man tried to do anything offensive, she would say, 'Now listen sucka, Ah dunno hoo-yoo bin' messin' with but don't ya pull that shit with me. I don't play with shit. Shit sucka, I'll cut yo' throat while yo' sleepin' if yo' fuck with me.' She definitely had a way with words.

During recent years, Alline had gone through a hard time making ends meet, but she wouldn't take any real handouts. Still, as a single mother, she fretted over her resources drying up. Tina saw an opportunity to return a bit of care to Alline and hired her as her personal assistant when on the road. As a very proud woman, this allowed Alline to keep her head above water while maintaining her independence and dignity.

Her relationship with drummer Ron Silico had blossomed and the two had married, much to Tina's distress. Ron was one of the few men that could drink as much as Alline. Their relationship was a feisty one — they'd bicker and argue on the road, get drunk, make passionate love and wake up the next day to start all over again. They loved each other in their own way, and that's how they expressed it in their marriage. But Ron showed up late one time too many, forcing Tina to find a last minute replacement. Tina fired him.

This put a real strain on Alline and Tina's relationship. Alline begged Tina on many occasions, 'Come on, Ann, hire Ron back.'

Tina would reply, 'No, Alline. You know what I'm like. I don't have time for unprofessionalism or nonsense. *I* hired Ron. He worked for *me*. You started dating him and decided to get married — that was your decision. I don't make concessions for family. You know that.'

But just because Ron was no longer on the road didn't mean that Alline stopped boozing. One night, before a show in Vegas, Tina waltzed into her dressing room and very grandly said, 'Alline, take my coat.'

Tina flung the magnificent fur coat towards her sister and as she caught it, Alline muttered through the cigarette dangling from her lips, 'Alright, Ann.' When the coat hit her, the cigarette in her mouth got tangled in the fur and burnt a hole in the garment. Alline brushed at the burnt area, not saying a word about the damage before hanging Tina's coat in the closet.

At that time, Alline wore her hair in braids decorated with beads, a hairstyle Tina disliked. Alline fetched Tina's slippers and knelt down to put them on her sister's feet. As she stood, her braids got caught on the dressing table and a few a few of them tore loose and flew off on to the floor. Tina, stripping herself of her jewellery in preparation to go onstage, snapped, 'Alline, pick up your braids right now. Why are you wearing that style anyway? You know your hair is too short to be wearing it that way.' Looking ahead at what could be the worse possible scenario in Tina's mind, she worriedly added, 'What if someone comes in and sees your hair lying on the floor? Just look at you. You look pathetic. I told you before, I hate that nasty hairstyle anyway.' Tina was so angry, she docked Alline's wages that week. Alline, incensed, retorted, 'Ann, this job ain't working out. Ah can't go on working fo' yo' no mo'. Nuh uh, Ah had enough. No mo'.'

By this time, Tina had discovered the burn in her fur coat, and while it did not make her feel any less guilty about the row with her sister, she did feel more comfortable about Alline's informal resignation. She told me, 'I realised after finding the burn that if Alline decided to stay on working for me, things would just get worse and worse.'

I flew to Vegas to sort out the finer details with Tina and Alline. I worried about stepping on Alline's toes and didn't want her to resent me because I was to take over her job. I was pleased, upon arrival, when Alline greeted me with relief. 'Ed, Ah'm glad thangs turned out the way they did. I miss mah Jackie and mah husband when Ah'm on the road. Ann's changin'. I wanna git back to my life an' mah friends. Ya don't have a life when ya'll be workin' fo' Ann. Well, Eddy, I want mah life back an' boy, Ah'm gittin' it. You do a good job, boy, ya hear? The sooner yo' catch on, the sooner Ah'll go home. Ann's mah sister an' Ah love her, but all this shit and glitter an' showbiz people ain't me.'

My meeting with Tina was brief. She told me, 'Ed, you won't be working while Alline is still here. I want you to sit right next to me and observe everything and everyone. You'll understand, then, how things work when you're on the road.'

Tina proved to be an unpredictable creature when on the road and she couldn't make it clearer that her comfort and happiness was all that mattered.

For instance, a new cologne came on the market called Kouros. I loved it but Tina hated it. She handed me a new bottle of Opium cologne while making her feelings known. 'Ed, I'm going to make myself perfectly clear. You will wear the Opium because I like it, and if I smell that Kouros on you again, you will be fired. Understand?'

That was Tina for you.

15

Bill Cosby could barely hide his amusement, as Tina raced up and down the corridor looking for her dressing room. Tina was sharing a billing with Lou Rawls and Bill Cosby in Las Vegas, and while she performed her hectic set on stage, Bill had camouflaged the entrance to her dressing room with tall, exotic plants, which made it impossible to see the entrance. Tina had ran off stage into the wings, then immediately wrapped her sweat-drenched body in a towelling dressing gown. Shivering, she ran down the backstage corridor towards her dressing room only to discover it had totally disappeared.

Bill watched her with a mischievous sparkle in his eyes. 'Tina, are you okay? Is something wrong?'

Tina, baffled, stared at the place where she thought her dressing room was. 'Bill ... my, uh, dressing room ...' Without finishing the statement, she turned and furrowed her brow, looking quizzically at the doors of the other rooms, wondering which one was hers.

Bill, with a concerned tone in his voice, enquired, 'What's the matter?'

'My dressing room. I'm sure it was there ... right at the end, ... but it's, uh, where is my dressing room?'

At this point, Bill couldn't help himself, and he burst out laughing. 'What's going on?' Tina demanded. Bill creased up, and could barely contain himself. By this point, other band members had gathered in the hallway and were all having a laugh over Tina's confused state. 'Bill!', Tina snapped.

Bill Cosby, his face glowing with amusement, walked to the far end of the corridor and started moving the plants out of the way to reveal the entrance to the dressing room. Tina stared with her mouth open for a moment, then playfully gave Bill a ticking off. 'I should have known! I need to watch myself around you!' Then she laughed, a bit embarrassed, and ran into the refuge of her room.

Bill Cosby was the sort of person that brightened up the spirits of everyone around him. You had to stay on your toes with him around because he was renowned on the circuit as a great practical joker who would, without fail, add spice to everyone's evening.

Tina freshened up and slipped into the audience to watch Bill's show. Tina liked playing Vegas, and you had to be a class act to get booked. She would dream up new routines over and over so her own show wouldn't become stagnant, and the bookings would continue pouring in. Her next booking was at a venue called the Thunderbird. Back then, it was not a prestigious place, considered to be a poor man's casino. Tina didn't mind at all because another act was opening for her while she headlined the show. It did Tina the world of good to have top billing.

Tina was absolutely correct in having me spend my first two weeks simply observing. It was the best form of training humanly possible for this type of job. During my training period, I watched Alline carefully, asked her numerous questions and stuck to Tina's side like glue. Only two days had passed before I found out how cutthroat the business could be. On the opening night at the Thunderbird, Gladys Knight was in the audience. I learned straight away that Tina did *not*, under any circumstances, want to know if a major singing star was in the audience. It made her feel she was being studied and scrutinised and meant that she might have to do something different, something diverse from her normal, strict stage routine.

On stage, Tina is not spontaneous and absolutely does not improvise. Everything is carefully rehearsed and performed with precision, right down to the laugh she let out at the beginning of her set when she performed 'Proud Mary'.

That night, before Tina went on stage, some security member of the hotel staff loudly mentioned that Gladys Knight was in the audience. It was the last thing Tina wanted to know, and she bristled.

But she knew how to be magnanimous, and, after doing a couple of numbers, she announced to the audience: 'By the way, we have a special woman in the audience tonight, a woman we all know, the woman who brought us 'Midnight Train To Georgia'. Ladies and gentleman, we have with us in the audience tonight, Miss Gladys Knight.'

The spotlight scanned the room and finally settled on Gladys, who stood up as the room erupted with applause while Tina said, 'Gladys Knight everybody ... Miss Gladys Knight.'

At that time, Gladys Knight and the Pips were one of the hottest bands in America and abroad. They had topped the charts with the most fabulous melodies, and it left Tina baffled as to why Gladys would go out of her way to see her perform in such a tiny venue. After her final set, Tina ran to her dressing room, sat in her chair and said: 'You know Gladys is gonna want to come backstage to say hello. Alline, get everything together.'

The room was already spotless but it had to be better than that. Alline had prepared and laid out the dressing room prior to Tina's arrival and completely refreshed it while she was on stage. Everything Tina touched, Alline buffed, so the room would sparkle when Gladys arrived. Tina, preparing for Gladys' arrival, said, 'Alline, get me my really, really good dressing gown.'

The one thing that irked Tina about people visiting her in the dressing room was that, inevitably, they would embrace her. Tina hated being embraced, cuddled or touched in any way. In her own gentle way, she would push herself away from the visitor after the obligatory cuddle. Gladys arrived with her mother, embraced Tina then started laughing and talking about old times. Tina fanned herself and kept glancing over at Gladys's mother, with a look I recognised as one of disapproval. Finally, Gladys stood back and in her soulful, country drawl, said to Tina, 'Giiiirl, yo' look good. Hot mama ... real good.'

Tina smiled and nodded before saying, 'Gladys, you're looking very well.'

Gladys then let out a soulful, 'Uhmmm, hmmm. Na-owe girl. Tell me who that good-lookin' keyboard player is. Na' Ah be tellin' ya'll, he's fine. Real fine. What's his name?'

Tina replied, 'That's Kenny Moore. He's been with me a while now. He worked for Carly Simon and Aretha Franklin. Young, very talented.'

Gladys leaned back and said, 'But do he sang?'

'Well, yes. You wouldn't have known it tonight but he does sing. In fact, he's extraordinary.'

But there had been a problem brewing between Kenny and Tina. His last pay cheque was short, and he complained to the person, who was in charge of those matters. He was told that it would be sorted out, but it wasn't, and Kenny got so angry he told Tina if his money wasn't sorted out by that evening, he would play his keyboard but he wouldn't sing. He told Tina, 'If ya'll are gonna give me only part of my money, then I'll only do part of my job.'

Tina said, 'Fine Kenny. If you don't sing tonight, then you better look for another job.' They were the two worst people to lock horns, because Kenny was as stubborn as Tina. Now, for the first time, the two tested each other's strong will and there was a major drama going on. Kenny sang all the harmony notes for Tina and doubled her voice in her show. He had the extraordinary gift of being able to sing exactly like the main performer. Unbeknown to Tina, Gladys had already heard of Kenny's reputation through the grapevine. She said, 'Well, Tina, I just gotta see if that boy is as fine in the flesh as he is up there on that stage.'

Tina innocently asked Kenny to the dressing room, thinking Gladys fancied him, and was glad to see them leave together. Once in the corridor, however, Gladys had a few quick words with Kenny, and they exchanged phone numbers.

The following day, Tina was informed that Kenny had left to work for Gladys Knight. She was livid, realising Gladys had come to the show not to see her, but to poach her prized keyboard player. I can't believe it. She only came backstage to say hello to me to get to Kenny. What am I going to do?'

Once home, Tina suggested I take some time to prepare myself to tour with her. That meant I had a lot of shopping to do. Living with Tina Turner gives you a taste for the better things in life. I would be travelling the world with her and needed to dress and appear as grand as my employer, knowing it would reflect well on her. I opened a charge account at Saks Fifth Avenue and spent like crazy while her words rolled around in my mind. 'Ed, you'll be at my side at all times and you must always dress suitably. I will have to attend numerous dinners and you will be my escort. I advise you to pack appropriate items. You know I like the band but they will stay in separate hotels to ours and I don't socialise with them very much. You're already stylish enough to carry yourself around me and you are very well spoken. At least I won't have to have Rhonda with me now ... that girl never dressed properly and ... ugh ... her speech!'

I stood in Saks Fifth Avenue, mulling over those thoughts while purchasing silk pyjamas, classy slippers, two large pieces of Louis Vuitton luggage, travel clothes and dinner clothes. I wanted all the latest designer stuff on the market, knowing Tina wouldn't be wearing anything that was noticeably last season's. I sighed, wondering how I would be able to keep up with her.

I was ready to embark on a San Fransisco tour when Tina told me, 'I'm not sure I'm happy being managed by Mike Stewart any more. I mean, I'm really fond of him but I'm not going anywhere. I want to be a big star, a big success but Mike can't see my dream. I want to record the sort of things that are happening today. I want to do rock 'n' roll. Mike thinks I should just stick to cabaret and recording rhythm and blues. I have to move on. I have to do it now or it'll pass me by.'

I was a bit surprised, but I realised how strong Tina was to reach that decision. She and Mike went back many years and he was like a father and guardian to her. For Tina, it would be like leaving home. I asked, 'Does Mike Stewart know you're thinking of leaving him?'

'Well, Ed, I'll put it this way. He knows I'm not happy staying put. I have to try to reach higher. It's now or never. I think he pretty much has an idea of my intentions, but I've only told you and Rava. I need to keep my eyes and ears open for the right sort of person who sees my dream. Someone who believes in me.'

Just before the San Fransisco engagement, Tina got a last minute offer to do an Olivia Newton-John special. Olivia was a hot property at the time, following her film success with *Grease* and her success as pop star. She was about to release her new project, *Xanadu*. Appearing in Olivia's special would be Peaches, of Peaches and Herb fame, Toni Tennile, of Captain and Tennile, Tina and, of course, Olivia. Unbeknown to us, Olivia Newton-John's show would be instrumental in changing Tina's life forever.

I had just got back to my place when my phone rang. 'Ed, It's me. Tina. Quick, get over here. Help me choose a song to do on Olivia's special.'

I arrived at Tina's and no sooner had I passed the threshold of her bedroom, she pushed me to the far end while saying, 'Just stand there ... stand there. I want to do this song for you. Just tell me what you think.'

She used one of the chairs from the dining room and had it placed in the middle of the floor. It was a slow, seductive song called 'Cat People' by David Bowie. She was straddled over the chair, singing like it was a cabaret number, then, suddenly, she stood up, kicked the chair away and started singing like I'd never heard her sing before — true rock 'n' roll. I suggested a few changes to make the whole thing more shocking for the audience, which she tried out and loved. She rehearsed the song ten times, took a short break then continued singing over and over until she was satisfied. As I watched her I remembered how Ike, when he had control over her, would force her to sing one single note endlessly, sometimes into the next morning. She was driven, and her need to perfect everything, even if it meant singing into the night, was all influenced by Ike.

Having perfected the song and choreography, Tina was ready to perform on the Olivia Newton-John special. Olivia was still being managed by the brilliant Lee Kramer, who had been her lover for many years. Olivia and Lee had recently ended their long romance but chose to maintain their business relationship. Tina did Olivia's show as a solo artist, choosing not to include her band or dancers but she let her pet friend-cum-dancer, Rava, tag along.

Lee Kramer, like all men except David Bowie, was bowled over by Rava. While the show was being taped, she perched on a chair with her back erect and played with her pearls while casually licking her lips. Every now and then she would glance over at Lee and bat her eyelashes. It didn't take much for Lee to fall for Rava's charms, and a hot romance ensued. Watching Lee and Rava's mating game was Kramer's partner, Roger Davies. Roger, a quiet Australian guy, shook his head with amusement before walking away.

Tina, needless to say, stole the show.

Some days later, after Rava had spent a passionate evening with Lee, she turned to him and said, 'Lee ... what would you think about managing Tina Turner?'

He looked at her, 'Well, she was brilliant on Olivia's special, and there's certainly no one like her but I dunno ... she hasn't had a hit record for far too long, she needs a lot of working on ... it would be a lot of work. But she's got something ... something special. She is talented, far better than I thought.'

After Lee left Rava's swish apartment, the tiny dancer rang Tina straight away. 'Tina! Tina! Guess what? I think Lee Kramer might want to manage you!'

'What! What did he say?'

'Well, I kinda got his interest Tina. I think you'll have to show him you can do it.'

'Oh, Rava, if Lee could do for me what he did for Olivia Newton-John ... oh, it'll be great! I'll show him I can do it! I'm not dead yet honey, I'm just starting!'

Tina contacted Mike Stewart and told him of the latest developments.

Mike, always keeping Tina's best interests at heart, took the news well and advised Tina on how to convince Lee Kramer to manage her.

'But remember, Tina,' he added, you are still in debt to me for a lot of money. There's also your taxes to sort out and the money you make presently just about keeps you afloat. He's gonna want to take on someone who can rake in millions, not small change.'

Tina sat in front of her altar chanting morning, noon and night, willing Lee Kramer into her life. She consulted her psychic readers to see what they had to say. They all told her similar things, that she was going to be the biggest of stars, playing stadiums, never tiny venues again. They told her she was going to bigger than Mick Jagger.

Meantime, Lee Kramer and Mike Stewart got down to the nitty-gritty. Mike explained that it wasn't just a question of taking her on. There was a lot of baggage that went with it. Tina was in debt to Mike for more than $100,000 and she owed a great deal in taxes. She made a certain amount of money which was just about covering her bills, but had to work on a daily basis as well as trying to get a record deal. Mike and Lee talked back and forth and Lee realised he would be taking on a lot, despite which, he was still interested. The only way it would work, though, was if he got her a big recording deal. It was a challenge.

Lee arranged another meeting with Tina, and I kept phoning her on the day to find out the outcome. It was a hideous day, pouring with rain, and I kept calling, but she wasn't in all day. Finally, I answered a knock on my door. There, soaking wet and bedraggled, was Tina. 'Ed, I did it! I just left Lee Kramer's house and came straight here. You're the first person I'm telling. Lee Kramer's going to manage me!'

We started jumping up and down and twirling each other in circles. When we had exhausted ourselves, I opened a bottle of wine and toasted Tina's good news. 'Ed, I played him a demo but made it clear I was looking for new material. We talked for a long time and he saw my dream. He saw it, Ed! And he wants to take me there!

'There's just one catch. He wants to see me perform live before he makes his final decision.'

I raised my eyebrows inquiringly at her. Tina lowered her eyes, slightly bashfully, and said quietly, 'Oh, please, Ed. Don't look at me like that. The deal is done. You don't really think he'll say "no" after seeing me on stage doing my thing do you?'

16

'**T**esting, 1, 2, 3.' It all seemed routine until Tina stepped in. I had never seen anyone conduct a soundcheck like her. She walked straight on the stage, picked up her microphone and said, 'Uh, okay, let's go. 'River Deep, Mountain High.'

Tina soundchecked as if she were performing to an audience. Hotel staff, who were setting up the dining room, ended up walking straight into each other. It was like a show without the costumes and by the end of the song, the band members were dripping with perspiration — and so were the people watching!

That evening, the show went off without any hitches and I was always ready backstage to help her change between songs. When she ran offstage, I would literally lift Tina from around her waist so she could quickly kick off her shoes. She would stand on the floor and I'd unzip her dress and pull it off. If her dress required a change of panty hose, I'd tug her hosiery down and while she stepped out of it, I would be bunching a fresh pair down to the toe area for her to step into. I would have already dampened the hosiery with water to reduce the chances of tearing the tights while they were rapidly tugged up Tina's legs. A dress was already bunched up on the floor which she would then step into. I would pull the dress up, helping her arms into the appropriate openings, then fasten the garment. Shoes were already waiting for her to step into which I would quickly fasten, if needed. Without saying a word, she would then snap her fingers and extend her hand, into which I would place her hairbrush. I'd hand her her jewellery then, finally, her lipstick, which she'd apply before studying herself in a long mirror. 'Okay, Ed, how do I look?'

I'd fluff her hair where needed or suggest, 'No earrings'. Then she'd look at herself once more before racing back onto the stage. The entire change rarely took longer than a minute.

Lee Kramer and Roger Davies, of course, were blown away. After the show the three of them met, and the deal was clinched. And Tina wasn't afraid to ask for changes. After the meeting she told me, 'Lee asked if there were any immediate changes I might require and I mentioned that I would like to replace Rhonda. He suggested I get someone in discreetly to study under Rhonda, rather than letting her go and leaving me in limbo. Rhonda does a lot, she's nearly indispensable. She senses it. She's running scared for her job. But I can't live in the past. She carries too much of the old Ike Turner baggage with her.'

Tina rang a few girlfriends in LA to tell them the good news. One girl suggested to Tina, 'These guys, Lee and Roger, have to put their hands in their pockets. Look Tina, you have the crappiest sound system I ever heard at your house and they're going to be listening to your demo tapes on that? You tell them that you need a proper sound system. A real good one. Tell them to buy it for you.'

We returned to LA the following day, and Tina immediately prepared for the meeting at her home with Lee and Roger. I served food and refreshments while Tina and her new managing team laid out their plans. They talked about recording new material and they listened to tapes she had of songs she wanted to perform. Amongst the small selection was a song I had written for Tina called 'Pain'. They discussed rehearsals, budgets and a new stage show. Tina decided to test Lee and Roger to see how serious they were about her. She decided she could measure their interest by the amount they were willing to invest in her. Just before they left, Tina suggested they should supply her with a good quality sound system to listen to her material on. Very wisely they did, but they had no idea of the significance of their actions. It made Tina feel very secure about their interest in her.

The management relationship with Mike Stewart ended straight away, but Tina still had six months worth of booking obligations to carry out which had been previously arranged through Mike's company. A financial arrangement over the percentages of those bookings had been worked out between Lee and Mike. But this didn't worry Tina. She was on top of the world, and believed her dreams of superstardom were becoming a reality.

If her career was looking up, her man situation wasn't doing anything. I recognised the mischievous sparkle in her eyes. I knew Tina well, and could recognise that she was ready for a new relationship. We had been talking about it when her former lover, Wim, phoned out of the blue. Tina's voice level rose in surprised octaves, 'Wim! How are you?'

Rather weakly, he replied, 'Tina, I'm in hospital, I've had surgery.'

Within a couple of hours Tina had dressed and was ready to see Wim. I studied her from head to toe and asked, 'Is there something going on with you and Wim again? How come he's suddenly back in the picture?'

Tina waved her hand around as if her fingers were butterflies, explaining, 'Oh you know what Wim's like. He's such a baby. He feels sorry for himself and wants sympathy. Poor thing ... in hospital ... I think I should go cheer him up.'

As she passed by me, I noticed an air of naughtiness about Tina. She paused at the open door, pouted her lips, winked, and flicked her hair before swanning to her Mercedes. I couldn't help but wonder what was on her mind. She wore a white, chiffon blouse with no bra underneath. The gossamer fabric failed to shield her large nipples. She wore a long pencil skirt and Armani jacket. Her shoes made her look like a teenager — a pair of men's-style brogues with wool socks rolled down to the ankle. To top it all, her hair was plaited in two schoolgirl style braids. I smiled to myself thinking that Tina would be the best medicine for any man.

A few days later, we were chatting away as usual when Tina suddenly came over all serious.

'What's up?' I asked.

She looked down at her breasts and said, 'I need to get these sorted out.' She was referring to her breast implants which had been troubling her. At that time, implants often hardened and patients would have to return to the surgeon to have their breasts 'cracked'. Cracking was done by clutching the breasts firmly and twisting them sharply to loosen the hardened implants. It was a short, agonising exercise which left women feeling delicate and sore.

Some weeks after getting her implants cracked, more trouble set in. Her breasts drifted apart, away from the center, to such an extreme degree that she couldn't get any cleavage at all. They stayed in that position for ages then started hardening again, but one more than the other. Tina was concerned that if a man touched them, he would notice one was almost rock hard. Her breasts constantly ached, causing chronic discomfort.

A bra couldn't alleviate the aches, and worst of all, they began looking unnatural. This didn't rest well with Tina. She was a perfectionist, always careful about her grooming and appearance. When she contacted the surgeon who originally did the implants, Dr. Larry Sieford, he told her, 'I don't want to scare you Tina, but it has been two years since you've had your implants. I think I will have to surgically enter and redo your breasts.'

Tina's reply was, 'Ohhh no.' Then she immediately recomposed herself and casually said, 'Okay, fine. Let's make an appointment.'

Tina went for her cosmetic correction which was carried out at the doctor's surgery. She was cut under her breasts and the old implants were removed, to be replaced with the finest fruits of modern technology. The new implants were different to the originals because Tina wanted slightly larger breasts, and the correctional surgery, which was a great success, reflected her wishes.

When Tina returned from the doctor's, she looked seriously flushed. I knew every nuance of Tina's body language so I raised my eyebrows in mock suspicion while prying with carefully selected words. 'Hello missy. You're glowing and looking lively, considering what you just been through. How did it go?'

'Well, uh, Ed, did I tell you about Dr. Larry?'

'No.'

'Oh! I didn't? Well, he's sort of cute, you know.'

Reading between the lines, I replied, 'Teeeeena, what are you up to? Come on. Let's have some wine. Then you can give me the real T. I want *all* the dirt.'

It didn't take much to persuade Tina — she was bursting to tell me about her new love interest from the moment she left the doctor's practice. 'Ed, I've arranged for Dr. Larry to meet us and a few friends at Le Dôme.'

'Oh, really, missy. And I wonder what for?'

'Ed, You always have sex on your mind.'

'Well Tina, at least I say it. You just hint around it, okay?'

I had to smile in admiration at the way Tina stalked her prey. She knew she was interested in Dr. Larry, but arranged to see him in a situation where she would be able to cry off with her friends rather than get stuck with him. As frisky as she was, she proceeded with caution. Tina thought Dr. Larry was sexy in his doctor's uniform, but once he was out of the office, dressed as a member of the public, whatever initially attracted her might be gone. She wasn't taking any chances, wanting the option of being able to bow out gracefully. 'What's the plan?' I asked, amused.

'Well, Ed, I think I'll invite Rava. If it turns out that I'm not really into Dr. Larry, then I'll pass him on to her. They'd be perfect for each other.'

I couldn't help but grin. Tina was more than covering her back.

We prepared to go to Le Dôme that Saturday. It was a prestigious bar, always frequented by the cream of LA's most rich and influential residents. Tina wore a fabulous Armani pin-striped suit and a net-weave top, revealing her soft skin and cleavage. The jacket teasingly hid what everyone really wanted to see. She wore light make-up and her hair was piled over to one side, held firmly in place by a clip. It softly framed Tina's glowing face, enhancing her youthful appearance.

We had arranged for Rava to meet us at Tina's house and, as she was half an hour late, we were on the verge of leaving without her. Just as we were about to go, the phone rang. Tina and I simultaneously rolled our eyes to the heavens, knowing it had to be Rava.

Tina lifted the receiver and Rava's piercing voice shrilled through, 'Tina, I'm ...'

Tina cut her off in a flash. 'Rava, why aren't you here? Where are you? If you're not here in ten minutes, Ed and I are leaving without you.'

'Ooohhh, but Teeena, I don't know what to wear. What are you wearing?'

'Come on now Rava. You know I don't do that girlfriend stuff when it's actually time to be leaving.'

'Teeenaaa, what are you wearing? I don't have anything to wear. Just tell me.'

'Oh, Rava! Okay. I'll tell you what I'm wearing. I'm wearing a white chiffon dress with straps and a long flowing shawl. Happy?'

I had to cover my mouth to arrest an attack of the giggles. Rava always wanted to dress like Tina, but that evening, Tina didn't want anyone copying her. Rava arrived 30 minutes later and I drove both women to Le Dôme. The car was noisy with our excited conversation, which focused on Tina's plans for the evening, and the possible outcomes.

When we arrived, the maitre d' escorted us straight to the bar, and we were sipping Kir Royales when the barman approached us with a message. Dr. Larry had rung to say he was running late but would be with us as soon as possible.

Rava was busy telling us about a new song by Jermaine Jackson called 'Let's Get Serious', then, without warning, she launched into a vocal routine of the number which left Tina and I choking on our drinks. Rava couldn't sing to save her life but that never stopped her from knocking out a number anytime, any place, anywhere. Thoroughly embarrassed, Tina kept turning in different directions, not knowing where to hide her face.

This continued until Dr. Larry entered the room. After letting him gently brush both of her cheeks with his lips, Tina introduced him to me and Rava. Always on the prowl, Rava started flirting with Dr. Larry before he had a chance to say 'how do you do'. Tina and I glanced at each other and rolled our eyes towards the heavens. I knew Tina wasn't having any of Rava's nonsense that evening.

With a few drinks down her, Tina went for Dr. Larry. She got a bit wild and came on strong, leaving the doctor in no doubt of his chances. When Rava saw the degree of interest he held for Tina, she realised she would have to hunt for another man. Enjoying Tina's company, Dr. Larry leaned closely to her ear and asked, 'Are you ready for us to go out and have some fun?'

Tina batted her lashes as she purred seductively, 'I'm as ready as you are.'

Tina and Dr. Larry decided they were in the mood for another venue called The Daisy in Beverly Hills. Before heading off, Tina discreetly whispered, 'Ed, take my car. I'm going to drive in Dr. Larry's new Porsche ... and Ed, make sure Rava drives with you.'

Once at The Daisy, I took delivery of the bottle of champagne that had been ordered, while Dr. Larry and Tina escaped to the dance floor. I glanced over at Tina every now and then until I noticed she was actually blushing through her tanned skin. Her deep red cheeks told me she was squirming inside with embarrassment. Tina spun and paused in my direction, contorting her face in a grimace of horror which left me creased with laughter. She kept pulling hysterically funny faces behind Dr. Larry's back, conveying what she thought about his dancing. Poor Dr. Larry knew two dance steps which he repeated over and over while bopping up and down like a buoy in the ocean.

When Tina and I had a small moment alone, she sympathetically whispered, 'Ed, poor Larry. Poor thing has no rhythm.'

I couldn't help but tease, 'Well Tina ... I'm sorry to remind you what they say about people with no rhythm. If he can't dance, then he can't fuck. Better pass him on to Rava ...'

'Ed! Stop it! Give the guy a break. Besides, I can always have fun teaching him how to dance.'

'Go girl.'

Tina and I gave each other a 'thumbs up' before she proceeded with the seduction of Dr. Larry.

I knew Tina wouldn't require any rescuing that evening so I decided to leave her and Dr. Larry to it. I told Tina I'd see her back at the house.

The next morning, I crept past Tina's room and was amazed to see her door open. I discreetly peeped in, not wanting to disturb her if she was still asleep, and immediately gasped in horror. It looked as if Tina's room had been ransacked during the night. Pillows were strewn across the floor and all the bedclothes were back to front. I scanned the heap with my eyes, searching for Tina, until I saw a nest of hair at one end of the bed. I leaned over and grinned. Her hair was pointing everywhere, like a porcupine's needles threateningly standing on end. Poking the centre of the blankets with my index finger, I gently enquired, 'Tina? Tina ... is that you?'

Slowly, the end of the blanket moved and I could see the tips of her manicured nails pushing the fabric off her face. She pushed the blanket down, exposing just her eyes and nose. She looked like a naughty little girl who just got caught licking the batter off a cake spoon. Then I heard a very tiny, 'Hi Ed.'

I put my hands on my hips and pursed my lips before replying, 'Well, good morning!' While waving one hand around the room, I enquired, 'And what, might I ask, happened here?'

She pushed the blanket entirely off her face and her eyes came to life as she gasped, 'Ohhh, Ed ... it was wonderful!'

I fetched some pillows off the floor and arranged them on the bed so Tina could sit up, while saying, 'Okay, gimme the dirt. I want the real T. What happened?'

Tina became alert, seeming to grab new energy out of thin air as she as she sat up and enthused, 'Ed, I was so naughty! We were in the car and started kissing and touching and stuff. We ended up back here. Ed, honey, you wouldn't know it by looking at him but that doctor knows his way around a woman's body.'

'My head started off here and before I knew it, it ended up at the other end of the bed!'

I burst out laughing while she added, 'After we did all sorts of interesting things, I looked down at my boobs and asked him, "Well, what do you think about your work?" He admired my boobs for a second and said, "Not bad". Then he played with them and said, "Not bad at all". So I said, "Well, Doctor, do you think I should come in for a check-up soon?" He suddenly jumped up, grabbed his stuff together and panicked like hell. He was saying stuff like, "Shit, Tina, I got to perform surgery at twelve noon today". Then he had himself a fast old wash and was out in a shot racing straight off to his office.'

The next morning Tina arranged to see Dr Larry, making the appointment through his secretary, telling me, 'Ed, he won't realise I'm coming. It'll be a surprise for him.

'I'll go in there and he'll ask me to remove my blouse so he can check me … then after he touches my boobs he'll lose control.'

'Okaaay Tina. If you say so.'

'Ed, can't you think positive? What else is going to happen? You think he'll just check me and send me home. I don't think so.'

Tina left to keep her appointment and was back an hour later, looking a bit down. She looked at me and said, 'Ed, he just didn't seem as appealing as he did the other night. I didn't feel that sexual buzz. I think Dr. Larry was just a one night stand.' After dropping her handbag on the table, she suddenly brightened up and, grinning from ear to ear, added, 'But he was a good one night stand, Ed. Really good.'

17

There was a new gambling resort, Sun City, being built in South Africa. It was designed to attract wealthy clients from all over the globe and they hoped big names in the entertainment industry would help draw in high calibre clients. There was one very large problem. South Africa was segregated and for that reason, very few big names would accept bookings. This resulted in mind-boggling offers to entice artists to play South Africa, then show them Sun City in the making, with hopes of securing a future booking commitment from the performer. The more the entertainers refused bookings, the more money was offered to tour South Africa. Tina Turner was finally offered a staggering $150,000 to play South Africa. It was an unheard of fee in those days for cabaret acts like Tina's. Sun City's offer was one that no entertainer in their right mind could refuse.

One evening Tina casually looked over at me an said, 'Ed, we've got a load of work to do. Lee Kramer has taken that gig in South Africa. We're going for six weeks. Ever been there?'

I nearly fainted. 'Oh ... my God Tina ... I'm really going abroad with you?'

'Ed, calm down. You're not coming with me to have a vacation. You are coming with me to work. Believe me, there won't be time to relax and barely enough time to sight-see.'

Flustered by the reality, I raced back to my place to break the good news to my friend and landlady, Helena Springs. Helena was an old friend from the *Soul Train* days, and had really gone up in the world. At the time she was dating both Bob Dylan and Robert De Niro! There was a car in her drive, so rather than disturb her and her guest, I walked to my little cottage situated across from her house, yet attached. I turned and looked back at Helena's house. I sighed before opening my own door, hoping Dylan was visiting her at that moment, not Robert De Niro. Bob was so civilised and polite, but Robert De Niro was unsociable and unnecessarily nasty.

I was fascinated with how Helena juggled her love life. Helena's shower had recently broken down and she had to nip to my place to freshen up before and after her lovers visited, which always guaranteed new gossip. No sooner had I got home than Helena was tapping at my door to use the shower. 'Ed, quick, hide in the other room. Bob is here and he needs the shower. You know he'll get all embarrassed if he knows someone is in here.'

'Helena, stop being silly. Bob and me get along just fine. It won't bother him.'

'No, Ed. Hide. Hurry.'

I shut myself away in my bedroom while Helena and Bob Dylan scrubbed each other's backs.

Meantime, Tina had endless meetings with Lee and Roger, chopping, changing and adding the odd new song to her act. She also had to hold auditions for a new singer/dancer to come on tour to replace Rava who had left the group. Finally, Rava suggested Tina audition a friend of hers called Annie Behringer, whom she thought would be perfect for the show. Annie was a recovering drug user who had been clean and sober for a year. She was a very nice girl, and she needed a job. Tina admired Annie's willpower and the strength it required to stay off drugs and drink for a year. She had waist-length thick blonde hair and when Tina saw how it swung all over the place on stage, she had to have her in the show. Annie was not the most skilled dancer but she did look marvellous. The other thing that attracted Tina was Annie's wonderful sense of humour; she didn't take Tina too seriously or fear her the way some other employees did. Lejeune, one of Tina's dancers from the Ikette days, was appointed with the enormous task of training Annie for the tour.

Lejeune, at her wits end with frustration, complained, 'Tina, I'm sorry, but this white girl just ain't got it. Annie cannot dance and you're gonna be sorry she's up there on that stage with you ...'

Tina sharply snapped, 'Lejeune, I didn't ask you that. All I'm asking you to do is teach Annie the dance steps and movements and get them down. I will make the final decisions.'

Lejeune was responsible for a great deal of the choreography in the show and always reported back to Tina. This time round, she was taken aback over Tina's reaction and didn't dare argue the point. Tina looked at me and said, 'Annie's got such a big personality that if she messes up on stage, she'll manage to just smile her way through it.'

During the final rehearsals, Tina was proven to be right. Annie made a lot of mistakes and each time she did, she simply swung her amazing head of hair in a full circle and fell into step again. Everyone, including Lee Kramer and Roger Davies, complained about Annie's inability to keep up, but there was something about her that made it very easy to forgive her anything, and Tina adored her.

Tina's son Ronnie joined the tour as her bass player and his best friend, Patrick Gammon, replaced the keyboard player, Kenny Moore, who had long since been poached by Gladys Knight. Patrick had an excellent voice and had done a lot of work with Anita Baker. Ronnie was a gifted bass player but sadly, at that time, he had a hideous drink problem which would become apparent while we were on the road. We would be accompanied by a delightful young man called Chip Lightman, a colleague of Lee's, who was placed on the road to observe Rhonda Graam discreetly with a view to taking over her job. Chip, a child of New York high society, came from very good stock. He started as an office boy for Lee Kramer and worked his way up. Lee felt Chip would be perfect as Tina's road manager. He was an unspoilt, eager, and a fast learner. He was very well educated, and adapted to any situation with ease.

A day or two before embarking on the tour, Lee brought Chip Lightman to Tina's house for a meeting to discuss the possibility of eventually taking over Rhonda Graam's job. The purpose of the meeting was for Tina to have a proper one-to-one chat with Chip, telling him what she expected of him and her likes and dislikes. When Tina met Chip, she discreetly buried her head in one hand while staring at me with her uncovered eye and whispered, 'Oh no, Ed. Here's this college educated boy going on the road with us ... This is going to be a disaster.'

Tina scared the living daylights out of young Chip, making him more nervous than he ever was. She mimicked a Southern accent as she lectured, 'Alright now, Chip. I know how you university educated boys are. An' Ah'm a-gonna tell ya' something, it ain't like that. On the road it's common sense. I don't want you askin' me a lotta questions. I don't even want you to think. When I ask you to do something, just stop and just do it.

'If I askya' toodoo sumthan', boy, just do it — don't go askin' no questions — don't go askin me nuthin.'

Then she stared at Chip and suddenly became sympathetic, realising how nervous she had made him. With her usual manner of speech restored, and in a voice laced with gentle kindness, she said, 'Chip, Rhonda isn't going to make this easy for you. She has a rough idea that her days are numbered and she's not stupid. It's likely she'll realise what you are there for. Whatever you need, tell Ed and he will relay it to me. I won't have time to wean you into Rhonda's job, and I need to stay focussed instead of being plied with questions day and night. It'll be fine, Chip, okay? Just fine.'

Poor Chip had never been on the road and there was a shortage of people prepared to help him. Tina shook her head after he left her, saying, 'Poor boy. He won't be able to hack it. He won't make it. What was Lee Kramer thinking of, putting this inexperienced college boy with us.'

Chip would, in a short space of time, prove us wrong and he would excel at things he had no knowledge of before.

The night before leaving for South Africa, I couldn't sleep for the excitement, waking every twenty minutes and dozing off again. Just as I dozed off for the fourth time, my phone rang and Tina's voice filtered through. 'Ed, it's me. Tina. So tell me, are you excited?'

I waffled on for twenty minutes, telling her how excited I was over the trip. I knew Tina genuinely shared my joy. She finally said, 'Now remember Ed. Be here at 8 o'clock. Do not, I mean absolutely do not, be late. We'll have a coffee together and go through the last minute details.'

Tina lived only a 20 minute drive away and with my car already loaded, I headed off at half past seven in the morning. As I backed my tiny red mini out of the drive of Helena's house, the driver's door, which I hadn't closed properly, popped open and wedged against the pillar of the exit. I pulled the car forward and desperately tried to close the door, but it had buckled, and hung open like a torn pocket on a pair of jeans. Half an hour rapidly passed while I tried in vain to repair the door. Realising I was meant to be at Tina's house at that moment, I panicked. I actually drove to her house with the car in that state steering while trying to hold the door closed at the same time. I took back-roads, hoping to avoid being spotted by the police. I was nearly in tears, thinking the police would see me, arrest me, then I wouldn't make the tour and Tina would fire me.

I finally pulled into Tina's drive one hour late, just as she was climbing into the limousine. When she spotted my little red car, her face was a mask of undisguised fury. She thundered, 'If you are coming on this tour, throw your things in the limo right now or you can just stay behind. I have no time to wait on you.'

She was furious with me. I tried apologising while pulling my belongings out of the mini, but Tina barked, 'I don't want to hear anything right now.' Just as she was about to climb back in the limo, she pushed her sunglasses down her nose and stared at my car. 'Ed, what is wrong with your car?'

While sweating half to death, loading my things into the limo, I nearly tripped over my words explaining, 'The door hit a post and jammed open — I had to drive and hold it closed at the same time — shit scared I'd be arrested — took all the hidden back roads — they would have thrown me in jail! — I was so worried.'

All of a sudden she burst out laughing, saying, 'Oh, Ed, you are something.' While pointing at my car, she added, 'Stick that thing in my car port. As a matter of fact, hide it. God forbid someone sees that in my drive, they'll think my luck has seriously taken a turn for the worse.'

Fortunately that was the only hitch of the day, and we settled comfortably onto the flight to South Africa. Chatting with Tina, I asked her opinion on a small personal dilemma I had. 'Tina, I think I should be moving out of Helena's. She was very nice to let me have the small outer house, and at such a cheap rent, but I don't really feel comfortable there and because of the shower situation, I'm not getting a lot of privacy. My mother suggested I move my things back home. I still have my room there. I spend most of my time at your place and she thinks it's mad for me to be laying rent out right now when I literally use my place to put my head down once in a while. Should I move back home?'

'Ed, I think it's a great idea! You're going to be on the road a lot now. It's crazy to pay rent when you'll barely be home. You have your own room at my house anyway so between my place and your mother's, you'll be fine. I second the motion! And Ed, think about it. You'll have more money to shop with!'

We clinked our glasses of champagne and drank to the unanimous decision. Tina then pursed her lips, and said, 'You know Ed, something a bit strange ... I didn't really like going round to your place because of Helena. She seems okay but I really can't get into her energy or aura. Hmmm.

'You know Helena is a singer, being Bob Dylan's backing vocalist and all ...'

'Yes, Ed. I know all that.'

I braced myself to tell Tina the whole Helena Springs story, starting at the very beginning. I became animated, my hands flying everywhere. 'Helena's childhood was a bit like yours. Her mother left when she was small and she was raised, with two sisters, by her father and grandparents. When she was reaching her teens, she went to Los Angeles to spend time with her mother but it didn't work out. They never got along.' I took a big sip of champagne and continued, 'Me and Helena danced on *Soul Train* together. We became so close, we told everyone we were cousins. She has a gift for making people laugh and I always thought she would go places — become something.

'Helena was always trying to get love from men, I think to compensate for being rejected as a child. The thing about her is that she perceives love and sex through a man's set of eyes and treats men exactly the same way men treat women. She doesn't sit around at home making booties. She's a go-getter. She started session singing and one thing led to another until finally, she auditioned as a backing vocalist for Bob Dylan. Honey, with her looks and voice, she got the job.'

I paused to refill my glass.

'Bob was having a thing with one of the other backing singers. Helena scoped the situation and decided, "Shit. That girl ain't that pretty. Honey, I'm gonna git in there and work that Bob."

'Helena told me she grabbed the first opportunity to sleep with Bob. She said she was so good in bed that she rocked Bob's world.

'It only took one roll in the hay with Helena. The other girl became history — Bob dropped her like a hot coal and kept Helena right at his side from that moment on. Helena had a way of talking like a little girl when she was after something and it worked time and time again on Bob. After her first tour with him, on the way back to LA, she told him she didn't have a place to stay and didn't know what to do. Bob immediately made arrangements for his office to find a home for Helena — the one she's living in now.'

I looked over at Tina, giving her a slick stare, before adding, 'And Helena makes good money working for Bob — about fifteen hundred dollars a week. Plus *per diems*. Plus she's allowed expenses. Plus she was going out with him so she never pays for meals or anything. She's Bob's favourite girl. He doesn't have lots of girls on the go at the same time. Bob's nothing like Ike, honey. No one's like Ike. Helena and Bob got along well, like real friends. Time rolled on and the relationship deepened ... Bob got hooked on Helena. But she was like a guy when she wanted something. A photographer started going on the road with Bob and all the women were after him. He was fine and, of course, Helena was the one to land him, which upset Bob no end. Helena started sleeping with the photographer on a regular basis. It really broke Bob's heart and things started getting messy. Helena stared Bob right in the eyes and told him if he was gonna lay every girl on tour then she was gonna mess around with whatever guy she wanted. That's what Helena's like. With sex, she may as well have been a guy. She'd tell a guy anything he wanted to hear to get him in bed, just the way men do to women. Helena had balls and it amused Bob. He couldn't believe her front. She saw off all his women and shit. Hell, at one time she wasn't even that pretty. Honey, she didn't always look the way she looks today. Back in the days of *Soul Train*, her personality was what made her, not her looks. She used all that money that was rolling in from Dylan to have loads of cosmetic surgery. Every time Bob saw her, she looked better and better! Well, Bob eventually went so nutty over Helena that he asked her to have a baby for him.'

I took a sip from my third glass of champagne, while continuing, 'One day, soon after Helena said she'd think about having a baby for Bob, she was driving through Beverly Hills right after having her hair done. At a red light, she looked over to another car and saw a guy staring at her. She pushed her sunglasses down her nose and winked at him. He pushed his sunglasses down and winked back. Some way down the road, she noticed the guy following her. He pulled up next to her again and took his sunglasses off. It was Robert De Niro! Helena told me she had heard rumours that Robert was into brown sugar so she flashed him her biggest smile. Then, with her fingers, she indicated she wanted him to pull over. He pulled over, then so did she. De Niro was understated and cool. They exchanged numbers and next thing I know, Helena's seeing Robert De Niro. Meantime, Bob was still begging a baby out of her.

'Helena was stupid. She should have had a baby for Bob. He would have set her up for life. He was real good to her and ... you know something, he really loved her. Robert De Niro was an asshole, a real nasty bastardly type person.'

'What, worse than Ike?'

'Tina, honey, Robert De Niro wasn't a nice guy — not at all. Anyway, Dylan kind of sensed something was different. He kept asking Helena over and over if she was seeing someone. Finally, one day Helena broke down in tears and confessed, in a half-baked Marilyn Monroe voice, that she was seeing another guy. Bob didn't even ask who it was. Helena finally said to him, "Bob, don't you want to know who it is?" Bob said, "Not if you don't want to tell me." Helena said to him, "It's an actor called Bob." She threw as many hints as she could before finally saying, "I call him Bob. His name is really Robert ... De Niro." She didn't get the reaction she hoped for from Dylan. He told her, "As long as you're happy." Helena was clever. She didn't want to totally blow out Dylan, just in case things with De Niro didn't work out. She told Dylan that she still loved him and didn't want anything to change because of De Niro, and Dylan was pleased to hear that. Helena started writing songs with Bob and he gave her the first big break she had with song writing. A couple of songs she co-wrote with Dylan went on one of Eric Clapton's albums and she ended up getting royalty cheques dropping through her door left, right and centre. She needed Dylan but the truth is, she had fallen in love with De Niro.'

I continued, 'De Niro had been married for years and Helena was certain he would leave his wife for her. She was wrong. De Niro had a brilliant arrangement with his wife — she got what she wanted and he got what he wanted. He had so many women that Helena lost count. But Helena believed in herself and thought she'd see the lot off, including the wife. De Niro didn't want that. His relationship with his wife made it easier to keep things very casual with the women he slept with. He couldn't make any sort of commitment to his lovers as long as he was married. It really suited him. And he loved his brown sugar. He'd see a white girl and say, yeh, she's pretty but he had no trouble turning them down. It was the black women that he couldn't resist.

'Heaven only knows why she went for the nasty one. Most women go for the creep, don't they, Tina? I can't tell you how many times I had to interrupt her love sessions to have De Niro move his car. He was always blocking me in and he was nasty as hell about it. Dylan blocked me in a few times but he was such a sweet guy, a real gentleman. De Niro was like a resentful, angry animal. Then he used to go mad at Helena because I knew all about their relationship. What did he expect? All I had to do was look out my window to see them under my nose. Once, when De Niro was due to visit, Helena bought him some very stylish underwear. He unwrapped the gifts and upon seeing the contents, threw the entire lot against a wall while shouting abuse at Helena. He was screaming his head off, saying, "Don't you dare buy me anything by that faggot designer. Everyone knows that designer is a fucking queer. I don't wear faggots' clothes. Don't buy me anything unless it's made by a man's man." Helena put her kittenish tone of voice on, talking like a little black Marilyn Monroe, pouting and shit, saying to De Niro "How can you be that way? You really hurt my feelings." De Niro turned on Helena without warning. Shit Tina, she was pregnant then! I felt like kicking his stupid ass but he's not worth breaking a fingernail over. I'll never forget what he said to her. "Helena, I want you to remember something. You're just my bitch in between planes. You'll never mean anything else to me and I don't want this baby. I'm not even sure if it's mine." De Niro stormed out leaving Helena in tears. He didn't beat her up but it scared the shit out of Helena. He would beat her up with his nasty mouth and words. Tina, honey, De Niro had a foul, abusive mouth. Being just outside the window, I had to listen to his shit all the time. Anyway, I'm glad he didn't like the underwear. I've got it on right now!'

I added, 'He did not want that baby. And De Niro's homophobic. During his savage outburst, he ranted like mad about how much he hated gays and bi-sexuals. Tina, you can imagine what he thought of me?' We both burst out laughing.

'The secret of Helena's success was to treat men the way they treat women. If you treat a guy the way he treats a woman, it hooks him. Men aren't used to getting a large dose of their own medicine. Tina, honey, just be a complete bastard to a man. Stop being so damn good to them.

'It's not that Helena does anything incredible or special in bed. It's what she does afterwards that gets the men. The second they're done making love, Helena just gets up to have a wash or do whatever. Meantime, the guy is saying "come back to bed, honey" just like a woman would. Helena just says, "Nope. I've got a busy day today." She's a great manipulator, carefully scheming and planning strategies. But she works damn hard at being a temptress. Since I been living in the house, Helena had her breasts enlarged, had two nose jobs and had her cheeks surgically enhanced. She drove men wild.

'You'd never believe what Helena did. She fell pregnant. She believed, or wanted to believe — until she finally *did* believe — it was De Niro's baby.

'In fact, the father was another white guy. Just a good lookin' guy who was a major fuck. He died in a horrible car crash. De Niro thought it was his baby. He was stomping mad over Helena getting pregnant.

'And there's more. Helena was still keeping a thing going with Bob Dylan. Can you believe it? Money was just pouring in. But Tina, that girl was worse than us with money. She spent it a week before it arrived. At least you and me wait until we have it in our hands before we blow it. So I guess we're not that naughty after all, huh?'

I returned to the economy cabin and spotted Tina's son Ronnie, with an ever-present drink in his hand, chatting up all the women from stewardesses to passengers. He was an extraordinary mixture of Ike and Tina, looking in many ways like both his parents. Amidst Ronnie's chat up lines, he made it clear he was with Tina Turner's band and that she was his mother. By the time we landed at our destination, everyone had eaten and drunk too much, talked too much and was tired and irritable. We all avoided eye contact, remembering what was revealed about each of us during the flight. We knew who was sleeping with who, who fancied who, who didn't like who, who had class, who didn't. There weren't any secrets left amongst us. By the time the plane landed, we were well and truly sick of each other, and we unanimously agreed to check into hotel, go to our rooms and stay away from each other.

After landing and passing through customs, I whisked Tina to a waiting limousine which transported us to our hotel. A bus was waiting for the band to take them to their hotel, which was at a different location to ours. All the luggage was tagged and collected by Chip Lightman, who would follow on to distribute the cases to the respective owners. By the time Chip arrived, we had already checked in at the hotel. As soon as Tina signed her name on the hotel register, I would escort her straight to her room and ensure it was suitable for her. I walked through the entire suite and checked for standard things, making sure her room wasn't facing a busy street, ensuring her sleep wouldn't be disturbed.

Tina sat down, kicked off her shoes and relaxed while I unpacked her hand luggage. By the time I had placed her cosmetics on the dressing table, her main pieces of luggage had started arriving. One by one, I would thoroughly unpack each while Tina read a magazine and had a drink.

It took two hours to unpack for Tina, starting with her bathroom goods, each bottle carefully placed just as they would be home. By unpacking the bathroom first, it gave Tina the freedom to have a refreshing bath or shower straight away, should she wish to. All the razors, soaps, bath mitts, shampoos and conditioners went on the counter at the side of the bath where they were in easy reach. On the bathroom counter went all her lotions, potions, masks, facial scrubs and beauty treatments. At the far end would be her perfumes and scented creams and gels, her favourite being Opium. I always packed a huge seashell which held her own personal selection of soaps. In the centre of the dressing counter would be all of Tina's hair products and brushes. The brushes and combs were laid out in order, starting with a round brush, a vent brush and a straight brush. On a leather Cartier travel mat were Tina's hairpins and ornate hair clips, her favourite being in tortoise shell. If the bathroom couldn't afford the space, I would set up a make-up vanity table where there was a source of good light.

Next, I would unpack all of Tina's nightgowns, undergarments and sleepwear. Tina always carried a wide variety of bathrobes ranging from white terry cloth robes to long flowing silk ones. Nothing in Tina's closet ever hung on wire hangers. They always hung on plastic ones designed for the specific garment; heavy duty for coats or hangers with rounded shoulders to keep jackets in perfect shape. I would transfer the lot to wire hangers before packing because the plastic didn't travel well. They'd sometimes snap and could easily ruin an expensive item of clothing by piercing it. I packed the plastic hangers separately, transferring all the clothes back on to them once at the hotel. I always packed Tina's outfits in sets, having first created a coordinated look at her house. For instance, I'd choose brown leather trousers with an Armani jacket, a silk top, a long silk scarf and belt — all those items would be together. All Tina had to do was see a jacket she wanted to wear and she'd know all the coordinating items would be hung directly adjacent to it. She could always mix and match, but more often than not, she'd go with the look I chose.

All her stockings were colour coordinated in drawers as well as her bras and panties. Spare belts, handbags, handkerchiefs and so forth were in drawers, in perfect coordination. She once told me, 'Ed, everything has to make sense when you pack and unpack. For instance, if there was a little closet in the bathroom, it would make sense that my robes, slippers and nightwear would go in there.' No matter where Tina and I stayed, she never had to ask where I put an item. She would just glance at the room furnishings, then look for the desired item where it would have been had she unpacked herself.

I always put her spiritual books by her bed. I would put her Cartier travel alarm clock by the bedside as well as her small Cartier diary and phone book. The larger diary would always go on the actual desk in her suite along with her Cartier pens and pencils. I would always leave a spare copy of her itinerary on the desk as well.

I would then set up the necessary chanting corner with fresh fruit nearby. Next, I'd set up Tina's stereo and tapes, items she'd started travelling with since I got her into listening to music. Finally I'd set up her own coffee maker, ground filter coffee and her coffee whitener, and her own sugar bowl with sugar, which travelled with us from LA.

I would spread her European magazines on the coffee table of the living room in her suite, then ensure there was a wine bucket and extra glasses for visitors. Lastly, I'd make sure there were fresh flowers in every room in her suite before I'd leave to unpack for myself. Just before leaving, I'd ask Tina if she wanted food or anything else. I wouldn't leave her until I was certain she was settled in and comfortable to the point where should she wake in the middle of the night, things were set up as if she had woken at home. Once in a while, before returning to my room, I'd massage her feet to relax her. The only time Tina and I spent apart was when she was chanting, sleeping or if I was running an errand. Apart from that, my job was to be at her beck and call at all hours, day or night, and I loved it.

That night, after studying the itinerary, we both fell asleep in our respective rooms, grateful to see we had the first two nights off after such a tiring journey.

18

Tina worked Wednesday, Thursday, Friday and Saturday, two shows a night, with Sunday, Monday and Tuesday off. The first week ran remarkably smoothly, and the promoter for the Sun City tour, a fella named Ronny, was delighted.

During the second week, one morning of a working day, I woke, carried out my routine then phoned through to Tina to see if she was ready for me. She drowsily said, 'No. I'll tell you what, Ed. I want to sleep a little longer. Come up in half an hour.'

I was all dressed, geared up to work and ready to fly out the door. When Tina said she wasn't ready, I got itchy feet and, needing to do something, I wandered to the hotel gift shop to buy some postcards and a few small gifts for my family. After choosing pearl and ivory jewellery and some hand-carved statuettes, I still had a few minutes to spare. I looked at my watch and thought Tina had sounded so tired on the phone I should give her another half hour to rest. Now, that was a bad mistake.

I dropped my shopping in my room then nipped a couple of doors over to Tina's, letting myself in with my key while gently saying, 'Hi, Tina, it's me.'

There was no reply.

I walked to her bedroom, thinking she might be in a deep sleep, but she was standing, in a flowing dressing gown, by a long mirror. I said, 'Oh! There you are. Hi. Are you ready for me?'

I could see her fingernails had been newly manicured, something I would have normally done. Tina glared at me, her eyes filled with borderline hate. To make her point, she stabbed at the air near my chest with her index finger as she began a short, angry lecture. Her deep red fingernail glistened with each poking movement, her face twitched and her voice was firm. 'Let me tell you something. When I tell you half an hour, I don't mean an hour. I don't mean thirty-five minutes or ten. I mean half an hour. When I tell you half an hour ...' Tina's anger had reached a fever pitch, embarking on a new sentence when only half finished with another. 'I tell you half an hour and you make it an hour. I'll tell ... You know ... I am really mad at you.'

I was shocked at how angry Tina was. I had previously experienced her mood swings, but they were barely worth noticing. I'd just potter around until she got past whatever was bothering her. I'd never seen her so angry as she was at that moment. At first, I simply got on with my job thinking Tina had said what she had to say and would quickly recover. I was mistaken. By the time half an hour had passed, I was panicking for my job. I tried to lighten the atmosphere and make small talk, but Tina did not reply to me once. She glared at me through her makeup mirror, her instructions spilling out of her mouth like ice cubes. 'Ed, I'm finished with you now. Go back to your room and I'll call you if I need you. I will know where to find you. You will stay in your room, yes?'

'Yes, Tina.'

Deeply upset, I rang Lejeune who had known her much longer than I had. After explaining the situation and Tina's frosty attitude towards me, I hoped Lejeune would tell me something reassuring. She was smart, never getting in the middle of things and I knew I should take on board anything she said. Lejeune advised, 'Eddy, welcome to the road. You'll learn about Miss Tina. Tina's not as easy as everybody thinks. I know you two laugh, have a good time together and you're close, but you'll learn about her. You'll discover another side to Tina. You're gonna learn and you're gonna learn quick.'

Tina performed two shows that night, hardly exchanging a word with me. I was constantly dismissed from her presence with an annoyed wave of the hand, as if she were swatting a flying insect.

Before I left to go to my room that night, where I had to stay like a prisoner so Tina could find me if she needed me, I tried apologising. I gently said, 'Tina, I am really sorry. I thought I was doing the right thing but it was a terrible mistake. I'm sorry to have upset you or let you down. It won't happen again.'

Wearing a twisted, almost heartless grimace on her face, she replied, 'Ed, I know it will never happen again. If I thought it would happen again, you'd be on a plane back to Los Angeles. Are you finished?'

'Yes, Tina.'

'Okay, Ed, you can leave.'

We were scheduled to have the following few days off and, originally, Tina and I were going to take a tour of Sun City, the sumptuous gambling resort that was still being built.

After a sleepless night, my phone rang the next morning and I assumed it was Tina. I thought I was having a nightmare when I heard Rhonda's voice. 'Eddy, you can go to Tina's room and pack for her now. Pack lightly, we're only going overnight. Oh, and by the way, you won't be going.'

'What?' I was gutted.

Rhonda, enjoying putting the knife in and twisting it, continued, 'Tina won't be needing your services. While we're at Sun City, you'll be free to do what you want. She won't be needing you.'

'Fine.' I put the phone down feeling extremely hurt and depressed.

I went to Tina's room and she still gave me the cold treatment as I tiptoed around her, plucking certain beautiful items from the drawers and closet. I carefully laid everything into the necessary cases and when I had finished, I heard Rhonda say to Tina, 'Duh Duh, shall I call for the porter now?'

'Yes, please, Rhonda. I'm ready.' Then she turned to me.

'You'll have the rest of today plus tomorrow off, but I left a small list of some errands I want you to run for me. Have a nice time, Ed.'

I had a quick glance at the list to make sure I had enough money to cover the shopping, and felt completely empty when I heard the door close behind Tina. I always kept $100 float in my pocket to spend on incidentals Tina might need. If I ran low on cash, I would go to Rhonda to exchange receipts for more money. I took the list, stuck it in my pocket and let myself out of Tina's suite. As I walked towards my own room, I couldn't remember ever feeling so lonely.

The phone wouldn't stop ringing the following morning and my head pounded as I reached for the receiver. 'Hi, Ed, it's me, Tina.' Her voice pierced straight through my hangover. 'Ed, you'd never believe what I did! I had so much fun last night! I did so many crazy things! I was wild, honey, *wild*!'

I clutched the remains of my thumping head with my free hand while Tina screamed down the phone. 'Ed! You're very quiet. What did you do last night?' Not waiting for a reply, she screeched '*Wake up*! I've got so much to tell you, Ed. I met this gorgeous guy! Why aren't you here?'

'You didn't invite me, Tina.'

'Forget about that, Ed. I wish you were here. You made me so mad. Damn it, you could have been here with me!'

'Tina, I didn't know you were going to get so upset over me letting you rest longer ...'

'Ed, that's the past. Anyway, I'm talking to you now. You and me are friends again. Anyway, I'm being brought back in a helicopter later. Okay? Just one thing, be there when I arrive — I'm dying to tell you about this guy!'

'Got a rough idea when you're arriving?'

'Yes, don't make any plans. I should get there around dinner time. Let's eat together and talk.'

By the time Tina arrived, I was handsomely dressed and waiting for her. I dashed to her room like a happy puppy and as soon as I let myself in, the first words out of her mouth were, 'Oh Ed, you'd never believe what happened. This guy was wild!' I grinned with the comfort of knowing everything was truly back to normal.

'Okay Ed, let's order up some dinner.' She glowed as she scanned the menu.

'Ed, I don't know where to start. We got there and I met this guy who was an entertainment manager at the resort. His name's Joe. He showed us a wonderful time!'

Tina stood, and her eyes sparkled as she animatedly continued, 'Joe's white, tall and good-looking. Anyway, we both knew what we wanted and agreed to do it at the end of the tour. Honey, I flirted for the gods and it was worth it. We made some heavy plans to meet up. It's exciting. I can't wait!

'Anyway, Ed, what did you do while I was away? I'll bet you didn't have as much fun as I did! Do anything nice? Meet anyone?'

'Tina, it was horrible. I went to this nightclub and at first they wouldn't let me in because I was black. They were going to have me arrested until they saw my American passport. When they saw that, they let me in to mingle with all the white folk. The white people treated me as if I was white just because I was American, but they would have arrested a black South African for trying to mingle with them! Today I went shopping and I smiled at all the black people I saw but they looked at me as if I were the enemy. They saw me walk in and out of shops where they would be refused, and get served.'

I felt withdrawn, and Tina sensed something was wrong. She asked, 'Ed, what's the matter? Did someone upset you?'

'Tina, I've never felt so degraded in my life. You'd never believe what happened. I popped into a restaurant to have lunch and they refused to serve me. I took out my passport but they said they didn't care what the law was, they weren't serving a nigger. When I left the restaurant, the white customers and staff turned their back on me, not wanting to see a black person in such close proximity to them. It was offensive and humiliating. Tina, don't go out there alone. Don't put yourself in that position.'

'Ed, why do you think I spend so much time in my hotel suite? I'll only go out if the promoters are escorting us. Believe me, I'm not putting myself in a position to be treated that way.'

Forlorn, I was staring down at my hands. Tina put her hand on my shoulder and said, 'I see, Ed. This kind of stuff never happened to you before. I've seen a lot of racism in my day. Haven't you ever been victimised for the colour of your skin?

'Well, there's a first time for everything. You see, the thing to do is don't look too hard at it and don't think about it too much. This is their karma. They were brought back to live their lives this way. They all have something to learn from it and we have to leave them to it. This is not our country and it's none of our business. Let's just do our jobs and get out of here.'

Tina and I went to stunning dinners, always as the guest of whoever was promoting that leg of the tour. Just before leaving Johannesburg, a wealthy promoter called Ronnie took us to a fabulous dinner in a private dining room of a hotel. The entire room was pannelled with hand polished wood, with every decorative detail carefully thought out, right down to the soft lighting. Attending the dinner were Tina, myself, Chip Lightman, Rhonda Graam and a few of Ronnie's close friends and family. Tina, who often dined with people within her own industry, would have me sit next to her so she would have someone to talk to when she became bored of the repetitive topic of music.

Ronnie was a charming man, very much a fatherly character who went out of his way to make that evening special for Tina. When the brandy was being poured, people shifted seats and gathered in their own little groups. A local socialite, sitting next to Tina and me, the only two black people at the dinner party, loudly announced, 'We treat our black servants like real people. We even take them on holiday with us.' She glanced at us while adding, 'Our blacks have a very good time.'

I noticed Tina shift, pretending not to have heard the woman's statement.

I asked the socialite, 'Do your black servants stay in the same hotel as you when you're on holiday?'

Horrified at the suggestion, she replied, 'Why goodness, no! Of course not. That is totally unacceptable. There are designated areas for blacks.' She smiled sweetly while explaining, 'There is accommodation attached to the hotel, in a discreet area of course, for the blacks to stay in. Of course it's not as grand as the main part of the hotel but I think it's rather nice, nonetheless, that accommodation is provided ...'

I calmly enquired, 'While on holiday, do the servants work for you?'

She answered, 'Well, yes ... yes they do.'

'Then they're not on holiday really, are they?'

The entire table went silent. Tina discreetly leaned towards me and whispered low enough for only me to hear, 'Ed, shut up.' I did as she requested, then excused myself so I could move to the other end of the table.

Ten minutes later, Tina came and sat next to me. I thought she was going to tell me off but she put her hand over mine and gently said, 'Ed, we are guests in this country. We are here working and when we are finished, we return home to our own freedom, our own lives and our own karma. We are not politicians, Ed, and we are not God. We can't change things here nor can we change the world. Let it go, Ed.'

We moved on to Capetown, a true beauty spot with breathtaking seafront views. As we took a guided tour of Capetown, particularly the waterfront areas, Tina kept diverting her eyes from the carefully displayed wooden signs stating 'Blacks Not Allowed On These Beaches,' 'Whites Only On These Beaches'. She kept smiling, deeply inhaling the salty fresh air, choosing to remain oblivious to anything that might rob her of the magic moment.

During the Capetown leg of the tour, she was told her schedule had to alter slightly that evening. She had to perform one hour earlier than originally scheduled because of the massively popular early 1980s television series, *Dallas*.

Dallas always brought Capetown to a standstill on the weeknight it was aired. Traffic mysteriously disappeared, shops emptied, restaurant doors closed, everything stopped for that hour. We were warned we had to finish our show half an hour before *Dallas* was aired, or not a single person would be present to see the performance, including the venue staff!

Just before leaving Capetown, we celebrated the birthday of one of Tina's backing singers. Tina took the band to the Hard Rock Cafe where we arranged for a cake to be brought to the table at the end of the evening. We were told the staff would also sing 'Happy Birthday.' When the moment arrived, we expected to see a cake with candles and hear the traditional American birthday tune and presumed we would all join in. The birthday song became an experience Tina talked about for months after. The kitchen door swung open and a large black woman in a cook's uniform stood holding the lit cake. With the kindest eyes, she looked at the flickering candle, and began singing a traditional African tribal song. Her voice was so astonishing that goosebumps rose on Tina's arms. It was an extraordinary tribal hymn, sung in her own language. Slowly, we could hear more amazing voices coming from the kitchen, joining into the main singer's tune. Then she started walking towards us and a train of black kitchen staff followed, creating the most exquisite rhythm we had ever heard in our lives. By the time the cake was put on the table, tears were streaming down Tina's face. We had never heard anything so beautiful in our lives and agreed we probably never would again. Rather than bursting into the normal birthday wishes when the song had finished, we all sat with silent tears trickling from our eyes. The stunned silence was broken by Tina's clapping hands, then we all burst into applause, telling the staff how wonderful their voices were and thanking them endlessly for doing something so special for us. It was days before Tina recovered from the experience.

It was nearing the end of the tour, and Tina twitched with anticipation over her planned meeting with Joe. He flew to Johannesburg and they kept to the intricate plans made weeks earlier. When Tina left to meet him, she was dressed for anything. She wore little make-up, but her lips and nails sparkled in a passionate shade of red. She wore sandals, big sunglasses, a Hawaiian-type print bustier and a matching gossamer sarong. The outfit was ingenious — it could easily move from a sunny sea shore to an elegant restaurant.

The day after they met, I entered Tina's suite to find her flushed from the excitement of the events the previous evening. Bursting to tell me the details, she started her account before I had barely had a chance to close the door.

'Ed, I have to tell you about meeting Joe last night. Just getting him into a room unseen made me feel like I got past the first hurdle of some sort of major spy mission. I left the door unlocked then he came in a couple of minutes later. Honey, as soon as he closed that door behind him we flew into each other's arms and fell right on the bed. It was just one of those wild nights.'

'Did you eat yet, Tina? Have you had breakfast yet?'

'You must be kidding, Ed.'

Tina's lips stretched into a smile filled with fond memories as she stated, 'You know, Ed, I don't think I'll ever see him again.' Then she hastily added,

'But it's okay ... it's alright. We both knew the score.

'I can have my breakfast in peace knowing, maybe even depending on the fact, that I won't have to look at him again. I won't ever have to look at him and think to myself, "Did I really do that?"

'Ed, listen. I'm staying here for another couple of weeks. I really need a break and I'm going on a safari. You go on home ahead of me and I'll keep in touch. I need a rest and I really want to do this, see all the animals in their own natural environment. I mean, it would be crazy to come all the way here and not go on safari! Let's have something to eat then we'll make a shopping list. I haven't got a stitch of safari clothes.'

'Tina, what's the real reason you're going on safari? I know it's not to get closer to nature or to have a close-up of a lion's tonsils.'

'Ed ... well ... there's things I have to filter. Things I need to think about.'

It was made clear to all those going on safari that they would be living a minimalist existence, meaning Tina couldn't show up with ten large crates of Louis Vuitton luggage. For once, she packed the very bare essentials and was travelling extremely light, leaving me to look after all her other goods. The safari company offered Tina a massive discount if she agreed to pose for some photographs for it. She readily agreed and, two days later, Tina and I flew off in separate directions.

19

Our next tour was to take us to Australia, so I flew out to Sydney on November 13, 1980, and meticulously set up everything for Tina's arrival four days later. I had packed so perfectly that when she flew out to join us, she didn't have to lug or carry anything except her small handbag. I was waiting in her room at the hotel and when she walked in her smile said it all. I had set everything up as if she was at home and she settled straight into that familiar comfort. This was to be a gruelling tour and I knew comfort would mean everything to Tina.

She arrived on Sunday, performed one show on Monday and one on Tuesday, then two shows each night on Wednesday and Thursday. Early Friday, we flew to Melbourne, where she performed two shows. Saturday, Tina made an appearance on a TV chart programme called *The Countdown*.

We had Sunday off, and on Monday Tina performed a private function for one of Australia's top newspapers. The following afternoon, we flew off to a place called Coolangata, where we would have a chance to settle in for a few days. During the flight, I had put my head together with the rest of the entourage, trying to work out what to do the following day, November 26, which was Tina's birthday. Unable to reach a decision on what to buy for Tina and how to celebrate, the only thing we accomplished was stressing each other out. By the time the plane landed, we were all in a state of total confusion. To make things worse, we arrived at the hotel only to discover it was an hour away from the venue where Tina would be performing. Our rooms were massive and set up more like apartments, but were hardly plush or elegant. I took one look around before uttering the words, 'Ugh! This is horrible. Are we really staying here?'

Tina shot daggers at me but didn't say a word. After her performance that evening, while being driven back to the hotel in a limousine, Tina sternly said, 'Ed, sometimes I think you're getting a bit too grand. You are staying in the same place I'm staying in and if you aren't happy with it, you can move to the accommodation where the band stays. I could make it very hard for you Ed, and I can be horrible if I want, but I'm not going to. But I want you to remember one thing — I will decide what I like and don't like. Don't you ever make a nasty comment like you did about our accommodation. I happen to like the rooms and if I like it, it will have to be good enough for you. Understand?'

'Yes, Tina.' I knew I was in the dog house.

'And, Ed, you can keep your opinions to yourself unless I ask. Understand?'

'Yes, Tina. Sorry, Tina. It won't happen again.'

'I know it won't, Ed,'

'Yes, Tina. Sorry, Tina.'

The following day, on her birthday, Tina had to perform one show. Hours before the performance, she got a fresh manicure and pedicure and I fussed over her hair. We discussed the evening's plans and it was unanimously decided, with Tina's blessing, that the entire entourage would take her to dinner after the show. In the middle of Tina's show that night, we presented her with a cake onstage while the band struck up 'Happy Birthday'. She was really moved and delighted by the sentiment, especially when the audience joined in singing.

This left her in great form, and we went on to the restaurant where we drank, danced, partied, laughed and had a ball.

On the way home, she got all sentimental and wanted her son Ronnie to join us back at our hotel along with Lee Kramer. Once in her room, Lee suggested he had some business to discuss with her. Tina, in a jovial mood, replied, 'Oh, Lee, look at my wonderful view. Why don't we just go out there for nice walk and not talk business. I'm not really in the mood.'

It was a hot, humid night and Tina excused herself to change quickly into a transparent, flowing cotton dress and sandals. While she was changing, she whispered, 'Ed, you and Ronnie have to come for a walk with me and Lee. I just don't trust myself with him — he's looking a bit too good tonight.'

'Oh, no, Tina. I'm exhausted.'

'Too bad Ed. Perk up.' She kept snapping her fingers to make me alert, then said, 'Look alive, Ed and go get Ronnie. You two are coming with me.'

The four of us walked along the beach and drank in the beautiful sight. Tina was a bit tipsy and flirtatious, laughing and making eyes at Lee. She suddenly kicked off her sandals and ran into the sea, encouraging Lee to follow. Ronnie and I rolled up our trouser legs and joined her, laughing like children while splashing each other. No matter how much Tina encouraged him, Lee was hesitant about getting his feet wet, behaving in a very businesslike manner. Tina reacted by saying, 'Oh, come on Lee, you're no fun ... come and have fun with us.'

Finally, Lee gave in and let his hair down, kicking droplets of water around while laughing with us. Suddenly, Tina in a fit of laughter, threw herself into Lee's arms. Realising she was flirting with him, Lee, pro that he was, didn't know how to react. During the rest of our walk, Ronnie and I kept nipping off on our own for the odd five minutes to give Lee and Tina time alone. Lee had hoped to talk business that evening but it was a lost cause. It was Tina's birthday and for once, business could wait until tomorrow.

We bade Lee goodnight and returned to our hotel where Ronnie had a room adjacent to hers just for that evening. I could see Tina was in the mood to talk so I pretended I was exhausted and went straight to my room. Tina then said goodnight to Ronnie and waited a couple of minutes before nipping out of her room to mine, where we sat up all night talking about Lee Kramer. Totally hooked, Tina gushed, 'Ed, did you see the way he looked at me? Did you see his beautiful eyes?' Tina talked on and on about her new love interest, determined they would become an item.

A few days later, we were due to fly back to Sydney. I got to the airport with Tina only to discover I had left my passport and valuables in the hotel's safe. I had no choice but to return to the hotel while Tina flew on. It was four and half hours before the next flight to Sydney, and by the time I arrived, Tina was livid.

She snapped, 'Me and Rhonda had to take care of my luggage and she did some unpacking for me and I can't find a damned thing. Not only that, you got an hour to get ready. We're going to an Elton John concert — you, me, Chip and Lee. Hurry up and finish unpacking my stuff. I have to get ready too, you know.'

We were staying in the same hotel as Elton John and Bette Midler. When we got to the concert, Tina sat next to Lee and within minutes of settling in, she popped open a bottle of wine we had brought. Tina and I had a plastic glass of wine. In the midst of being merry, one of Elton John's assistants approached Tina and asked her if she would join Elton on stage for an encore. Tina was delighted.

She looked young and sexy with her hair in a ponytail, dressed in an Armani suit with a grey teeshirt which made her breasts look amazing. We all grabbed our belongings and were ushered backstage where Tina waited to do the encore.

Elton ran offstage and the audience erupted, begging him to come back on and sing more of his famous tunes. He ran straight up to Tina, gave her a big hug and asked her if she was ready to come onstage with him. She said, 'Well, what song do you want to do?' Without waiting for a reply, she whipped off her jacket and handed it to me. 'Ed, quick, take this. Hold it for me.' Then she turned her attention back to Elton, who suggested a song. Tina replied, 'Oh no, I don't know the words to it!' Elton called someone over to write the lyrics out quickly for Tina who stared blankly at them. She was slightly tipsy and started laughing while trying desperately to focus on the handwritten words.

Elton went back on stage to sing one song, then he announced to the audience, 'I have a real surprise for you. A good friend and one of the greatest female vocalists today, the fabulous Tina Turner.' Tina waltzed onstage with a huge smile and the audience went wild over the unexpected treat. Tina and Elton sang 'The Bitch Is Back', and between focussing on the audience and the lyrics in her hand, she managed to work the audience into a complete frenzy. She left the stage and the crowd went nutty, prompting Elton John to invite her back. They had a brilliant time, and when they left the stage, Elton said, 'Listen, Tina, Bette Midler is having a birthday party tonight. Why don't you and your friends come along? That's where I'm going tonight.'

Tina threw her hand to her head, replying, 'Ohhhh, gosh ...'

Lee grabbed her and discreetly said, 'Tina, you have to go. Think of the publicity. It'll be great. Just do the right thing.'

It didn't take much to convince Tina who actually wanted to go, anyway. We poured into a waiting car which followed Elton's limousine. Tina, flushed, asked, 'Ed, how do I look?'

'Tina, honey, you look fantastic.'

'Ed, I was tipsy. I can't believe I couldn't remember the words to that song ... and I recorded it on my first solo album!'

When we arrived at the venue for Bette's party, I was still well and truly sloshed from the wine I had drunk on an empty stomach. Elton greeted Bette by saying, 'Sorry I'm so late, I had a show to do.'

Bette merrily replied, 'Well it's about fucking time you got here! You know honey, you keep me waiting on my own fucking birthday! Why didn't you just leave the concert and tell them you'll make up for it tomorrow night!'

Elton burst out laughing then announced, 'Don't you start on me, because I have a big surprise for you. I got a birthday present for you!'

Bette was feisty, fiery and very funny. In an extremely camp manner, she batted her eye lashes while gushing, 'What is it? Whaaaat?'

He toyed with her, 'Are you ready?'

'Oh, come on. Get on with it!'

Elton moved to the side and pointed our way, and when Bette saw Tina she nearly fainted. Bette was an avid fan of Tina's, and screamed, 'Oh my God! Tina Turner! Come here! Oh my God! You are so beautiful!'

Tina didn't have a chance to take one step forward before Bette ran over straight into her arms. They gave each other a hug, laughed together and posed for loads of photographs. Bette then asked Tina to come sit with her.

Meantime, Lee Kramer and Chip Lightman were behaving like typical managers, staying discreetly in the background while keeping an eye on their interests. I was out of my face on drink, and it wasn't long before I started making a complete ass of myself. Very loudly, I was talking to Bette while imitating her at the same time. The only difference between the real Bette and my imitation of her was the simple fact that I was slurring! Suddenly, Elton, Tina and Bette were rounded up for press photos and I kept drunkenly jumping into the photographs, ruining the entire lot of them. Lee Kramer looked on in horror. I overheard Lee say to Chip, 'That boy is out of control. Tina is going to have to get rid of him. We can't have this.' I knew he was thinking back over the events of the day. I had stayed up drinking until 4am in the morning the night before. I had missed a flight because I'd left my items at the hotel and all Lee could see was that I was out of my face again. He had decided there and then that I was a very bad influence on his artist. At that point, I was so drunk that I didn't care what Lee Kramer thought.

When we returned to the hotel, Tina and I staggered to her door then stumbled into her room. We both fell onto her bed and rolled around with laughter. Finally, she got up and wiped her make-up off before falling back onto the bed. I then spent twenty minutes tugging her clothes off and falling all over the place trying to tuck her into bed. I staggered, singing loudly in the hallway, back to my room. The next morning I ordered room service and wolfed down breakfast as the events of the night before came flowing back. With each thought came panic and a general feeling of illness, accompanied by a steady, painful thumping in my head. With me being the worse for the wear, I wondered how Tina was feeling. I abandoned my breakfast, showered and raced round to her room. While I picked up her articles of clothing that I had thrown all around the place the night before, I suddenly heard her quiet voice.

'Oh, Ed. What did we do last night?'

I felt like running to a corner and hiding. I didn't volunteer any information about my behaviour at the party the night before, wanting to see how much she actually remembered. Tina suddenly glared at me, her face momentarily looking furious, then, out of the blue, she suddenly started laughing. She kept regaining her composure, having an annoyed look on her face but each time our eyes met, we both cracked up. Suddenly, Tina stopped laughing and blurted out, 'Bette Midler's coming to my show tonight!' Then she looked at me and we both burst out laughing again. She kept saying, 'Ed, Ed, Ed, I'm going to kill you!' Each time she opened her mouth, it resulted in another laughing fit which did nothing for my pounding hangover.

That night, when Tina ran offstage for her assorted costume changes during both shows, she'd say things like, 'Yep, Ed. I'm going to do it. I'm definitely going to kill you!' Then we'd start laughing and she'd beg, 'Ed, don't make me laugh ... please, stop, stop!'

Tina had a two hour break before her next show that evening and one hour into her break Chip Lightman showed up at the dressing room door. 'T, can I have a word?'

Tina snapped, 'What is it, Chip?'

'Well, I thought you should know that Bette Midler will be in the audience for the next show and she'll be with John Reid, Elton's manager.'

Tina already knew Bette would be there but she had rules which she had made clear to Chip when he joined us on the road. Annoyed, she snapped, 'Chip, I told you before, I don't care who is in the audience. I never want to know. Those are my rules.'

Chip, who was now nervously bopping up and down while speaking, replied, 'T, I know that, but after last night I thought you might have to do whatever you do to relax for the next performance and give it your best.'

Although Chip had a valid point that evening, Tina was insulted and further annoyed that he had broken her rule. As he nervously bopped out of the dressing room door, Tina said, 'Oh, Ed. Come on. Put the towel down.' I knew what that meant. She had to do some deep breathing exercises and meditate.

In the middle of her second performance, she announced to the audience, 'I have a new friend in the audience tonight. It was her birthday yesterday and I'd like everyone to wish Bette Midler a happy belated birthday.' Tina and the audience sang 'Happy Birthday' to Bette, then she immediately asked her if she would join her on stage for a song. Bette nearly broke her ass running up to the stage where she and Tina immediately launched into a rendition of 'Hollywood Nights'. When the audience erupted into a frantic applause, Bette turned to Tina and bowed to her, honouring her as the queen of female vocalists. Tina teased the audience by saying, 'Do you want more?' The audience went berserk. Tina sang a song and said, 'If you want more, then you'll have to come back tomorrow night.'

Tina ran offstage to the dressing room where I peeled all her clothes off. She was standing stark naked while I dried the perspiration off her body with a towel when Bette Midler burst into the dressing room. She stood open-mouthed for a moment, then finally blurted, 'Oh my God, Tina, look at your body! What an amazing body! Shit Tina, I wouldn't even get undressed in front of myself let alone anyone else!'

Tina, totally flattered, replied, 'Oh, Bette. Stop it.'

Bette didn't stop. 'I gotta be honest with you Tina. I was just a little girl when I saw the Ike and Tina show in Hawaii and I been a fan ever since. Tina, honey, you are the queen. Everyone raved about Janis Joplin, but you were there first. There ain't no one like Tina Turner. Every major female singer worth her salt emulates a bit of Tina Turner.

'Come on. Let's go get something to eat. Let's go do anything. Even just have a coffee. I just want to talk with you.'

Before Tina could reply, Bette turned to me and said, 'And you. Both of you. I don't know what planet you and Tina arrived from last night. Shit. You pushed me right out of my own birthday pictures!' My black skin turned bright red.

Totally embarrassed by my behaviour the night before, I replied, 'Bette ... I'm so sorry.'

She cut me off by saying, 'Don't go apologising. When you lot arrived last night with Elton, it made my party. You turned it into an evening to remember!'

The conversation sparkled, and Bette amused us by telling us stories of how she, Cher and Diana Ross have a huge drag queen following. She said, 'Thank heaven for them. Those drag queens keep us alive. And Cher is crazy. Wait 'till I tell you about her! She cursed me out like she was a sailor!

'Anyway, Cher and Diana Ross are best friends ...'

Tina chipped in, 'Yes, I heard that somewhere ...'

Bette continued, 'Cher was going out with Gene Simmons, then all of a sudden, Diana was going out with Gene Simmons ...'

Tina said, 'Yes, I heard their friendship got strained over that little matter ...'

'It did hit a rocky patch but you know, everyone is scared of Cher.'

'Noooo, I never got that feeling from her. I mean ... well, she is outspoken, but ...'

Bette cut Tina off by saying, 'Well, honey, she scared me. Let me tell you something, Cher cursed me blind. She was putting a big Las Vegas show together, the focal point being the beginning of the show. It opens with these drag queens, who look the spitting image of me, Diana Ross and Cher. The audience thinks it's the real stars on the stage, got it? Okay. This is how it works. The drag double of Diana Ross says something like, "I never get a chance to work with Cher". Then I, or the drag double of me, stomps onto the stage saying, "You and Cher never invite me. I had to invite myself". Then the drag double of Cher comes on the stage saying something like, "Then us girls should do a number together. Let's get real funky". The audience by now is going mad thinking they came to see Cher and got two more big stars thrown in with it! You see, the doubles are perfect, but the voices really do belong to Diana Ross and me. We made a talking tape for Cher to use. All of a sudden, the real Cher comes from the wings demanding, "What's going on here? I am Cher!" It's a great Vegas type opening. Anyway, this is why I said that Cher scares me. She had an idea to do that opening and she phoned Diana asking for her to lay down her talking voice off a script for her. Diana thought it was a wild idea and agreed straight away. Then Cher phoned me asking me to do it and I told her I wasn't that crazy over the idea because there were at least a couple of hundred drag queens out there doing me already. I told her I'd pass on it.'

Bette suddenly stopped what she was saying and looked at the table, then she stared up at us wide eyed, adding, 'Cher went crazy. She yelled down the phone screaming blue murder. She said, "Who the fuck do you think you are? If it weren't for the drag queens you wouldn't even be Bette Midler." She kept cursing me and, for once, I was speechless. By the time she came up for air, I actually felt intimidated and heard myself muttering, "Calm down Cher. I'll do it."'

Tina asked, 'Then what happened?'

'Well, I went to a studio to do it. Cher marched straight up to me and instead of saying thanks, she said, "I'm glad you came to your senses." I'm terrified of her now. I'm scared she might go off the handle again.'

Tina and Bette really enjoyed each other's company and promised to see one another again. Although they exchanged numbers, that occasion never arose. It was one of those road things where it was magic for that moment and everyone went their separate ways truly liking each other.

We flew on to the Southeast Asia leg of the tour, where things proved problematic from the start when we discovered we had to share rooms because of arrangements made by the local promoter. Also, Customs decided some of Tina's outfits were too revealing and when they later sent them on, there were huge, black ink customs stamps over the crotch and breast areas of the stage costumes, making them impossible to use and damaging them so much that they had to be discarded. When the damaged batch arrived just before Tina was due to go onstage, she was level-headed and rational. The outfit she used to open the show couldn't be used, and rather than panic with only a few minutes left to go onstage, she simply said, 'We won't have enough time to try to clean off the stamps. We'll just have to improvise. Ed, see what I've got that's similar to this costume.' Tina was unflappable.

The promoter had us working on days off and playing two shows where one was only booked. Our itinerary was no longer to be relied upon once we were there. When Tina learned we would be working straight through without a day off, her level of professionalism became very apparent. She simply said, 'Fine. Then we work.'

We did three days in Bangkok, leaving for Hong Kong on December 23. Rhonda and I helped Tina with her Christmas list, with Tina buying a lovely gift for everyone in the entire entourage. The band and Tina spent Christmas morning exchanging gifts and that evening we worked. Afterwards, Tina suggested we all go for a Chinese meal and although we did, our enthusiasm and energy level had slipped to an all time low. The entire band, including Tina, was ready to go home. Meantime Lee Kramer's colleague, Roger Davies, had flown over to see what subtle changes had been made to the show. With most of Olivia Newton John's commitments seen to, he now had time to concentrate on Tina. Tina joked, 'Now, just look at Roger Davies. Whenever he gets bored with goodie-goodie Olivia Newton John, he flies out to us to have some fun.'

I woke up early the following day to pack the few remaining items of Tina's and, while there, I heard a knock at the door. Tina said, 'It's okay, it's Roger Davies. He said he needed to talk to me before we fly out today.'

I let Roger in and he joined Tina on the balcony where I served them coffee and snacks. Each time I walked onto the balcony, Tina looked more and more upset. Her voice vibrated a little as she said to me, 'Ed, leave everything right now. I need to be alone with Roger. I'll call you as soon as our meeting is finished.'

When Tina called me to return to her room, I could see she was unsettled. I asked, 'Tina, are you alright?'

She crunched her forehead and threw her hands forward while saying, 'Ah, Ed ... there are lots of things I have to do. A lot of thinking ... a lot of things I have to sort out.'

'Do you want to talk, Tina?'

'No, uh, I can't talk about it right now. I have to sort things in my head ... we'll talk later. Just finish packing me ... yeh, finish.' I knew something was gravely wrong.

I chose an Armani suit and silk blouse for Tina to travel in and laid it out carefully on the bed in preparation for our journey back that day, which was New Year's Eve. She walked in and solemnly said, 'Ed, uhm ... listen ... seeing how Roger is here, why don't you travel to the airport with the band. I'll see you at the airport.' That was a very unusual request, considering I was always at Tina's side from the moment she stepped out of her room. I thought she might have a few more things to talk about with Roger, and wouldn't argue a request of Tina's, anyway.

We were all milling around the airport foyer waiting for Tina when I saw her angrily stomping towards me with Rhonda in tow. When Tina spotted me, she stormed my way with a really mean look on her face. I thought to myself that she was still in a strange mood so I just waited for her to reach me and when she did, she snapped, 'Ed, in my suite was a kimono. A silk one that the hotel leaves in the room for guests' use. It's gone. Do you have it?'

'No, Tina. The cleaning lady came in at one point while I was packing your baggage and she took away the used towels. She removed the kimono, too. I knew you wouldn't need those things so I had her leave one fresh towel just in case, but let her take the other stuff.'

'Well, Ed, the hotel charged me one hundred dollars for the thing.' She turned to Rhonda. 'Take one hundred dollars off Ed's pay.' Then she turned back to me and said, 'It was your responsibility so I want you to know you will pay for it. Rhonda, are you writing this down? Take note. It is to come out of Ed's pay. Got it?' Rhonda dutifully whipped out her notepad and wrote Tina's instructions down.

I realised that more and more, Tina was treating me like a child, especially as I developed my own wild social life. I slowly began to realise that unless I cleaned my act up, my job would become insecure.

I knew Tina was carrying a heavy burden. After all those years together, I could recognise every bit of her body language. When she had something weighing heavy on her mind, she developed a nervous twitch in her foot. She would cross her legs, fold her hands and her foot would vibrate like crazy. It was happening at that moment, but it would take me a month to find out what was happening to her.

20

'There's going to be some changes, Ed. Remember when Roger and me were on the balcony and I asked you to leave and come back later to finish packing?'

'Yes, Tina.'

'Well, that's when it all happened.'

'What happened, Tina? I did pick up a strange vibe.'

'Roger sat down and talked to me about my life, where I'm going and how to do it. He felt that the way to get through the next transition, to get record companies interested, was to make some new demos and get rid of my whole show. Get rid of the costumes, the dance steps, the whole act and ... uhm ... get rid of all the band and entourage.'

I kept a brave face. 'I see, Tina. I guess you're telling me this is my last day working.'

'Ed, I wanted to get rid of Rhonda anyway and Roger felt you should go too. He was rattled over our behaviour at Bette's party and our all night gossip sessions and drinking. He just thinks, as a personal assistant, that you're a bad influence on me.'

'Okay, I see.'

'Roger wanted everyone to go. Especially people that were around from the Ike days. He wants to surround me with fresh, young, talented blood.'

'Tina, I'm only 23. Is Roger saying I'm too old or past my sell-by date? So it's over for me.'

Tina took a sip of coffee and stabbed at the table with her highly polished index finger while making her following point. 'Ed, you see, after a lot of thinking, I came to a conclusion. The fact is these people, Roger Davies and Lee Kramer, they work for me. After a lot of soul searching and arguing back and forth, I just put my foot down. You're staying Ed and I was adamant about it.'

I released a huge sigh of relief. 'Thank God, Tina.'

'I simply drew the line. When I finally told them, they really didn't have much choice. I told them I'm keeping you, I'm keeping Lejeune and Annie as dancers and they kept complaining to me that Annie wasn't any good as a dancer. But I put my foot down. As far as Rhonda is concerned, she's been with me a long time and she helped get me back on my feet and back on the road. I couldn't leave her out in the streets so I talked them into giving her a job. She'll be working with Lee Kramer at his office. I don't want Rhonda handling any of my day to day personal things. I don't want to have to have contact with her right now.'

'Tina, thanks for insisting I stay...'

She quickly cut in. 'Ed, having fought to keep you on there is something I have to make clear to you. There have to be some serious changes.' Her face became firm as she lectured, 'You will have to conduct yourself differently now. You'll have to conduct yourself better. When Lee and Roger aren't around, we can be ourselves and have fun. We'll just tone it down when they're around and we'll be serious and professional. Understand? It's the only way it will work. Don't make me regret locking horns with them over you.'

'You won't regret a thing, Tina.'

'I know I won't. I'll tell you something. I think they were a bit insecure because of your sexuality. They don't really understand you. They're uncomfortable because you're a free spirit. I tried to explain to them that you're gay, but they're just not comfortable with your sexuality.'

'They do flatter themselves, Tina. They don't have anything to worry about. Neither Roger or Lee is my type.' We burst into a fit of laughter.

'I want you to hear what I'm saying, Ed. They do not want you around. They'll scrutinise everything you do trying to find a reason to fire you. Be in control, Ed. Don't lose control. If we're alone at home with the music loud and being silly and dancing, that's between you and me. We're not going to be able to be silly around other people any more. They get jealous and feel left out. You know we do leave people out, Ed. Once we're together, it's not like we include anyone else, is it? Be a step ahead of them because they'll be nit-picking, understand?'

'You bet, Tina. Besides, you're not the only actress around. I can do them Oscar performances too, you know. Don't worry. I'll behave.'

'Do you want some wine, Ed, or should we get back to work?'

I stared at Tina for a long moment and replied, 'No, maybe we should get back to work.'

'Ahhh, I was just testing you. I knew I could rely on you and you passed the test. Now let's have some wine to celebrate!' Before I could object, Tina, as the boss, had made her decision.

Chip Lightman was to take over Rhonda's former duties as road manager. I was glad he had that position because we got along brilliantly. He once went as far as telling Roger, 'Ed's not that bad. He and Tina are like two peas in a pod. Eddy's good for Tina. He understands her moods and when she's on a low, he seems to know what to do to bring her out of it. You don't really want to lose that.'

The next part of the agenda was for Roger and Lee to get Tina a record deal. She had to cut new demos and choose new songs. We spent hours listening to tapes of potential recording material that had been sent over from Roger's office. Tina told them she wanted to cover a Rolling Stones song. She wanted to do material like Rod Stewart and Mick Jagger. Roger had managed a group called The Sherbs who had a song called 'Crazy In The Night'. Tina loved it and wanted it on the demo. She chose another song sent in from Chris Blackwell, a number that really showed she had a fantastic range to her voice. Tina also chose 'Pain', the song I had written for her. Roger totally objected but, once again, Tina put her foot down.

Roger and Lee managed to get a man to produce Tina's demo under the agreement that if it worked, he would be contracted to produce her actual album. The next problem was that Tina's new management claimed they couldn't finance the studio time and told her she would have to pay for it. Tina raised a loan against her Mercedes to pay for the studio time which ran between five to ten thousand dollars. Roger hired top studio musicians, the very best in the business for Tina's demo. February 16, 1981 was Tina's first day in Sunset Sound on 5650 Sunset Boulevard, Hollywood. I drove her to the session and as we pulled into the security parking lot, Tina gasped, 'It's so weird, I've been here before.'

Once we got in, she muttered, 'I've definitely been here before.' We got talking with studio staff and they told Tina the establishment had been around for years but in days gone past, the entrance was formerly at the front. Tina whispered to me, 'Let's nip out and go round the front. I want to see it.'

A staff member came with us and showed us where the entrance once was but it had long since been bricked over and closed off. Tina stared and said, 'Okay. I remember now. Ike and I recorded here once, a long, long time ago.' Suddenly, she got an energy surge and vibrantly perked up. 'Ed, me and Ike, we did good work here at one time. I've got a really good vibe.'

Tina was incredibly switched on that day, and very excited about taking the first steps of change. She saw herself as a female Mick Jagger fronting an all male band. She no longer wanted the beaded costumes and glam image. She wanted to go onstage wearing jeans, boots, teeshirts and just grab the microphone and be one of the boys. She was wearing black leather jeans, Maud Frizon boots, dyed to look like leopard skin and a sexy, trendy top. From where we stood, Tina suddenly looked very rock 'n' roll.

Lejeune arrived to lay down background vocals and Tina suggested Waddy, one of the session guys who had worked with Linda Rondstadt and The Eagles, should sing, too. Waddy and Tina got along brilliantly. During a break, Tina sat with him to share a beer. The sight was amazing. Waddy had a gorgeous mane of thick blonde, curly locks. He was pencil thin and wore John Lennon style glasses. He looked like a real rock 'n' roller and Tina looked like a rock 'n' roll bad boy, too. Tina had had an idea and, overnight, she had become one of the lads, just as she had envisaged. They had a ball while laying down the background vocals to the Stones' 'Out Of Time'.

At one point, the backing vocalists couldn't reach a note on a particular song. Tina leapt up and said, 'Don't worry, I'll do it.' She left the control room and went into the recording booth and when she sang the backing lines, one technician gasped, 'Fuck me. Tina Turner can really sing!' There was no doubt left in anyone's mind that day that Tina actually had an amazing voice and wasn't just a screamer.

Tina then asked everyone to get ready to record the next song but the band, utterly exhausted, begged for mercy. Tina clapped her hands and said, 'Boys, ya' gotta keep up with me. Come on. Let's do it.'

One of the technicians turned to Roger and asked, 'What's she on?'

Roger stared proudly at Tina through the soundproof glass and replied, 'She's on life, man. Life. She's like that all the time.'

During the drive home, Tina played her new tape over and over and we sang to the tracks while driving through Beverly Hills. We let ourselves into the house and Tina, still on a high from the day's recording, suddenly said, 'Everyone we decided to let go of, including Ronnie, has been informed that their services are no longer needed.'

I could see Tina was relieved that matter was out of the way and didn't allow feeling or emotions to creep in. She said, 'Ed, it's not a question of losing old friends. I'm embarking on a new life. I started losing people in my life at a very young age. My mother, my father ... the list has got to be a mile long. When I was with Ike, musicians and Ikettes came and went. My whole life's been like that. I just learned to let go at an early age.'

Tina had a way of letting people go out of her life. Once she decided it was over with a person, she had a way of detaching herself. Since childhood she developed as a loner and never depended on people. I looked at her and wondered at that moment how long I would last, would I be the one left behind?

Tina, still in a buoyant mood, talked of her immediate plans. 'Ed, it's so exciting. I'm auditioning a whole new band! Well ... nearly a whole band. I'm keeping that synth player, Chuck — he's young enough and he minds his own business. Roger and Lee want fresh, young talent so he'll do just fine. If you know any talented new blood — real talented, let them know, Tina Turner is putting a hot new band together!'

Tina twirled around the room as if she were dancing on top of the world. She fell asleep that night with the past well and truly behind her, knowing she would open her eyes the next morning to a new life, new dreams and new ambitions.

Tina had endless meetings with Lee Kramer and Roger Davies, going through lists of potential musicians, while finetuning their plans. Not only would Tina take on a new band, she had to record with them and tour live as well. This posed a problem for her. It's easy to play with people you've never met before in a recording studio, but performing live is a different matter. To perform live, she needed one other person that was her musical twin on stage, a person who knew her style and every note inside out. Tina always needed an Ike Turner on stage and there was only one person talented enough to carry her if she vocally slipped while performing — Kenny Moore, the guy Gladys Knight had whisked away from right under Tina's nose in Vegas. Kenny had enjoyed working with Tina and when he got call to come back, he leapt at the opportunity. He had worked for numerous top female vocalists but the one he was happiest with was Tina. They had had a terrible battle of wills and on the surface, Tina had lost but in reality, Kenny lost too because he wasn't happy working with any other artist. On stage, Kenny and Tina were one and it wasn't until he left that they realised it.

March 9 was the first day of auditions, and the trail of musicians that came through the studio door was endless. We had all sorts, all sizes and all colours. This was a bizzare event for Tina because she would normally check a person out once the numbers had been narrowed down. This time round, Tina had to see every single musician herself. This was her band, a band that would be a major part of her future and her opinion meant everything. She was the one who had to be on stage with them, not anyone else. Kenny Moore was on cloud nine. He was back with Tina Turner, sitting at her side, advising her about the hopefuls she would be seeing and telling her about their assorted musical backgrounds. Kenny was very much in charge of the auditions and he felt confident, having been given another chance to work in an environment, and with an artist, that he actually enjoyed. Kenny never got the recognition and applause he deserved when he worked with Aretha Franklin and Gladys Knight. He was their right hand man on stage, but Tina was the only artist that would tell the audience how important Kenny was.

Sitting facing the stage, Kenny, in his wonderfully soulful voice, said to Tina, 'Awraaat na T. We got a guitar player comin' on'. An all American white boy.'

Kenny didn't miss a trick and noticed Tina, for a flash, getting slightly rattled when she saw the next musician walk on stage. His name was James Ralston. He was around six feet tall, with layered blonde hair just above his shoulders, a long face and slim body. Having observed Tina's reaction, Kenny slowly glanced at James Ralston to see what turned her on so much. As soon as Kenny saw him, he reacted just like Tina. His face lit up and being bisexual, there was no doubt what he was thinking. Kenny and Tina were attracted to the same type of man. It was obvious Tina and Kenny fancied poor, innocent James Ralston, and it was simply a question of James' preferences and who would get there first.

I watched Tina's body language with amusement. When she was upset, her foot would shake. When she was smitten with a guy, if in a sitting position, she would point her toe like a ballerina while her foot twirled in tiny circles. I looked down at her feet and saw one of them twirling like helicopter blades. It wasn't that James Ralston was particularly great looking, but he was extremely confident and cocky and that shone through on sight. Kenny worked his way to his piano and asked Ralston, 'Hey, man.

What stuff d'yoo know?'

James replied, 'Some James Brown, some ...'

Kenny got up, leaned over his piano and whispered to James, 'Now, dude. If yo' want this job, don't go mentionin' no James Brown. Don't mention anything R and B. Think of the boys, the boys. Ya'll know what I mean, thank of the Rollin' Stones ... stuff like that ... an' yo' get the job, man.' Kenny discreetly sat back behind the piano.

At that time of his life, James was good but he wasn't great. He strummed on his guitar while Kenny played the piano, but Tina was next to oblivious to the sound coming out. She took an instant shine to James and decided on the spot that he would be in the band. James wasn't aware of that at the time. Tina decided to start having fun with her new toy straight away. She did something totally uncharacteristic, she went on the stage with an auditioning musician. She looked at James Ralston and said, 'Come on. Play something.' He was struck rigid. Tina then said, 'Alright. I'll sing and you play to my tune then you play and I'll sing to your tune ... then maybe we can meet in the middle someplace. Come on.' She turned to Kenny and said, 'You hit something, Kenny, then you start, James, then I'll follow. Okay?'

Kenny started playing 'Proud Mary', and Tina took the microphone out of its stand and started singing to James Ralston. I stared at the scene and thought, 'There's Tina's new boyfriend, only he doesn't know it yet.'

Finally, when the choices were made, Tina's new band was made up of Kenny Moore on keyboards, James Ralston on guitar, Bob Feit who would work with James, Chuck Olsten on synthesiser and Mark Williams on drums. Blonde-haired Annie, who never could keep up with the steps, stayed on as a dancer with Lejeune. Lejeune and Annie were also backup vocalists but when playing live, the technicians would turn off Annie's microphone because she couldn't sing, either. It didn't matter to Tina — she liked Annie and insisted, against Roger's and Lee's wishes, that she stayed. Rehearsals started the following day, March 10, lasting for 5 days. I always had a look in at rehearsals because Tina would ask my detailed opinion later. Often, in the evening, Tina would put on a show for me, asking my opinion and testing out certain suggestions I would make.

One night, Tina jumped up and said, 'Ed, I've got it! I've got a great idea. I'm going to open the act with Rod Stewart's song, 'I'm Gonna Kill My Wife'. I'll start singing it really slow, then turn my back to the audience and go over to Kenny, who will slip me a gold rope noose ... then I'll suddenly come alive and start going in circles twirling the noose all around in the air and singing like a crazy woman, "I'm gonna kill *his* wife", instead of "I'm gonna kill *my* wife." Got it?

Tina ran to the end of the room and started singing very quietly and slowly:

No one can stop me now
I'm about to take a life

Can't stop me now,
I'm about to kill his wife.

By the time she had finished a few lines, she was nearly in front of me. Then she turned her back on me and walked slowly away. She paused in front of a chair and reached as if she was taking something in her hand, then she turned and went nutty, singing like a crazed woman on a killing spree, twirling a belt all over the place as if it were a hangman's noose, while the words burst out of her mouth, 'I'm gonna kill her ...'

I sat speechless. She casually said, 'What do you think, Ed?' By the time she perfected this idea, it would leave people stunned and sweating in their seats.

On the third day of rehearsals, Tina said, 'Ed, leave your errands for today. Stay with me for the rehearsal.'

I noticed she was dressed out of character for rehearsals. She wore a designer jogging suit over a one piece green leotard. The difference with this particular outfit was that she oozed sex appeal in it, an effort she wouldn't make under normal circumstances. She would always be well turned out, but not necessarily as sexy as that. I stared at her from head to toe and asked, 'Excuse me, missy, where do you think you're going?'

She grinned like a naughty little girl, gave a twirl and replied throatily, 'Rehearsals, darling. I told you already!'

'Ohhh,' I cheekily said, adding, 'I guess "rehearsal" is a new word for "love mission."'

'Shut up, Ed, and let's go.'

While singing with the band during the rehearsal, Tina was flirting like crazy with James Ralston who seemed oblivious of Tina's actions. Tina stood in her leotard and tracksuit bottoms while she sang a couple of numbers. After a while, she discarded the bottoms, affording a good overall look at her fabulous body in the skimpy, revealing leotard. She wasn't wearing a bra and her nipples stood as erect as her breasts, the fine detail and outline clear for all to see. She wasn't wearing underpants and the tight leotard was slightly transparent.

By the time rehearsals finished, everyone picked up on the fact that Tina fancied James Ralston — everyone except James himself. If he did know, he made a splendid job of pretending otherwise.

Tina kept old favourites in the show like 'Proud Mary' and ended the act with 'Rolling On The River'. The only difference was how she interpreted the songs in the new show. Instead of screaming at the audience, she purred at them, snarled, growled and licked her lips, working them into a frenzy. Gone was all the wild dancing on her part — she left most of it to the girls, although she did a little bit of dancing with them knowing a large part of the audience would expect her to. Instead of all her wild movements, she concentrated on romancing the audience and making them feel like they were right up on that stage with her. She started prowling to the edges of the platform like a wild cat, close to the cheering crowds. She started using spiky high stilettos, walking in the difficult shoes as if she were walking on air. No one could walk in stilettos like Tina Turner. Finally, Tina had to decide what the bands costumes would be like. In the shows gone past, her band would wear tuxedos but with the new budget, Tina really had to cut corners and come up with a cheap idea that would be a cross between cabaret and rock 'n' roll.

Finally, again overriding Roger Davies, she decided that the band would wear Karate suits, with each member wearing a different colour belt. She chose Bob Mackie costumes for the girls with very little glitter, but her own stage wardrobe had to undergo a total change. She had read somewhere that miniskirts were coming back into fashion so we went through her stock of old costumes from the Ike days. We found a tiny, short dress made of gold chains. She held it against herself and asked, 'Ed, what do you think.'

I immediately replied, 'Well alright, Miss T, that dress is fierce!' On Wednesday, March 18, Tina opened her new show at the Fairmont Hotel in Knob Hill, San Fransisco — the very same venue where I had started working on the road with her as her personal assistant one year before. She had a new look, a new band and more importantly, a future. A new chapter in the history books of rock and roll was about to be written.

21

ina's new hairstyle was long with a fringe. The roots were dyed dark brown and the ends an ash blonde. It was swept into a hairband on the very top of her head, the ponytail spraying out like a palm tree. She called it the 'waterfall' look because she had so much human hair in her multilayers of weaves, that the ponytail sprayed out like a fountain.

It was a mark of bravery that Tina was willing to risk change and face an audience familiar with her former image. But the one thing Tina couldn't face was her management being present at the opening night. She begged them not to come and they finally agreed to her wishes. To make things more unbearable, everyone was tense and kept trying to hide it, which only made the fact more obvious. Tina and I had a light bite to eat while the band set up soundcheck. Charged with the energy of anticipation, Tina entered soundcheck while the band were going through a number and became tense when she sensed they weren't as tight as they should be.

Everyone was walking on needles. This was a first night band with first night nerves, but it wasn't playing with a new band that worried Tina. She was worried whether the change over to rock 'n' roll would be well received.

'Ed, round everyone up. I want to see them in my dressing room before the show.'

Once everyone had gathered in her room, Tina said, 'Okay everyone, this is the score. I know you're all a bit nervous, but you must watch my cues and watch me. You know I got private sign language for you guys. Follow the sign language and listen to Kenny's cues and to mine.' Tina had a way of raising her hand and fluttering her fingers which looked as if it were body movements involved with the number she was singing. In fact, the hand fluttering down was sign language for the band, telling them they were playing far too loud and to lower it. If the band didn't do it fast enough, Tina would take the mike in her hand, turn her back on the audience and flash the filthiest look at the band before turning to the audience with a huge smile on her face. If it ever came to that, then the band knew she was not happy, and to pick it up. Now.

Tina continued her lecture, 'Let's just do a good show. Now go have a good rest and I'll see you out there shortly. We're gonna do a great show.'

Tina was clever. She didn't transform her show past the point of all recognition. She knew change is hard for some people to accept and so she kept several of her trademark songs. She compensated for the rock 'n' roll flavour by getting the audience very involved. She sang to them and they felt her energy and stage power. They loved it. One of Tina's mottos was never to allow the audience to lead you. Always stay in control.

The band had settled down, but there was one major problem. Her drummer, Mark, couldn't keep up with the rest of the band and had to be replaced quickly. He was talented enough but needed more experience and Tina, with several important bookings waiting, couldn't afford to nurse him through that stage of a musician's career. Someone suggested she try a drummer called Jack Bruno and on the hush-hush, Tina flew him over during the second week of the engagement. He discreetly checked into the hotel and went down to the top secret rehearsal where he would quickly audition for Tina without her own drummer being any the wiser.

Much to our horror, Mark unexpectedly walked in on the audition. The shock and hurt on his face was too much to bear. He was going to be replaced but he was the last to know. He was distraught and humiliated. To make things worse, Jack Bruno was thumping away during the audition on Mark's set of drums! For Mark, it was simply too insulting and he made it clear to Tina that he wouldn't be available for the remaining days that she was booked at the Fairmont, leaving Tina well and truly stuck.

Tina, calm and unflappable when faced with the unexpected, simply threw her hands up before announcing to Jack Bruno, 'Well, I guess we'll really have a chance to see what you can do. Work him hard guys. Jack has a lot to learn by tomorrow night. He has to know this show inside out.'

There was a lot more to being a drummer for Tina Turner than just being able to keep a beat — you had to be a very perceptive showman with it. Sometimes, Tina would flip her hair around wildly and suddenly stop, and at that point, the drummer would instinctively know to stop too, affording the audience the full intended impact of the moment. Jack Bruno was, indeed, heaven sent. He and Kenny Moore turned out to be Tina's best musicians and, as I write this book, Jack is still with Tina today.

Tina hadn't played LA in so long that she twitched with nervous anticipation over the two night booking at The Country Club in Reseda that Roger Davies had arranged in early April. She knew it was considered a major coup to win a local audience — all California based singing artists believe that if you crack the audience on your own ground, your potential for national, even worldwide success is very real. Tina's nervous tension gave way to certain confidence when the news broke that her show had sold out for both nights. Tina whipped the audience into a frenzy. The crowds went wild over her performance and couldn't get enough of her, begging her back on stage over and over. They kept chanting, 'Tina, Tina, Tina' and she raced back on stage and said, 'You want more? Well, I'm going to give it to you ...' Then she burst into song. The majority of that crowd was young and what they saw on stage was a something that really appealed to them — a young, energetic woman with the most amazing stage charisma they had ever seen. Not one person stopped to think that they were looking at a woman of over forty. Tina was hot, sexy and as seductive as ever, and that crowd was left wanting more.

The media reviews on Tina's show were scintillating and they set the public's tongues wagging. This new interest in Tina Turner would open the doors for record companies to start looking at her in a different light. After reading the reviews, Tina teasingly said, 'So Ed, it looks like I'm not the only star in this house!'

The reviews highlighted Tina's amazing version of 'Help' and told how she brought the house down with a new song 'Pain', by Eddy Hampton and Jeannie Cunningham (with whom I'd written the song). On stage, Tina made 'Pain' sound like a sado-masochist number and made it very raunchy and seductive which sent audiences wild. We found ourselves dancing in circles over the reviews on her performance and my song.

Good Friday, April 17, found us flying to Vancouver, Canada, so Tina could perform on a Tom Jones television special. Tina, Chip Lightman and I were taken by surprise over the cold, crisp Canadian weather and shook like leaves while checking into our hotel. We arrived at the venue the following day, early enough for rehearsals. Tina and Tom performed a duet together, a Rod Stewart number called 'Hot Legs', then, Tina, performed 'Pain'. She raced offstage to where I stood and as I dabbed at her perspiration with a towel, Tom Jones suggestively asked, 'So tell me Tina, what sort of pain are you into?'

Tina, completely flustered, replied, 'Oh, no, no. I'm the innocent one. I just sing the song. You'll have to talk to my assistant here. He's the one who wrote it.'

Tom stared at me with a wicked grin on his face and asked, 'Tell me the sort of pain you're into.'

I became totally flustered as Tina burst out in a hearty, naughty guffaw, and kept prompting me, 'Come on Eddy, tell me what it's about.'

Finally, after Tina and Tom had exhausted themselves teasing me, I said, 'This song is actually about emotional pain but for some reason, when Tina sings it, it sounds like an S & M number. Okay, I wrote the song but Tina makes it suggestive.' Finding the opportunity to tease Tina, I added, 'You see Tom, I think it's Tina who can give you the answers you're looking for ...'

Tina didn't know where to run and hide. Tom finally said, 'Tina, are you thinking of putting it on vinyl? If not, I'd be interested ...'

Tina cut him off by politely saying, 'Tom, Ed wrote that for me and yes, I will be recording it.'

While walking away, Tina kept glancing back to ensure Tom was out of earshot and when she thought we had sufficiently distanced ourselves, she burst into a hearty laugh. Barely able to get the words out, she said, 'Ed, I have to tell you a story. Years ago, when I first played Las Vegas with Ike, I had a beautiful black dancer called Dee Dee. She really was something to look at. Anyway, we were opening Tom's show and Dee Dee couldn't stop flirting with him. Dee Dee told us she was a Tom fan since she was a young teenager and always wondered if 'it' was true ...'

'If what was true, Tina?'

'I'm getting there, alright, Eddy? Anyway, the band and I were making bets whether Dee Dee would sleep with Tom or not and sure enough, when we came off stage just before he went on, you could really sense something between them two. Tom and Dee Dee flirted so much that they were ready to tear each other apart in bed. I knew I'd win the bet. Anyway, I heard Tom say to Dee Dee, "Let's meet up in a couple of hours, after the show is over, and have a drink together." Dee Dee was going, "Yes, yes, yes!" I hurried to the dressing room to tell everyone but she burst in right after me going, "Alright honey, I'm tellin' ya'll guys, Ah'm datin' Tom Jones tonight and Ah'm findin' out if that thang is real!"'

By this point we had reached Tina's dressing room and she sat in a fit of laughter with her head in her hands. Finally, wiping the tears of laughter from her cheeks, she continued, 'Ed, she went on the date and I couldn't sleep. I told Dee Dee that she'd better come straight to my room and tell me what happened. She came in sparkling and the first thing she said was, "Ah'm tellin' ya'll, that ain't no sock! Nuh uh. Tom Jones is all man!"'

Nick Ashford and Valerie Simpson were the hottest writing team for Motown records. They were an Afro-American married couple and had, by writing some of the world's best-known number one songs, become frighteningly rich. Their heady, success began with a Ray Charles hit they penned called 'Let's Go Get Stoned'. They conquered the charts during the disco era writing memorable songs like 'I'm Every Woman' performed by Chaka Khan and stars such as Whitney Houston have recorded versions of their songs. Tina was playing New York and it was Nick Ashford's birthday, so we were invited to the party held at his home. It was very hard work getting Tina to go, but finally Roger talked her into it by saying it was a press exercise and she had to be seen and photographed as much as possible. Also, Roger was on a never ending quest to find new material for Tina and hoped that Ashford and Simpson could work their magic and write a hit song for her.

Ashford and Simpson lived in a lovely, informal brownstone house. The door was open, music gently flowed and there were countless happy people mingling and laughing. The party was very laid back and the catering was fabulous, all traditional soul food such as candied yams and black eye peas. The atmosphere was like a house party except that most of the guests were well known celebrities. When Ashford and Simpson spotted Tina, they went over immediately to greet her warmly and thank her for coming.

Suddenly, although the music continued, all the people fell silent. Making one of her trademark memorable arrivals was Grace Jones. At that time, Grace was a huge star in her prime. She wore a big hat, long gloves and glided through the crowd that stood frozen at the amazing sight. Grace certainly made the most of the effect her presence had on people. At another party a few days later, Andy Warhol would say to me 'She's like a beautiful black panther stretched into a human body.' While swanning past the revellers, Grace grandly demanded in her French Caribbean accent, 'Valerie? Nick? Where are you? My darlings, I'm sorry I'm so late.' As the crowd parted to allow her to glide along, Grace's eyes landed right on Tina. As she strode forward, Grace said, 'Tina. That was a fabulous show last night, darling.' Standing with us was Roger Davies and his beautiful wife, Nanette. Upon seeing the couple, Grace made a beeline for them. She snaked dramatically towards Nanette who was an elegant, stunning woman who looked a bit like a young Jackie Onassis, and carried herself with the same grace, style and class. Grace made it clear that she thought Roger and Nanette were a good looking couple and she fancied both of them. As Grace turned to attractive, fair haired Roger, she seductively cooed, 'Darling, who are you?' Tina and I struggled to stifle a laugh as Grace eyed Roger and Nanette from head to toe while suggestively saying, 'Mmmm, you two look good ... why don't you come with me later, darlings, then we can *really* party.'

Roger and Nanette stayed at the party while Tina and I returned to the Berkshire Hotel. We laughed, joked and enjoyed each other's company during the journey and once in her room, we ordered a bottle of wine. We started talking about the guests. Tina said, 'That Grace is something else. She's too much. I like her but that girl is too wild. You don't know what she's going to do.'

While we were talking, an urgent phone call came through. It was Roger Davies and I could hear him screaming through the earpiece, 'Tina! You won't believe it! Grace Jones tried to get Nanette and me to go home with her! She told us we could be her dinner! She finally started talking to someone else and I grabbed Nanette and shot straight out of there!'

When Tina put the phone down we creased with laughter and couldn't stop for a solid twenty minutes. Everytime one or the other came up for air, we'd launch into another laughing fit after saying things such as, 'Could you picture Roger trying to squirm out of it!'

We were on a high. Tina's reviews were amazing, arousing immediate interest which led to a sudden flurry of interviews with newspapers and magazines. Los Angeles and New York were two areas an artist doesn't really play if they don't have a current hit record. Tina was one of the very few able to do so with astounding results. Combined with Tina's astounding talent, Roger's brilliant strategies were working. He had carefully put a plan together, changed Tina's image with great results and networked himself half to death getting the media and public interested in her. It became apparent that Roger Davies was a determined, very focussed hard worker, something he had in common with Tina. They were both daring, fearless and willing to take chances. Roger and Tina meeting and joining forces was like a match made in heaven.

Roger had seen first hand of the repercussions of lovers in working relationships. He had just watched Lee Kramer and Olivia Newton John suffer a separation after a long relationship. It made business very difficult between Olivia and Lee, a fact which wasn't lost on Roger, and he didn't know how to deal with the relationship between Tina and James Ralston. Due to past experience, Roger felt people shouldn't mix business with pleasure and hoped Tina's interest in James would soon fizzle out. Far from it. Tina couldn't wait to go on the road because it meant she would be able to be with James.

Early June, we flew to Toronto for a two week engagement, consisting of two shows a night. The band and dancers flew in a couple of days ahead of us to set up the show. Tina had been looking forward to this booking, which would afford her time alone with James. She had noticed that her dancer Annie had taken a shine to James, which proved a bit unnerving for her. After mulling over the problem, Tina came up with a strategy to see if anything was brewing. She cornered Annie and suggested, 'Let's make a deal, Annie. If you sleep with James, tell me, because I don't want to sleep with him if you get there.'

Annie replied, 'I'm not interested in James. You can have him.' This worried Tina because when Annie claimed not to be interested in a man, it usually meant the exact opposite.

We arrived in Toronto two days after the band and checked into the Royal York Hotel. Tina was in a great mood and soon after arriving, she suggested we hunt down the band. She looked at her watch and said, 'They'll be heading for the restaurant.' Tina had stayed at the Royal York before, and with the confidence of a person familiar with her surroundings, she whisked me straight to the hotel's eaterie. Within minutes of being seated, Lejeune and Annie joined us at our table. Every now and then Tina craned her neck towards the entrance, looking for some sign of James while Annie noticeably squirmed in discomfort. Tina and I both noticed Annie was behaving oddly.

Tina suddenly asked, 'Where's James?'

Annie piped up in an unusually high tone, 'He must be somewhere here!'

Tina and I glanced at each other for a moment then she locked eyes with Annie while playfully stating, 'Annie! You didn't! You slept with James!'

'Tina! I didn't!'

'Annie, I'm going to give you one chance, now don't lie to me. You slept with James, didn't you?'

Annie looked at Tina then looked away. After a long silence she blurted, 'I was gonna tell you, Tina. But you just got here and I didn't have a chance.'

Tina snapped, 'We made a pact. You said you would tell me! I don't believe it!'

'You didn't give me a chance. It only just happened. Right here! During the two days we were waiting for you.'

At that moment, it was hard to know if Tina was more livid than hurt. Tina wasn't about to let Annie or anyone else in the group know how upset she really was, so she played it off in a girlfriend fashion, asking Annie if there was any other gossip rather than flipping. I could tell Tina couldn't wait to get out of the restaurant, so we wolfed down our food and left. As soon as we stepped into the foyer, Tina said, 'Damn that Annie!'

Tina should have made her position clear to Annie by telling her not to mess with James. She could easily have dismissed her from employment, but didn't. The thing that stopped her was remembering how all her dancers had slept with her husband in the past. In a strange way, half of her was saying 'that's the way things are'. It was as if she was trained to expect that her friends would sleep with her man. This incident made Tina realise something. She had fallen head over heels in love with James Ralston. She was extremely hurt, more than I had ever seen her be over a man.

Tina was fuming and didn't want to look at the four walls in her suite so we took a taxi to the cinema to see a film called *Mommie Dearest*. The film was about Joan Crawford's violent relationship with her adopted daughter. Faye Dunaway played the role of Joan Crawford. There was one scene where Joan goes crazy, going through her daughter's wardrobe, then rips a hanger out of the closet and wakes her sleeping daughter to beat her with it. I looked over and saw tears streaming down Tina's face. I didn't say anything and left her to it. When we left the cinema, Tina blurted, 'You know Ed, it's always the same old stuff. Everytime I find someone I'm interested in, they're not interested in me. I've been chasing after James and he doesn't give me the time of day. He doesn't care about me, he's not loyal to me and he doesn't value our friendship. Annie is my dancer and he picked her over me?'

I said, 'James Ralston is living with someone. Do you think he's really worth it? You will never be part of his life as long as he has a home situation with someone else. Come on Tina, be sensible. You're wasting your tears so stop crying over him.'

I put my arm around her shoulder while we slowly walked. After a long moment, Tina said, 'Something about that film made me think of all that. Then the scene when Joan beats her daughter with the wire hanger ... well ... that's what Ike used to do to me. He did it a lot. And I'd be curled up on the floor, bleeding and crying and begging him to stop but all I could see was his hand raising over and over and he hit me and hit me ... sometimes with a hanger, sometimes with a wooden shoe tree ...'

She was in tears. All I could do was reassure her that it was over and no one could ever do that to her again.

The following evening, an hour before Tina was due to perform, Chip nervously bopped over to me and said, 'Don't tell Tina, but I heard Shirley Bassey is coming tonight!' I nearly shrieked. I knew Tina was fascinated with Shirley. Towards the end of the second performance, Tina ran offstage into quickchange to prepare for the encore while the audience begged for more. She said, 'Ed, we've got two days off. Two more songs then I'm out of here'. Yeh. Mmmhmm.'

People, by this point, were banging their champagne glasses on the table chanting, 'Tina, Tina, Tina'. She smoothed her dress down and said, 'Listen to them. They're wild. Honey, I think they're drunk!' She peeped through the curtain wing and said, 'I'm going to do 'Higher'. What else should I do?'

''Hollywood Nights', Tina. They always love that.'

Then she ran back onstage, belted out the two favourites, teasing and tantalising the audience, working them into a sweat. Tina had this sort of effect — she could turn a sober audience into a gang of bad boys and girls. There was something raunchy and wild about her that made people want to let their hair down. She raced off stage and I wrapped her sweat soaked body in a towel. She immediately flopped on a chair and everyone knew when she did that, they were not to say a word to her until she got up. She rested over the chair like a rag doll, letting her legs and body go completely limp. She had her eyes closed and breathed evenly, bringing her pulse rate down. While she did this, I gently wrapped her hair in a towel and patted her face and body dry. A few silent minutes later, she suddenly came to, stood up and said, 'Let's go to the dressing room.'

While Tina removed her make-up, I buzzed around the dressing room, putting everything in its rightful place while humming a tune. Tina snapped, 'Ed, why are you humming? You're making me nervous. Go sit down for a minute.'

'No Tina, I think the dressing room should look really nice ...'

Tina, quick as lightning, said, 'What's going on Ed? Something's going on ... do you know something I don't?'

'Noooo Tina.'

Tina glared at me with suspicion, then she suddenly piped up, 'You've got a date! Ed! Who is it? That's why you're so happy! Tell me who it is!'

'Tina!'

At that point, Chip tapped on the door and let himself in, nervously bopping up and down while saying, 'T, someone asked to come backstage ...'

Tina snapped, 'Chip, I'm not seeing anybody. I don't care who was here tonight ...'

Chip quietly muttered, 'It's Shirley Bassey ...'

Tina slowly turned to look at me and said, 'So that's why you were so happy. You knew Shirley was here. Now, you know I just have to see Shirley!'

I brushed Tina's hair out, put away the towels and fled to find Shirley. Just as I entered the ballroom, I saw her stumble, shriek and send a whole table full of dishes, cutlery and champagne crashing to the floor. The lights went up and Shirley was a sight, laying in the middle of the floor in an elegant long dress, her hand dramatically pressed against her forehead, with tableware spread all around her. I had to call on all my powers not to laugh when Shirley started explaining herself. 'Darling, I was so excited over Tina's show. I felt my heel catch in the tablecloth and I must have tripped or fainted!' She dramatically signalled for all those present to help her up and as she stood, she said, 'That bloody table cloth. Don't people realise how dangerous it is to have them trailing on the floor that way!' Then she brought her hand to her forehead and dramatically added, 'I could have ... I could have ... been killed!' She fled to the ladies room just like an actress would have in an old 1920s film.

While Shirley was in the ladies, I ran to Tina and yelped, 'You'd never believe what happened. Shirley's heel got caught in a tablecloth and she fell or fainted!'

Tina smiled as I added, 'And she was so grand! She was laying there like it was an acting scene from an old film, dramatically bringing her hand to her forehead, posing and in such distress. I don't understand ...'

Tina put one hand on her hip and pointed at the door with her free index finger while saying jokingly, 'That girl didn't trip or faint. Shirley's been having a good time. I bet she was tipsy. Honey, I've known Shirley for years. We shared the same label. She does this stuff all the time. Watch, Ed. She'll come in here and tell us the whole story scene by scene.'

Sure enough, Shirley waltzed to the doorway and dramatically posed with her hands gripped over her heart while bellowing, 'Tina! My darling! My sister! It is so good to see you!'

The two women fondly embraced and I noticed Shirley was the only person Tina didn't push away. After they loosened their embrace, Tina asked Shirley, 'What happened out there?'

Shirley said, 'Darling, one must sit there, oh dear, Tina, I must tell you.' Once seated, she spoke as if she were performing on stage. Her lips pursed, her hands fluttered and her eyes excitedly darted in all directions as she continued, 'I was slightly tipsy. Darling, you know I had to give them a bit of drama. I didn't want to look the fool so I said my heel caught on the tablecloth and I tripped or fainted. When I saw I pulled the whole tablecloth down, I had to give them Sarah Bernhardt.' Tina and I burst out laughing while Shirley continued, 'I waved at my manager like, "Don't touch me, let my lay here for a minute." Then I put my hand over my head and in my best proper English accent, blamed the tablecloth!'

We shared a bottle of wine while Tina and Shirley reminisced, many of the stories sending us into fits of laughter. Before she left, we had Chip take pictures of all of us together, not knowing when Shirley and Tina would bump into each other again. Shirley's visit left Tina on a high. She was one of the very few people Tina was genuinely happy to see.

Just as Shirley was about to leave, she suddenly said to Tina, 'I noticed they got you, too.'

Tina, bewildered, replied, 'Got what, Shirley?'

'The pickets. All them people protesting against your show because you played South Africa. I nearly didn't get in here tonight, there were so many.'

We had all hidden the fact that the show was being picketed because we didn't want to upset Tina. She looked daggers at me while Shirley waffled on, 'I told all my fans that I didn't go for any political reason. I needed the money. My fans love me. They understand.' With her tongue in her cheek she continued 'Anyway, Tina, I'm looking again. I must find a lovely man. I'm having the worst time dating but I'm seeing this guy who's family is in oil. I'm trying to hook him. I'd just love a rich husband. I don't know how you do it, Tina. I don't know how you manage.'

Tina replied, 'Well, I gave Ike everything. I don't care about all that. I just had to get on with starting over again. Things are working out. So do you think your oil gentleman will get you down the aisle?'

'I'll keep you posted, Tina.'

And off she went. Tina and I went up to her suite, where we laughed for hours over Shirley. She was so grand, animated, dramatic and entertaining that she was one of the very few artists Tina really enjoyed.

We returned to LA where Tina made an appointment for both of us to have a reading on July 3 with Carol Dryer, her favourite psychic. Tina said, 'I have to find out what's going on with James. I'm sure Carol will see something.'

The night before the reading, Tina said, 'Ed, I made a list of questions for you to ask Carol. There's some things I want to know about you.'

Normally, after Carol finished her reading, she would ask if there were any questions. Tina made my list. She wanted to know if a scar on my leg, similar to a birthmark on her arm, had some connection which indicated we had a past life together. She also wanted to know if my songwriting career would take off. Carol told Tina that we had shared many past lives together, sometimes as brother and sister, sometimes as sister and sister, and once as brothers. We had never been lovers and Tina was always the older of the two. We once had an Indian life and danced many sanctified tribal dances together. She said Tina and I had been branded as punishment once and left scarred, that's why we carried similar body markings in this life. She also said that I would leave Tina to pursue a life of my own.

'You and Tina will be together for a long time. Then the time will come when you will have to spread your wings. You will have to let Tina go and she will have to let you go.'

Neither of us wanted to hear that.

A publicity shot from 1977, as Tina relaunched her career with a new look.

Top: Tina at the grand opening of Bolic Sound Studio where I first met my Rock 'n' Roll Angel, Ms Turner.

Below: Ike and Tina kiss for the cameras at Bolic Sound's opening party.

Top: Ike and Tina Turner Revue. Ikette Vera (*left*), Tina (*centre*) with Ester (right) in the early 1970s.

Below: Tina on the phone at Bolic Sound, 1971. In the background is Ike's mural of a man and a woman making love.

Ike and Tina. Holding onto her man was just a stage act.

Top: Tina and Shirley Bassey backstage in Toronto after Shirley's 'Sarah Bernhardt performance'. Tina once stripped to Shirley's song, 'Hey Big Spender'.

Below: Bryan Adams, Tina and my road brother Kenny Moore, backstage at the Birmingham NEC.

Top: Tina and her mother Zelma
at a smart Hollywood restaurant.

Above: Bernadette, and Tina's
son Craig. Bernadette was like
a daughter to Tina.

Right: Kidding around with
Kenny Moore.

Top: Tina at a local radio station.

Below: Tina dancing at a pool party at her Royal Woods home.

Top: Tina gives all American boy James Ralston a good beating!

Below: Fancy dress party at Tina's home, with Kathy and Chip Lightman, 'Wicked Witch' Tina and Dracula!

Top: Axel, Tina's playboy boyfriend.

Below: In Italy after a show, Tina's millionaire ex-boyfriend Adrianno centre left. At the head of the table Chip, Kathy, Tina and me holding hands.

Top: Backstage at The Ritz, NYC, Keith Richards, Tina and David Bowie.

Below: The Ritz, NYC. Keith Richards checks out Tina, Tina checks out John McEnroe and David Bowie looks on.

Top: Lejeune, Tina and Annie before a show in 1981.

Bottom: Jack Burns the drummer hitches a ride from Ms Turner, on the road in the Middle East.

Top: Tina telling everyone at my surprise birthday to wait while she makes a speech.

Middle: Back stage in New Jersey at the Rolling Stones *Steel Wheels* show. Tina opened for the show. Roger Davies, the manager, Tina wearing a Rolling Stones T-shirt cut down the middle and me.

Left: Tina and I, before clubbing in London.

Top: Linsey Scott, Anna Marie Shorter, Lee Kramer and Tina at Le Dome on Lee's birthday.

Above: Tina smiles at Lee Kramer's birthday party at the famous Hollywood restaurant Le Dome. One of my favourite pictures.

Right: Tina in a bikini in Australia. Despite the outfit, Tina cannot swim.

Top: Rava and Tina at Kathy Lightman's wedding at Tina's Royal Woods home.

Left: Ms Turner fooling around at a photo session.

Right: Touring in the Middle East. Sexy Tina and Kenny Moore pout at our Thanksgiving meal.

MUSIC

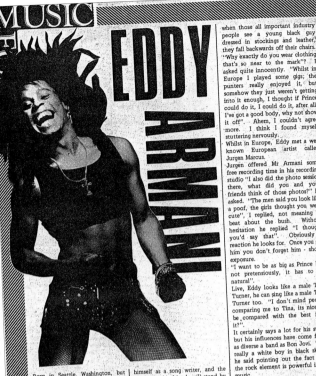

EDDY ARMANI

Born in Seattle, Washington, but growing up in Los Angeles has probably had a lot to do with Edward Armani's musical background, but its in England that he sees his future.

"Its the pure energy that's around that I like about England" he told me recently. Personally I thought all the energy was leaving for the States. Anyhow, when talking to Eddy you notice an enticing, almost overpowering sense of energy that kind of rubs off on you as you exchange views. Believing in

himself as a song writer, and the belief that his friends will stand by him obviously lend a lot to his energy.

But Eddy Armani is different from most struggling musicians or artists. He feels that he's already at the top and that he is more professional than most performers. Having seen him twice I have to agree. "I need a manager but they all think I'm wild and back off". The problem in Eddy's case is that he is still able to shock in an industry that's supposed to have seen it all, so

BY EDWARD FERMOR

when those all important industry people see a young black guy dressed in stockings and leather, they fall backwards off their chairs. "Why exactly do you wear clothing that's so near to the mark"? I asked quite innocently. "Whilst in Europe I played some gigs, the punters really enjoyed it, but somehow they just weren't getting into it enough, I thought if Prince could do it, I could do it, after all, I've got a good body, why not show it off". Ahem, I couldn't agree more. I think I found myself stuttering nervously.

Whilst in Europe, Eddy met a well known European artist called Jurgen Marcus.

Jurgen offered Mr Armani some free recording time in his recording studio "I also did the photo session there, what did you and your friends think of those photos?" he asked. "The men said you look like a poof, the girls thought you were cute", I replied, not meaning to beat about the bush. Without hesitation he replied "I thought you'd say that". Obviously a reaction he looks for. Once you see him you don't forget him - shock exposure.

"I want to be as big as Prince but not pretensiously, it has to be natural".

Live, Eddy looks like a male Tina Turner, he can sing like a male Tina Turner too. "I don't mind people comparing me to Tina, its nice to be compared with the best isn't it?".

It certainly says a lot for his style, but his influences have come from as diverse a band as Bon Jovi. "I'm really a white boy in black skin," he said pointing out the fact that the rock element is powerful in his music.

I actually caught Eddy, Eric Robinson (reviewed) Mike McCovoy, Ratchel Fury, Jermane Stuart, Boy Marylin and an assortment of other singers/musicians jamming recently in London.

He'll be returning to the states for two months, but in the meantime catch him on the Metropolitan Line.

Eddy Armani; "My image is my statement!!!"

FORUM

SAT 12

LONDON Charing Cross, Astoria, WC2:
Parker + Chariot + Eddy Armani + Equestrian Statues + KGB + The Level + Salvation Sunday + Another Fine Myth + Nancy Peppers + Q.A.X. + Christie + Das Eliphoney Kiks + Hour In The Shower + Big Business + Da Dat + The Motivators + And He Said

"A curious line-up of fairly unknown bands, Eddy Armani will probably steal this show. A powerful and persuasive performer, Eddy unashamedly lifts his image from Prince and Tina Turner. He pouts, preens and poses with great effect, his voice is ballsy, gritty and gutsy and his delivery is utterly superb. Musically, the set is a bit humdrum (relying heavily on average rock 'n' roll), but Eddy's stage craft will always pull him through. Definitely one of the discoveries of '85, Eddy Armani deserves great success."

Top: Some of the press I received while gigging in London.

Live at the Marquee *(bottom left)* with ex-Sex Pistol Glenn Matlock and *(right)* gigging at The Ad Lib Club .

Tina at 57 still 'Rollin' on the River' on the *Wildest Dreams* Tour, 1996.

22

Dallas, Texas. The Fairmont Hotel. We had noticed, for a couple of nights running, a man of wealthy appearance taking the centre table and watching both performances each evening. The first night, he sent Tina a dozen red roses. The following night, roses again accompanied by a bottle of fine perfume. The third night he sent roses, a bottle of champagne and a note asking Tina if she would kindly join him for dinner. He signed it 'Tex'.

Tina was flattered and the attention couldn't have come at a better time. Because we would be in Dallas for three weeks, the band invited their wives or girlfriends to join them. The women, including James Ralston's girlfriend, had arrived and Tina decided it would do James good to see she had an admirer.

'You know what I think, Ed, ring that Tex gentleman. Tell him Tina Turner thanks him very much for the flowers and gifts. Tell him I am flattered by the dinner invitation but it might not be possible because of my work schedule.' She paused for a moment before adding, 'What do you think, Ed? I'm not saying no and I'm not saying yes right now. I'm just leaving it open.'

'It can't do any harm, Tina.'

I dialled the number and a receptionist answered, indicating the business was office supplies. I asked to be put through to Tex, explaining I was Tina Turner's personal assistant.

When Tex came on the line, I conveyed Tina's message and sentiments, explaining, 'Tina will be happy to send you an autographed picture or say hello to you after the show.'

In a strong Western drawl, Tex replied, 'I don't need an autographed picture, thank you very much. And another thing, I didn't realise Tina Turner was above calling a person to say thank you herself and has an assistant do it on her behalf.'

I quickly said, 'It's not that at all. Miss Turner is still resting and is asleep. We felt it was best not to leave the courtesy call too long.'

He barked, 'Well that's just fine. You tell Miss Turner, when she wakes up, that she is welcome to call me herself and I'm a patient man. I can wait.' Click.

Tina had her ear pressed near the phone, clenching her mouth closed while rocking from foot to foot like a high school girl. As soon as I put the phone down, she said, 'Well, he seems determined! I'll wait an hour and then I'll call him.'

When she phoned, the first words out of Tex's mouth were, 'I must tell you, Miss Turner, you're the most brilliant performer I've seen in my life. I've been a fan for years. When I heard you were coming to town, I booked every show. I'd love to take you out to dinner and show you our lovely town.'

Tina replied, 'I can't really do that for the simple fact that I don't know you. I'm happy to have a coffee with you here in the hotel lounge.'

'Would you feel safer if I took you and your entire band to dinner? Restaurants are closed after your show finishes but I'll make an arrangement for one to stay open just for you, Miss Turner.'

Tina lit up. 'That's very nice of you, Tex, but you couldn't possibly take all of us out.'

'I wouldn't have offered if I couldn't. How about Sunday?' Tina excitedly agreed. He made arrangements and phoned me with the details half an hour later. Tina was impressed. Tex rented a restaurant to stay open to serve us. Suddenly she became suspicious and asked me to phone the restaurant to confirm he really made the arrangement. The concierge at our hotel told us it was one of Dallas' finest restaurants, and they confirmed the private booking. Tina and I were amazed.

He sent a two stretch limousines to collect Tina, me, the band and their partners. The restaurant was fabulous with beautiful candles burning everywhere. We were brought by a formally dressed maitre d' to two huge double doors, and when he swung them open, a stunning banquet room lay before us. There were place cards at the table, indicating he had gone the trouble to find the names of everyone in Tina's entourage. We were seriously impressed.

We were all seated when the huge wooden double doors dramatically swung open again, framing the host. Tex had the air of a count. He was tall, over six foot, well groomed and very elegant. He walked straight over to Tina, gently lifted her hand and kissed the air just above her skin. He said, 'I've wanted to do this for a long time. This has been a dream of mine and I want to thank you for making the dream come true.'

Tina actually blushed. Not only was he a perfect gentleman, he was clearly wealthy as well. The moment was like something straight out of a movie —handsome rich Texan sweeps the woman he always dreamt of off her feet. During the evening, Tex told Tina about a local craftsman who designed fabulous leather clothes, and he wanted him to make a special outfit for Tina. Tina said she couldn't possibly accept such an extravagant gift. Tex insisted, saying, 'The dress is already being made for you, so you can't turn it down. Just go make sure it's to your perfect measurements.'

Tex insisted that Tina and her guests ordered anything they wanted. He ordered red and white wine for all. After dessert and brandies, Tina thanked Tex for the lovely evening. Being a gentleman, Tex never asked Tina if he could come back for coffee. He simply said, 'Thank you for joining me for dinner. I'll just see you to the limousine and the driver will deliver you safely back to your hotel. I'll contact Eddy to give him the details of where you should go for your fitting. I hope you like the dress.'

Tina said, 'Well, I can't wait to see it!'

Tex quickly replied, 'Now that's what I like to see — a woman who knows how to accept gifts, because I get a great deal of pleasure giving them.'

Tina went for her fitting and the dress was gorgeous. It was soft red suede, cowgirl style with suede tassles dotted with hand painted Indian beads, beautifully tailored to Tina's every curve.

Before leaving Dallas, Tina gave Tex her home number, telling him, 'If you ever come to Los Angeles, give me a call and I'll take you out to dinner.'

Tex replied, 'When I come to Los Angeles, I'll be staying with you and I will be taking you out to dinner by night and out shopping by day.' Tina swooned.

Our next port of call was Florida, which proved far too hot and humid for us. The August heat caused our clothes and hair to stick to our bodies within minutes of stepping outside, and we found ourselves playing seedy clubs filled with shady characters. The Florida hospitality of some people involved with the venues or bookings was different to anything we had ever known. They gave the boys in the band cocaine as a thank you for playing the venue. Some of the entourage, as well as myself, indulged while making it clear that Tina was never to know because she was firmly anti-drugs. We discreetly used the gifts and stayed very cool about it, hoping Tina was none the wiser. We left Florida August 23, with a few band members and myself agreeing that we hated Miami at first, but warmed to it once we got in the swing of Sunshine hospitality. We still had some coke left on us and decided to nip to the airplane conveniences to polish them off.

Cocaine was still very new to me and I was invited to have a go. However, I was worried because Tina was in first class and I knew I'd be nipping in to see her. I was concerned she might sense I had taken something. Two hours into the flight, some of the guys were higher than the plane itself and I found it all too tempting. Finally, I took the communal cocaine and went to the toilet to experiment with it. I scooped out the goods and inhaled a mountain of white powder up each nostril. It was Miami powder — powerful stuff — and no one told me I should take it in small quantities. I thought I was meant to feel something straight away and when I didn't pick up any unusual sensations, I shovelled another mountain up each nostril. I carefully returned it to the band member who gave it to me. Within minutes of taking my seat, I was in a better mood than ever, talking non-stop and getting into deep conversations. I got so high that I thought I could reach one hand out of the plane window and touch heaven. Next thing I knew, the entire band was making fun of me, knowing it was the first time I had got a buzz on cocaine. Kenny said to me, 'I done told yo' ass. You did too much, boy. Yo' eyes are bigger than basketballs. Boy, yo' betta sit yo' ass down.'

'I'm thirsty as hell, Kenny. I need to get a drink.'

'I'll git it boy. Yo' stay put. Sit there, by the window. Shiiiit. I be comin' back with water. Eddy, boy, you are higher than the stars.' Everyone burst out laughing at me.

I had a glass of water, checked on Tina and, much to my relief, she lazily looked at me and said she was going to sleep. I returned to my seat, put my sunglasses on and spent the remainder of the seven and a half hour flight staring out of the window as if my eyes were propped open with matchsticks. I was praying that I'd come down from the effects before landing at LAX. I nervously escorted Tina home and started unpacking for her, completely unaware that I still had my sunglasses on. Tina suddenly said, 'Ed, why are you wearing sunglasses in the house? Take them off so I can see what you're doing.'

'No, no Tina. My eyes hurt. They're a bit sore. They feel better if I keep the glasses on.' The truth is that my pupils were nearly as big as my face and I was scared to death that Tina might realise I had taken drugs. It seemed I got away with it and soon, we were back into our normal routine, preparing for Tina's next engagement.

Roger got Tina a slot on Johnny Carson's *Tonight* show, a real coup considering she didn't have a hit record on the market. On the August 27, we excitedly made our way to Burbank Studios, where the show was to be recorded. She had spent the last three days rehearsing the band half to death, whipping them into perfect shape for the high profile program.

We arrived at Burbank Studios, did a soundcheck, rehearsed and had three hours to kill before the live show. While in Tina's dressing room, she turned to me and said, 'Ed, go and tell Kenny all eyes will be on me and him so we have to stay tight. Tell the rest of the band no drinking and groom themselves well. We have to look good and sound great.' Then, pretending it was an afterthought, she added, 'Oh yes, tell James I want to see him to discuss him picking up my cues.'

I rolled my eyes and replied, 'Tina, why didn't you say to just go get James. You didn't have to go through all the rest of the rigamarole.'

'Just go and get James for me. And give the rest of the band the original message, anyway. Thank you very much.'

I went to the band's dressing room to relay the message and finally added, 'James, Tina wants to see you in her dressing room. Something about picking up on her cues. She will explain it to you.'

Straight away, the entire band started teasing James, saying things like, 'Woooo. Gooo James. Miss T has requested you. Go boy. Woooo. Woooo.' James turned beetroot red. I pottered around the dressing room while Tina and James played around, joking and every now and then, Tina would run her fingers through his hair. There was a very good vibe between both of them.

Tina suddenly suggested I take the next hour or so off, saying she was fine with James and when he left, she'd have a small rest and do some breathing exercises before the show. I killed time by hanging out with the band in the games room while taking advantage of the very generous food spread the Carson show had laid on. Around fifteen minutes before Tina was due to go on, I remembered she wanted to do breathing exercises so I raced back to her dressing room to prepare an area on the floor where she could lay on her back. The dressing room was top notch, lots of open space and all the latest mod cons. Straight across from the door, was the large, light bulb trimmed mirror and sturdy make-up table. In my mind, I imagined the generous floor space in front of the make-up table would be the perfect place for Tina to do her breathing exercises. I flung the door open to see Tina, perched on her dressing table, back against the mirror, with her legs spread in the air. There was James, his trousers down around his ankles, with his naked little white bottom pumping away. Tina had a towel wrapped around her, pinned at the bust, pulled up over her waist.

It felt like being in a car accident, the final moments before impact seeming to pass in slow motion. I thought I had stood in shock for ten minutes when, in reality, only seconds had passed. Tina looked at me. I looked at Tina. James looked straight ahead in the mirror at my reflection and I looked at his mirror image. All our mouths dropped open and I realised Tina and James were equally startled. I was the first to blink and, rather than turn to leave, I stared again, hoping I hadn't really walked into such a private situation. Upon second inspection, there was no doubt because Tina and James had only paused for a second then carried on with business as if I wasn't there. I suddenly snapped out of my stunned state, took one large step back into the hallway while saying, 'Sorry!'

My body suddenly doubled as a barrier as I stood like a sentry in front of Tina's dressing room, ensuring no one else could intrude on her moment of lust. I nervously looked at my watch, hoping she'd hurry it up because she didn't have long to prepare herself for Johnny Carson's live show. The second thought paramount in my mind was disbelief that Tina and James didn't lock the door. I shuddered when I thought of what might have happened if Johnny Carson had walked into Tina's dressing room rather than me. When I heard rustling, I knew James would be leaving so I made myself scarce. I waited ten minutes, then went to the dressing room, entering as if nothing had happened. I pottered around, saying nothing, waiting for Tina to be the first to speak. Two agonising minutes later, she playfully snapped, 'How could you? I can't believe you walked in and caught us.'

'Well Tina, it's better that I walked in instead of a security guard or Johnny Carson.'

'But Ed, you just stood there and gawped!'

'Teeenaaa, I was in shock!'

Tina leaned back in a chair, fluttered her hand in the air and stated, 'Well honey, it was good. Let me tell you something. Honey, I don't know how it happened. I was sitting at the make-up table and James was just standing there talking to me and his crotch was in my face! I mean, he was just standing there and I just started unbuttoning his pants and one thing led to another!'

She turned to her mirror, powdered her face and enthusiastically applied her cosmetics while telling me how she seduced James. She suddenly asked, 'How do I look?'

My smile stretched from ear to ear. 'Honey, you look gorgeous! You are really glowing!'

'Yeh, I need this more often ... don't I?' She breathed, as a stagehand knocked on the door to give her her five minute call. 'Ed, while I'm on, I want you to see if James is watching and looking at me. Tell me how he's acting. You have to be my eyes. You have to report back to me.'

Tina ran straight on stage and sang like I hadn't heard before. She hit notes I didn't know existed. Her performance was spellbinding, leaving the audience and Johnny Carson hooked. She sailed through Carson's interview and she pranced offstage glowing with confidence. On the way back to the dressing room, She enthused, 'You see Ed, a little action before a show does me good ...' We both burst into a naughty laugh, still chuckling when we entered her dressing room. We took a limousine back to her house, laughing about the James incident during the entire fifteen minute journey home. Just before getting out of the car, Tina said, 'You know ... I think I'm falling for James ...'

I cut her off by saying, 'Oh, no Tina. Not that. Please don't. Not yet ... slow down, please.'

'It's a bit too late for that, Ed. I want James. I want him to be mine.'

I knew better than try to dissuade her. There was something different with James. She really liked him, his simple approach to life and his indifference to material things appealed to Tina's root sense of earthiness and wholesomeness.

I stayed with Tina for the following two days, preparing to depart on the August 29 to a Las Vegas Riviera Hotel booking. Las Vegas had taken a new turn, with many hotels beginning to compete with Caesar's Palace for entertainment showcases. The Riviera wooed some of the biggest stars, matching the high fees they commanded at Caesar's Palace which lost out on quality performers. Diana Ross was one of the first to be tempted away, along with Tom Jones. The star wars of Las Vegas had begun.

Diana Ross was playing the Riviera and we arrived on her closing night. We checked in and, while unpacking, Chip popped to Tina's room, informing her that Diana's manager had arranged the best table for us should we wish to see the show. Tina replied, 'I don't really feel like it.'

It was no secret that I was a fan of Diana's, so I asked Tina if she would mind if I caught the show. Tina said, 'You want to go and see *her*? No. It's not okay for you to go.' I was stunned. Noticing my reaction, Tina said through very tight lips, 'Chip, I'll tell you what. We'll take the table for Miss Diana's last show. Yes ... let's check out Miss Ross. See what she's really all about.'

I squealed with delight. Diana had just signed with RCA records, scooping the largest record deal ever at the time for any female artist. This was Diana's new show to coincide with a new album. Everyone said her act was unmissable and as a fan, I couldn't believe she was playing in our hotel that night and that we would be her guest. Moreover, Diana had always been a fan of Tina and had made it well known.

Diana's show was superb and she had countless costume changes, the standing joke being that she and Cher were in direct competition to see who could change more often during their act. After the show, her manager invited us backstage to say hello. We were walking along the long corridor when Diana dashed out of her dressing room like an enraptured schoolgirl, barefooted and wearing only a lavish terrycloth dressing gown emblazoned with her initials. She held her arms out and yelled down the long corridor to Tina, 'Girl, you better get down here!'

Tina, a bit taken by surprise over Diana's enthusiasm, kept herself in check, remaining reserved while whispering to me, 'It's not like we're best friends.'

As we neared Diana, she put her hands on her hips and swayed her head while stating, 'Girl, you look good!' She waved for us to enter her dressing room with an enthusiastic, 'Come in, come in!'

Tina carefully looked over the dressing room, knowing it would be hers after that night. Diana was being very cordial, pouring us wine while making nice conversation. She took an immediate liking to me and said, 'I'm sure I've met you before, Eddy. You look so familiar and have such a nice smile!' I was deeply flattered that Diana Ross was taking such a great interest in me. Tina sat there, not getting too familiar, but not being cold, either.

Everyone who works for Diana calls her Miss Ross. A personal assistant came in and said, 'Excuse me, Miss Ross.'

Diana cut her off by saying, 'Not now. Not right now. I'm entertaining.' The girl quietly left. She turned to Tina, 'What are you doing now? What's going on?'

Tina told her about her new band and new management, the same team managing Olivia Newton John, adding, 'I've got sold out shows, fantastic press. But things seem a bit slow getting a record deal.'

Surprised that Tina wasn't signed to a label, Diana snapped straight into business mode, offering Tina help and advice. 'Listen, I've just signed with RCA and have a bit of clout there. Let's see what I can do for you. I'll make a few calls. We can't have this — you're too fabulous. You have to be on top. You are fabulous. There's no one like you. Tina, let's exchange numbers and I'll see what I can get rolling.'

Tina's back suddenly became erect, and she seemed almost as if she were perching in her chair as she evenly replied, 'No. That's okay Diana. It's not necessary. I believe my management have something in the pipeline.'

At that point, Diana's personal assistant reappeared, saying, 'Miss Ross, I'm very sorry to intrude but this is very important. It's imperative you sign these checks now because we have to courier them to New York.'

Diana sent the girl away, repeating that she was entertaining and did not wish to be disturbed. She then apologised to us for being disturbed by her staff, adding, 'I just got new accountants. I'm afraid all financial transactions are passed through me. I once discovered an error of nearly $100,000 and, ever since then, I oversee everything. No one is allowed to sign a check on my behalf. Only I can sign them. Tina, girl, let me give you some advice. All money spent and any checks signed should always have to come to you so you are aware of how every penny you earn is spent.' She had gone from offering Tina help to get a record deal to advising her about her finances. Diana was giving very good advice, and was being nice and helpful, but I could see Tina was borderline insulted and her back further stiffened.

She replied by saying, 'Diana, it was wonderful to see you, but I must be going now.'

'Well, let's have your number and I'll make some calls first thing.'

Tina turned to Chip and very matter of factly said, 'Give Diana Roger Davies' number.'

Diana raised an eyebrow because, under normal circumstances, you would exchange home numbers, and she realised at that moment that Tina wasn't keen to take any help. Diana was known for helping many people in the business, including Michael Jackson, reach the top. She loved talent and believed there was plenty of space at the top for others, and she wasn't afraid of competition. She also knew some people were too proud to accept help and she assumed Tina was one of them. The two women hugged and promised to see each other again but that moment wouldn't arise for some time. Before leaving, she also gave me a huge hug and said very warmly that she hoped to see me again. When we were a safe distance from Diana's dressing room, Tina snapped, 'That was a nice encounter, wasn't it?'

I excitedly replied, 'Yes, Diana was so friendly and sweet! I had no idea she was such a caring person. It was so nice of her to give all that advice and offer to help.'

Tina shot me a sharp look while growling, 'Are you hungry?' Then she quickly recomposed herself and evenly asked, 'Would you like to go out for dinner?'

'Love to. I'm starving.'

'Let's go to Benihana at the Hilton.'

We decided to walk the short distance from the Riviera to the Hilton and, for some reason, Tina seemed to be in a temper. She quickened her step, causing me to perspire just trying to keep up with her. Suddenly, she flew off the handle, saying, 'Who does she think she is? How dare she? She ... she ... she's going to call up and arrange a record deal for me. And telling me I should be signing my own checks!'

I stupidly offered my opinion when I should have kept my mouth shut. 'Tina, I think she was genuinely offering to help you. It's no secret Diana's done this kind of thing before. There's not a lot of people that would do it. I'm sure her intentions were only good and her heart was in the right place.'

Tina stopped in the middle of the pavement, crossed her arms and glared at me while accusingly saying, 'Oh, yeh, sure. You were sucked in by her telling you that you got a nice smile and she's so sure she met you before and she likes your vibe and all that I saw. You just grinned and sucked it all in. We only met a couple of times briefly and suddenly she's treating me like I'm her best friend.'

As soon as we arrived at Benihana, they gave Tina star treatment. I was relieved, because Tina had to stop ranting about Diana. As soon as we were seated. Tina tightly asked, 'Would you like some wine?'

'Yes, thank you, that would be nice.'

Her voice sharpened as she snapped, 'Oh, yes. I'm sure you'd like some wine. There you were just sitting in her dressing room, while Madame Diana poured and served you glass after glass. You were just loving it, weren't you?.'

'Tina, I think she genuinely likes you. That's why she was so nice to all of us.'

'Oh, you would say that, wouldn't you? She's got the biggest record deal, and you keep going on about Diana playing in Central Park, Diana this and Diana that. Diana buys a $100,000 necklace ...'

I found myself sinking in my seat, wishing I hadn't said a word about Diana.

Tina drank some saké and finally mellowed out and much to my delight, we started laughing and joking again. Suddenly, in the middle of the light-hearted mood, Tina said, 'You know, maybe you were right. Maybe Diana genuinely wanted to help.'

I didn't say a word, worried that any opinion of mine concerning Diana might set Tina off again.

September 28 brought us to New York to play the Ritz where we stayed at the Berkshire Hotel on Madison and 2nd. Roger Davies had gone ahead of us, getting Tina an astounding amount of publicity through interviews and photo sessions which kept tongues wagging.

By now, we were well accustomed to the Ritz, a lovely old theatre with a high stage and no seats on the main floor, affording abundant standing room for fans. The next level was a beautiful old balcony, with seating, which stretched around the entire interior of the venue.

Tina's shows had sold out and, on the opening night, we had the treat of our lives. Rod Stewart was in the audience. Tina performed two of his songs in her act and added her sexy twist to the numbers, blowing Rod Stewart away. She opened her show with 'Kill His Wife', and during the set she sang another of Rod's popular tunes, 'Tonight's The Night'. Rod was wildly impressed. Tina was one of the first female Rhythm and Blues singers that hugely influenced Rod in the early stages of his career. After the show, Rod raced backstage to have words with Tina, inviting her to perform 'Hot Legs' with him on his taping of the hugely popular American show *Saturday Night Live*. Roger Davies was over the moon. He had recently parted company with Lee Kramer, and was looking after Tina himself. What more could he hope for than Tina performing with one of the hottest artists that year, Rod Stewart, on one of America's most highly rated shows. He knew everyone would be talking about the newly revamped Tina Turner.

Rod's manager arranged for Tina and his client to rehearse 'Hot Legs' at a rehearsal studio in New York. The traffic was so bad, and Roger and Tina were so nervous that we all jumped out of the limousine and ran the remaining few blocks to the studio. Tina walked in, gave Rod a hug and said she was ready. To tune in to each other, they sang *acappella* for a minute, then Rod told the band to start playing.

Vocally, Rod and Tina were meant for each other, their voices and body movements complementing each other perfectly. Rod was bowled over. After they finished singing, he laughed and said, 'I can't believe it. I'm standing here singing 'Hot Legs' with the woman who has the hottest legs in the world!' They went through the number a few more times, and the sexual energy Rod and Tina generated together made the act irresistible. They were knock-out.

After the rehearsal, we climbed into a waiting limousine which would take us back to the hotel. While sitting in the back of the plush car, Tina grabbed my hand and squeezed it tightly, saying, 'Ed, it's starting to happen. I can feel it. Something huge is on the horizon ... I just know it ...'

After Tina's Friday night performance at the Ritz, we raced back to the hotel and I went through her clothes while she gave herself assorted masks and beauty treatments. We frantically put numerous outfits together, trying to work out what she should wear for her duet on *Saturday Night Live*. We settled on a black tuxedo jacket and trousers cut off to shorts. She tried them on and looked like a million dollars.

Saturday October 3, Tina performed her act at the Ritz, then she showered and freshened up before racing over to perform with Rod on the live show. Rod had failed to mention to the show's production team that he had invited Tina to do a duet with him. The show's organisers strongly objected so Rod gave them an ultimatum; either Tina performed with him or he wouldn't perform at all. With Rod being one of the hottest male artists in the world at the time, the show's team caved in.

There was a new face, very shy and overwhelmed by Tina and Rod, who was making his debut on *Saturday Night Live* that night. He had a huge smile that matched his high hopes and, wondering who he was, Tina asked a stagehand, 'That guy there, the good looking shy one who keeps staring at me and Rod, who is he?'

The stagehand replied, 'A newcomer, real talented. He'll make it. His name is Eddie Murphy.'

'Oh.' The she added, 'I wish him success. He has a nice smile.' Then she walked away to join Rod and his wife.

The performance, needless to say, was incredible. Rod and Tina, both oozing this fantastic sex appeal on stage, proved to be a quintessential male and female rock act. Their voices rasped with an intensity matched only by their physical performance, and the response was amazing. Tina still had a second performance at the Ritz, for which she was now running thirty minutes late. When she finished with Rod, we raced back and I poured her into a gold chain stage costume which I had earlier set out in readiness. While dressing Tina, I could hear someone onstage explaining to the audience that Tina had just taped a show with Rod Stewart and was running thirty minutes late. Suddenly, we heard the man say, 'I just heard Tina is in the building! It won't be long now!' The audience erupted with applause and started chanting, 'Tina, Tina, Tina, Tina ...'

Tina slowly walked on stage, rolled her eyes around while the audience was going wild, then she broke into the opening number of 'Kill His Wife'. Normally, after the song, she says, 'Are you ready for me?' But this evening, she did something different. After the song, she said, 'Thank you for waiting for me. And because you were so nice and patient, I'm going to give you a real treat. You waited for me ... and now ... I'm gonna give you all of me!'

The audience went wild. Tina added, 'I just did *Saturday Night Live* with Rod Stewart. I know a lot of you will have set your video recorders to tape the show. When you get home to watch it, you'll be seeing me again, and this time with Rod Stewart. I'm dedicating the next song to Rod. Rod, this one is for you.' The audience erupted once more in applause and Tina did a sizzling rendition of 'Hot Legs'.

She did encore after encore and finally she said, 'Thank you, you were a fantastic audience tonight. I love you. Good night. See you next time.' But the audience, including all the stars present, begged for more. She did one more encore then left the stage, her booking at the Ritz completed. Tina was on cloud nine.

For the final show, friends of mine had come out of the woodwork. Two people flew all the way from Los Angeles, and numerous people I knew who were in New York phoned me for precious tickets to her performance. When I got to my room, the visitors never stopped knocking. It was mayhem. At one point, I left half a dozen people in my room for three hours while I got on with my job of being Tina's assistant. Finally, I settled Tina in her room and returned to mine, where I opened a few bottles of wine to share with my countless visitors. It was very late, perhaps three in the morning, when there was a loud, insistent banging on my door. My visitors went silent and one opened the door to find Tina standing there in her dressing gown, her face covered in a beauty treatment, a thick white face mask. The people in my room nearly dropped their wine glasses.

Tina shrieked, 'Oh my goodness, Ed! I didn't know you had visitors!' Splaying her fingers over her potion covered cheeks, she added, 'I have to go! Hi, hi, hi, bye — bye — bye!' She ran back to her room and phoned me, saying, 'Why didn't you tell me you had company?'

'I didn't get a chance, Tina.'

'Ed, I can't believe how many people were there staring at me. You're getting a bit too popular here. I don't know why all those people are bombarding your room. I mean, people must be thinking you're the star or something.'

I teased, 'Strange you should say that. I was just telling everyone that you're the star and that they should be bombarding your room ... so I sent all them over to you. They should be arriving any second now ...'

Tina screamed, 'Ed! No!'

Then I burst out laughing and Tina followed in relief, realising I was just joking with her.

The following day, the vibe was unbelievable. Our phones didn't stop ringing. Word had spread that a superstar was on the rise and all the media were suddenly fighting to get a piece of Tina. Chaos reigned supreme. Roger was at one end of the hotel looking for Chip Lightman while Chip was at the other end searching for Roger. Flowers and messages of congratulations poured in while people tried every trick in the book to get near to Tina. The attention was overwhelming. Roger was as alert as he was nervous, looking after Tina, knowing how close they were to the door that would lead to superstardom.

But as Tina's star was starting to rise to greater heights, I was beginning to feel that my life was not taking the direction I wanted. Against all odds, I had managed to ferret away a hefty sum of money, and I decided it was time for me to find my own home. I wanted it to be near enough to Tina's so she could always reach me easily, but I had reached the point of life where I desperately needed space. On the flight from New York to LA, I had a feeling of emptiness. I wanted to be able to hang my clothes in my own closet. I wanted to jump into a bed of my own. Tina was still performing my song 'Pain' on stage, and I wanted to explore new avenues of songwriting and performing.

I went to first class to check on Tina. She looked like like a kitten who had gotten the cream. She was popular, in demand and she knew America was beginning to notice her again. I was so happy for her. I simply smiled and left her in peace. Back at my seat, I dwelled on all the excitement of the last couple of years. Worldwide travel, swish hotels, caviar, champagne, limousines and parties. Through being with Tina, I had sat casually with megastars, sipping wine and laughing like old friends. Most people would give anything for a lifestyle like that, yet suddenly I felt lonely and empty.

I wanted to be able to turn my music up loud, dance in the mirror and act the fool. Once in a while, I yearned to wake up when it suited me and have the day to do what I wanted. A lover — that's what I really wanted. A lover. I was in my mid-twenties and didn't have a steady partner. No one and no relationship had a chance because no one could compete with Tina for my affection, devotion and love. I was lonely. I raced to the first class cabin and sat next to Tina, softly telling her I was going to find my own place when we got back to LA.

Shocked, she replied, 'No Ed. Why?'

'Tina ... I need some space. I need *my* space.'

She objected, 'Are you telling me my house isn't big enough? Do you mean there's not enough space in my home?'

'Teeeenaaa ...'

She stared at me long and hard then her eyes softened. 'It's okay Ed. I understand ... really, I do.' We squeezed each other's hands and I went back to my seat, where I seemed to rest more easily having made my decision.

When we got to LA, I had no problem finding a place, a stunning, original 1930s building on Sycamore Street, just off La Brea, and within two days I had moved in.

I started gathering my furniture out of storage, my luggage from Tina's and assorted bits I had at my mother's. Knee deep in boxes, my phone rang. It was Helena Springs. She said, 'Ed, listen. I need a big favour. I'm really stuck. I got Miles Davis's ex-wife Betty singing back-up for me at the Country Club. I'm opening for Chuck Berry. Can you come sing and dance with me? You, me and Betty will open the show.'

I was chuffed. Tina had brought the house down in the Country Club only a few short months back and next, I would have my crack at fame on the very same stage. I told Helena I'd do it. I immediately phoned Tina. 'Guess what, Tina? I'm singing at the Country Club this weekend, opening for Chuck Berry!'

'You what, Ed?'

I explained everything to her and she was elated. She said, 'I said it before and I'll say it again, Ed. You'll be a star. You got what it takes, especially the songwriting. I won't be able to come but make sure you phone me straight after the show. It doesn't matter how late it is. Good luck, Ed!'

Helena, Betty and I rehearsed, Betty's voice and mine moulding together perfectly. I developed a hot dance routine with Helena, who was the lead singer, and the show went without a hitch. I did so many inventive hot dance steps with Helena that the audience was mesmerised and roared with approval. Two days later there was an article about Chuck Berry's show in the newspaper and most of what was written was about me. I raced over to Tina's and showed her the newspaper. We sat over coffees while she read it aloud, quoting the paper, ending with, 'Eddy Hampton stole the opening act. He had more moves than a champion chess player ...' Tina was delighted. 'Ed, honey, that's why I'm never letting you on stage with me. You'll end up stealing my show!'

'Tina, nooo. You know I wouldn't do that to you ...'

'I know you won't, Ed, because I'm never going to give you the chance.'

'Tina ...'

'I said no, Ed!' We both burst into a fit of laughter. After we calmed down, I said, 'It's funny, this business. There I was for years working in the background and suddenly I have this yearning to be up front. I really want to be on stage. I want to sing and dance and be a star ...'

'Yes, Ed. But right now, *I'm* the star and this star's got a stint coming up in New Orleans. We'll have to start preparing.'

I snapped out of my dream world and laid out plans, with Tina, for our forthcoming trip. Five days later we were on the road, checking into the Fairmont Hotel in New Orleans which would be our home for the following two weeks. As soon as we arrived, Tina said, 'Ed, some of your family is from New Orleans, is that right?'

'Yeh.'

'Great, honey. I'll tell you what we'll do. This hotel has the best Creole restaurant in the US. Let's go downstairs and tuck into some of the local goodies. Your family comes from here, so a taste for Creole will be in your blood!'

I excitedly prepared myself for dinner. We had red beans, rice, salt fish, gumbo and we stuffed our faces. The waiter asked if we'd like dessert and Tina just burst out laughing. We finally decided to share a peach cobbler between us and our bellies ended up so bloated that we were in agony. We wobbled back to Tina's suite, flopped on her sofa and rubbed our bellies while laughing and talking. Suddenly Tina said, 'Ed, I hate you! How could you let me eat so much food? I was going to invite James up but how can I let him see me naked with my tummy so bloated?'

'Well, look at my stomach. Okay, no one's gonna see it but still — it's enormous!'

Tina rubbed at her stomach and said, 'No Ed. Mine's much bigger than yours.'

'Oh well, Tina. Looks like it's gonna be an early, quiet night for you. No nookie with James ...' Tina responded by throwing a cushion at me. We both exposed our bellies and stood next to each other studying our reflections in a mirror. We faced forwards, then turned sideways, then I said, 'You're right Tina. Your stomach is much bigger than mine.' We giggled and tickled each other's bellies, rubbing at the mountain of food hidden inside. Suddenly the phone rang and Tina made a great show of carrying her swollen tummy to the desk. She put the phone to her ear and Tex's strong accent came bellowing out of the receiver. 'Tayna. It's Tex.

Ah'm camin' to New O'leans.'

Tina was in her element. She had James, with whom she was madly in love, and now Tex. Tina agreed with Tex that he could visit during the second week of her show and told him she would take care of the arrangements. After putting the phone down, Tina said she was in a dilemma. 'Ed, what should I do? Should I let him stay in my suite or should I get him his own room?'

'Tina, you don't really know the guy. I don't think it's wise or safe to let him stay in the same room as you. You'll have to get to know him better. We don't really know anything about him apart from the fact that he's generous with his coins.'

'Yes, you're right Ed.'

Our conversation was interrupted by a knock at the door and when I opened it, I was presented with a massive arrangement of flowers for Tina. It was so large and stunning that Tina and I stared at it for a solid minute before reading the card. It said, 'Darling Tina, By the time you hang up the phone, you will have received this. Can't wait to be with you. Tex.'

Tina gasped, 'He must of have gone through a lot of trouble to arrange the timing on this. This is like something out of the movies!'

Tex was clever. He was wooing and courting Tina in style, just the way she always imagined a man would treat her. She suddenly said, 'Ed. I want to have a band meeting in my suite. Let's put the magnificent flowers there, and the card right there ... good.' She rubbed her hands together, adding, 'If I have a band meeting, they'll see the flowers. I know what I can say at the meeting. You know, Ed, the same stuff I say to you. I'll tell them, "Okay guys. Most of you have never been to New Orleans. It's exciting, wonderful and there's a lot to see but remember, you're here working. You are not on vacation. Enjoy yourselves but stay focussed on our show." What do you think, Ed?'

'Perfect Tina. Great idea ...'

Tina cut me off by saying, 'The band will come down and everyone will notice the flowers and James will get jealous. He'll read the card. Call the band and tell them I want a meeting in here.'

I rang around gathering the band, and as soon as I put the phone down, Chip Lightman appeared at the door, his head bopping away as usual. He started telling Tina a few things about the arrangement of soundcheck the following day when he stopped and asked, 'Who are the flowers from?'

Tina casually replied, 'Oh, those. They're from a friend. There's the card.'

Chip bopped over to the card and had a peep while Tina signalled me with excitement, pointing at Chip behind his back. She was having a test run of how she would react if James asked her about the flowers. Chip read the card and nervously bopped up and down while saying, 'You know something T, that Tex guy ... something about him gives me the creeps.'

Tina piped up, 'Don't be silly, Chip. You just don't understand that sort of man. This is romance. If you're a grown man and have money, this is how it's done. This is how to romance a woman. Tex is a gentleman.'

Tina stayed in her bedroom while the band arrived and settled in her suite, giving them an opportunity to look around and notice the flowers. Tina gave me strict orders to watch James carefully and listen to everything that was said about the flowers. I walked out of Tina's bedroom and said, 'Hi guys. Tina will be ready in a few minutes. Make yourselves comfortable and I'll get you some coffee.'

Kenny Moore, reliably nosey as hell, asked, 'Man, Ed. Where these flowers from? Shit. Thang's so big looks like a funeral or sumthin'.'

I casually said, 'Arent they beautiful? They were sent to Tina.'

James was the next to speak. 'Wow. They must have been expensive.' Then he wandered over to the card, opened it and started to read.

Without stopping him from reading the card, I immediately objected, 'James! Really! That's taking liberties!' I poured a cup of coffee and went to Tina's bedroom and pushed open the door nearly knocking her out. She had been leaning with her ear pressed against her bedroom door, struggling to hear what was being said in the main part of the suite.

Tina immediately asked, 'How do I look?' Dressed in jeans and a smart top, she looked gorgeous, and I told her so. She casually strolled to the sitting room and said, 'Hi everyone.' Then she went on to explain about the tempting sights of New Orleans but told them not to not lose track of why they were there. She told them to shy away from the strip joints and not to stay out boozing until six in the morning, considering we would be doing two shows per night, apart from Sundays. After the meeting, she dismissed everyone, not seeing them again until soundcheck.

That Saturday we held a small birthday party in Tina's suite for band member Chuck. Tina and I had already planned that I would discreetly get rid of everyone at the right moment, affording her and James a chance to be alone. The party was wonderful, and when I noticed Tina and James flirting, I suggested to everyone that we should move to the bar and party like mad because we didn't have to work on Sunday. Thinking about the jazz clubs, bars and bright lights, the band seized the opportunity to leave the suite and go do all the things Tina told them they shouldn't do, falling right in line with the secret plans Tina and I had hatched. The band slowly dispersed, with James being the only one lingering behind, just as Tina had hoped. The band hit town, revelling in the carnival atmosphere for which New Orleans is famous. There were live jazz and blues bands, many musicians striking up tunes in the streets, people walking around late at night, swigging beer from bottles while munching on crab claws and crawfish. The gay area was as entertaining as the rest, many people dressed in drag while preparing for the Halloween festivities in two days time. The town buzzed with excitement.

Meantime, Tina passed on the famous local hospitality to spend a splendid, passionate night with James, letting him know what he'd be missing after Tex's arrival. Tex arrived three days later and Tina warmly welcomed him. After their greetings, she told him, 'Tex, we are still getting to know each other and I wouldn't want you to have the wrong impression of me. I'm not a loose girl and I don't jump into bed with anyone. I booked you into your own suite, near to mine, so we can both have our privacy while we learn more about each other.'

Tex replied, 'What kind of man do you take me for? Did you think I was gonna come along and invade your privacy? Throw myself at you and take over your bedroom? I'm a proper Southern gentleman and we don't do that kind of thing.'

Much to our surprise, Tex had pre-booked the centre room table, right in front of the stage where Tina performed, for each night he was there. The guy had style, which impressed Tina, and she dedicated a song to him on the first night of his visit.

During the two hour break between shows, Tex came to Tina's suite. I left them alone and pottered around in the spare room. An hour later, while I was listening to some music, Tina raced in with only a fluffy terrycloth white towel wrapped around her radiant body. Her face glowed as she asked, 'Ed, how long do we have?'

'Actually, Tina, I was just thinking that I should start getting you ready.'

Tina breathlessly replied, 'I'm just going to jump into the shower.'

Our eyes locked and a knowing look passed between us. I suddenly whispered, 'Teeeenaaa ... you didn't!'

With a smile broader than the Grand Canyon, Tina nodded her head up and down while replying in a whisper, 'I did! I'll tell you about it later!'

After Tina finished cleaning herself up, I blow dried her hair while Tex jumped into the shower. Afterwards, he walked into the dressing area, sauntering with a macho air, while announcing, 'Tina, I'm just going to go to my room. I ain't bothering putting my stuff back on. I'll just go in this towel. I'm gonna dress for the second part of the show. Maybe, if you have a little time, we can see each other after the show.'

I finger fluffed Tina's newly dried hair while she girlishly replied, 'Yes! Of course!'

Tex left, and as soon as the lock of Tina's door turned, I half screeched, 'Teeenaaa! Tell me what happened!'

With her fingers animatedly fluttering all over the place, Tina replied, 'Well Ed, I don't know what happened. I just don't know ... I went into the room and he just grabbed me and started kissing me. One thing led to another!' Excitedly clasping her hands between her rocking knees, she continued, 'Next thing I know he's got me thrown over the bed and we're making love. I mean, look at this. I don't have sex for months and all of a sudden I'm juggling two men at one time. Honey, I'll tell you something.' Then she switched to a Southern accent, 'That Tex, waaail, it ain't just the hats that're big on the men in Taaaayxas!'

We both burst out laughing. Barely able to coordinate my hands, I dug my fingers back into Tina's hair while saying between giggles, 'Pull yourself together girl. I gotta get you ready.'

Halloween was my birthday and there was a buzz of excitement in the air. Everyone involved with the show was especially wonderful to me that day, giving me cards and thoughtful gifts. Still, I knew something was going on. Tina sent me on assorted unnecessary errands and missions while everyone else tried to occupy my time with false emergencies or lengthy conversations. I made it easy for them — I didn't want to alert their suspicions that I might know something special was going on, so I played along. While the show was on, Chip arranged for Tina's suite to be decorated and for catered food to arrive. Tina arranged for an array of Halloween masks to be there so we all could dress up. She also arranged for Tex not to be at the show, letting him in on the party secret. She told me not to go to her room because Tex was in there in a state of undress.

After the show, Tina asked me to go to my room to get something and no sooner had I got through the door, than Chip arrived to talk business, clearly sent by Tina to keep me busy for ten minutes. I finally said to Chip, 'I know why you're here.'

Chip laughed and said, 'Eddy, don't ruin it. Tina said you're so nosey that you're the hardest person in the world to surprise.'

Just then Tina phoned and savagely snapped, 'Ed! My dressing room! I can't believe you did this! Get to my room right now!' Then she slammed the phone down. I raced round to her room and just as I was about to insert my key, Tina snapped the door open and everyone shouted, 'Surprise!'

Wine, champagne and booze flowed. We turned Rod Stewart up to full volume and Tina and I danced, fell over and rolled across the floor, clutching each other in fits of laughter. I noticed that everyone's girlfriend, except James', was present, having been invited by their partners. At that moment I wondered what psychological effect Tina's visitor Tex was having on James, considering the absence of his girlfriend. I was snapped out of my thoughts by some of the band encouraging me to open a present resting nearby. I opened it to find an enormous vibrator, and we all burst into laughter while assorted people grabbed it and used their imaginations to amuse!

The vibrator became the star of the party. We ended up playing a truth or dare game with it. Afterwards, Tina asked me to open my other presents. There were four shockingly expensive goblets that I had pointed out one day when Tina and I were on a shopping spree. At the time I had commented that I adored them. In beautiful wrapping were the very same goblets, given to me by Tina. Moved by her thoughtfulness, I gave her a bear hug and the party raged on for hours.

Totally merry, Tina stepped into Tex's huge shoes and said, 'See the size of these feet! Let me tell you guys something, it's true ...' Annie and Lejeune creased with laughter. We cut the cake, and, around four in the morning, the band and entourage slowly dispersed to their rooms. James kept lingering until finally he was the only one left apart from Tina, Tex and myself.

Finally as I was about to leave, I said to James, 'Don't you think it's time to be leaving. Miss Turner needs her rest.' James shot daggers at me, not liking the words he heard. I walked out with James, leaving Tina to another magical night with Tex. The following day Tex left to return to Texas while I nursed my well-deserved hangover. But nothing can sober an abused body more than a shock can, and the news we received that afternoon was certainly a shock. Tina would be opening for the Rolling Stones in New Jersey in four days time.

23

Keith Richards clutched a half empty bottle of Jack Daniels tightly in his hand, a burning cigarette dangling from between his teeth when he approached Tina. In his distinctive English accent, he asked: ' 'Ere. You fancy a gig with us in Jersey, Tina?'

This was a couple of months ago in New York, but weeks had passed and we didn't have a confirmation until Roger Davies informed us that he had sealed a deal and the Stones gig was on. Rather than returning to LA, we flew straight to New Jersey from New Orleans on November 5 for the concert, which Tina would open that night.

Opening for the Stones was an opportunity money couldn't buy, therefore she accepted a very small fee in exchange for her services. Out of that fee had to come the band and entourage's hotel and living expenses. We ended up checking into a dated, unmodernised hotel.

Tina's suite had brightly coloured shag pile carpet with a round bed and mirror and cork squares pasted to the walls. The bathroom had stairs up to the round, sunken bath which must have been state of the art in the 60s. Even the bathroom had shag carpet and psychedelic drapes. I quickly unpacked before we made our way to soundcheck.

The Stones had a special stage constructed which dipped and dived in different directions. It created chaos. Tina was singing 'Proud Mary' and because of the slopes all over the stage, she would take one small step and find one leg down one bend while the other was still up on the platform. The backing singers and dancers were slipping and sliding all over the place, and momentary panic was etched on all their faces. Although slightly panicked, I could see the whole of Tina's group determined to get past the sloping nightmare of the stage, with each member willing to break every limb if necessary to play up there for the Rolling Stones. They stayed on stage until they cracked routines that would work with the uneven flooring.

Dripping with perspiration, Tina stormed into the dressing room while complaining, 'I'll break my neck tonight on that stage. I just know it ...'

Roger Davies tried to soothe her by saying, 'Darling, darling, calm down.

This is the best thing that can happen to you ...'

'What ... you mean breaking my neck?!?'

'No darling ... gigging for the Rolling Stones. Think of the audience! These people have got to see the new you. Everyone will be talking about Tina Turner.'

Tina muttered, 'Yeh, but I hope they won't be saying things like, "Poor Tina Turner, broke her neck at the Rolling Stones concert ..."'

An hour passed and the Stones arrived and set up for their soundcheck while Tina calmly waited for someone to tell her when it was time to rehearse 'Honky Tonk Women' with Mick. He wanted Tina to come on stage during his act and do a duet with him. I had to laugh watching Tina and Mick during rehearsals. Tina is very disciplined, does nothing impromptu and all her shows are precisely identical in body language and movement to the one before. Mick is another story. Although very professional and an absolute perfectionist, he loves the unexpected, never sticks to a routine and God knows what he'll do next on stage.

Mick and Tina were astonishing together, belting out 'Honky Tonk Women'. Just as Tina was about to leave the stage, Mick said, 'It'll be great tonight, Tina. I got a few surprises for you ...' Tina's face dropped and she just stopped short of saying, 'Oh no'.

Back in the dressing room, Roger enthused, 'Tina! It's going to be great!'

Tina casually replied, 'Yeh, I know. I did this stuff with the Stones before.' Then she grinned like an excited school girl while adding, 'The thing is, you never know what that Mick will do!'

Roger suddenly suggested, 'Tina, I think you should dress down tonight. No flashy costumes with wings. Something more rock 'n' roll.'

She thought for a moment and replied, 'Okay.' Then she turned to me and asked, 'Ed, what do we have?'

I suggested black leather jeans and leopard-print boots with a strappy tank top. At that moment, someone walked into the dressing room wearing a Rolling Stones tee shirt. Tina stared at the shirt and said, 'Take it off.'

The stagehand replied, 'What?'

Tina repeated, 'I said, take it off.' The bewildered boy did as he was ordered. Tina grabbed the shirt and while Lejeune and Annie tried on their outfits. 'This is what I'm wearing tonight when Mick calls me on stage to sing with him. Ed, get me some scissors.' She snipped the shirt to pieces and slit it right up the centre showing off her lovely breasts and tummy. It was very naughty-girl rock 'n' roll.

Having got the outfit together, Tina removed all her clothes and just as she was reaching for her dressing gown, Mick barged straight into her dressing room without knocking, waffling, 'Tina, what do you think of the number?' Meantime he stared at Tina as if she were fully dressed while Roger and I stood, our hands suddenly covering our own fully clothed bodies, while our mouths gaped open in shock.

Tina laughed and said, 'You guys can relax. Mick always does this. Back in the days with Ike when we used to gig with the Stones, Mick never knocked. He'd just barge right in. He's still the same, aren't you, Mick?' Not waiting for a reply, Tina slowly tugged the dressing gown on, adding, 'Mick does that so he can get a good look at my girls and me. Uh huh. Mick would walk right in and get an eyeful of me and the girls. It was like he had some sort of radar. He always barged in right when we were completely naked, just to get a good look at us, didn't you?'

Mick burst out laughing and turned slightly pink while objecting, 'I never looked at the girls ...'

Tina cut him off by playfully snapping, 'Yes you did, you took Claudia Lenear from us! Then you took PP Arnold and now you're eyeing up my two girls here trying to work out which one you'll have next. You probably want both of them, you naughty boy.'

Mick replied, 'No I don't. I don't want your blonde dancer, she looks like my old lady.' Then he stared at partially clothed Lejeune, who was still frantically trying to make herself decent, and started chasing her around Tina's dressing room like a randy old man. We were creased with laughter. He finally paused to stare at himself in a mirror and asked, 'By the way, Tina, what do you think of my new hat?'

Tina tried not to laugh while saying, 'It's ... uhm ... very interesting.'

Mick further admired the leopard print apple-cap in the reflection while saying, 'You like it? I call it my nigga-hat.' Then he quickly turned to me, Lejeune and Tina, the only blacks in the room, while saying, 'I don't mean that in a bad way. This my cool hat. That's why it's my nigga-hat. I gotta tell you how I scored it.'

He made himself comfortable, commanding our full attention as he told us, 'I was in the limo on the way to the hotel and I asked the driver to take me to a real 'blues' area so I can get a feel of what New Jersey's all about. There, walking along was this skinny black guy, drinking some sort of booze out of a bottle, you know, the bottle covered in a paper bag like no one's meant to know there's liquor in it. I shouted to the driver to pull over. I jumped out of the limo, ran up to the guy and he looked at me from head to toe and said, "Hey." I said to him, "You're cool!" The guy says to me, "Yeh, yeh. Whadooyoo want?" I said, "Your hat. I like your hat. Can I have your hat?" He says to me, "No you can't have my hat. I had this hat for years, man. This hat has more history than a fat ol' school book." I said to him, "But I want your hat." The guy says to me, "Boy, you better get away from me, you scrawny little thing." I said, "I got some money." The guy leaned back and said, "Man, how much money you got? You know, money does talk na'." I said, "Gimme the hat and I'll give you some money." He says, "No way man. Uh uh. I been on the streets too long for that number. You pull up in your big limousine askin' fo' mah hat. No way." I whipped out a hundred dollars and handed it to the guy. He took the money and handed me his hat while saying, "Man, you can have mah hat. Mah friend over there, Charly, he gotta hat too." Then the guy yelled, "Yo. Charly. Come here you fucka and gimme yo' hat." I started laughing and thanked the guy and jumped back into the car.'

Mick twirled the hat in his fingers and put it back on his head while saying, 'I'm gonna wear this hat tonight.'

Tina said, 'Look, I'm going to wear these boots.' Mick held his cap by Tina's leopard-print boots and they both agreed that they'd look great on stage together. Tina suddenly said, 'Mick, I want you to do me a favour. Someone gave my assistant here, Eddy, a birthday card a few days ago. The cover of the card is an old black and white picture of you. Would you autograph the card for Ed?'

Mick looked over at me and said, 'Of course I will. Let's see the card.'

I showed it to Mick and he leaned back while staring at the card and said, 'Wow. That was a long time ago. Where did they get this card from? That picture is from way back. This picture is from the mid-sixties ... you know something ... I look kinda good there ...' He seemed momentarily lost in thought, and while still studying the old photo, added, 'I look like I could use a few good meals, but this picture was taken well before I made it. Well before my career took off.'

Mick scribbled a few words on the card and signed it then said, 'Eddy, Eddy, Eddy. You just made my day. I got my nigga-hat on, Tina Turner has her leopard boots and now there's this old picture of me. It's gonna be a good night, ain't it?'

I grinned and took the card back while saying, 'It's gonna be great, Mick.'

Mick departed and we started getting ready for the show. The audience went mental over Tina's performance and during the long intermission that followed, the Stones arrived at Tina's dressing room to tell her how great she was. While the Stones performed, Tina dressed in the ripped teeshirt, leather jeans and leopard boots and patiently waited to be called to the stage. An assistant collected us and we stood in readiness in the wings until Mick finally said to the cheering crowd, 'What did you think of Tina Turner? Did you like her?' The audience erupted in cheers and applause. Mick said, 'Keith and me think she should do a duet with us.' The audience erupted again then the familiar opening bars to 'Honky Tonk Women' began. Tina ran on stage with an identical cordless microphone to Mick's and they rocked the crowd. During the instrumental part of the song, Mick and Tina danced around, then Mick suddenly ran round Tina and stuck the microphone between her legs, right in her crotch, as if it were a vibrator. Tina nearly jumped out of her skin while Mick chased her around. When they finished singing the song, Tina left the stage during the rapturous applause that followed. As soon as she was offstage, she laughed, 'See what I mean about that Mick. You never know what sort of stuff he'll pull next.'

Tina quickly changed and we raced to take our reserved seats in the audience to watch the remainder of the Rolling Stones concert. Tina stared at the tens of thousands of heads in the huge stadium and squeezed my hand while whispering, 'Ed, see all this? It'll be me someday. I'll be playing to audiences like this. You'll see. I'll be headlining the show and someone else will be opening for me. I'll be inviting people like Rod Stewart and Mick Jagger to come on stage and do a song with me. That's my dream Ed. Before I leave this earth, I'm going to do it.'

'I know you'll do it soon. Real soon, Tina.'

Before the following night's show, Tina was engaged in a deep business conversation with Roger Davies when there was a tapping at the door, followed by Keith Richards letting himself in with Mick hot on his heels. I stood scratching at the soles of Tina's stage shoes, making them abrasive so she wouldn't slip or fall while performing, when the phone started ringing. I answered it and it was a request for Chip to come to the back door. No sooner had he opened Tina's door to exit, than we could hear a loud rustling and a disturbance in the corridor. It was none other than Tex, who had flown into New York, taken a taxi to the gig and arrived loaded down with luggage in total disarray. His hanging suitcase was half open, and a hat box under his arm had a stetson threatening to fall out and amidst clutching all these items, he held a bouquet of flowers for Tina which were now half crushed. Tex angrily marched into the dressing room, ignoring the fact that there were several other people present and wailed directly to Tina, 'Ah dunno what it is. Ah thought you had things all togetha'. They kept me waitin' there backstage and threatened not to let me in ...'

Mick Jagger stopped in his tracks and stared at Tex while Roger Davies nervously ran his fingers through his hair. He then clutched his head and muttered to me, 'Oh God, why did she invite this guy here?'

Seeing Mick and Keith in a state of befuddlement over Tex, Roger grabbed Chip Lightman and said, 'Get rid of this guy.'

Tina overheard and said, 'No Chip. I'll take care of it.' She took Tex to a corner and told him, 'Please calm down. You're making a bad impression.'

Tex suddenly yelled, 'Ah don't give a fuck. You invited me here, didn't you?'

Ignoring Tex, Roger marched straight up to Tina and asked, 'Are you okay? Do you need some help here?'

At this point Tex dropped his Southern gentleman image and started acting terribly camp, almost like a gay drama queen, complaining about everything. Tina suggested Tex should go to the hotel and freshen up, but he firmly objected, saying he was staying put. Mick Jagger stood in a corner with his mouth open, then started imitating Tex's drama queen actions behind his back. Half those present covered their mouths so as not to burst out laughing over Mick's performance, while Roger looked sick as a parrot. Someone finally started laughing while Chip Lightman bopped so nervously that we thought he might spring through the roof. Chip was in a bad position. His boss Roger had ordered him to get rid of Tex while his other boss, Tina had ordered him not to. Tex, still throwing a tantrum, stood in a corner with Tina until Chip persuaded him into a private conversation. Being remarkably diplomatic, Chip managed to calm Tex down.

Tina sat in front of her mirror staring at Tex in the reflection, I could read the look on her face, and I could tell see was seeing him in another light. She had a look of humiliation as she studied him, her new boyfriend, her new lover, her new embarrassment. She wished she hadn't invited him. There were so many important things going on with people suddenly tugging at her from all directions that she didn't need her petulant lover present as well. Tex simply didn't fit in.

The show was as great and successful as the night before, her professional attitude not letting anything get in the way of her performance. Tina returned for her duet with Mick and he couldn't get near her that night onstage. Every time he chased her around during the song, Tina ducked and dived to avoid him springing any more saucy surprises on her. Mick knew what she was doing and he loved it, motivating him to further flirt and tease her during the song, which only served to drive the audience wild. The electricity between Mick and Tina shot straight into the audience, earning the duo a deafening, rapturous applause.

Afterwards I rushed Tina to her dressing room which had suddenly turned into a meeting point for America's Who's Who. Andy Warhol, Liza Minelli, Bruce Springsteen and countless others arrived. Andy spent a few minutes with Tina, his soft, mysterious voice soothing her. This came as a total surprise to Tina who had always felt a bit frightened of him. He then asked Tina to come to the Stones' dressing room where everyone had decided to gather. This made her a bit uneasy. She knew several superstars would be there and she never felt comfortable around celebrities or those in the public eye. She was never overwhelmed by them, she just never really wanted to meet them. She had little in common with those in the showbiz world and I knew why she felt that way. I thought back to the Bolic Sound Studio days, nearly a decade before, when stars would come in droves to compliment Tina on her performance, then Ike would drag them off to the party room with Tina always excluded. Somewhere deep inside she felt showbiz people liked all the things Ike Turner adored, and that they always abandoned her in favour of courting Ike's interests.

Tina popped to the Stones' dressing room, said hello to everyone present and speedily left to return to the hotel. Once in her suite, she asked me to pack everything. Roger then came in and ordered me to unpack. He had arranged for Tina to stay to do her duet with Mick again, but that everyone else, including myself, would return to Los Angeles. The following day I returned to Los Angeles taking most of Tina's luggage with me, leaving her a small selection of clothes to wear.

I got to Tina's house, let myself in and turned off the alarms, then carried on with the meticulous task of unpacking for her. I had music on, a bottle of wine open and was grooving along when the doorbell went. It frightened the daylights out of me. No one ever showed up at Tina's without a prior arrangement.

I crept down the stairs and looked out of a small, discreet window and, much to my surprise, saw Tina's son Ronnie. I pressed the intercom and said, 'Hi Ronnie. Yes, what is it?'

He replied, 'Oh, hi Eddy. Is my mother here?'

'No.'

'But I thought she was meant to be back. It's really important.'

'She's not here, Ronnie.'

'Well, can I come in?'

'No Ronnie. You can't. You know I can't let anyone in when your mother isn't home. I'll take a message and give it to her when she gets here. She's meant to arrive sometime over the next few days.' I knew exactly when Tina would be back but I didn't want anyone to know her specific movements. It was my way of protecting her.

After I said goodbye, I secretly kept watching him through the window. He didn't leave immediately and nervously paced back and forth. He was behaving suspiciously and it made me uneasy. I started wondering why on earth the pedestrian front gate was unlocked. I watched Ronnie leave, then I raced up to a spare bedroom and peered out of the window where I could get a view of the street beyond Tina's property. To my horror, I saw Ike Turner. I fought off the crippling feeling of fear, knowing I was safe because of Tina's alarm system which I had set as soon as I got into the house. The alarm wouldn't go if there was movement, but it would sound if any windows or doors changed position. My knees like jelly, I made it to a phone and left a message for Tina to ring me right away.

While waiting, I dashed out and locked the front gate then raced back in and reset the alarm. I carried on with my duties, the only difference being that I didn't switch the music back on so I could keep my ears open for suspicious noises. I prepared a meal and turned the TV on without volume when Tina's call finally came through. 'Ed. What's wrong?'

I told her about Ronnie and Ike. After a long silence, I asked, 'Tina, are you there?'

'Yes Ed. Don't say anything. I just need to think for a second ... I just need to think.'

Finally, she said, 'Ed, what are you thinking? I don't want to freak you out. Just don't leave the house. Forget about all the errands and dry cleaning. Don't leave the house until I get there. I'll talk to Roger about it.'

I agreed. After putting the phone down, I thought about sleeping in Tina's room where she kept her gun, but I remembered I had never touched a gun and had no idea how to use one. I started getting flashbacks of the days of when Bernadette's car was set alight and the gunshots fired into Tina's house. Ike always made a point of letting Tina know he knew her movements. I was scared. I decided, although inexperienced, I would sleep in Tina's bed where her gun was in easy reach.

In my warm pyjamas I snuggled under Tina's luxurious duvet and I lay in her bed thinking about her children. Craig, upset over Bernadette leaving him to marry Len Swann, the famous American footballer, and determined to make something of his life, had joined the Navy. Michael was spending time with his real mother, Lorraine. He was still suffering emotional problems and bouts of depression. Ike Jr. had been travelling back and forth from St Louis, staying at his father's house. He hustled the best he could to make ends meet. Ronnie was sucked back into his father's clutches, having been fired from Tina's band when she put the new show on the road. Craig was the only one who seemed settled and he was very proud of his life in the Navy. The other three were still lost and confused and, suffering from the feeling of not being wanted, they drifted around in aimless circles.

Ike Turner's world was rapidly crumbling — his finances were dwindling and Tina's apparent success with the Rolling Stones irked him. One thing was for certain, Ike still knew all of Tina's movements and had arrived just when she was originally due back. Had it not been for the Rolling Stones, Tina would have been in residence when Ike showed up. I worried myself to sleep. Early the next day Tina phoned to say she was on her way home and Tex would be arriving with her. I was surprised, considering she had seemed to go off him only the night before. Tina instructed, 'Make sure there are fresh flowers all over the house including my bedroom. You know how I like it. Make sure the house is spick and span. Please Ed, I need you to help me out. I know you're excited about your new apartment and you're dying to go but don't make any plans because I want you to spend a couple of days with me so I can settle in. Tex will be staying and I have a feeling I've made a mistake but I got myself into it and I'll have to work it out. I need you at the house with me.'

I couldn't understand how Tina would have time to entertain Tex. We had less than a week to prepare for a foreign tour, she had to rehearse with the band, go over new material and songs and have numerous business meetings with Roger Davies before departing. This was the worst possible time to have a house guest.

I phoned Tina's florist to deliver flowers and then I nipped into her Mercedes and drove to Gelson's to stock up the fridge for Tex's tastes, filling it with things Tina would never eat such as dips and easy-to-prepare snacks. When I heard the limousine arriving, I greeted Tina and Tex in the driveway, both of whom were laughing and getting along famously. While walking through the front door, Tex waffled on about his plans to go to Universal Studios, museums and sightseeing. Tex was aware that we would be on the road a week later and that it would be impossible for Tina to accompany him on all his planned jaunts. In reality, Tina just wanted to come home and relax between the necessary things she had to do related to business. She had had it with airplanes, airports and hotels. She was tired of the routine of having dinners with people within the music industry and sick of having to receive well-wishers after each show when she was thoroughly exhausted and just wanted to collapse. She always had to find an extra ounce of energy from somewhere to be a polite hostess when all she really wanted to do was go to her room, give herself a beauty treatment and go to sleep. She longed to be in her own bed, in her own home and at this point, she would have rather slept alone.

Rather than make a burden of himself, Tex disappeared during the day, returning late in the evenings. After a couple of days, Tina told me I could go home because she felt Tex was harmless. I still hadn't unpacked my belongings or decorated my apartment, so I nearly burned a trail racing out of her front door.

As soon as I got home, I listened to my messages and ended up taking a quick shower and racing to a friend's birthday dinner at a restaurant called the Rose Tattoo. It had live entertainment, was grand, intimate and expensive. Upstairs was a popular disco called Studio One, frequented mainly by gays. After dinner we all popped upstairs to listen to the music and as we pushed our way to the bar, I saw something that stopped me in my tracks. Tex was on the dance floor being extremely friendly with a young man, occasionally giving him a kiss on the cheek while whispering in his ear. My friend Sam said, 'What is it, Ed?' I pointed at Tex, who was now holding the other man and dancing with him closely. I wanted to make sure it was definitely him, so I worked my way across the dance floor and bumped into him while passing, causing him to spin and come face to face with me. I acted totally surprised and said, 'Tex! What are you doing here?'

He stared at me as if he had seen a ghost. Tex was shocked at me seeing him making out with a man at a gay disco and I was shocked that he was there. His partner affectionately stroked Tex's arm while asking, 'Tex, what is the matter?'

I said, 'Tex, I'll see you later.' Then I quickly disappeared through the crowd. I couldn't get down those stairs and out of the disco fast enough. I was dying to get to a phone so I could tell Tina.

As I worked my way to a phone, I suddenly thought that Tex would probably do the same thing. I resolved to let him make the first call and let him hang himself. I knew it was unwise to get in the middle of a close friend's relationship. I decided to wait until the next day when I would talk to Tina on the phone as per normal, while having my morning coffee. I'd know if Tex confessed because she would tell me straight away. That morning, I was woken by a call. 'Hi Ed. It's me. Are you still sleeping?'

'Yeh, Tina.'

'Okay, phone me as soon as you wake up.'

'I will ...' Click.

I turned over to go back to sleep but memories of the night before came flooding back, and I dashed to the phone. I dialled Tina and she was surprisingly vibrant and chirpy. I immediately realised that Tex hadn't confessed to her about his double preferences. Tina said, 'Ed, let's go to dinner tonight.'

'Tina, I can't. I haven't stopped long enough to unpack a single box in my apartment. My coffee maker isn't even set up. I went out to a friend's birthday last night which set me further behind.'

Proper, authoritive and in a mother hen voice, Tina replied, 'Ed. I told you before, life on the road means you won't have much time left for socialising and friends. You have to conserve your energy.'

'I see. Does this mean you need me?'

'Will two o'clock be okay? Can you get here by then? And come to dinner later in the evening?'

'As if I'd say no.' We both laughed and I arrived at her house at two sharp. I let myself in and the first person was Tex, jovially saying, 'Hi Ed! Ha' are you?' Tina and Tex seemed to be getting on beautifully so I gritted my teeth and decided the timing would be appalling if I mentioned Tex's preferences to her then.

Tina piped up, 'Ed will be coming to dinner with us tonight.'

I glanced over at her and she gave me a knowing look. I suddenly thought that she did know something. As soon as Tex left the room I turned to her and confessed, 'I would have said something sooner but I don't think it's a good idea to interfere in your love life. I know you should have heard it from me before hearing it from anyone else. I didn't know I'd end up at the gay disco and bump into Tex making out on the dance floor with some young stud ...'

'What are you talking about Ed?'

Much to my horror, I then realised Tina didn't know anything at all. I stuttered, 'I went to a gay club and saw Tex making out with a man on the dance floor.'

Tina's lips thinned to pencil lines. She crossed her arms and glared at me before replying, 'I can assure you Ed, Tex is all man.' She threw her hands around and said, 'You guys, you and the band members, sometimes even me, you all go to gay clubs all the time and dance with men and goof around. I dance with the girls and play around and act the fool. So what? It doesn't mean everyone is gay.'

'Yeeesss Tina. But it wasn't like that.'

Tina put her foot down and said, 'Honey, I can guarantee you. Tex is not gay.'

'Okay Tina. I'm sorry. I didn't want to say anything and it was a dilemma for me. I didn't want to get on your bad side.'

'Ed, I always told you. If you have something to say just say it. Don't beat around the bush and don't ever let me find out from somebody else.'

'Okay, fine. I told you. End of subject. I don't want to upset you. I saw your boyfriend making out with a guy, I told you, it's done, out of the way, over. Friends?'

'Of course, Ed.' Then she turned on her heel and marched away.

We ended up not going to dinner that evening, getting a takeaway instead and eating in the house. Dinner was strained because Tex knew or sensed I had told Tina about his nighttime exploits and Tina knew I was telling the truth. I knew her well. Her mood towards Tex had dramatically changed and I knew he was finished and she couldn't wait to get rid of him. He left the following day, never to return. That was the end of Tex.

24

Just before Christmas, we were off to New York for Tina to play the Ritz for the third time. A friend of mine called Renée, who lived in New York, phoned me at the Berkshire, telling me I should come to her warehouse with Tina. Renée had loads of designer goods which she was shipping out for the sales and said Tina and I could have first choice of precious items at knock down prices. Tina and I couldn't wait to get there because Renée stocked Claude Montana, Armani, Calvin Klein and other good labels. Her thousand dollar jackets would be going for one hundred dollars each, a bargain Tina and I refused to miss.

Come Sunday, the day Tina and I had arranged to go to the warehouse, she emerged out of the shower to announce James would be coming with us. I was not happy about it. James was very negative when it came to top designers, referring to them as a bunch of faggots. He was not a fun shopping partner. Tina bought loads of things and I went equally nutty, with Tina telling me not to go too crazy but to choose anything I wanted and she would cover it for me. I chose several items of clothing including a stunning leather jacket. James shopped much lighter, choosing only one leather jacket similar to mine. After we'd paid for all the items, Renée escorted us towards the exit. Tina thanked all the staff, then turned and noticed James and I both wearing our new leather jackets. She put her hands on her hips and stared at both of us while saying, 'You two look great in your jackets but it looks silly with both of you wearing them. One of you will have to take your jacket off.'

I looked at James and said, 'I guess you better put your jacket back in your bag.'

Much to my humiliation, in front of my friend Renée, Tina ordered, 'No, Ed. Take your jacket off so James can wear his.' Renée glanced over at me and I could feel my cheeks heating with embarrassment.

In front of Renée and everyone I firmly replied, 'I guess because James is so important to you, because he's your boyfriend, you have to embarrass me in front of my friend and her staff by ordering me to take off my jacket as if I have no choices in my life. Well, I don't want to but I will because those are your orders, missy.' I crumpled my new leather jacket into a ball and stuffed it carelessly into a bag.

Tina went rigid. As soon as we were in the elevator and it began its descent, she exploded. 'How dare you speak to me like that in front of people?'

'You embarrassed me.'

She wagged her index finger in my face and stated, 'Get it right Ed. I did not embarrass you. You embarrassed me! Just get it straight. Remember who works for who.' When the elevator door opened Tina grabbed James by the arm and marched off ahead of me down the snowy streets of New York. In the distance, I could see Tina stop at a street corner where there was a man selling roasted chestnuts. Tina had always raved about them, telling me I must try them next time we were in New York. I finally caught up with her and I realised she had already put the incident at the warehouse behind her, but I still felt terribly offended, hurt and angry.

She cheerfully turned to me and sweetly said, 'Ed, these are the nuts I was telling you about. They're really wonderful. Shall I buy you some?'

I gave her an evil look and nastily replied, 'No, thank you!'

That did it. I had never seen her face like that before. Tina was shocked. I had never questioned her or stood up for myself before. Now, I had done it twice in the space of fifteen minutes and, worse, in public. She glared at me as if I would never have a chance to do that again. When we got back to the hotel, I put her bags in her room and was about to start unpacking them when she firmly said, 'Ed. I want to get one thing straight. For the rest of our stay in New York, I will call you when I need you. You are not to call me. That's how I feel right now. Before I say something or do something that might upset both of us, just leave my room right now.'

'Alright.' I marched straight out, got to my room and felt no regret at all. I didn't understand what was happening to me, but all I knew was that I had a life and I wanted to be treated like a human being, not like a second rate citizen. In my own way, I had conveyed that message when we were at the warehouse and it made me feel good.

Two hours later, she delivered the first snub. She rang me and said, 'Ed, I'm ready. Meet me in the lobby.'

Normally I would collect her from her room and escort her through the hotel to a waiting limousine. Once in the car, I tried to make small talk and Tina cut me off by cold. 'Ed, I have nothing to say to you.'

'Alright,' I muttered.

We got to the Ritz and all through the routine of getting ready to go on stage she said very little to me. When she did speak, she was as cold as ice, barking out orders or instructions. That's when I started worrying, wondering if I had gone too far. During the ride back to the hotel that evening, Tina icily told me, 'Ed, as soon as we get back, go to my room and pack up my things. I won't need your services for the rest of the night. In the morning, go to my room and get my luggage and I'll meet you downstairs.'

That night I tossed and turned in bed. My stomach was knotted with nerves and it made me feel worse than ever. Finally I got out of bed and got on my knees and prayed for God to get Tina and me past our difference. We loved each other too much for this.

At JFK airport, everyone was in a jovial mood, except me. By the time we boarded the plane, everyone knew something was going on because of the noticable distance between me and Tina. Kenny Moore took a seat next to me and asked what was going on. He said, 'Man, we all noticed Tina's giving you the cold treatment. What happened?'

I felt miserable. I replied, 'I really need to be alone right now.'

Halfway through the six hour flight, Chip Lightman came nervously bopping down the aisle and told me he needed to talk to me in private. We went to the back of the cabin and he said, 'Eddy, I'm really sorry. Tina asked me to give you this.'

He handed me a letter from Tina. Chip stood next to me while I read the letter. While reading each word, I felt like I was caught up in a living nightmare. The letter was written on Tina's company paper, dated the day before, December 13. Tears spilled out of my eyes as I read the words, 'Dear Eddy, Your services are no longer required as assistant to Tina Turner. You will be paid one week severance pay. Merry Christmas. Tina Turner. Chip put his hands around my shoulders and he told me how very sorry he was. I stumbled to my seat and put my sunglasses on, burying my head in a corner by a window.

Somehow I pulled myself together in time to disembark from the flight and I loaded the waiting limousine with her goods. Ten minutes into the journey to her house, I pitifully blurted out, 'Tina, I'm sorry, I'm really sorry ...'

'Ed, I have nothing to say to you. You should have thought of that before. I can't have you working for me anymore.'

'Tina, I'll never do anything like that again. I'm really sorry. Just give me one more chance.'

'Ed, life is not like that. Not everyone gets a second chance. You had great opportunities, you've been on the road and travelled the world with me. Now it's over. We'll stay friends but right now I have to say to you to give me some time.'

I knew Tina too well. It would be futile to beg for another chance once she had made up her mind. I had seen her time and time again cut people with whom she was once inseparable, out of her life forever. Now it was my turn. It was actually happening to me. Suddenly, the little boy from Seattle rose in me. I idolised Tina from the age of eight and was employed by her by my fourteenth birthday. I wasn't going to let her go that easily. Just as we pulled into her drive, I pleaded with her once more but she snapped, 'I said no. All I need for you to do for me is go in and unpack, carry on with your job because you are paid to the end of today. After you are finished with that you are more than welcome to leave. I don't need you to stay around, I don't want to discuss it. We won't be sitting down. I told you I need time and space right now. Hopefully, we will be friends but I will never have you work for me again.'

I knew then it was truly over.

When I had finished unpacking, Tina stood at the front door and snapped, 'Goodbye, Ed. *Goodbye*.' She closed the door behind me and I loaded my suitcases into my car and drove home through a haze of tears. I had been eliminated from Tina's life. That night, I cried myself to sleep. The next morning, the reality intensified, increasing my feelings of anguish and loss. I phoned countless people, each one of them trying to soothe me by saying Tina and I would be friends again, but none of it rang true.

Tina was due to record a live satellite show with Rod Stewart and Kim Carnes, a concert which was being recorded for an album. I had looked forward to that booking and Tina and I had enthused about it before we fell out with each other. Suddenly the phone rang. It was Chip Lightman saying, 'Tina told me to say this in her exact words. She knows how much you love Rod Stewart and she wouldn't be so cold as to not let you come to the show. She is leaving one ticket for you, but no backstage pass. You can come to the show and that is all.'

All my friends told me not to go. They said I would be a fool to show up because she was just rubbing my nose in all the things I'd be missing. I knew they were right but I went anyway. Lejeune found me in the audience and came up to give me a big hug. She said, 'Eddy, I know how you feel. I've known Tina for years. I know how cold she is — that's why I keep my distance from her and never became close with her. Honey, that woman is cold but I love her and I need my job. If you need anyone to talk to, you can always phone me.'

'Lejeune, do you think I'll ever get another chance?'

'No, Eddy. When Tina is through with someone, she's through. You've seen her do it before. Musicians and dancers from years gone past, Tina will go out of her way to not see them. When it's over, it's over. You should know that a lot better than anyone else. Ed, it's best you just accept it and get on with your life.'

After Tina's performance, I watched the chosen few get access backstage with their precious passes. I felt heartbroken, lonely and left out. I stayed for the longest time hoping someone would come for me and take me backstage. Finally, the lights went out and I was the only one left in the vast venue. I knew no one would be coming for me.

Over the next couple of days, I pulled myself together, spending time with my friends and family as it neared Christmas. Two days before Christmas, I had a thought which brought me a ray of hope. I would carry on with the tradition of baking her a cake and exchanging gifts. This time, I made two butter cakes and a triple layer German chocolate cake. I phoned Tina and when she answered, I cheerfully said, 'Hi Tina, it's Ed.'

She curtly replied, 'Yes. Can I help you?'

'I got you a Christmas gift and baked two butter cakes and one German chocolate cake for your family.'

'Thank you very much Ed. I appreciate that and I know Alline and the family will appreciate it too.'

'When shall I bring them over?'

'Tomorrow, Ed. I need to run errands so if you could get here early I would appreciate it.'

As I pulled into Tina's drive, I was surprised to see Craig who was home on leave from the Navy. We greeted each other warmly. Tina appeared from the side of the house and said, 'Hi, Ed. You can take the cakes to the kitchen.'

I did as she instructed and returned to my car where she stood. I reached into the vehicle and said, 'Here's your present, Tina.'

She snapped, 'Well put it under the tree.' Then she pointed to the front of the door and said, 'There's your present. I didn't have a chance to wrap it.'

I gasped. It was two antique side tables I had once admired in an antique shop. 'They're wonderful! Thank you Tina!'

'You are welcome, Ed.'

I started to ask how things were before she cut me off short. 'Just fine Ed. Merry Christmas and Happy New Year. Goodbye.'

I got in my car and left.

From that moment on, I did everything I could not to think about Tina. I partied every night, hung out with friends and became more sociable than ever before. In the New Year, I joined the unemployment lines and, when they asked why I was fired, Chip sent them a letter saying I was laid off due to lack of work. I fell back on my cosmeticology education and did loads of hairdressing and beauty work on a private basis. I set up a lucrative business making housecalls to the wealthy women of Beverly Hills, coiffing them in the privacy of their own, luxurious homes.

Having worked in the industry since my early teens, I was already familiar with the business. I was earning royalties on my song 'Pain', and wanted to expand within the writing and performing side of mainstream music. I threw myself into my career so I wouldn't have time to think about Tina and how much I missed her. I met a man called Allen Zentz, the producer and owner of the recording studio where Michael Jackson's phenomenal album *Off The Wall* was recorded and mastered. We had a chat and I sang a couple of my own tunes which resulted in Allen encouraging me to team up with a gifted artist called Mars Bonfire who wrote Steppenwolf's worldwide smash hit 'Born To Be Wild'.' Between us both, we hoped to create new, contemporary songs for major performers. I went to Mars' apartment off Hollywood Boulevard, a throwback to the 1960s, everything about it frozen in time from the hippy era. Three young kids, two girls and one boy ran around the sparsely furnished rooms like wild, playful tiger cubs. I introduced myself to Mars and he said, 'I hear you're gonna sing me a couple of songs. I have this philosophy. If you're gonna do it, just do it — or you're no use to me.'

Mars took my tape from me, slapped it on and I jumped up in the middle of the floor and performed my songs like I had never done before. He snapped his fingers and said, 'Good! There's something there. But I want you to do this ... on the second verse, quicken the tempo, and let's sing so I can feel those things you're singing about. Start at the top.'

Mars picked up his guitar and strummed out the tune he had just heard, quickening the tempo on the second verse. My first impression was that I had been put together with an eccentric hippy, but when he started playing his guitar and directing where the song should go, the true genius of Mars Bonfire became apparent. I got to know him on a personal level, often developing a new song in between Mars playing mother. He referred to himself as a single father and, although devoted to his kids, said that he felt the strain of single parenthood was taking its toll on him.

While doing all this, I still visited Tina's sister Alline and their mother Zelma, each still regarding me as part of the family. Alline and Muh would tell me stories of Tina's childhood and we would laugh and talk for hours. Late February, during a visit to Alline's, she told me Tina hadn't hired anyone to take my place and had decided instead to carry out my former duties herself. While I listened to Alline, I felt the familiar longing to be on the road again with Tina. As hard as I tried to put it all behind me, I missed her and the band. I snapped back to the present when Alline said, 'See. Na' yo' see. Na' yo' know what Ann's like. That's why Ah gave you the job. Shiiit. Lemme tell yo' sumthin' boy, Ah ain't goin' back on the road with Ann. One of us'll end up killin' each other.'

Meantime Muh, sitting cozily in a big, downy chair, lazily said, 'Alline, don't be like that 'bout yo' sista.'

As I was leaving, Alline stopped me at the door and said, 'Yo' just leave Ann doin' that shit for anutha coupla weeks. She be callin' yo' ass then. Ah know mah sista.'

Meantime Annie, Lejeune and Kenny sent me postcards while on the road, telling me the latest gossip. They wrote saying Tina was like an evil wet hen, lugging all her shit through the airport. It gave me a ray of hope and made me feel good. I grinned affectionately, picturing Tina in my shoes. One postcard told me that after two months of fuming, Tina was even angrier at me, once snapping, 'Damn that Ed. Why did he have to make me so mad at him?'

Some time in March, Lejeune phoned me and said, 'I tell you ... that Tina. Eddy, why don't you just get off your pedestal and make it up with her and come back on the road. We can't stand it any more. All she does is complain.' I grinned from ear to ear when she added, 'Kenny was watchin' Tina tryin' to get her shit together before a show and she was preparing her dressing room the way you do. That girl was sweatin'. She didn't realise how much damn work it is lookin' after her. She was flyin' around the way you do, only she was mad, so Kenny goes and teases her and says, "Hey Teeeee, stop acting like Eddy." Tina exploded, goin', "Darn it. I don't act like Ed. If anything, he acts like me. I'm so mad at him."'

It had been nearly three months since I last spoke to Tina. Missing her more than ever, I threw myself into my career, and, with Allen Zentz's help, things started gelling with my music. Flying with it, I networked like crazy and my phone never stopped ringing. Then, one sunny March day, I put the receiver down, only to hear the phone ring again. I picked it up to hear the words, 'Hi, Ed. It's me, Tina.'

25

Thrilled to hear Tina's voice, I asked, 'How are you, Tina?'
She spoke to me as if nothing had happened, as if we had talked every day. She confessed, 'I'm tired, Ed. Real tired.'
'Why are you so tired, Tina?'
'Don't give me that, you know why I'm so tired!'
We both burst out laughing. While nattering about anything and everything, a small fear crept over me. Over the past three months I had become very independent, living my life for myself, not for Tina. Yet as soon as I heard her voice, I melted. I knew, then, that I would always be putty in her hands. I asked,'Where are you?'
'On the road. Listen, Ed, my housekeeper is having a few weeks off.'
Rather than making a request, she ordered, 'I want you to do a few things for me. Tidy the house, keep the flowers fresh, take care of the dry cleaning, stock up the fridge for me – Ed, you know how I like things done. You can make some extra money, twenty dollars a day.'
Tina was very clever. She kept asking the band and girls if they had heard from me and wanted to know every small detail of what I was doing. Alline kept Tina up to date on my goings on and she knew she could phone me as if we had never fallen out. I nipped round to Tina's accountants and re-collected my set of keys. While caring for her lovely home, I continued cosmetic house calls, writing music and testing out my new material. When I had a tape ready, Allen Zentz invited me to Sunday lunch so he could listen to my songs.
It was a beautiful, sunny day when I met up with Allen at a swish outdoor restaurant. We seemed surrounded by positive energy. Beautiful, young, sexy girls slowly swayed along the promenade, wearing tiny shorts and little tops, allowing the sun to kiss their firm, bare midriffs. Shiny cars kept pulling up, the passengers protecting their eyes with designer sunglasses as the sun poured through the open-top vehicles. Tall, elegant women in tiny designer dresses strolled along, their little pedigree dogs in tow with expensive leads attatched to their delicate dog collars. It was a

typical lazy Sunday on Sunset Boulevard.

Allen and I soaked up the atmosphere and, after an enjoyable lunch, he told me he would phone me after he had got a chance to listen to my tape.

As well as recording and mastering *Off The Wall*, Allen had mastered recordings for many other stars including the Pointer Sisters, Leo Sayer, Donna Summer and the supergroup Kiss. I didn't hang any high hopes on Allen knocking my door down to offer me a songwriting contract, feeling I couldn't possibly be in the league of the big boys yet, but I knew I had talent that would eventually get me there. I was stunned when he enthusiastically called me a couple of weeks later. During the days leading up to his call, Tina had returned home and I arranged to let myself in the following morning, falling into the same routine I formerly had when I first started working for her as her housekeeper and cook.

I got to Tina's around ten in the morning, let myself in, opened the curtains and windows, started a fresh pot of coffee brewing and carried on with all the things involved with my past routine. I laid out a tray, silver service, with fresh coffee, toast, and eggs and carried it to Tina's bedroom. As I pushed the door open, I heard her familiar, sleepy, early morning voice gently purring, 'Good morning, Ed.'

I spoke as if we never had parted, casually saying, 'Morning Tina. Ready for breakfast?'

I fluffed up her pillows, helping her lazily shift her tiny body into a comfortable position and fussed over and pampered her. I placed the breakfast tray in front of her and poured out a cup of fresh coffee while saying, 'I'm going open the rest of the rooms and air them out. Give me a shout when you need me.'

Tina patted a space on the bed by the side of her and said, 'No, no. Don't go. Sit here and tell me what's been going on.'

I sat facing her and said, 'There hasn't been much...'

Tina's voice suddenly sounded as if she had been awake for hours as she stated, 'Don't give me that stuff, Ed. I've been talking to Lejeune and Kenny and they've told me what's going on. You've been singing and writing. What's this all about?'

I didn't act overly enthusiastic, calmly telling her, 'I had a go at it and I really love it. I know that's what I really want to do, Tina. I know the business pretty well and always adjust to the contemporary stuff and a lot of important people have taken interest in me. You know, Tina, spending all that time on the road with you really made me crave the stage. Seeing you out there performing made me want to do it too. It's my dream!'

She replied, 'Yeh, yeh... that's good.'

I rattled on in great detail about networking, meeting people and how one thing led to another. She listened with interest and laughed occasionally over my exploits. Finally Tina said, 'I've got a week off and I've got a lot of things I have to do. Will you be able to help me out or do you have other things going on?'

'I'll work things out around your schedule.' I wanted to kick myself as soon as I said that. I still couldn't refuse her.

That night at dinner, Tina suddenly said, 'Ed, I been thinking about the past and, uhm, I don't like the way you spoke to me and I want to make sure this situation never happens again. We made an agreement in the beginning and I expect you to stick to it. Besides, I missed you, you silly boy. I want you to come back on the road with me in two weeks.'

I leaned forward and said, 'Tina ... this writing and singing thing... I want to give it a chance. I want to give it a try. I left a tape with Allen Zentz and I got a call from him that he wants to produce my songs.'

Tina knew who Allen Zentz was. She stirred uncomfortably and became a bit quiet. She said, 'Ed, I'm really happy for you...'

Then I said, 'Tina, I really want to go back on the road with you. I really missed you. Besides, while these things tick over, you know there's a lot of waiting in the business, I could do with making some real money. Can I think about it? Can you give me a little time?'

Tina sat erect and said, 'Sure, you can think about it. I'm not promising the job will still be available if you're going to drag your feet, though. I need someone now. You know I can't do all this, Ed. You're putting me in a bad spot right now and I'll be forced to get somebody.'

A week later she told me she had hired drummer Jack Bruno's wife Lori to be her assistant on the road. She added, 'But I want you to stay on at the house and look after things while I'm away. You can earn some money while seeing how things turn out with your music.'

Tina was bursting with energy and enthusiasm on her return. Roger Davies had persuaded John Carter of Capitol Records to let them tape a demo at the Capitol Studios in Hollywood. John Carter watched over the rehearsals and recording and I developed a good relationship with him and his wife Jeannie. Tina was offered a deal, but Capitol dragged their feet with the matter. Roger became nervous and contacted a friend of his called Richard Perry, a top producer known for his work with Carly Simon, Barbara Streisand, Diana Ross, the Pointer Sisters and many others. Together with Richard, Tina recorded the Beatles song 'Help', my song 'Pain' and a third song. Richard came up with the idea of beginning 'Help' just as the Beatles did it, then the body of the song would be in Tina's style, before ending like the original version. It worked brilliantly. But despite all of this, negotiations still dragged on. Out of the blue, Roger Davies got a call from London where a top British group called Heaven 17 were recording an album made up of several known artists covering certain tunes. They wanted Tina to cover a Temptations song called 'Ball Of Confusion'.

Tina flew straight to London to record the song. At one in the morning, LA time, Tina rang me in a state of wild excitement. 'Ed! This group Heaven 17 are really big pop artists here in England. These guys are really young but they're great. I have to tell you about the studio! It was so exciting! I went in thinking I was gonna see a big band but there weren't any musicians except a guitar player. All the music a live band makes was done with a small machine. They call it a Fairlight. It's like a real band, maybe even better! I have never seen or heard anything like it in my life! It's like something from some futuristic movie!'

Tina was bowled over by the new technology. It was one of the most exciting things she had experienced during that era. 'Listen, Ed. I'm going to play this song for you over the phone.' I could hear her fiddling with a tape and inserting it into a machine. I heard her pressing buttons and after a few seconds of silence, Tina's stunning voice filtered through. The song was fabulous. Tina did her own background vocals and I noticed something different about her voice. It was in a slightly deeper style than usual and it really suited her. She rewound the tape and wanted me to hear it a second time. I thought it was brilliant and told her so, then she informed me the song was to be released in a couple of months.

After talking about the song for a while, Tina told me how much she was enjoying herself. 'I've been shopping, and guess what? There's this great thing called a filofax and it's the biggest rage here. I'm bringing some back. Ed, I can't wait for you to see London. It's you. You'll love it!'

Our relationship went on like this for months. Late August, at around two in the morning, my phone rang. 'Ed, are you awake? It's me, Tina.' Characteristically, not waiting for a reply, she said, 'Wake up! I have something to tell you. I met Steve Forbert last night!' Steve Forbert was a pop-folk musician. I absolutely idolised him and Tina really liked his music.

I snapped awake. 'Oh my God, what was he like?'

'He was great, Ed. Lots of people came backstage after my show last night, including David Bowie and Keith Richards.'

Keith Richards later told friends that he found Tina irresistible. 'Well Tina,' I told her, "I think Keith is kinda cute ...'

'Oh, please, Ed. I not going there. No way. Anyway, Steve Forbert was really sweet, like a little boy from Louisiana. He got all flattered when I told him that someday I'm going to do one of his songs. See what you're missing not coming on the road with me?' Click.

When Tina returned home, she threw her hands in the air and said, 'Come on now, Ed. Let's stop this foolishness. It's time for you to come back on the road.'

Allen Zentz and I were putting together some good material but the clockwork of the business was very slow. I was a young artist and had a very long way to go. I took one deep sigh and said, 'Alright.'

'Ed, I'm going to throw you a birthday party. It's just around the corner, on Halloween, so let's make it a fancy dress party. I'll tell everyone that it's a surprise birthday party for you and they're not to breath a word. It's nicer when guests think they've surprised someone.'

As it neared October 31, 1982, Tina came up with a crazy idea. 'Ed, I've got it. I want you to dress up as me!'

'Whut?'

'Yeh, Ed. As me! Use my costumes. All my stuff fits you... some of it looks better on you than it does on me!' Tina's mind ticked away and she kept on improving on the idea. 'Come out as Tina Turner in my normal clothes then disappear and come back in my stage costume and do one of my numbers! That's it! That's what we'll do, Ed!

'We'll get the musicians' wives to dress up as Ikettes. Chip can video the whole thing and it'll be a birthday you'll never forget!'

We spent days trying on everything in her closet, not to mention some of her flashiest stage costumes. When we finally settled on the two sets of clothes I would use, we celebrated. 'Okay, Ed. Remember. Stop at a phone booth and call me so I know exactly when you're arriving. I'll gather everyone together to toast your birthday as I swing open the door. And remember, make sure you act surprised!'

On the way to Tina's that night, I pulled into a petrol station to call her, completely forgetting I was wearing one of her dresses and high, shiny stilettoes, not to mention one of her wigs and full make-up. I'll never forget the looks I got as my high heels clacked on the ground whilst dashing towards the phone. When I finally arrived at the party, I rang the buzzer and the door swung open. More than a hundred people shouted 'Surprise, surprise!' Music started, people laughed and drank while admiring each other's costumes. I had around twenty friends there and Tina invited loads of people she knew within the industry, plus the band and their families. Tina's sons were not present, but Alline and Muh were.

I gathered the wives of the musicians and dragged them to Tina's bedroom where we discreetly changed. The girls dressed as Ikettes and I put on a gold chain dress of Tina's that she had used since the days of performing with Ike. Finally Tina got everyone's attention, saying she had an announcement to make. 'Listen everybody. I have a special treat for you tonight. We all know Ed is my biggest fan. Tonight, for Halloween, he will entertain us along with my musicians' wives. Ladies and gentlemen, put your hands together to welcome, live, Tina Turner and her Ikettes!'

The music started right on cue and the wives and I put on the show of our lives with Tina particularly enjoying the entertainment. I knew all her moves as well as she did, having watched her rehearse and perform night after night. While everyone was shouting and screaming, just as they would do for the real Tina, her mother stood in a corner shaking her head disapprovingly while saying, 'Lord, Lord, Lord. Just lookit that boy! Tsk. Tsk. Tsk.'

Alline turned to her mother and with a cigarette dangling from her lip, she said, 'Ah dun toldya'. Shiiit. That boy dun watches everythang Ann does. He knows Ann's shit betta than she know her own shit. Shit!'

I couldn't help but think of when I was a little boy, looking at Tina on television. I had prayed, way back then, that someday she would be my best friend. Eighteen years on, the lady I had prayed about had thrown me the mother of all birthday parties to celebrate my twenty-six years of life. Tina's own birthday was three weeks away and I wanted to do something special for her. I took her to a new restaurant opened by Cher's ex-husband, Sonny Bono. Tina objected, 'Ed, you can't afford that!' I insisted anyway.

Having known each other in from the old days, Sonny Bono greeted Tina like an old friend. He immediately sent over a bottle of champagne and suggested that he choose the menu. Tina replied, 'I like that, a man taking charge. I'd love for you to do that for us.'

Sonny gave Tina star treatment and the food never stopped coming. Finally Tina begged, 'Sonny, stop it! If I eat another thing, I'll never get back into my dresses and I'll have to blame you!'

They laughed and talked for a while and when it came time to pay the bill, we were informed that it had been taken care of by Sonny Bono with best wishes for Tina on her birthday. Tina asked to see Sonny and when he came to the table, she insisted we should pay the bill. Sonny put on a comical, deep masculine voice, and said, 'Tina, you said you like a man to take charge so I insist we don't argue about this.' We all burst out laughing. Sonny's restaurant became a success story, turning into an exclusive who's who establishment.

A few days later, when I was talking to Allen Zentz, he asked me to put Tina on the phone. She had met him at the Halloween party and they chatted the way people in the industry do. I felt uncomfortable about asking Tina to come to the phone and talk to one of my friends, but Allen insisted. I heard Tina saying to him, 'Yes. Yes. Sure I will. That'll be fine. See you then.'

After she put the phone down, she told me Allen wanted to record one of my songs with me in lead and asked her to sing backing vocals. I nearly fainted, thinking Tina would be furious that someone should ask her to do such a thing. Instead, she warmly smiled and said, 'I told Allen I would. We're doing it in a couple of days. Don't go telling Roger. He'll only get upset with me.'

I couldn't believe my ears. A few days later, I recorded a song called 'Deal Me In' with Tina's amazing voice as background. She had never sang backing vocals on anyone's songs, but, later that night she told me, 'Ed, I'm really proud of you. And that Allen really believes in you. I get a good feeling about him. You're writing some really good songs. Really good. By the way, I'm having that ballad of yours that Allen played for me. I'm going to record that one.'

Mid-December, Tina phoned in a panic. 'Ed, I need some help. I want to get a big Christmas tree. I decided this Christmas I'm going to decorate the house and have all the kids and family over. I'm not going to have the housekeeper cook. I'm not going to have you cook. I'm going to do all the cooking myself.'

'Tina. You know you can't do all that cooking.'

'Okay, Ed. I'll let you help out a little. You can bake some of your wonderful cakes!'

Christmas Eve, while elbow deep in flour, juggling eggs and batter, the phone rang. 'Hi, Ed. It's me, Tina. I've just got the turkey... I've got my turkey. I'm just about to put the turkey in the oven. How do I do it? Do I do it with foil or without foil?'

I didn't even bother to ask if she had taken it out of it's wrapping yet or if she'd even stuffed it. I said, 'Tina, I'm bringing the cakes over later. Why don't you wait until I get there and let me look after the turkey. We can have a glass of wine together.'

'Oh. Okay, Ed.'

I got to Tina's and seasoned and stuffed the turkey. Tina started managing everything, telling me what vegetables she wanted while I gathered them, cleaned and peeled them and prepared them for cooking. Tina also had cornbread, ham and a few Southern soul food goodies. She wanted to do the soul food greens herself, and everytime she nipped out of the kitchen, I added essential seasonings to the bubbling pot. Everytime she came back to taste the broth, she exclaimed, 'It's funny Ed. Everytime I taste this, it just gets better and better! Honey, I told you I know how to cook!' Smiling approvingly, I didn't say a word. With everything cooked, we went down to the tree and she asked me if we should exchange gifts then. I suggested we wait until the following day, promising her I would pop by in the evening because I was spending Christmas day with my family.

After my family Christmas, I went to my friend Michael's at 4 p.m., just as I had originally planned, and we were going to make our rounds visiting and exchanging gifts with mutual friends. While at Michael's, I decided to give Tina a call to see how her family Christmas was going. I could tell straight away that something was wrong. I asked, 'Tina, what's wrong?'

In a quiet voice she replied, 'Ed, no one showed up.'

Her words hit me like an arrow in the heart. I told her I would come right over.

She replied, 'No, Ed. You got all your friends to visit. You're always with me on special days, my birthday and Christmas. You helped me cook all this food. You need some time for yourself and your friends. Don't let them down just because of me.'

I told her, 'I'll go visit all of them then come straight over to you.'

We talked a bit more then she wistfully said, 'You know Ed, maybe because I didn't spend enough time with them, maybe they thought I really wasn't into it. Maybe they thought I wouldn't be that much fun. When I called everyone to invite them, they all said they would be here... but no one came.'

'I'll be over soon, Tina.'

'Listen, Ed. Bring your friend with you, the one you're with now, Michael. He's the one you told me about, an artist or something like that?' I was heartbroken for Tina. She went through so much trouble to have a family Christmas and she had spent the day alone. Now she would be spending the remains of it with me and my buddy Michael, a total stranger. I worried like hell on the way over. She was very down and Michael sat in the passenger seat of the car telling me, 'We're going to Tina Turner's and we're gonna party. Yeh. We're gonna show that lady a good time!'

Michael had an amazing personality, always positive and full of energy. I begged, 'Please, Michael. Tina's not like that. She's really very down at the moment.'

He replied, 'I know, Ed. But by the time we're finished, she's gonna have had the best Christmas she's ever had. Ed, no one should be alone at Christmas, especially Tina Turner.' I kept my thoughts to myself. Tina had reached the point where her kids had to contact her through the office and the gap between her and her family had widened enormously. I wasn't surprised that they had other people they planned to be with at Christmas. The last person they imagined would ask them was their own mother.

We drove up to the house and all the outdoor light decorations were blinking and sparkling. Tina ran out to open the gate and once we stepped through her door, she turned to Michael, shook his hand and said, 'Hello, Michael, I'm Tina.'

Michael's first words were, 'Come on girl. Where's the music?'

Tina stared at him for a moment and said, 'Uhm... okay.'

Michael was so informal, energetic and witty that Tina leaned over and whispered to me, 'He's funny. I like him!' She poured champagne and ended up laughing and dancing within minutes of our arrival.

An hour later, Michael was still playing DJ when Tina confided to me, 'The family, they phoned. Everyone met up at Alline's, started eating and ended up staying there. The kids wanted to see their friends. I told them their gifts were here and they asked if they can come tomorrow. So Ed, everyone is coming tomorrow.'

Michael and I had already eaten three times that day. We nearly fainted when she said, 'Come on, guys, let's eat.' All the food was spread out in heated serving trays where you would walk along and serve yourself. Michael and I loaded our plates with food and ate the entire lot. We just wanted Tina to be happy so we didn't tell her we had had three family lunches already that day! After resting for a while, we ended up dancing and laughing again and partied for another couple of hours. Tina and I exchanged gifts and, as the evening wore on, she seemed tipsy. I suggested she went to bed while Michael and I tidied up. She objected, saying we should just enjoy what was left of the day and she would clean the party mess herself. I tucked her into bed and Michael and I drank a bottle of champagne while clearing away the food and restoring the house to its pristine condition.

The next day, around one in the afternoon, I was woken by the ringing phone. I sleepily answered, 'Hullooo...'

Alline's Southern soul accent burst through the receiver, 'Boy, whereareyooo? We here at Ann's, waitin' to have dinna an' stuff...' Then she lowered her voice and whispered, 'Na' Ah know Ann didn't cook this here dinna.'

I rubbed my eyes and giggled. 'What time is it, Alline?'

'Time to git yo' ass over here.' Then she confided, 'Ya' know we feel so bad about all this stuff... anyha', git yo'self on over here ratna', ya'll hear me boy? Ratna.' Click.

I got to Tina's and the atmosphere was wonderful. The kids were there exchanging gifts with Tina and along with Muh and Alline, we all sat down and ate. Right after lunch, the boys wanted to leave. Always formal with Tina, they each said, 'Love you, mother. Thanks for the gifts.' With just Muh and Alline and her daughter Jackie left, they started telling me loads of stories about Tina's youth and her early days of singing. Tina and I were both creased with laughter at Alline and Muh's memories. After two hours of laughter, Jackie suddenly said to Alline, 'Come on, Muh, there's a party I gotta go to. We gotta get back, na'.'

Alline barked, 'Alright Jackie, naaa.' Yo' have some respect fo' yo' Auntie Ann.'

Tina cut in, 'You know I don't get to see much of you, Jackie.'

Jackie replied, 'But Auntie, I got a party I want to go to. It's time fo' me to blow this mutha.' Tina laughed. Jackie was definitely her mother's daughter.

With Christmas over, Tina had one last gig to play that year. A new club, The Palace, formerly a theatre, was opening opposite Capitol Records. Roger had informed her she had to attend the grand opening as a guest because it was very prestigious. Meantime Tina had some cosmetic dental work done and was fitted with temporary caps. Roger was insistent that Tina attended the party, and only later would we see why her presence was so important.

Tina made it through the party, holding a beautiful handkerchief near her face as she spoke to newsmen, just in case her temporary caps showed. She sailed through the evening without any problems and the next day the papers were full of Tina Turner at the grand opening. This resulted in the club booking Tina for New Year's Eve. Once again, Roger's genius was working. It was a sell-out performance and Tina nearly blew the roof off the club that night. Unbeknown to her, the gig was attended by loads of Capitol Record bigwigs, the same people who had been dragging their feet signing her. Soon after, we were back on the road, and off to Texas once more.

We were happy to be playing Texas because it was a two week booking which meant we could settle in as if it were a second home. Tina and I stayed at the stunning Hyatt Regency Hotel, and the band stayed at a less expensive hotel nearby. Tina's suite was fabulous and modern and I stayed in an adjoining room with communal inner doors, which we would keep open and wander to each other's rooms. We were so comfortable with each other that Tina would stroll in with a face mask on with a towel wrapped round her body while I was brushing my teeth or lying in the bath. Sometimes I would sit in the bathroom while Tina was soaking in a scented bath and we would gossip or lay out our plans for the following day.

Even James Ralston adjusted to our routine. He would spend the night with Tina and early the next morning I would stroll through in my pyjamas while he lay in Tina's bed, stretching out like he was king.

Tina noticed James had been shunning her in favour of going out with the band most nights and Kenny Moore, nosey and observant as ever, picked up on this. He was a real shit stirrer and created lots of dramas in other people's lives as a form of entertainment — but he did it all in good fun. Noticing Tina's uneasy feelings about James' absence from her bed, Kenny chose the perfect moment to wind her up. He sat back in Tina's dressing room, chatting away while I helped prepare her for that evening's performance. He casually blurted out, 'Us boys just love this old town, especially James.'

'Oh, really, Kenny? I'm glad. Uhm, what do you boys like about this place?'

'I'll tell ya' T. There's this club we go to every night. It's jumpin'. We eat an' drink and do all sorts of thangs. It's real good 'cause all the people workin' there know us na'. And there's this real cute waitress always chasin' James around. Anyway, I gotta go get ready for the show. See ya'll later.'

The nightclub was near to the hotel and was like an old fashioned tavern with a live jazz band and easy atmosphere. People dressed in jeans and stetsons stood at the bar knocking back shots of tequila. Others sat at round wooden tables tucking into chicken wings, fries, onion rings and barbecued ribs. It was like something you'd see in an old western movie, a roadside bar where the cowboys would stop, eat, get drunk and have a good old shoot-out.

Almost as if she was angry at herself, she said, 'Why am I so crazy over him? Why? There's something about him...'

'Tina, I told you before and I'll tell you again. I think James, subconsciously, is a little bit predjudiced.'

'Oh, Ed, you just think that because he doesn't understand you and you two are always getting into arguments.'

'Tina, face it. James is from a real white background. This honky white boy isn't gonna fall in love with Tina Turner. The sort of background he's come from almost dictates that white and black people simply aren't supposed to be together.'

'Just watch me, Ed. I'll have James eating out of my hands. You'll see you're not right about that racist stuff.'

Tina had slowly changed over the years. Where she would pursue something in the past, she now felt it should come to her instead. She developed an attitude that she was Tina Turner and she deserved the things she wanted. If it became a struggle, it could go. That's how she felt about James at that moment but the reality was that Tina, for some reason, was addicted to him. She could never cut him out of her life the way she did others.

But it wasn't to be with James Ralston, for he soon fell head over heels for a gorgeous flame-haired dancer called Bernadette. She was astoundingly beautiful with one of the most stunning bodies I had ever seen. She was a brilliant jazz dancer and was totally committed to her profession. James always had a weakness for redheads and Bernadette rocked his world.

Tina knew she had lost James forever.

26

Over a period of time, Tina became very fond of Chip Lightman's fiancée Kathy, an all-American beauty. Kathy was a Beverly Hills girl who knew absolutely everybody. She had a vibrant personality and loads of energy, making her very compatible with Tina. During a two week gig in Las Vegas, Kathy talked Tina into a blind date with a friend of hers called Don. Tina was bringing me on her blind date, so Don brought a mate of his called Chris Kontos.

Tina nervously prepared herself in her suite and when Don and Chris arrived, I introduced myself, made the men comfortable and got them drinks before racing back into Tina's bedroom. I told her, 'Oh, no! This guy Don isn't your type at all!'

'We'll just go out with them for a couple of drinks then make some excuse to leave early.'

'Well, Tina, I don't know about that. Don might not be your type, but the guy with him, Chris, is something you'd die for!' She was suddenly interested. 'Tina, Chris is gorgeous. He's elegant, stunning and has an animal magnetism like you wouldn't believe.'

'No. No. No. Ed, I'm finished with that sort of man. If he's got that sort of charm, I'm really not interested at all. I'm not going, Ed. Go make some excuse...'

I cut her off short. 'You have to go!'

Tina held her finger to her mouth and said, 'Shhh! They'll hear you! Go out there and keep them busy. I'll finish getting ready.'

As much as Tina tried to resist, she and Chris got along like a house on fire and she insisted we leave early, hoping she could forget she ever met Chris. We made the excuse that we had two shows the following night, and politely left. The next morning she told me, 'I couldn't fall asleep last night. I couldn't stop thinking about Chris Kontos. I really have to fight this one off. You really have to help me. Listen, Chris and Don invited us to a club after my show tonight. I want you to call them and say I'm just too tired.'

'Don't do that Tina. They're Kathy's friends. The whole band is going.

EDDY · HAMPTON · ARMANI

You'll be safe. Come on! I promise we won't stay long.'

Tina dressed beautifully after her show and Chris took everyone to a very chic, exclusive Las Vegas club. Meantime Don, who was originally Tina's blind date the night before, took a shine to Lejeune, whose marriage was on the rocks. Don and Chris were big spenders and showed everyone the most fabulous time. Every now and then, Tina glanced over at James Ralston, who was deeply involved with his beautiful new love, Bernadette. By the end of the evening, Chris and Tina were in a world of their own. In the midst of all this, Kenny Moore, who was like a big brother that always bossed me around, ran over, grabbed me and dragged me to the gents. He opened something similar to a woman's compact and nestled in the center was a mountain of beautiful, pearly white cocaine. 'Kenny! I can't do that right now. Not with Tina around. Suppose she notices something different about me?'

Kenny replied, 'Shut up boy, and take yo' medicine.' After I filled my nail with mounds of powder, I snorted it up each nostril before closing the compact. Kenny handed me the box and said, 'When you get back to the table, give it to Don.'

'What? You mean this is Don's stuff?' I knew that if Don was a party boy, then Chris Kontos had to be, as well.

As I left the gents, Kenny warned me, 'Be real discreet.'

I got back to the table and Chip's fiancée Kathy said, 'Come on, Ed, let's dance.'

I whispered, 'I can't, Kathy. I got this thing full of cocaine in my pocket and I'm scared it might spill all over the place!'

'Oh! You have it!' blurted Kathy. 'We been looking for it! Give it to me and come to the bathroom.' I followed Kathy into the ladies' room where again I dug my nail into the product and had myself a bump. Suddenly a security lady knocked on the door, saying, 'Is there a man in there? You must leave the ladies' room immediately.'

I handed the compact to Kathy and fled, stopping for a split second to glance in the mirror to ensure there weren't traces of white powder all over my shiny black nose. During that era, it was actually chic to indulge in cocaine, known as the rich man's drug. When people used the expression, 'I'm gonna go powder my nose', that's exactly what they meant! Don and Chris escorted us back to the hotel and in the foyer, Don slipped a wrap of cocaine into my hand and whispered, 'In case you're not finished partying.'

Tina waltzed past me and paused for a second, giving me a peculiar look, then she walked on. I followed her into the bar where a few members of the band were present and as soon as Kenny Moore saw me, he barked, 'Eddy, man, Ah think you need to go to the bathroom.'

Bewildered, I replied, 'No, I don't.'

He grabbed me by the arm and dragged me out of my seat. 'Yo' goin' to the toilet, boy.' As soon as we got there, he dragged me in front of the mirror and said, 'Look at yo' face.'

To my horror, under my nose and resting on the five o'clock shadow of my

· 236 ·

upper lip were chunky crystals of cocaine with one huge rock dangling out of my hairy nostril. I nearly fainted. I wiped at my face with frantic swipes, while nervously asking, 'Shit, Kenny, do you think Tina saw it?'

'I dunno boy, but yo' ass is finished if she did.'

I had just got back to working on the road with Tina and the last thing I wanted was to lose her again. I stamped my foot in frustration, and with my hands clenched, I shouted 'For *fuck's* sake!'

I returned to my seat, nearly bursting into tears of nerves and noticed Tina chatting happily, looking over at me occasionally while smiling from ear to ear. It was a safe indication that she was none the wiser and I immediately calmed my wretched nerves. When Tina was ready to go to her room, she asked, 'Ed, you have the keys to my suite, yes?'

'Yes, Tina.'

'Okay, I'll see you in the morning.'

It was obvious Chris was going to walk Tina to her room. We had a little code so she could be bailed out if she didn't want him to stay so I asked, 'Should I call you later?'

She dreamily answered, 'No, you don't have to.' With a victorious smile stretched across her face, she walked away arm in arm with the man I knew would become her new love.

The next morning, Miss T was glowing. There was vibrancy in her every word as she gushed, 'Chris walked me to the room and I asked him in but he turned me down! I was so disappointed until he said, "If I go in, I'm not having a cup of coffee, I'm having you."' Tina had a huge smile on her face while adding, 'I told him not to be silly, he could control himself during the space of time it takes to have one drink. He told me he couldn't promise me that. He didn't trust himself but I'll tell you, honey, I'm having him tonight – Ed, I didn't know you did cocaine.'

I nearly fainted on the spot. Sweat leapt off my brow as I blurted, 'Once in a while... I did it before... I mean nothing much...'

She cut me off by asking, 'How long have you been doing it? I've never done it in all my years.'

'Well, I don't know, I mean... I never bought it. I just try it if someone gives it to me.'

She clasped her hands in front of her and with her back like a schoolmistresses, she said, 'Okaaay. You know how I feel about it, don't you?'

'Of course I do, Tina.'

She started waving her hand around dismissively while saying, 'Everybody thinks I'm a fool and that I don't know they're doing it. I know everyone that does it and I know when they're on it. As long as they don't do it when we're due to work, as long as it doesn't interfere with their work and as long as they keep it far away from me, I turn a blind eye.' Tina then named absolutely everyone that did it and she was one hundred percent correct about them all, not leaving one person out. She continued, 'I just want you to know I know you do it. Although I must say I'm surprised. You never seemed to be on it. Don't ever do it around me or when we are working. Just to let you know I know. And Ed, you don't seem to have a problem but if you think you do, I'll get help for you. I'll pay for it.'

It was for reasons like this that I loved her more and more. Tina was nobody's fool. I answered, 'Thanks, Tina. Don't worry. There's not a problem.'

Tina's eyes widened as she said, 'Ed, I couldn't believe you walked through that hotel and sat and ordered drinks with that big rock of cocaine hanging out of your nose.'

I could feel my cheeks heat with embarrassment as I replied, 'Tina! Why didn't you say anything to me?'

She grinned and rolled her eyes to the heavens while explaining, 'Ed, to be honest with you, I was so into Chris that you could have had two tons of cocaine hanging out of your nose and I wouldn't have said anything to you. Honey, I was in another world!'

Romance was rife during those months, not only with Tina and Chris, but also with Kathy and Chip Lightman, who decided to marry in Los Angeles. Tina, who adored the couple, insisted on hosting their wedding. She was grateful that Kathy had brought Chris into her life and wanted to do something special in return. Chip and Kathy were overwhelmed and made all the wedding arrangements to be held at Tina's magnificent home. Meantime Chris returned to his LA home and remained solid with Tina, always calling her when she was on the road and spending every moment with her when she returned.

One day, while making love at his house, Tina and Chris were disturbed by an unexpected guest. They suddenly heard the doorbell ring. The buzzing was followed by the words, 'Chris, it's Mommy.' Then they heard the woman letting herself in with her set of keys. Tina grabbed the covers and pulled them over her head.

Chris' mother walked straight into the bedroom while saying, 'Chris, darling, I was worried about you!'

'Why, Mom?'

'Because you never leave your car sitting in the drive, darling. I was driving past and noticed...'

By this point, Tina was crouched under the covers, holding her hand over her mouth struggling not to burst into laughter. She told me, 'It was the funniest thing ever. There was my fast boyfriend who drives a fast car suddenly being henpecked by his mother. It was hysterical seeing him suddenly turn into a little boy.'

While Tina hid, Chris' mother suddenly said, 'Chris, darling... you look pale. Have you been eating? I'm going to make you some breakfast.' Chris immediately objected but his mother marched off to the kitchen with Chris, dressed in a toweling robe, hot on her heels. He gulped the meal down and persuaded his mother to the door and by the time she left, Tina had been under the covers for nearly an hour.

Over the following couple of months, Tina spent every moment of her spare time preparing for Chip and Kathy's wedding in the finest detail. Being deeply in love herself, she threw herself into the wedding as if it were hers. Just before the wedding, Tina's son Craig was having his Naval graduation and Tina asked me to attend the event with her. Not wanting to look like an old mother, Tina chose her clothes carefully, portraying an image of fresh elegance. She wore a smart trouser suit and very little makeup. The Naval officers gave her star treatment, fussing over constantly and inviting us to take lunch with them at their table.

It was Craig's big day, though, and Tina didn't want to steal his thunder, making every effort to ensure that he was the shining star. She swelled with motherly pride when the officers told Tina that her son Craig was a very good recruit. She got emotional, her eyes filling with tears when she watched Craig graduate. That day, Tina was a mother, her son as proud of her as she was of him. That day, Craig put all their problems behind him and at that moment they were truly mother and son. Before leaving, Tina and Craig held each other closely and their eyes swelled with tears as she whispered, 'Craig... darling.. you know that I love you. I haven't been the best mother but I'd like for us to have a relationship. I want us to spend more time together.'

Craig held her closely and replied, 'Mother, I love you. I know what you've been through.' They said a long, emotional goodbye.

During the drive home, Tina said, 'I haven't been the mother I should have or could have been. It's so hard to work and travel and be a mother at the same time. I know I'm responsible for their lives. The kids suffered because I was away from them a lot. Ed, I didn't know how... I was compromised by Ike and the pressure he put me under to work at the studio all the time. I wished for so many years that I was a better mother. But today... today I'm proud of the mother I was able to be for them.'

Tina saw a roadside diner and asked me to pull in. As we entered the diner, she said, 'In the old days, we lived on food from these places.' We tucked into patty melts, french fries, milkshakes and other fun junk foods, ending the meal with hot apple pie and ice cream. Pushing her plate away, Tina wistfully said, 'If I had it all to do again, I'd do it right. I'd hire a nanny and take the baby on the road with me. I'd love a little girl, like Bernadette, but not as naughty.' I saw a gleam in her eye and my eyebrows raised. I felt she was toying with the idea of trying for a baby.

Back at her house, Tina and I drank two bottles of wine while she reminisced about life on the road and her children, particularly Craig. Suddenly, she stood up and said, 'Ed, I want to show you something.'

We went to the den where she opened a large chest, revealing beautiful silks, linens and satin bedclothes, all made to fit a baby's crib. I gazed at the bedclothes and exclaimed, 'Tina, all these are miniatures of your own bedding.'

She shook her head up and down. 'Yeh, I had them made.' Then she went starry eyed and said, 'Don't you think Chris and I would make a beautiful baby together?'

'Hold on, Tina. Don't you think you're moving a bit fast? Are you using pills or protection of any sort?'

She shook her head back and forth while saying, 'No.'

I covered my mouth in horror and she quickly told me, 'I haven't used precautions. Just nothing ever happened. I simply didn't fall pregnant.' She suddenly looked up and pointed her finger at me while saying, 'I'll absolutely kill you if you tell a soul about what I'm going to show you.'

Tina went downstairs and came back up cradling a baby in her arms. I never sobered up so fast in my life. My heart pounded while wondering where this baby could have come from. I slowly moved to the bundle in her arms and when I gently pulled back the fluffy, soft blanket, I realised it was a very lifelike doll – an exact replica of a newborn baby. We ended up spending the entire evening dressing the doll in a vast assortment of beautiful clothes Tina had bought. She had spent at least $10,000 on baby goods. There were booties, bonnets, rattles, little spoons and even a christening gown. Tina and I ended up on another planet, letting our imaginations run riot, designing a baby room and nanny's quarters on paper. Both of us wore ourselves out, then we hid the baby and its accessories and climbed into our pyjamas. The last thing she said that night was, 'I want just one more. Just one more baby.'

The following day Lejeune arrived for the two day job of preparing Tina's hair. Tina had informed everyone that we would be out of town for a couple of days, affording us absolute privacy to get on with the mammoth, time-consuming task. Suddenly, the door bell rang and Tina barked, 'Who's that? I'm not seeing anyone. Don't answer the door.' The bell rang again and I suggested I'd see who it was, considering no one visited without prior arrangement. In a state of distress, begging to see Tina, was Craig's ex-fiancée Bernadette. Tina said, 'I haven't heard from that girl for at least nine months. Quick, Ed. Let her in.'

I had already removed Tina's old hair wefts and unwoven her tight braids, and she washed and prepared her hair in readiness for Lejeune. While Lejeune started the complex process of re-braiding Tina's hair, Bernadette explained to Tina why she had arrived unannounced. 'I've been dating Michael Jackson's brother, Randy.'

Tina cut her off by saying, 'Bernadette, why do you keep messing with Randy Jackson? And why didn't you phone me and tell me all this stuff before?'

'I haven't called you because Randy is insanely jealous. I mean crazy. Because you and me are so close, he kept accusing me of having an affair with you and said he'd kill me if he found out I saw or spoke to you. I told him you and me are like family and that his accusations were totally untrue. I dunno, he just has this thing in his head.'

Bernadette sipped some water and continued, 'As long as he was still living with his girlfriend things were fine, but as soon as his girlfriend left him and moved out, Randy became more possessive than ever. Once we started being together on a full-time basis, I saw the other side of him. He started grabbing me by the arm and shaking me. He never beat me but I sensed it might happen soon and he really scared me. Anyway, we got in a big argument today and he went all wild-eyed. He walked towards me, looking like he was going to kill me. I got shit scared and ran for my life. And... uhm... here I am.'

Bernadette's eyes were now red from crying, and she asked Tina if she could use the phone.

Tina replied, 'Don't call him! Don't! You poor girl. All I see is me. This is the way I used to be. Why do you want the phone, to ring Randy?'

'Nooo. I won't call him.' She fidgeted for a moment and asked, 'Tina, can I go to the kitchen and get something to eat?'

'Sure, Bernadette, you know where everything is. Make yourself at home.'

As soon as Bernadette stepped out of the room, Tina whispered to Lejeune and me, 'She's not getting anything from the kitchen, she's going to phone Randy. Mark my words. I know... I know because I used to do the same thing with Ike. Just watch the phone, you'll see. The light will go on.'

We all stared at the phone and five seconds later, the button illuminated. Tina slapped her thigh, exclaiming, 'What did I tell you? I knew she'd phone him. I knew it. Poor girl, I used to do the same sad thing with Ike.'

When the light went off, we scampered back to what we were doing so Bernadette wouldn't know we were any the wiser. She walked into the bedroom and everyone started talking, with Tina proudly telling Lejeune and Bernadette about Craig's Naval graduation ceremony the day before. Bernadette, who was still very fond of Craig, held on to Tina's every word of the event. Finally, a little shamefaced, Bernadette looked down at her slim fingers and admitted, 'I.. I phoned Randy when I went to the kitchen.' None of us said a word and her eyes darted at each one of us before she continued, 'Randy's got a lot of emotional problems. His family is crumbling fast. They're all at each others throats since Michael split from the family. And there's some things about Randy that are weird. He's, uhm, a little sick... sexually.'

I fled out of the bathroom with a towel under some dripping strands of hair and Lejeune froze mid-braid while Tina's eyes widened. We all gave Bernadette our undivided attention as she told us of her sex life with Randy. When she told us what he made her do, sexually, we all paled. I actually had to sit down for a moment because the details made me feel ill. I could practically see Tina's skin crawling. Her voice hoarse with distress, she said to Bernadette, 'Why? Girl, why do you go along with it? Why do you do it?' Tina took a few moments to recompose herself but she still sounded a little shocked as she added, 'Bernadette, you have to get rid of that man. You've just got to.'

We were all snapped out of our state of shock by the ringing of the phone. I answered the call to find Randy Jackson on the line and Tina flipped. 'Damn it Bernadette, why did you give that sick bastard my phone number?' Bernadette ran to the kitchen to take the call in privacy while Tina twitched with anger and nerves.

Suddenly we could hear Bernadette screaming, 'Randy, I'm not coming back. You lied and lied and lied to me...' Tina, Lejeune and I tiptoed towards the kitchen, hiding around a corner so we could eavesdrop on every word. Bernadette ranted on then slammed the phone down, leaving us scampering back to the bedroom to retake our positions as if we had been there all along. Bernadette returned to the bedroom shaking, her face twitching with fear. Her voice shaking, she said, 'I can't go back to him. He knows my every movement, he follows and stalks me. I mean, I can come out of a food store or the gym and he'll be there, hiding behind something just watching...' She rubbed the goosebumps on her arms and said, 'He phones around and checks up on me to see if I'm where I said I was going... and he picks and chooses who I'm allowed to see...'

The phone rang again and Tina grabbed it, calmly but firmly stating, 'Do not phone my house again. Bernadette is a guest in my home and I won't have you intruding. She does not want to speak to you tonight and I'm sure you two can sort things out tomorrow. Meantime, you are not welcome to phone my home.' She slammed the receiver down.

An hour and half passed. Suddenly the doorbell rang. We all glanced at each other, I pressed the buzzer, asking who was there. The uninvited visitor replied, 'This is Randy Jackson. Is Bernadette there?'

I replied, 'She's not here. She's left.'

Randy frantically replied, 'I know she's there. I know she is! I've got to see her. I've got to come in.'

Tina threw the towel that was on her lap onto the floor and sprung out of her dressing table seat. She wagged an angry finger at Bernadette while announcing, 'I'm not having this. I'm not having it. Do you understand? This is my house, my home. I went through all this with Ike and I'm not having it again.' She pounced on the intercom button and barked, 'You ring my buzzer one more time and I'll call the police. You are to leave my property immediately.'

Tina slowly paced her bedroom with her arms folded across her chest. I knew she was silently chanting to herself to calm her anger. She let out a few deep breaths and paused in front of the vast sliding glass doors, the light from her bedroom casting her shadow onto the garden of her dream home.

She paused for a moment, enjoying the stunning moonlit view of the tree-filled terracotta pot garden in bloom. Satisfied, she took a few deep breaths and composed herself before rejoining Bernadette, Lejeune and me in her dressing area.

Tina glared disapprovingly at Bernadette, chastising her with her angry eyes as she repositioned herself in front of her large make-up mirror. She was fed up with Bernadette and made no effort to hide her disappointment while making her feelings clear to the girl who was once her son's fiancée. To make her point, Tina lifted her index finger and wagged it furiously, her trademark red nails glistening as she spoke.

'Bernadette, I don't know why you keep messing with these guys. And after all the things you've seen and all the things I've told you.'

As soon as we saw Tina wag her finger, we knew she meant business and knew to stay silent. Bernadette quietly wept and mopped the tears from the corners of her eyes while Tina delivered a stern lecture.

'So why did you bother with him in the first place? Because he's Michael Jackson's brother? That doesn't mean anything. That Randy Jackson's no good! He's like any other man getting their kicks scaring their women. And you put up with him running his mouth all over town saying you and I are lesbian lovers. Who does he think he is?'

Tina's hand reached for a glass of white wine. She took a large sip and pursed her angry lips. 'And you gave him my phone number and address. How *dare* he keep pressing my intercom. If he presses that intercom one more time, I'll call the police. He'd better get off my property.'

I left the dressing area, passed through the large opened partition and walked across Tina's bedroom to the adjoining bathroom to check on the hair I had just coloured and washed. Alone, I listened to Tina as she continued delivering the motherly lecture to Bernadette, nodding my head in agreement.

'Bernadette, let me tell you something, you've got yourself an Ike Turner there. You'd better get rid of him. I know you're scared. Aaagh.' Tina was furious, and she threw her hands up in disgust. 'I know what it's like Bernadette. It's best you stay here tonight. Just make sure you get rid of that Randy Jackson first thing tomorrow.'

But no sooner had Tina spoken, than the noisy shuffling of footsteps could be heard outside. I paused and watched her from across the bedroom. The worry on her face was unmistakable. Bernadette had already scared the daylights out of us with horrifying stories of Randy's violence. Lejeune and Tina remained still and silent as the intrusive sounds outside continued. There was a momentary eeriness, and then, without warning, one of Tina's huge, treasured terracotta pots burst through the glass doors, exploding on impact. Shards of razor-sharp glass sprayed like darts throughout the bedroom. There was soil and terracotta everywhere.

Everything else that followed seemed to happen so quickly.

Randy Jackson leapt through the broken window and paused for a moment, breathing and sweating heavily. Then, as he moved, glass fragments on Tina's plush cream carpet could be heard crunching beneath his hard, determined steps. He seemed possessed, and his wild eyes rapidly scanned the bedroom. It only took a split second to focus on what he had come for. Like an animal stalking prey, he walked towards Bernadette, muttering like a crazy man about how much he loved and needed her. In all the years I had spent with Tina, she had drilled me over and over on certain safety procedures should an intruder gain entry into her home. We had always though if it happened, it would be her ex-husband Ike. On this particular day, we were wrong. Worse still, everyone froze in shock, forgetting Tina's meticulous safety drill.

The only one to spring into action was Tina herself.

She calmly and purposefully walked into the bedroom, where her eyes immediately darted to the framed pictures on her bedside table where she laid her loaded handgun. Without looking away from the table, her hand whipped out with shocking speed and grabbed a second gun — a shotgun — from behind the freestanding oval antique mirror just next to her. She cocked the weapon, then turned and aimed the loaded barrel at Randy Jackson's head. Her body stiff and her aim steady, she said with true determination, 'Freeze, or I'll blow your brains out.'

Randy did stop, but only for a split second. Locking eyes with Tina, he ignored her warning, and lunged for Bernadette. Tina, still several feet away from Randy, raised the gun a blew a hole in the ceiling. Randy, his face a mask of brutality, charged straight at Tina like a raging bull.

Still in total control, Tina moved the barrel slightly to the side and fired towards the doorway. She pointed the gun at Randy. Randy, suddenly terrified, leapt through the broken windows, fleeing for his life.

There was a silence as we all stood, shocked by the scene we had just witnessed. Then Bernadette snapped out of her trance and raced in hot pursuit of her lover. Tina, Lejeune and I stood in stark amazement listening to the voices in the distance. Bernadette's voice was breathless and tearful as she professed her love and loyalty to Randy. Only then did Tina's body start shaking, and, although in shock, she had the presence of mind to press the panic button beside her bed. Like a robot, I handed Tina a white towel which she numbly wrapped around her half-finished head of hair. Lejeune, whom I had rarely seen touch any form of alcohol over the many years I had known her, uncharacteristically swigged straight from the bottle of wine.

Over the next few minutes, none of our eyes met. We couldn't believe what had just happened. Like zombies, we stepped over the debris of the elegant bedroom which now appeared as if a bomb had hit it. Barely able to breathe, we all sat on the bed, completely stunned. It wasn't until we heard the police sirens in the distance that we were jolted back to reality. Tina, still slightly dazed, nervously ran her sweating palms down her thighs, smoothing the fabric of her designer knit sweat suit. She glanced at herself in the mirror and took several deep breaths, calming herself. Then she held her head high and adjusted the towel tightly wrapped over her hair in readiness to deal with the uniformed officers.

After the police took their report and asked Tina if she would press charges, they left us to get on with the task of clearing away the debris, not to mention the fact that we still had a long way to go in finishing Tina's hair. Randy phoned to apologise to Tina but she said, 'I have nothing to say to you. Don't ever use my number again. I have given the police all the details they need to contact you.' Then she put the phone down. Bernadette phoned too, and apologised over and over, begging Tina not to press charges on Randy. While an emergency service busied themselves boarding up and temporarily making safe the door area of Tina's bedroom, Tina coldly told Bernadette on the phone, 'Bernadette, I can no longer have you around me. As long as you have this guy in your life, I don't want to know you.' Goosebumps raced over my arms. I knew when Tina cut a person out of her life, she meant it. I had been the rare exception.

The following day, a man arrived with an envelope with several thousand dollars in it, sent from Randy Jackson to cover expenses due to the damage caused by his breaking and entering. Tina refused the cash, firmly saying, 'I don't do things this way. My assistant will give you my accountant's details and the monies can be sent to them, or a check, and they will give a receipt.'

Tina, after discussing things with Roger, decided not to press charges. Roger very rightly felt that Tina's reputation would be damaged and people might think she was like Ike Turner. By not pressing charges, it did not make the newspapers and the incident became a matter of police record.

Over the next couple of days, we put our lives back in order. Tina put the incident behind her and, along with it, Bernadette became a thing of the past.

27

studied Tina carefully as she buzzed around preparing for Chip and Kathy's wedding. She had changed so much in the years I'd known her. There were certain things that were no longer welcome in her life, the Randy Jackson incident being abrasive and, at this stage of her development, beneath her. It reminded her of the tacky, low-life years she had spent with Ike. Tina was now a woman of elegance and impeccable taste.

Kathy wanted a sweet old-fashioned wedding, but Tina talked her into a modern one. We went through the house with a fine tooth-comb until the house was gleaming. Tina couldn't afford the thousands of dollars it would cost for a professional floral service to supply arrangements so we went to a flower market which supplies the trade. Retailers gathered at the market and we stood amongst them at half past four in the morning, waiting for the bell to ring indicating it was time to trade. As soon as it did, the place went as crazy as Wall Street. We pushed a massive industrial trolley around the market, choosing at trade cost roses, orchids, lilies and other stunning blooms. We loaded the car, packed to the roof and by half past seven in the morning, had the entire lot spread across Tina's lawn.

With hours left before the ceremony, Tina and I panicked and worked our fingers to the bone to create stunning arrangements in time for the wedding. As the sun rose and became stronger, sweat dripped down our bodies into our rubber wellies, mingling with dirt which was stuck to our heavily soiled bodies. We were a shocking mess as the caterers arrived along with hired serving staff. Tina, exhausted, started fading fast and said she had to put her head down for an hour.

I raced home to get my clothes and as soon as I saw my bed, I couldn't resist lying down just for a few short minutes. Next thing I knew, I heard the phone ringing and as I answered it, I saw that several hours had passed. Tina freaked, 'Ed, I been calling you for hours! I left loads of messages!'

'Oh my God, Tina! I fell asleep!'

'Just get here fast, Ed.'

I was racked with panic, thinking Tina might get angry and fire me because I had nodded off. I raced to her house and when I walked in, she quickly ordered, 'Don't talk to me. Just go make sure the flowers are in order, check the hors d'oeuvres, champagne, ice — everything! Go supervise those people while I do my hair.'

I did as she instructed and, forty minutes later, I heard a blood-curdling scream. I knew it was Tina and I dropped the vase of flowers in my hands, shattering it on the floor and fled straight to her bedroom. Tina was gripping her head, tears in her eyes as she stared at her reflection in the mirror. Her hair had turned fluorescent, golden green.

It wasn't a question of removing a wig. Her extensions were hand-sewn to the base of her roots and nothing in the world could make it come loose. Her hair was fucked. She wanted to try a colour enhancer which would make her hair more golden but it had turned bright green instead. I found a bottle of de-toner, applied it to her hair, conditioned it and she jumped in the shower to rinse the concoction out. We were hugely relieved to see her hair had toned down, but when she dried it, the colour changed once again to a clear green with golden highlights. We stared at her reflection in dismay when we heard the doorbell, indicating that the guests had started arriving. We applied the de-toner again and when she rinsed and dried her hair, it had massively improved, turning an ash blonde but still with a hint of green. Tina decided it would have to do. We dressed ourselves and went to receive guests and before we knew it, the ceremony was in full flow.

Tina's eyes swelled with tears as the stunning young couple, Chip and Kathy, took their vows on Tina's vast, flower-filled bridge. Rays of sun kissed the couple and everyone stood in silence on Tina's meticulously manicured lawn, admiring the newlyweds as they were pronounced man and wife.

It was a beautiful sunny day and everyone was happy, enjoying the opulent reception. After the ritual of throwing rice on the newly married couple, Tina noticed her lover, Chris Kontos, was nowhere to be seen. She talked to guests as she worked her way around the inner and outer limits of her vast property, trying to catch sight of Chris. I could see her bite her lip occasionally and once in a while, a familiar look of fear crept into her eyes, and I knew she was suffering from a gnawing gut suspicion that the man she loved was being unfaithful. When she finally did find Chris, they had a small spat then returned to the wedding guests. Tina wanted everyone to know Chris was her man and they spontaneously gave each other a gentle peck on the lips.

With the wedding behind us, we flew to Toronto where Tina was booked to perform. During the entire time there, she talked my ear off about Chris Kontos and when I fell asleep from exhaustion, she'd sit on my bed and ring James Ralston from my phone, talking his ear off too. They had settled into a comfortable friendship with James often giving Tina good, sound advice.

The first couple of days in Toronto, Chris and Tina argued endlessly over the phone, with Tina often left in floods of tears. She lay face down with her head buried in her pillow, crying her eyes out. I touched her gently while her body convulsed from her heavy sobbing. Her words were choked as she pleaded, 'Ed, you've got to help me. Please, please help me...' There wasn't a single thing anyone could do. Realising this, Tina sat up and fought to compose herself, this time losing the battle. Around half an hour later, she wiped her swollen face and said, 'Ed, stay here with me. I know what I need to do and I need moral support.'

Finally she asked me to go to my adjacent room, wait for her and she would fetch me when she was ready. I felt so sorry for Tina. Ten minutes had passed before Tina appeared on my balcony, numbly saying, 'Ed... I did it.. I phoned Chris and broke up with him.'

We walked back to her room and I sat on her bed while saying, 'I thought he was good for you at first but now, considering everything, you know you did the right thing.'

Tina lay comfortably with her head on the pillow, engulfed in a new peace that comes from acceptance. 'Ed, Chris told me everything. He broke down and told me the truth. He's been seeing another girl for months while I was on the road and now it's starting to get serious. He was just waiting for the right time to tell me.' Suddenly, she burst into tears. She wailed for a few minutes then recomposed herself, propped herself up and said, 'Ed, I do pick them, don't I? Here I am, sitting in a hotel on my night off, with no lover and everyone else around me has found happiness. Chip and Kathy are married, James and his girlfriend are sure to do the same, everyone is happy. I've got an ugly habit of loving men who don't love me back. None of my relationships work. I always end up alone and hurt. Forty-three years old and I'm still alone.'

I told her, 'Tina, you are a very special lady and when you're in love, I've never seen anything like it. You really devote yourself to your men and you are unique. The truth is you need someone just like that. A person who's not selfish and who will put their all into a relationship. It's just a question of having the right man. Nothing less will do. Tina, it might sound empty and hollow right now but there is a perfect partner for you somewhere out there. When the time is right, he'll be brought into your life.'

I went to my room where I could hear her crying herself to sleep. I tossed and turned thinking how unfair life had been for Tina when it came to romance. The following day, Tina had recovered enough to be able to control the tears. Her swollen eyes hidden behind sunglasses were the only clue of her heartbreak. Later that day, while she was talking to Roger on the phone, I heard her voice suddenly change to one of jubilation. After she put the phone down, she said, 'Guess what, Ed. Roger gave me some news. Just what I needed. I can get out of the country and give myself a little break. I'm going back to London to record a few more songs. That last recording I did was well received. He got me a gig at an open air concert to cover the cost of his and my travel and expenses. Only me and Roger are going. There's a stage band I'll be using so my guys don't have to go. I can't wait to get away from here.'

'What's the song you're going to record?'

'Oh, it has to do with some arrangement that Heaven 17 made with Roger. I don't know anything about that stuff. Roger and Heaven 17 picked the songs.'

She had only been gone a couple of days when she phoned to tell me, 'I did that open air gig and I'll tell you something, them boys have some funny equipment. Oh yeh, I just finished recording a couple of songs. Remember that old Al Green song, 'Let's Stay Together'? Well, I recorded that one too. It sounds really good. I can't wait for you to hear it!'

Meantime, Roger had a gift for timing and making all the right moves. He rapidly organised a thirty-nine date tour of Europe and the Middle East, leaving in October and returning in December. The Europeans really loved and embraced Tina. It had been decided 'Let's Stay Together' would be released as a single in England in several weeks time and Roger, quick as ever, made sure Tina incorporated the song in her show, familiarising fans with it by the time it received airplay. Thirty-nine dates and extensive travelling meant I had to work my ass off to prepare for the tour. I nearly went grey ensuring we didn't forget to pack something we might need. In the evenings, Tina and I would talk about the direction we hoped our lives would go. She always dreamt of having a home in Paris and I always wanted a home in London.

Suddenly, I made a snap decision. I looked over at Tina and announced, 'I'm not coming back home.'

'What are you talking about, Ed?'

'Tina, at the end of the tour, I'm not coming home. I'm gonna stay in London and pursue a music career.'

'You don't really mean that, do you Ed?'

'Yes, Tina, I do. Right now, I'm still young. I'll never get this chance again.'

When Tina realised she couldn't talk me out of the decision, she threw herself into helping me with my plans. She went as far as arranging my wages so I would have a decent amount of cash left at the end of the tour. We agreed I'd travel as light as possible and leave all my furnishings and belongings in a storage hold in LA. In the midst of all this, she said, 'You know, Ed, I been thinking about it. If I were in your shoes, I'd do exactly the same thing. I guess it would be crazy to let it all pass you by. You know I'll miss you.'

I was in a constant state of excitement, not knowing what would happen when the day came for me to stay in London. I didn't know anyone there but that's where I was determined to chase my dreams. I was attracted to the culture, the fashion, the people. I simply had to do it. While I was home, packing my goods for storage, Tina rang asking, 'Ed, those antique tables I got you for Christmas, don't sell them or store them. I'll have them back

THE · REAL · T

and I'll look after them until you need them again. And, Ed, I've just realised I'm going to have to replace you!'

I went round to Tina's and we put our heads together, coming up with the idea of replacing me with Chip's new wife, Kathy. It was decided she would come on the road with us and learn the ropes, hoping she would be suitable to take over my job when the time came. In the midst of all this, the doorbell went 'Who can that be? No one ever shows up without being invited.'

I pressed the intercom and asked, 'Who is it?'

'Ed, I know that's you. I need to see my mother. It's me, Ronnie.' I told him to wait a minute.

Tina told me, 'Tell Ronnie he knows I'm not seeing him until he's apologised.'

Although Ronnie was just a year younger than me, I spoke to him through the intercom as if he were a child. The previous week, Ronnie had stormed into Tina's house demanding his bass guitar back, which Tina had retrieved from the pawn shop. I gave him Tina's instructions, but he was insistent. I finally told him, 'Your mother is not coming to the door. I think it's best to do as she says.'

He kept pressing the buzzer. Eventually Tina, furious with the constant noise, slammed her hand on the intercom and barked, 'Ronnie. You heard what Ed said. Those are not Ed's words, those are my words. Those are my instructions. Leave right now or I'll call the police.' Back in her bedroom, she snapped, 'These kids will drive me crazy. Every time I look around it's one thing or another.'

She marched to her dressing room and sipped some wine while furiously pacing back and forth. Suddenly she stormed, 'Craig got out of the Navy and I let him stay here. It was constant loud music and he never helped around the house. He turned his room into a complete mess. I had to get him out of here within days of him arriving. We get along better when he's at his place and I'm at mine. I don't know, Ed, the kids just irritate me. They drive me nuts.'

All of a sudden, we could hear rustling in the bushes outside of Tina's bedroom, the noise sending Tina silent. She crept across the bedroom and switched off the lights so no one could see in, then she quietly muttered, 'Oooohhh no.'

Suddenly we heard, 'Mother! Mother!'

Tina switched the lights back on and yelled, 'Ronnie, I told you to go!'

Ronnie was insistent on seeing Tina. 'He's trying to make me open a door. I'm not stupid. As soon as he puts a foot in he'll try to push his way into the house.'

Suddenly she became strong and said, 'After that Randy Jackson business, I'm not having this. This is my house. I'm phoning the police.' And she did.

A few minutes later sirens were blaring and after Tina opened the door to the police, one officer pointed to Ronnie and said to Tina, 'This man says he's your son. Is this true?'

Tina confirmed Ronnie was her son and said he was disturbing her. The officer said, 'I understand. Shall I release him, Miss Turner?'

Tina, with her arms folded across her chest, replied, 'Yes, he is my son, and I won't press charges.' Then the police officers said they could not release Ronnie because he had numerous parking violations. They ended up taking him down to the station. Tina did nothing to help the situation, as she felt a shock like this may help Ronnie take responsibility for his life.

Tina had reached breaking point and couldn't wait to get on the road which would take her as far away as possible from all the recent incidents in her life. Meantime, leading up to the tour, I spent as much time with my family and friends as I could, knowing I wouldn't see them again for a very long time. In the midst of my packing Tina drove to my place to pick up my album collection, all perfectly preserved records of Ike and Tina Turner that I had been collecting since I was eight years old. It was the only complete collection she ever had of her work.

During the week leading up to the tour, I moved into Tina's and attended five going away parties, with everyone wishing me success for my stay in London. Tina was feeling down, and the only time I saw her smile was when she got caught up in the excitement of my planned adventure. I was 28 years old and it was now or never, and Tina did everything she could to provide me with moral support, unselfishly spending hours on end preparing me for the career I was about to embark on.

The night before our departure, Tina said, 'Ed, someone special is coming to Europe with us.'

Taken by surprise, I asked, 'Who?'

She reached behind her and revealed our new travelling companion, her lifelike baby doll. Tina softly said, 'Make sure you pack all the things our new travelling companion will need.' And I did.

Finally, I gave into exhaustion knowing everything was in order. I was able to sleep peacefully knowing Tina, her baby doll and I were thoroughly prepared and ready to travel to Europe and the Middle East the following morning.

We played a few one nighters in Oslo, Stockholm, Luna and Helsinki then flew on to Bahrain where we played the Hilton. Towards the end of November, we flew to Abu Dhabi then Dubai, where we would celebrate Thanksgiving and Tina's birthday. We had a small party in her suite, presenting her with gifts of vases, pots and ornaments made of copper and brass. Throughout, Tina made every effort to be jovial but it was clear she wasn't with us, seeming occasionally to drift deep into her own thoughts. At those moments, when her lips were smiling, her eyes were telling a different story. On Thanksgiving we all gathered in a private dining room adjacent to the hotel restaurant when, out of the blue, someone pulled out a packet of marijuana, saying, 'Can you imagine what the turkey is gonna be like? We better get munchies first or we'll end up not eating at all.' A large joint was rolled and Tina reached over and took it, lighting it and having a few puffs before passing it on. Soon after smoking the joint we all started getting stoned and, thankfully, the food arrived right after.

We all held hands while Tina was saying grace. All of sudden, mid-prayer, she let out a small laugh and said, 'Oh Lord! I can't even bless the table properly... I feel a bit wheezy. I'll tell you one thing, I am starving.' Then she sat down, still holding hands with those on either side of her, and managed to finish saying grace. We tucked into the meal like a pack of wild animals, all fighting to quell our raging munchies. The entire spread of food was devoured.

The next morning, I phoned Tina and asked, 'Are you alright?'

'Ed, quick! Get to my room!'

I let myself into Tina's suite to see her sitting cross-legged in the middle of her bed, rocking back and forth with a big smile on her face. Referring to the marijuana she had smoked, Tina enthused, 'I see why people like that stuff. I had so many amazing dreams last night! I'll tell you, that stuff gave me the munchies and I just couldn't stop laughing. It was fun but I'm not taking it again or I won't be able to control myself laughing, and it hurt my chest!'

While performing in the Hyatt Regency Ballroom in Dubai, we learned top tennis players Vitas Gerulaitis and Björn Borg were in the audience. After the show, the two tennis players arranged to meet Tina and tell her how much they enjoyed the show. Vitas and I got on like a house on fire and easily entertained everyone with great conversation. Tina played music and we laughed and talked when Vitas suddenly whispered, 'I left something in the bathroom for you.' I raced to the bathroom where I found a generous line of cocaine hidden under a tissue. I snorted it, returned to the main room and thanked Vitas for the treat.

Vitas told everyone that after a match, he liked to spend his evenings going to local bars to jam with the musicians. He then said, 'There's no bars here in Dubai, so do you guys want to go downstairs and jam?'

Kenny Moore was on for it. Vitas asked Tina if he could borrow her band and tried to persuade her to come along. She replied, 'I already did my jamming tonight. I need to get some rest. Take my band if you want to but I'm played out.'

Alone with the band in the ballroom, Vitas laid out lines of cocaine for anyone who wished to indulge. The lines disappeared pretty quickly. Vitas and the band jammed then he and I sang together. Revelling in music and laughter, everyone enjoyed themselves until three in the morning.

Around this time we started getting feedback from London informing us that the response was good for 'Let's Stay Together'. This snapped Tina out of her blue mood and she threw herself into her work with fresh enthusiasm. Night after night, I watched her perform that song and each time it seemed as if she was singing it to herself, about herself. The emotion in her voice mesmerised the audience and the song seemed to serve as some sort of release mechanism for the emotional pain she was suffering over the split with Chris Kontos.

We flew to London then went on to Sheffield where Tina was booked to appear on a national pop programme called *The Tube*, hosted by Jools Holland and Paula Yates, former wife of Live Aid hero Bob Geldof and lover of the late Michael Hutchence. Tina was given a fifteen minute set and when she saw members of Heaven 17 had come to see the show, she invited Martin Ware and Greg Walsh to sing back up with Annie and Lejeune when it came time to perform 'Let's Stay Together'. It was a hot number and the public loved the combination of Tina Turner and the heart-throbs from Heaven 17.

The Eurythmics were on the same bill performing a song called 'Sweet Dreams'. Later, while dining, Tina noticed a pretty young girl who kept walking past our table, shyly looking over hoping to get our attention. Tina asked me who the girl was. I explained it was Annie Lennox and that she was a very popular, talented singer. I always had to tell Tina who certain people were. Pop stars were always fascinated with Tina, some even idolising her, which was something Tina couldn't understand at the time. Those people already regarded Tina as a living legend. Soon, the public would also share that view.

The exposure Tina got on *The Tube* proved to be a major turning point, boosting record sales which sent 'Let's Stay Together' soaring into the British pop charts. After a flurry of press interviews and live performances, Tina shot into the top twenty. Tina hadn't had a record success since leaving Ike and the good news left all of us joyfully dazed.

Barrie and Jenny Marshall owned a company called Marshall Arts and they had been Tina's European agents for years. The relationship with Tina and the Marshalls was a close one, all of them being genuinely fond of each other. Tina told me on many occasions that Barrie and Jenny had been very good to her. She arranged for the Marshalls to give me a guiding hand in my quest for stardom after the tour was over. I would be staying in London and, not knowing anyone, I networked like crazy to make contacts and friends. Maggie Ryder, a backing singer with the Eurythmics, offered to help me find accommodation. In a few short days, I had secured several contacts and phone numbers, all of which would make settling into London much easier for me.

Meantime, Roger Davies' adrenalin was pumping. All his hard work was beginning to pay off. We flew to Stockholm, Sweden, Denmark and various parts of Germany then returned to the Bahrain Hilton for a second time. The success of 'Let's Stay Together' came as a surprise for everyone and the venues we were committed to weren't the sort of places to play if you're promoting a record – just hotel banquet rooms, really. While there, Tina gave a journalist permission to interview me about my role as her assistant. Before the interview started, she whispered, 'Just make sure you don't tell him anything about my personal life!'

I ended the interview by telling the journalist, Richard Cohen, that I would be leaving soon to embark on my own career. He would, in later months, contribute to stirring interest in my own live performances. Tina sent Chip into the room to say to the journalist, 'If you are finished with your interview, Miss Turner would like to have Ed back.' We all laughed and I returned to Tina's suite where she was bursting to hear about the interview. When I told her what I said about embarking on my own singing career, Tina quietly commented, 'I wish I loved the business the way you do. I wish I had the enthusiasm. You know, Ed, it's always been work. In the early days it was exciting and I thought there would be a big star on my door but none of them dreams ever came true. I'm just sick of it.'

Surprised by her words, I replied, 'Tina, get with it. You got no time to be sick of it right now. You're gonna get everything you ever dreamed of. You have a hit record in Britain!'

'I know, Ed. Every night I just want to call Chris and play the song to him over the phone. But I can't. I just can't seem to find real happiness.' Tina looked lost and her eyes darkened with sadness. With all the good things that had started to happen, she had no lover that she could share it with.

'Tina, fuck all the men. You got a hit record, you're gonna have more, you'll be a fabulously wealthy superstar. Then you can pick any damn man you want.'

She brightened up and said, 'Ed, you always find a way to make me smile.'

With a hit record, something she hadn't experienced in years, she was still down in the dumps and seemed to focus on her doll the way a child might focus on their favourite old teddy bear. After a while, the baby doll no longer stayed in her suite, with Tina often clutching it in her arms in public. The doll was so realistic that most people thought she was holding a real baby. The band started teasing the doll, with Kenny Moore, of course, usually initiating the games. We all travelled on a tour bus when playing Germany and, after a while, everyone started taking turns holding the baby. They even got broody and mushy over the doll, with Lejeune begging, 'Ahhh, lemme hold the baby.' Then Annie would ask to hold it, then Chip or Kenny Moore.

Everyone noticed the change in Tina and saw that as hard as she tried to be jolly, she had clearly lost her sparkle. With that, everyone agreed that the baby doll somehow worked as a tool to console her over the loss of the only man she ever truly loved. As crazy as it may seem, we all came to adore the baby knowing that it was the only thing that brought Tina any form of comfort. Just like Tina, we all began treating the doll as if it were real, dressing it and putting it down for naps. Once, Kenny Moore asked to hold the baby and when James asked for the doll, Kenny threw it across the bus to him. When the doll went flying, Lejeune and I screamed, and James chastised us by saying, 'Keep the noise down, the baby is trying to sleep.'

Another time, when we arrived at a hotel, I grabbed some hand luggage and asked Tina to nestle the baby in my free arm. Tina objected, 'No! I'll carry the baby!'

I argued, 'I want to carry the baby.'

'No, Ed, it's my baby and I'll carry it.' Sometimes she would say backstage, 'I think the baby should stay in the dressing room, it's too smoky out here and it won't be good for her.' On the occasions the baby wasn't allowed in the wings, Tina would come off stage after the show, I'd dry her off then she'd run straight to the dressing room where the baby lay and pick it up to give it a long, loving cuddle.

Meantime, Tina kept preparing me for my career, giving loads of advice and tips. Finally, we decided that I would have to have a catchy stage name and Lejeune suggested I take the name of my favourite clothes designer, Armani. While on the tourbus, Tina said, 'Fine, from this moment on, you are now Eddy Armani. Now go make an announcement.'

I went to the front of the bus and asked everyone to be quiet because I had an announcement to make. 'As you all know, I shall be leaving soon to embark on my own singing career...' Someone threw a sweet wrapper at me and said, 'Shuuut uuuup.'

'Now, please audience, control yourselves. I want to say that it has been decided that my new name, from this moment on, is Eddy Armani, and I'm to be called by that name at all times.' The band started hissing and booing and throwing things at me. I returned to Tina who was in fits of giggles over the incident and told her, 'Hmm. That went down well!'

Tina told me always to vocalise before a performance, meaning to spend a half hour going through the music scales. My mouth fell open and I said, 'But Tina, in all the years I've known you, I've never seen or heard you vocalise before a performance.'

She waved her hand around and said, 'Please Ed. When you've been singing as many years as I have, you just go on stage, open your mouth and do it. Honey, I haven't vocalised in twenty years but I don't know any other singer that dares not to.'

While in Italy, Tina's Euro promoters Barrie and Jenny Marshall flew out to join us. Over dinner, Tina reminded Jenny, 'Please look after my Ed. You know he's going to need a lot of help getting his career off the ground.' Jenny raised an eyebrow and studied me carefully and from that point on, she took me under her wing.

While in Rome, Tina looked up her ex-lover and old friend, Adrianno, the lovely Italian promoter that loaned Tina money to redecorate her dream home. Tina still owed Adrianno $2,000 and Chip made the arrangements for the cash to be available. She arranged for Adrianno to see her show and afterwards, he raced to her dressing room and swept her into his arms. They were so very happy to see each other. Adrianno, along with his girlfriend, took Tina, Chip, Kathy and me out to dinner. Tina, who absolutely adored Adrianno, joked, 'Adrianno, honey, I'm glad you've got a girlfriend because this tour has been so hard on me that I don't have enough energy left to fight off a man tonight!'

Adrianno had us in stitches, telling us about the time he threw Tina's shoe out of the car and Tina piped in, 'Out of all those shoes you bought me, you never did replace that pair!' We all creased up with laughter. Tina had arranged for Chip to give Adrianno the remainder of the money she owed him. I have never known Tina not to pay back a loan in full, no matter how long it took.

With Tina's record hot as a griddle, Roger and the Marshalls got her booked into a London club called The Venue which was owned by Virgin tycoon Richard Branson. Ticket demand was such that extra dates were added and she packed the place out for four nights running, taking London by storm. Her dressing room was right next to Annie and Lejeune's and she could hear everything they were saying through the thin walls. One night, she heard them complaining to each other about their wages and so forth. Annie said, 'Tina's got a hit record and we don't get shit. We should be enjoying it, too. I think it's time we all got a raise. We should be cashing in on her success, too.'

Chip nervously bopped into Tina's dressing room and came right to the point. 'T, the girls think it's time they had a raise.'

Tina went mental, yelling like a crazed woman. I had never seen her like this before and thought she was actually losing control of her mind. She raged, 'Who do they think they are? I might have prestige right now but the money is not coming in. Who do they think has to pay for their hotels, travel and meals? Me! That's who – yes, me!' I'd seen Tina angry before, but not like this, and I prayed she'd find some happiness soon. Tina's final words on the matter of the girls having a rise were, 'If they keep this up, I won't use *any* girls in my show.'

When Tina makes her mind up, even if it's a snap decision made in anger, she sticks to it. Little did Lejeune and Annie know at the time that it would be their last tour with Tina. Their cards had been marked.

Even though Tina had had European success with 'Let's Stay Together', America refused to push the song. Mid-December 1983, we held an end of tour going away party. Everyone was there from crew, soundmen, dressers, band – the lot. Absolutely everyone involved with the tour was invited. Dave Stewart was there with his singing partner, Annie Lennox, while Tina's dancer, Annie, flirted like mad with a band member from the then hot group, Blondie. Later, Tina sat next to me and said, 'Ed, I'm going to miss you. There won't be anyone else like you. It's unfortunate you're going just when everything is happening for me.' Now that it was really happening, I became terrified. Tina covered my hand with hers and reminded me, 'Don't go getting scared. Just go out there and go for it. This is what you wanted and this has been your dream for a long time. Look at it this way, you travelled the world with me, you learned the business onstage and offstage because of me... Ed, you've been involved with this business since you were just a teenager. You started my first fan club and by the time you were 16 you were night managing Ike's studio. Ed, you got more going for you than most people in this business and now that you're nearly thirty years old, you better dig your heels in before opportunity passes you by. I've had some assistants in my time, Ed, but there will never be another you. Do you know you're the only one I ever sat up all night with talking? I never did that stuff with anyone else. I don't think I ever will. I'm sure there are people out there who can do the job with your efficiency, but no one will ever replace you. There's only one Eddy.'

Jenny Marshall came to the table and asked me to bring in one of my tapes and she would guide me with management and so forth. She was an amazingly kind lady and offered to let me stay in the hotel for an extra couple of days after the band left, giving me enough time to find accommodation without panicking. Tina suddenly said, 'Now listen Jenny, if Ed gives you any problems just call me. I'll get on the phone to him right away. I'm the only one that can put him straight!' We all laughed and talked about plans for my future.

Tina and I posed for goodbye pictures and we became sad as hell. Annie, who was taking the photos, suddenly snapped, 'Stop it you two. No sad faces and no crying. Tina, you got a hit record and Ed, you'll probably have one soon. So be happy!' Tina and I looked at each other and burst out laughing. As she left, Kathy was hot on her heels, just the way I used to be. I watched the scene as they left the party and my insides tightened with sadness.

28

woke up on Christmas Day all alone in a hotel. I phoned Maggie Ryder, the backing vocalist with the Eurythmics and she told me to pack my bags, jump in a taxi and spend Christmas at her family home in Richmond, just outside London. Maggie was a white girl with a black woman's voice and was one of the most successful session singers in London. She introduced me to a girlfriend of hers who lived in London's Wandsworth and I rented a room from her for a couple of months. Maggie tried to guide me, making sure I was immediately clued up on the right places to be seen at and the right functions to attend so I wouldn't waste valuable time hanging out in the wrong places.

Early New Year, my phone rang and when I drowsily answered I heard the familiar words, 'Hi, Ed, it's me, Tina. Happy New Year.'

'Teeenaa! How are you? How was your Christmas?'

'It was a busy Christmas, Ed. I haven't stopped. Now, Ed, you're not getting rid of me that easily. Roger's got me crazy with loads of interviews and live shows. I thought *I* was run off my feet but that Roger Davies, honey, he's the only one I know that works just as hard, if not harder, than me. He got me booked to open for Lionel Richie's new tour! I'm returning to London to record a new album called *Private Dancer* or something like that. Anyway, that Kathy... you'd never believe what happened!'

I had been wondering if Kathy was succeeding in filling my shoes. I settled down to hear Tina talk about my replacement. 'Ed, when I ran offstage for quick change, that girl had me step into two different shoes!'

I burst out laughing. Tina added, 'Ed, Kathy is sweet and all but a lot is happening now and I'm gonna need you while I'm in London. I know you have your career plans but if you don't mind taking a couple of weeks off for me, I'd really appreciate it. Besides, I miss you.'

'Tina, I can't wait!'

During the two months that I hadn't seen Tina, Jenny Marshall had listened to my tapes and she and husband had decided to manage me. Jenny told me, 'We simply can't throw you out there to the wolves.' I later found out that Tina had made an arrangement that if I went broke or lost my way, she would cover my costs. She had also stipulated that I wasn't to know about this arrangement. Jenny rang to inform me that it was decided that my material was too American and it wasn't for the British market. I wrote a selection of new songs, which she approved of and responded by arranging for me to record them. After the recordings were completed, Jonny listened to the tapes and said she and her husband would now try to get me a record deal. A few days before Tina was due in London, Jenny phoned again, this time to make arrangements for me to work with Tina. She said, 'I just spoke to Tina and she wants you to contact her as soon as she gets in. She has loads of things for you to do. Eddy, I think you're going to be very busy so I wouldn't make any plans for the next couple of weeks. Oh, Tina also said she needs you to make a wig or something. Got a pen? Write this down. She'll be staying at the St. James in Mayfair.'

I was amazed. The St. James was a hotel which catered to the world's wealthiest people, and the fact that Tina was booked in there indicated that things were going in the right direction for her. I phoned the St. James on the day Tina was due to arrive and left my phone number and a message for her. Two hours later, my phone rang. 'Hi, Ed, it's me, Tina. Ed, I'm exhausted. I spoke with Jenny and she told me you've been very busy and I hate to do this to you, but I need you. I'm really tired so I'm going to rest tonight. Come here at ten in the morning and we'll have coffee together.'

I arrived at Tina's suite at the St. James and it was manic. Roger was examining new sets of pictures that had been taken of Tina and there were cassettes everywhere – new songs Roger and Tina had to listen to. There were several stylists in the room who brought a vast array of designer clothes. Tina had to choose outfits for photo shoots and so on. Roger and Tina gave me a huge list of errands to run, things which catered to their personal and business needs. Tina said, 'It's lucky that you've been living here for a couple of months. You know your way around. It makes things a lot easier.'

The days passed quickly, with Tina buzzing around recording songs, doing interviews and having several business meetings. I barely saw her for the first week. I was in her suite when she raced in, threw a tape my way and asked me to put it on so she could hear it. Then she jumped in the shower – she was so busy that she could listen to a new song only if it was played while she was showering. While stepping out of the shower, she said, 'Ed, call Alline in Los Angeles. Tell her she has to run out and buy some things for me and have them sent over by courier. I need some new wigs, Ed. Get Alline to buy the hair and all the other stuff we need to make my wigs. I want all the stuff here by tomorrow then you can make a couple for me. I want you to start the second the package arrives.'

I told her it wouldn't be a problem, but my fingers got sore just thinking of the task that lay ahead. Whenever I made wigs for Tina, my fingers would bruise and my nails would bleed, it was such a difficult job. She broke my thoughts by saying, 'Ed, I've got a photo session to do. I'm really excited. It's with a top photographer and it's going to be really special. It's for the album cover. Listen Ed, it looks like I'll be here for another three weeks. There's a lot we have to do. I've been working really hard and I'm going to take a day off. I'll let you know when I can do it then you can stay the night and we can gas until the sun comes up.'

I was over the moon. We hadn't had a good session in ages.

A few days later, as soon as I arrived, Roger Davies grabbed me by the arm and dragged me to a room to look at the delivery of Tina's new photos. They were incredible. Suddenly Tina came through and said, 'I thought I heard Ed's voice. Ed, come with me. I've got something to show you.'

As soon as we got into her bedroom, she said, 'Ed, quick, ya' gotta hear this! Don't let Roger in, I'm not meant to let anyone hear this at all!'

The first song on the tape was called 'What's Love Got To Do With It?'

Tina said, 'I don't want you to say anything yet. Just listen to all of it before you say anything.' With my ear tuned in to the London scene, I knew she had cut a great tune. I raised my eyebrows at Tina and she looked away. Next was a tune called 'Private Dancer'.

'I want to make a million dollars
I wanna live out by the sea
I want a husband
And I want a family'

The hairs rose on my arms. Those words perfectly reflected something she had been telling me for nearly fifteen years. Everything on there was her dream. She saw my expression and said, 'I know, I know...'

Next was 'Steel Claw' and Tina jumped around the room singing to the song. She didn't like a line in the second verse and changed it by putting my name in it. I burst out laughing when I heard it and she winked while saying, 'A little treat for you, Ed.'

After listening to the entire tape, I told Tina, 'Okay. This is what I think. "What's Love Got To Do With It" is going to be your biggest hit.'

'But I hate it. I can't stand the song. Roger literally forced me to do it, I hated it that much. I did three takes with Roger staring at me through the control room. I was so mad that I was singing it that while I did it, I just stared up at Roger and made my voice like gravel like I was telling him off while singing. And you know something funny? Them boys in the control booth went wild. They loved it. They told me they didn't know I could sing like that and why didn't I ever use that style before. It only came out that way because I was having a dig at Roger while singing.' Tina was totally disappointed that I rated the song so highly.

Apart from Roger, the producers and Tina, I was the only one to hear the tracks before they were sent to EMI Europe. Tina said, 'Tomorrow I'm recording a song called "I Can't Stand The Rain." I decided to sing it like that white guy you like, you know, the one that sings like a black man.'

'You mean Paul Young?'

'Yes, that's him. Paul Young.'

We drank champagne and much to my surprise, Tina lapsed into talking about Chris Kontos again. With all the things happening in her life, she still couldn't get that man out from under her skin.

Finally, at one in the morning, Roger chucked me out by saying, 'If Tina talks any more, she'll end up without a voice. And she's going to be needing that voice tomorrow!'

A week before Tina was due to leave, she said, 'Ed, that day off that I've been looking forward to, well I'm doing it tomorrow. Why don't you stay tonight, here in my suite, and we'll have dinner and do whatever we want to. I'm not going to budge or lift a finger tomorrow. I'm just going to rest.'

'Sounds good to me, Tina.'

She was dying for me to try a new dish she had discovered at the St. James, a treat called Potato Beluga. She ordered room service and I marvelled at the dish she had talked so much of. It was a baked potato, which had been spooned out and mashed with sour cream and herbs, then restuffed back into the whole skin and topped with a generous heap of beluga caviar. The cap of the potato lay on the side, also topped with a mound of caviar. It was the most gorgeous thing I had ever tasted. Tina and I kept making pleasurable noises with each bite of potato until finally, we both realised we sounded like we were having a major session of low-down dirty sex. Realising what our moaning and groaning noises sounded like, we burst into a fit of laughter.

We drank and ate and laughed just like old times, easily slipping back into our old routine. We sipped our glasses of champagne and I said, 'Tina, girl, you are living the life... look at you, the best hotel, eating potatoes worth $100 each and drinking the finest champagne... alright, missy!'

Afterwards we looked through the final selection of photographs for her planned album cover, taken by top photographer Brian Aris. Tina said, 'What do you think of the new make-up? Interesting, isn't it? You know how funny I am about make-up artists. Well this time, I threw the rag in and let the make-up girl, Sue Mann, do what she wanted and it was the best decision I made.'

While studying the pictures, Tina added, 'To show my appreciation to Sue Mann, I've invited her and her fiancée Jeff Banks to dinner. Jeff's in the clothing business. Kathy will be there too so why don't you join us? It's at the end of the week.'

The next morning, I showered and borrowed a pair of Tina's jeans and a jumper and went off to rehearse with a new band that Barrie Marshall had put together for me. A man called Eric Robinson who worked with Sylvester, The Weather Girls and Patti LaBelle, conducted the band for me. We rehearsed the first day and the second day we recorded a song and the week passed quickly.

I lifted my ringing phone to hear the words, 'Hi Ed, it's me, Tina. Listen. Dress really great. The St. James Club here in the hotel is really grand. It's for the richest of the rich, you know what the English are like, darling, very classy.' I arrived and Tina, Kathy and I went to the restaurant where I met Sue Mann and her fiancée Jeff Banks. We got through three bottles of champagne and the most lovely food I had ever tasted. Tina seemed a bit down and she whispered, 'See what Chris Kontos is missing...' She still hadn't gotten over him.

Everyone was laughing and joking while Tina slipped into a morose mood, the champagne making it worse. She started acting a bit of a fool, then out of the blue, she started criticising me. She blurted, 'Ed, here, so knowledgeable about everything, predicts I'm going to have a big hit.' I shot her a look of annoyance.

Everyone was interested in what I was saying about my own recording session when all of a sudden she started having a dig at me and got a bit ugly about it. Her voice got very loud as she sarcastically slurred, 'Ed here is gonna be the new Tina Turner, aren't you Ed? And every song you pick is gonna be perfect, just like you predict. "What's Love Got To Do With It?" is gonna be my biggest hit. I hope you don't make big mistakes with your own predictions, Mr Know-It-All. You know nothing.'

A deathly silence followed. All of a sudden Tina snapped out of it and waved her hand dismissively while saying, 'Oh, Ed, don't be silly. You know I didn't mean it.'

We went to her room and I told her I was leaving. She asked me to stay but I objected by saying, 'Tina, I'm a grown man now. I can't be the way you want me to be and do the things you want me to do any more. I have to go now.'

'But Ed, sometimes I just get so mad. Sometimes I get so angry.'

I felt sorry for her. We held each other for a long time, then I left Kathy to put her to bed.

Tina returned to the States to prepare to tour with Lionel Richie. He was rocking the world with hits and had been nominated for several Grammys. While Tina was touring with Lionel, I recorded my song 'Pain', and another called 'Joke' which I wrote with Mars Bonfire. I had a three day deal with the studio and much to my horror, I lost my voice for the first two days. By some miracle, on the third day, my voice returned when I had to record and within an hour of finishing, it had vanished again. A man came in from a studio next door and told me he was A&R for Zomba Records, part of a company which had Def Leppard and other known bands. With my voice gone, I wrote down the number for Marshall Arts and told him to contact them. I tried a remedy Stevie Wonder uses when he loses his voice. He mixes a teaspoon of cayenne pepper with hot water and gargles with it. I tried it and it didn't work. A few days later, my voice started slowly returning. Up to that point, all my communication was in sign language.

Zomba Records decided they wanted to record 'Pain' and contacted Marshall Arts. For some reason, Barrie decided it wasn't a good idea and put them off. This left me feeling fairly depressed and I seized a chance to search further afield after I had a call from America. It was my old friend Helena Springs, lover of Bob Dylan and Robert De Niro. She told me she had decided to move to Germany, and two weeks later I was on my way to Munich to stay with her. I discussed it with Barrie and Jenny Marshall and they both thought it was a good idea for me to go make contacts in Germany. In a sense, I felt I was in the way because they had so much to concentrate on with Tina and her movements. Barrie and Jenny were the hardest working couple I had ever met. They handled everything themselves when it came to looking after their working artists. I felt that with the excitement of Tina's recent hit, they didn't have enough time to concentrate on me. I was still very inexperienced, but I felt when things started working, they would put the same sort of time into me.

I was only living on £100 a week so rather than fly, I took economical transport to Germany – a train. The journey was stuffy and dirty, a far cry from the limousines and flights I took with Tina. Meantime Tina was getting great reviews from touring with Lionel Richie. Her new show was hot and every time I turned on the radio or opened a magazine, I seemed to read or hear something about Tina Turner. I finally reached Helena's apartment and, after the nightmare journey, I was looking forward to the comfort of her home. When she opened the door, I got the shock of my life. Her apartment was made up of one single room with a small kitchenette inside. The only other room was the bathroom. And she had her daughter there, too. I wondered how we would all manage to stay in that one room but I was grateful to Helena for inviting me. I was only going to be there for two weeks and I knew we would manage. We were family, and terribly close.

One thing I learned straight away was that the Germans loved black recording artists. While there, I went to museums, film premières and, having bumped into two people I knew from the States, I ended up going to a lot of swish restaurants. During my whirlwind of socialising, I met a man called Jürgen Marcus who owned his own recording studios and churned out many European hits. After he listened to my demos, he asked me to write some new material and record new demos in his studios. I kept Marshall Arts informed of my movements. During my third week in Germany, Ariola Records heard my new demo and wanted to strike a recording deal. They contacted Marshall Arts and Barrie wasn't happy about it. He explained to me that he wanted me to get a British record deal because it was more prestigious. He then told me that Tina's new songs were getting airplay in England and the response was very positive. I smiled to myself, remembering that I had heard those songs in the privacy of Tina's suite before anyone else did.

After speaking with Ariola Records, Barrie agreed to a new photo session, new demos and new songs, all to be put together in Germany.

Boy George was very big at the time and because of him, the trend for male pop artists wearing make-up became very fashionable. I created an amazing outfit for the photo shoot. I wore Maud Frizon boots and black fishnets under torn, leather jeans. My hair was wild and my eyes were enlarged with eyeliner – the photos made me look like a cross between Prince and Billy Idol. The record company told me I was the first black artist they had worked with that was able to step into the style of white boy's rock 'n' roll. But, after all the work recording and sitting for photo sessions, Barrie still wouldn't make a deal with Ariola.

I ran out of money, had no income at all and had hit rock bottom when former Ikette, Judy Cheeks, asked me to stay with her for a month and help her out as a stylist. She was another black American artist who had made it very big in Germany. I moved into her flat and came down to earth with an almighty bump. I ended up being her maid and servant for a month. I cleaned and cooked for her as well as helped her with her hair and make-up on a daily basis. I realised she wanted me to be to her what I was to Tina. But I couldn't do that for anyone else at that time. If that's what I wanted to do, I would have still been with Tina. Not only that, I loved Tina enough to pamper her the way I did and I wasn't exactly in love with Judy. I had my head under the bathwater one morning and when I sat up and suddenly wondered what I was doing with my life. I wanted a singing career, not a career as Judy's servant in Germany. I packed up and moved into an empty apartment that Jürgen Marcus owned.

Meantime Tina was doing her thing on the Lionel tour and was working like mad putting a new band together for a tour of her own. Her *Private Dancer* album was about to be released; the tour would be without Annie and Lejeune, and included a few new band members. After a few weeks in Jürgen's empty apartment, I felt terribly lonely and phoned Tina. When she answered, I burst out crying. I told her everything that had happened, that I was broke and lonely. Tina, solid as ever, gave me the encouragement I needed to keep going. I packed my bags and returned to London.

Jenny Marshall arranged for me to live in a furnished flat in Kilburn, North London. Once in London, I was determined to make it, for myself and for Tina because she encouraged me and believed in me. I had set out to climb a hill a few months before and suddenly it had turned into a mountain. I thought about Tina's success and hard work and determination and it gave me further encouragement that I needed not to fall apart. I got a band together with James Holloway on keyboards. James was formerly with Alison Moyet and Leo Sayer. I had Glenn Matlock, former bass player for the Sex Pistols, and James Stevenson on guitar, formerly with Generation X and The Cult. We rehearsed ourselves to death and got our very first gig at a pub called the Ad Lib. I burst onto the stage wearing black leather cut off shorts, fishnets, an American tank top and a jean jacket. Introduced as Eddy Armani and his band, the music started and I sang Hot Chocolate's tune, 'You Sexy Thing'. The revellers went wild and I did the most outrageous show imaginable. It was a huge success and I sat in my dressing room, basking in the glory, all alone just wishing I could share that moment with Tina.

I knew then I had graduated from the school of Tina Turner. People started filling my room, telling me how great the show was, and what made it special was when Barrie and Jenny Marshall walked in and said they were very proud of me. They told me they had hired someone who would act as my road manager and would tour with me. His name was Nic Cooper. With Tina's tour being set up, Barrie and Jenny had their work cut out. I was no longer worried that they had no time to devote to me because they had hired Nic which gave me the confidence that in time, things would work out. I played several gigs and started getting good reviews, then I stopped to record another song.

I phoned Jenny Marshall to keep her informed of what I was doing and she told me, 'Tina is in town and she's been trying to get hold of you. Call her straight away at the St. James Club.'

When Tina answered her phone, I could hear loads of noises in the background. It sounded like there was total mayhem in her suite, with busy people doing several things at once. She said, 'Hi Ed. How are you?' Not waiting for a reply, she continued, 'I need you. I want you to work for me as my personal assistant while I'm here. Can you come over right now?' I was thrilled with the idea of seeing Tina after six long months and when I walked into her suite, she looked ravishing.

She pulled me straight into her bedroom and told me, 'There's no more Kathy or Chip Lightman. Kathy told Chip he should be on a percentage and when the idea was turned down, things just didn't work out anymore. Chip had to leave and of course, his wife went with him.'

We gossiped a bit longer, then Tina explained she urgently needed a new wig and handed all the supplies.

She laughed and said, 'Ed, I'm so excited about playing the NEC in Birmingham. I can't wait. It's such a big venue. Remember that musician you liked, the one from Canada, Bryan Adams... well he's opening for me on my tour! Can you believe it? And I'm gonna be playing the places that the Stones and David Bowie play. It's really happening, Ed. It's really happening. They'll all be coming to me now instead of me going to them.'

We talked for another four hours before she finally said, 'Well Ed. The next time I see you I will be in Birmingham. By the way, it's going to be taped live. Oh yeh, I got some things for you.' Tina always had gifts for me. She gave me a denim jacket, some Armani teeshirts and £200 cash to cover my expenses while working for her.

Jenny Marshall and I travelled to Birmingham together by train. While taking a taxi to Victoria train station, she told me, 'We have to stop and pick up a large order of sushi. Tina phoned and asked me to get it for her and David Bowie. By the way, she told me to tell you she rehired Ann Cain to look after her house in Los Angeles.' I wasn't surprised.

We walked into the NEC to find the place crawling with cameramen, lighting guys, men with walkie talkies and mobile phones. There were cameras and wires everywhere. Tina was jumping around on stage with Kenny Moore, and when she twirled and saw me, she raced straight off the stage right into my arms. Like a little girl, she suddenly asked, 'What do you have for me? What's in that bag?'

'Your wig.'

Tina peeped in the bag and jumped back, gasping, 'I can't fit all that on my head. That's a lot of hair!'

'Trust me, Tina. It's a new look.'

We got to her dressing room where she immediately removed her wig and popped the new one I made on, pinning it down tightly. She spent a good few minutes staring at the hair at every angle imaginable. Life had become a lot easier for her since she gave up wearing hairweaves. They took days to put in and wigs were a fast, easy option now that she no longer had enough spare time to have her head weaved. After scrutinising the wig, her eyes began to sparkle and she grinned from ear to ear while saying, 'Ed, how am I going to wear all this hair?'

It looked amazing. Up to this point, everybody saw Tina with straight hair. The wig I made was just a massive mound of layers and layers of blonde hair, slightly wavy, very shaggy and very big. It was a totally new look. Jenny Marshall came in, took one look at Tina and enthusiastically agreed that it was amazing. Tina leapt up and said, 'Let's go. Let's see the reaction out there.'

She walked past the stage and Kenny Moore yelled, 'Yo! Teee!' Tina glanced over and Kenny sucked in his cheeks and soulfully murmured, 'Uhmmmm Hhmmmmmmm.' That was an old Southern expression that said a million words.

Tina beamed and I became overwhelmed with pride that her great new look was my innovation. I glanced around and noticed how many people in her staff had changed. She had a new girl called Jenny Bolton who was training to take over Kathy's position. As I studied all the new people, I realised Kenny Moore and I were the only black faces around. I looked at Tina and for some reason, didn't count her as black anymore. She was totally comfortable in that environment. Tina sang a song with Bryan Adams, then with David Bowie, then she ran through a couple of numbers on her own. As I watched her, I remembered when she used to get invited onstage by the big boys, and now they were going up to join Tina.

After rehearsals, we returned to Tina's dressing room and loads of people followed. There was a two hour break before the next rehearsal so everyone decided to hang around. David Bowie came in and we were reintroduced; Bryan Adams and I had a nice long chat and, after a while, it felt like a class reunion. Suddenly a photographer asked for Tina, David Bowie, Bryan Adams and Paul Young, who had played at the NEC the night before and had hung around to catch Tina, to pose for a photograph. They all settled onto a long settee, and Tina layed across like Cleopatra over three hunky rock stars. She tilted her head back while David Bowie fed her grapes. It was wildly erotic with David running the grapes over Tina's red lips and Tina licking at them with her pink tongue.

After the next rehearsal, a few of us retired to Tina's suite. Paul Young, who had seen my show at Crazy Larry's in London, told Tina how wonderful my act was. She winked at me and said, 'You'll make it, Ed.' I felt proud that a recording artist of Paul's stature took the time to compliment me. As the champagne flowed, everyone got tipsy, and Tina and David Bowie started flirting with each other. She was fashionably dressed in knee-high socks, little boots, suede shorts rolled up around her thighs and an oversized button-up shirt which was completely open but tucked in at the waist, revealing a sexy little crop top underneath. She looked stunning and oozed sex appeal, looking more delicious because of her wild, abandoned hairstyle.

She kept flicking her new hair and letting the shoulder of her shirt slip, which was sending Bowie wild. Tina and David were flirtatiously debating a song by a group called Foreigner, and they became so loud, that everyone was listening to the friendly debate. Tina loudly said, 'No, no, no. This is how it is, David. That song is about sex. Just getting out there and doing it. It's about sex.'

Bryan Adam's mouth fell open. He was a gentleman and very well-mannered and found the whole exchange somewhat shocking. Paul Young, who was a bit quiet by nature, went totally silent. David glanced over and upon spotting the stunned duo, broke into a broad, naughty grin.

Bryan stood up, thanked Tina for the wonderful evening and said he had to rest up for the taping. Paul said his goodbyes and told Tina he was looking forward to the show. I was working assisting Tina, but her new official assistant, Jenny Bolton, started preparing the suite so Tina could retire to sleep. I heard Tina say, 'Noooo, David. You have to go now.'

David left and I tidied up the suite before bidding Tina goodnight. As I was leaving, I said, 'Tina, honey, I have worked today. Since I arrived I haven't stopped. I'm dying to get my head on a pillow.'

Tina, applying moisturiser to her face, said, 'Ed, I really need you right now. I really need this favour. They just can't get it about quick change. Look at it, Ed. I've got Jenny Bolton as my personal assistant. I got a dresser called Teamer and between them both, they can't get it right. You did more work than both those people put together and nothing ever went wrong. I never had to ask you for a thing. You knew everything I needed and when I needed it. Nobody can seem to get it right.'

'Hey, don't worry Tina. I'm here.'

'Okay, Ed. Tomorrow I want you to do the costume change. Don't let anyone help you. Set it up just the way you used to in the old days. I know you've already been through my costumes. I need you Ed.'

We kissed each other on both cheeks and I returned to my room where I fell into an exhausted sleep.

The next morning, my phone was ringing off the wall. 'Hi, Ed. It's me. Tina. Don't bother taking off your pyjamas. You have to come to my room right now!' Click.

I raced over in pyjamas and slippers and when I got to her room, she was already standing there with the door wide open. 'Hurry, Ed. Come in, come in. I've ordered breakfast already. Shut up! Let me tell you what happened! After you left, I went through my routine then took off my wig and put it in the bathroom. Then the doorbell went and I thought, "I bet that's Ed. What does he want now." Thinking it was you, I didn't bother putting my wig back on and I was just about to swing the door open when some funny instinct stopped me. I asked who it was and the visitor said, "David Bowie." I said, "Just a minute". I tore back to the bathroom and pinned one of my spare wigs on then I answered the door. David stood there saying, "I want you now." I told him it was late but he said he had to have me. I thought, "Oh no". Anyway, I just gave up. I told him, "You want it. Fine. Come in. Let's do it now."

I drew my hands to my face and let out a scream.

Tina continued, 'Honey, that boy worked overtime and I had to do everything to not burst out laughing. I wasn't into it at all but when he got going, I started getting interested. You know I've never been attracted to David but I'll tell you what, it wasn't bad. After, he went to take a shower and I lay here in bed thinking, "I can't believe I just did that!"

Then Tina started laughing and added, 'I heard the shower water stop, then two minutes later he walks out stark naked wearing that great wig you just made me! He started singing "Rolling On The River" and was dancing like me and shaking a tail feather. I was curled up on the bed in stitches. Imagine that. Me and David Bowie ...'

I quickly replied, 'Well honey, I'm glad!' Then we both burst into laughter.

We reached the NEC where Tina gave her band a pep talk, telling them, 'Focus only on me and follow my lead and Kenny's cues. Don't let the audience control you. Watch me, not them. Remember, the cameras will be on us. Be happy and look like you're having a really good time.'

The show was about to begin and Tina was being announced to the audience when she suddenly turned to me and asked, 'Ed, how do I look?'

'Fantastic!'

'Well, Ed, that's how I feel.' She raced onto the stage and sang like I never heard before. She looked fresh, young, new and her songs were absolutely amazing. She flew offstage for quick change and I forcefully shoved a crowd of people out of the way. I peeled her dress off and slipped her into a hot number made of black leather that was so tight it looked like stretched PVC. I dried her face, put fresh lipstick on, and gave her a traditional push back onto the stage.

When Tina did her duet with David Bowie, the whole audience broke into applause. David appeared at the top of a long flight of stairs on the stage and Tina turned his way and looked at him lustfully.

After the NEC, Tina was hot. She made the cover of *People* magazine, and was nominated for several Grammys. Meantime, I returned to my own shows and played several London hotspots, resulting in a half hour slot on

London's Capital Radio. When I did my slot, Capital's phone lines didn't stop ringing. But it wasn't long before Jenny Marshall informed me that I would have to leave the country for a minimum of three weeks so as to not contravene Home Office rulings. If I didn't do this, I would have overstayed my agreed visiting time and would have great difficulty in the future gaining entrance into England.

I decided to return to LA to visit my family.

Tina contacted me from abroad and said, 'Ed, will you be in LA for a while? Don't leave yet. I want you to come to the Grammys with me. I want you there to assist me. I'm going to do my make-up myself, but I just want you there. I have a feeling this is going to be my year.'

'Girl, it better be. Look at the facts. "What's Love Got To Do With It" hit number one and you got another climbing the charts.'

On the night of the Grammys, I dressed fabulously and worked my ass off backstage. I had never seen so many famous people in one place in my life. Prince, Bruce Springsteen and other greats all had nominations that year and everyone's entourage, family and friends were packed in the private area. Tina arrived in a fabulous long black fur coat, and Roger immediately escorted her to assorted different rooms for quick interviews which would be broadcast before and after the Grammys. Tina spotted me, gave me a huge hug then threw her huge fur coat into my arms. From that point on, I trailed her like a shadow. Everyone surrounded Tina as she worked her way to her dressing room, saying things like, 'I'm so happy for you.' and 'It's great to have you back'. It was clear that Tina was the star and it was her night.

I helped her get dressed and suddenly there was a knock at the door. It was Tina's date, Richard Perry, one of LA's most elegant bachelors, looking utterly dashing and distinguished. With Richard was Steve Bower who played opposite Al Pacino in *Scarface*. Linked arm in arm with him was his new wife, actress Melanie Griffith, as cute as a button with her soft voice and fabulous body. Tina was as polite as she could be as she shook Melanie and Steve's hand, but it was clear that her spirit was somewhere else. I ran around gathering items she needed when there was another knock at the door. It was Tina's son Craig. She introduced him to the other guests and then went about preparing for her performance. Craig, shy and retiring, really didn't fit in. After standing on his own for ten minutes, he said, 'Mother, I'm going to take my seat so I can watch the show.'

'Alright, darling.'

Craig kissed the air by Tina's cheek and before departing, saying, 'Good luck, Mother.'

Tina stood and looked at herself. She was wearing a bright red, figure-hugging, glitter-beaded dress. She slipped high, black stilettos on and looked ravishing.

There was another knock at the door and Tina snapped, 'Now who is it?'

It was Cindy Lauper, also up for a Grammy, wishing Tina the best of luck.

She said, 'Tina, I know we are up for the same award but you are the one who deserves it.'

Cindy wandered off, Richard, Melanie and Steve took their seats and, once alone, Tina started getting nervous. She asked me, 'How do I look? Ed, powder me down, powder me down.' Just as I started, there was another knock at the door. Tina yelped, 'Damn it, who is it now?'

It was Chaka Khan saying, 'Tina, step it up. You're about to go on.'

I thanked Chaka then closed the door. Tina snapped, 'I don't know her. Why is she knocking on my door?'

A stage organiser knocked and said, 'Tina, it's time.' She ran her palms down her sides and I escorted her towards the stage wing of her entrance. She had to climb a huge flight of stairs and when the curtain opened, she was to walk down them onto the stage. The music started and Tina started down the long set of stairs which seemed to go on forever. While slowly stepping, she started singing and the audience erupted on the spot, applauding like crazy and giving her a standing ovation – and she'd only just opened her mouth! I watched her from the wings and saw she was in her element, truly enjoying the very special moment. When she was about to leave the stage, she was asked to wait for a moment and, while standing there, collected her first Grammy award.

She raced offstage, into my arms and gave her Grammy to me to hold. She picked up another four Grammys that night, slinging each one into my waiting arms.

On my return to London, I found out that Jenny Marshall had booked a tour for me because my reviews were so good. I embarked on the tour with my road manager Nic Cooper and we played several dates at venues that felt so small after seeing Tina at the massive NEC. While I was away, Nic found me a flat in Hampstead. The area was charming, green and very much in demand – stars such as Sting, George Michael and Boy George all had homes there. The first piece of post I received at my new home was a funny postcard from Tina. It read, 'I'm having a small break then heading to Australia to shoot *Mad Max* with Mel Gibson.' She had drawn a Mercedes symbol and written next to it, 'You know what that means!' Tina had always wanted a Mercedes jeep and it clearly meant that when she went to Germany, she would be buying one. Little did she know that along with the jeep would come a man that would be her partner for the following twelve years.

29

I went on tour playing to audiences consisting of no more than 100 people, but halfway into the circuit, I started receiving bookings from top London clubs including the Hippodrome, Limelight and the famous Marquee, a venue Mick Jagger still sometimes gigs at. Roland Gift of the Fine Young Cannibals and Siouxsie from Siouxsie and the Banshees became friends of mine. I suddenly had a night life and a day life and I can't remember when I paused long enough to go to bed. I became a hit as a live showman and people kept asking when I would release a record, which only served to frustrate me. For some reason, Barrie Marshall felt it wasn't the right time. Barrie and I started arguing endlessly, with me constantly jumping down his throat. I was getting terrified, feeling that my chance had arrived and now it was slipping past me.

When Tina was due back in town, I cleared my calendar and rushed over to the St. James to see her. As soon as I got to her room, she ordered Potato Beluga and Crystal champagne. She started filling me in on news straight away. 'Ed, my Mercedes jeep was waiting for me in Germany, and there was a guy from the record company who was assigned to escort me everywhere. His name is Erwin Bach. Hmmmmm.'

I knew that noise well. Tina was nearly in love. I asked her to tell me what Mel Gibson was like. 'Cute. Nice eyes. But he's a bit of a little boy, you know – not my type.' She suddenly leaned forward with her eyes as wide as saucers while saying, 'And, Ed, They shaved all my hair off and glued this big old blonde wig on my head! By the way, Ed, can you make another wig for me? I'll be here a few days. I have to knock out some vocals for the *Mad Max* movie. They want me to do something called 'I Don't Need Another Hero'. I think that's what it's called.'

Over the following days, I made Tina's wig and hung out with my new friends Boy George, Marilyn and Billy Idol. After a heavy night, I picked up the phone to hear a low whisper. 'Hi, Ed. It's me. Tina. The most awful thing happened to me. It's never happened in my whole life. I went to sing the vocals for the *Mad Max* movie and nothing, but nothing came out. Ed, I can talk but I can't sing!'

I told her the Stevie Wonder remedy and she snapped, 'That Stevie Wonder. I was with Ike years ago and I spotted Stevie and asked him for an autograph for my boys. He cheekily told me, "I know you don't want it for your kids, you really want it for yourself". Imagine that nerve!'

I went to the hotel the next day but Tina was gone, so I assumed her voice must have returned. She left me a pair of riding boots and some shirts with a note that read, 'Ed, I might not see you for a while. Keep in touch. Love Tina.'

Meantime Marshall Arts wouldn't entertain the idea of a record deal for me so I consulted a lawyer which sent Barrie mad with fury. He agreed to cover my expenses for another month and to write off the £50,000 he had spent on developing my career and told me, 'You want to go, then go. Now you can find out what the real world is about.' I was gutted. I really loved Jenny Marshall who had a lot of patience with me and they had kept me afloat and put a lot of time into me. I sorely regretted our parting of ways. I stayed in a spare flat pop star Marilyn offered to me while I worked out what my best next move would be. With all that going on, I knew I wouldn't see Tina for another six months, an interim that would find me hitting rock bottom.

The flat, situated in London's beautiful Maida Vale, had two bedrooms and a lounge overlooking a large green. The carpet was filthy and the furniture was soiled and full of holes. One bedroom was covered with silver foil and black wallpaper and pictures of Marilyn all over it. The bed itself was frightening. There was no stove, no refrigerator and no hot water. I spent the first five days scrubbing the place from top to bottom. Totally depressed, I spent money I didn't have and in the middle of the madness, I picked up a cigarette and lit it. I had never smoked before in my life.

Boy George was great. He popped by the flat and when he saw I didn't have milk, he nipped out and returned with loads of shopping, forgetting I didn't have a fridge. I moved to another friend's flat in Hampstead and I cooked and cleaned to pay my way. I worked hard trying to find management and I managed to record new material in Trident Studios, a song called 'Talk Trash', which secured me a management deal. But the details seemed dodgy and I didn't sign.

Meantime Boy George was exposed as a heroin user and Tina, knowing I was friends with him, phoned me in a state of alarm.

'Ed, it's been all over the news in the States and everywhere. Now I know you and that Boy George spend a lot of time together. Are you into that stuff, Ed? Are you taking heroin? If you are taking drugs I'll pay for a de-tox. Are you?'

'Tina, honey, I never touched heroin and never will. Don't worry. I'm fine. My only problem is the press chasing me everywhere trying to get a story about George.'

'Okay, Ed. As long as you're not doing that stuff. Anyway, I have to go. Bye.'

After a while, I decided that when she phoned again, I would tell her exactly how bad things were for me. I started singing in a Russian restaurant, dressing in drag as Tina Turner, just to earn a meal on Sunday evenings. By day I still pursued some sort of recording deal, but I reached the point where I had to do something, anything, to put food in my stomach or earn a few coins. Tina rang out of the blue to have a little gossip and to tell me she was heading to London. After a brief conversation, she asked me if there was anything I needed. 'Yes Tina, I need money.'

She immediately changed the subject, saying, 'Ed, the other line is flashing.

I'm just going to put you on hold so don't go away.' Ten minutes later she came back on the line and said, 'Ed, I never told you. I'm doing a book! I got a big advance and guess what I did with the money? Remember the house I rented and the lady refused to let me buy it, well Ann Cain told me it was for sale and I bought it for Muh. Hold on a minute, don't go away. I have to pick up another call.'

Two minutes later Tina came back on the line saying, 'Muh wants the same patio furniture I have and Alline wants a Jaguar car like the one I used to have. Now they want to live grander than Tina Turner. I'm not having any of that. I'm buying new cars for everyone and sorting them out in their own homes. Nuh uh. I'm givin' them all homes and cars and that's all they're getting from me. Now Ed, how are you?'

'Not very good, Tina. I pawned my watch and my mink.'

Tina went mad, snapping, 'Oh, Ed. You know how much I loved that coat.' Then she started speaking softly, saying, 'Well, Ed, you were there. You know how much I was forced to sell after Ike.'

'I didn't have as much as you had to sell.'

'Well ... how are you surviving, Ed?'

I sighed and told her. 'I'm performing in a Russian restaurant doing you in drag, that's how I'm surviving. I get a good meal out of it but no money. Oh, yeh, thanks for the loan of that dress...'

Tina began one of her famous lectures. 'Ed, I had to sell my fur coats and jewels then I spent years playing little dirty, greasy clubs and venues. You know that.'

I tearfully blurted, 'Tina, where did I go wrong?'

'You were there, Ed. It wasn't easy after Ike. I had to start all over again. I think it happened too easy for you, Ed. You needed to hit rock bottom to see what it's really like. You're probably going about things all the wrong way again. Jenny Marshall looked after you and everything was first class. You wanted a record deal before you even stepped one foot on stage. You weren't ready Ed and now it's all been taken away. You can't start at the top. Now that you been knocked off your pedestal, you have to start at the bottom. I did it. And now you see where I am today. Hang on, the other line is flashing again.'

I held for half a minute then Tina was back on the line. 'Ed, I'm getting a house in Holland Park. I'll be doing the book there and I'm recording a new album, *Break Every Rule*. And Herb Ritts, the photographer, he's flying over to do pictures for the book cover. I'll phone you as soon as I get there.'

'Okay, Tina. I'm looking forward to seeing you.'

'I got Muh holding on the other line.' Tina took a deep, dreamy sigh before adding, 'Ohhh Ed... all this beautiful money. Now that all this money is pouring in, I'm going to have a ball! Talk to you soon! Bye!' Click.

My friendship with Boy George had led to my becoming a prisoner in my own home, with the press camping outside of the apartment for days on end, all waiting for a story. It became too much for me so a friend of mine, Eric Robinson, famed for being signed to Motown at the age of 16, told me to escape and stay with him. I seized the opportunity. I was still penniless but at least I was living in a civilised environment when Tina rang. 'Ed, it's me, Tina. I'm here, in Holland Park. The house is great! You have to come over right now so I can show it to you. I have so much to tell you!'

I wrote the address down then Tina said, 'Take a taxi. I'll pay for it. See you soon!'

As the taxi driver pulled up to the huge house, he said, 'Are you visiting Madonna?'

'No,' I replied.

'Oh. She must have moved out. Madonna was living here with that Sean Penn actor. I dropped them off once.' I grinned and wondered if Tina knew she was living in Madonna's former house.

Jenny Bolton opened the door just as Tina's voice boomed from the top of a grand stairway. 'Ed, is that you. Come on up. You have to see this house!' Tina, who would be in London for three months, explained it was Roger's idea to rent a house. With all the work pressures and the need to be within easy reach of each other, he suggested they stay in the same premises with Roger taking the bottom half of the house and Tina taking the top. It was one street over from Kensington High Street and hidden behind a surrounding brick wall. It was Victorian with vast, high ceilings. The fireplaces were original and ornate, beautiful old pieces of art. Through two old wooden gothic doors was Tina's marvellous bedroom. I gasped when I saw her luggage, twenty eight pieces of oversize crate cases – Tina had brought every creature comfort from her home with her, including her linen.

It was so much work looking after Tina now, that her assistant Jenny hired her own assistant. Tina called Jenny upstairs and told her, 'Tell the maid it'll be lunch for two. Ed and I will dine up here.'

Roger's rooms were on ground level, the entrance opening into a large hallway with the great staircase which led to Tina's part of the house being the main focal point. Through the hallway to the left were three large bedrooms, one belonging to Roger. The kitchen had a huge table the size of those you'd find in a park, with matching benches and other large pieces of country kitchen furniture. There were large panes of glass and doors which revealed the splendour of their green, manicured garden.

Back upstairs, Tina took me to her living room and we flopped down, sinking into the expensive, down-filled cushions of the settee. Tina said, 'The album I'm recording, Mark Knopfler is producing a couple of songs on it.'

'Teeena. Don't you remember I told you about Mark Knopfler before? He's with a group called Dire Straits and he's really talented. I told you about him when he went to Memphis to produce something for Bob Dylan. Helena Springs ended up with a big crush on Mark.'

'Yehhhh. I'm not surprised Helena got a crush on him. There's something about that Mark that makes my palms go all sweaty ...'

'Teeeenaaa.'

'Yeh, Ed, I know. He's married. Anyway, I think I have a new boyfriend!'

'Who?'

She pointed at several photographs around the lounge and said, 'Him. It's the guy from the record company in Germany. Erwin Bach.'

Late lunch was served, we blessed the table and toasted our reunion with crisp, white wine. We munched through our meal while Tina spilled loads of gossip about people we knew in LA. Then she suddenly said, 'Oh yeh, Kurt Loder, the guy who's writing my book, is coming in a few days. I have to scratch my memory over all those awful years I spent with Ike. But it's okay, it'll be good.'

I studied her for a moment and said, 'Tina. There's something different about you, I mean the way you look. You look great... but different.'

She sat back in her chair, put her hands on her hips and announced, 'Ed. I had corrective surgery on my nose! You don't miss a trick. It's a mess. My sinuses were deviated from Ike hitting me, and I was having problems flying. Look closely, Ed. See the gap just here?' Tina stabbed at area on her nose with her red nail while saying, 'I'm having cartilage taken out of my ear to fill that gap. Can you see it?'

I went up close and studied every centimetre of her nose and replied, 'No. I don't see anything.'

'Look closer!' For the life of me, I couldn't see any imperfection. Tina sighed and said, 'Just eat, Ed. I'll talk.'

I munched away while Tina revealed the details of her new fancy. 'Lucky thing I got the idea of using a jeep. You know, the Rolling Stones and David Bowie all use jeeps now because it's not fashionable to go around in a limousine any more. Because of my Jeep, I met Erwin. Anyway, the Germans came to LA and took me and Roger to dinner. Roger picked up on the fact that I liked Erwin so I told him to run my career, not my life. Anyway, after dinner, I asked Erwin to stay. I told him I liked him. He said, "What!". Anyway, we kissed and it was nice and I've been calling him regularly ever since.' She took a sip of wine before announcing, 'Well. Ed. I am Tina Turner. I'll tell a guy if I want him, now. If they turn me down, they turn me down. But I don't think it would be wise of a man, do you Ed?'

I'd started getting tipsy when Tina said, 'I know you don't have any money. I got some American dollars. Take them and cash them into sterling. Don't spend it stupidly and Ed, I mean this, don't go shopping!' When I told Tina in great detail about my living situation, I asked her if she would give me a loan so I could move into my own flat. She said she would rather I worked it off instead of taking it as a loan. I agreed and found a flat with the £1,500 forwarded to me against my wages. During that time I met a wonderful partner called Kim and, in every sense, it was love at first sight. With Tina back and me living in a flat of my own with someone I loved, I felt my life would go in the right direction.

Tina was busier than I had ever known her to be. I thought I had seen it all with *Private Dancer* but the business and work involved with *Break Every Rule* surpassed even that. There were interviews, photo sessions, rehearsals and, of course, recording sessions for the album. Tina was moving at the speed of light, with Roger Davies exercising his strategies and calling all the moves. Roger knew how to do it, Tina was willing and between the two, they would create another album which would soar into the charts. Tina put me on a schedule to go to her home five times a week to help her out. Added to her hectic schedule was the writing of her book. Kurt Loder would submit material and Tina edited the material every night. When she read through Kurt's pages, she would do it in a very guarded fashion, always leaning over the work so no one could glimpse a single word. One day, while whizzing around her room doing things as Tina read, I asked, 'What have you said about me in the book?'

Tina answered in a sing-song voice, 'You'll seeee...'

Mark Knopfler didn't produce or perform on the *Private Dancer* album but for *Break Every Rule*, he was committed to two songs.

I noticed a familiar sparkle in Tina's eye as she said, 'You have to see this Mark. You know I don't like men who are too good looking, well Mark's really sexy, tall with big old hands and feet.'

I asked what major changes there were to the show and Tina answered. 'You know I fired the girls right after "Let's Stay Together" and there were some of the same old problems with Kenny, taking drugs, so I got rid of him. It didn't go down too well. The audiences really missed Kenny and they missed having sexy girls dancing. So Kenny got his act together and he's back and I'm going to bring some girl dancers back, too.' Almost as an afterthought, she added, 'Guess what? I re-hired Rhonda Graam.' I was speechless.

Tina snapped her fingers. 'Ed, I've got it! I've got to go to a studio tomorrow and Mark is gonna be there. You have to see him and tell me what you think. Come with me and check him out.'

Tina was real funny about recording studios. Ike used to force her to stay up all night and sing a single note over and over and all she wanted to do was escape from the building. Consequently, when Tina goes to a studio, she knocks the tracks out in the shortest time imaginable, then nearly burns a trail leaving. This day, Tina was in no rush to leave. Her palms started sweating when it came to recording with Mark Knopfler. Mark asked Tina to do a 'guide vocal', a rough track for the musicians to build around. Tina wanted to impress him. Sitting at a control desk behind a glass enabling him to see Tina, he had no idea her mind was on him, not the song. Tina said, 'Ed, I was so worried about bursting out into a sweat when I started singing. I was just praying, "Oh dear Lord, don't let me sweat." I wanted to stay dry and look good because Mark could see every inch of me from behind that glass.' She rubbed her hands together. 'Ed, you should have seen how I played him. I was acting like I was tied to a train track and he was the only man that could save me. I kept asking him things like, "Did I do it right?" "How do you see it going?" "Should I try it a different way?" Men love feeling important and needed. And it's really exciting for them when they have to rescue a damsel in distress. Mark was so pleased with the test vocal that he said he might use it on the final mix. I panicked. I told him, "No, no... I can come back and do it again."'

Mark was married to a very nice lady called Lordes, whom Tina immediately befriended. Tina had a girly day with Lordes and I joined them. Tina was genuinely fond of Lordes and told her how great she thought Mark was.

I started talking about Helena Springs, and how she had fallen for Mark.

Tina sat erect and said, 'Now this is a coincidence. Mark told me he knew some backing singers he wanted to get hold of and I'm sure he said something about Helena...' She rubbed her forehead for a moment then threw her hands in the air.

Stretching her arms, she added, 'Ed, I've been working real hard and I deserve a night out. You come with me. Roger's a bit crabby right now so we won't invite him. We'll invite Lordes instead.' We went to London's exquisite Café de Paris near Piccadilly Circus. It's famed as a celebrity haunt, attracting stars, socialites and the world's wealthiest people. As soon as you enter through the foyer, there's a champagne bar to the rear. Straight ahead is a staircase leading to the right and to the left up to a circle bannister where people dine and can see everyone on the vast dance floor below.

That particular night was hot, with all the current faces present. Amongst the revellers were Boy George, Marilyn, The Cure, Siouxsie and the Banshees, Mick Hucknall of Simply Red, Sade and members of Motorhead. We took our seat on the balcony and, soon after arriving, the DJ played Al Green's version of 'Let's Stay Together' then immediately followed it with Tina's version. Tina and I went wild, bopping, laughing and joking and drinking glasses of fine champagne. A figure suddenly leaned over and tapped Tina on the shoulder, nearly making her jump out of her skin. It was Andy Warhol.

Tina squealed, 'Hi, Andy!' He sat with us and seemed terribly shy and when he did speak, he just mumbled and Tina couldn't understand a single thing he said. She just smiled and nodded her head as if she had heard everything. I got the gist that he wanted to make a poster of her and when I whispered that fact to Tina, she nearly wet herself with excitement. I dragged Lordes to the dance floor and when I returned, Andy had gone. Tina started to get tired and decided it was time to leave.

During the drive home, Tina all of a sudden, asked Lordes, 'Are you and Mark planning for any children?'

Lordes confided they did want children but were suffering a bumpy patch in their relationship at the moment. Tina replied, 'Don't you worry. Bumpy patches are normal in marriages. All bumps have a way of getting smoothed out.'

Tina's life was moving as fast as a meteor and two months had rapidly slipped by since she arrived. She said in a panic, 'I've only got one month left. One month for me these days isn't enough. I'm fitting an entire year's worth of work in a month these days.'

Roger was constantly busy, too, always flying around the house with several things going on at once while Tina continued to edit the new pages of her manuscript. She consulted with Roger on one matter. Tina wanted the public to know she had a scalp problem dating back to childhood. Roger thought it was a bad idea, worried some nutter might stalk her and try to pull off her wig. Tina sighed, almost surrendering. She said, 'I'm coming clean with a lot of things, Ed. And I'll tell you something. Muh isn't gonna be too happy when this book comes out.'

I finished what I was doing and seeing Tina was busy, I went straight home.

No sooner had I let myself into my flat, then the phone rang. 'Hi, Ed, it's me Tina.' Then she exploded, 'I can't believe this. I've had enough. I didn't like the idea of sharing a house with Roger and Jenny. They should've stayed in a hotel. I'll tell you one thing Ed, it'll never happen again, not as long as my name is Tina Turner.'

'Tina, darling, what's happened?'

'Sit down, Ed. Wait 'til you hear this. I'm busy as hell and Jenny is giving me attitude about her choice of clothes. There are constant conflicts and I've had enough. We had a row.'

I could hear Tina pacing back and forth and her breathing was heavy as she continued, 'Then Jenny gave me the filthiest look and turned on her heel to walk away. Now, Ed, you know what I'm like. I'm considerate. I told Roger what happened and he said that I couldn't blame Jenny because she had her own ideas about what to wear. I told him the facts.'

Tina huffed and puffed while adding, 'Nobody there has a job without me. Tina Turner pays *all* their wages. I told Jenny to pack her bags. She looked at me and arrogantly said, "Whatever". Roger snapped at me saying, "You're being ridiculous". Then he walked off with Jenny. I'll never rent a house with him again. I told both of them to stay out of my sight. They stay downstairs and I stay up.'

The following few days in Tina's house were silent ones, no one daring to cross her path. Roger tried to make his peace but Tina couldn't forgive Jenny for the way she spoke to her, telling Roger, 'There's something you're forgetting. You people work for me. I don't work for you.'

Roger found Jenny another position in the organisation, overseeing the band's styling and working as his personal assistant. There was nothing Tina could do about that and Jenny remained in the house but kept out of Tina's way.

Roger often had little parties downstairs and didn't invite Tina. She phoned me once saying, 'Ed, listen, can you hear all that party noise? They're having a party downstairs in my house and weren't polite enough to invite me.'

I explained to Tina that she was the boss and sometimes things happen that she might disapprove of. Therefore she couldn't always be included. Still annoyed with Roger, Tina confided, 'He was good to me and I was good to him. I made a lot of money because of him and he made a lot of money too. I've been looking into other avenues of management, though, and if things don't work out with Roger, I'll make a move after this album.' As it happened, Tina realised it would be silly to blow the great relationship she had with Roger because of her personal assistant.

During the final weeks at Holland Park, Kurt Loder flew in with the final drafts of Tina's manuscript and thanks to Rhonda Graam, who Tina had suddenly re-employed, the book was filled with photos of days gone past, and they were able to work off all the itineraries Rhonda had kept over the years. Herb Ritts was due to fly to London to take snaps of Tina. In preparation for the session, she had a London plastic surgeon nip cartilage out of her ear and place it in the gap she insisted she had in her nose. Afterwards, she complained that her nose looked like a beak and she panicked, hoping it would settle down in time for Herb's arrival. With her nose still a little swollen, Herb took his cover shots in the back garden of the Holland Park house.

Three months had flown by, and while I packed for Tina in preparation for the mass exodus from Holland Park, my lover Kim simultaneously packed to leave me. I couldn't believe it. Kim left just when Tina did and with both of them absent, I suddenly felt abandoned and alone. Again, I had no income and my money dwindled away. I had never been so unhappy in my life. It was nearly two years since I had left Tina to embark on my own career and after all that time, I had nothing. Penniless, I packed my belongings in boxes in preparation to leave the flat. I had no idea where I was going but wherever it was, I went with the certainty of knowing that Tina had everything she wanted.

30

Two months would pass before I'd see Tina again. In the interim, a friend let me stay in his flat and introduced me to his barrister, Rupert, a kind, proper English gentleman. Over drinks, I told Rupert I was a performer and he expressed a great deal of interest in young, fashionable music. I told him I was performing at the Hippodrome, explaining that if he really wanted to get a grip on what was happening today, he should come to see the show. Rupert did see my show and thought I was talented enough to invest in. We struck an agreement that if I ended up with a recording deal, Rupert would share the profits. It was a proper business gamble, one we both believed would pay off.

Rupert wrote out a very large cheque for studio time, demo tapes, a salary for myself plus all my expenses including a flat of my own. By the time Tina arrived back in London, I had fallen on my feet and felt like the world was my oyster. She arrived to tape a live special at a venue called the Camden Palace. She wanted the act to have a 1960s theme, complete with dancers like the Ikettes. She asked me to make a long, straight wig for her like the ones she wore in the Ike days, but when she tried the creation on, it made her look very old. The wig was immediately relegated to the deep recesses of a chest. To complete the theme, Tina decided to have Wilson Pickett fly in to do a duet with her to add an R & B flavour to the show. Also, she had recently covered Wilson's classic 'In the Midnight Hour'. The public were keen on duets at the time, and Tina and Wilson were the ideal R & B union. Tina planned to do 'In the Midnight Hour' and a few other classics with him. Keen on the idea, Wilson laid out his terms: $10,000 cash, two first-class return flights and top hotel accommodation to be paid for by Tina.

Wilson and his wife checked into the Mayfair hotel and arrived at the Camden Palace while Tina was rehearsing. He walked straight up to the stage and being an old seasoned professional, broke straight into song with Tina. Everyone watched with amazement while Wilson got low-down dirty dog with the band and the entire venue vibrated with his astounding sound. Agreeing the rehearsal was a raging success, he retired to his dressing room caravan. As soon as he reached the caravan, he started complaining and never stopped. Camden Palace's situation was such that it only had one dressing room backstage. All other dressing rooms were outdoors in these plush caravans. Wilson snapped, 'I can't walk out in the cold right after singing. I'll fuck up my voice.'

Tina had been given the indoor dressing room but, wanting to accommodate Wilson, she had me move all her things to an outdoor caravan so her guest could be inside.

Wilson still wasn't satisfied, complaining about anything and everything, especially that there was no alcohol present. He made a huge list of the things he wanted, included a vast array of spirits before ordering the road manager to fetch the lot for him. The road manager took the booze list to Tina and she flipped. Putting her foot down, she barked, 'You tell Wilson I don't run that sort of show. He's welcome to all the booze he wants but only after he tapes my show. And don't water it down! Tell Mr. Wilson Pickett what I said in my exact words.'

When Wilson was informed of Tina's feelings, he went crazy. 'Who the fuck does she think she is? Just because she has a couple of hit records, she thinks she can tell me what to do? I remember when that bitch sang for *me*, and she better not ever forget it.' The woman with him, pale, thin and covered in a fur coat, was hugely embarrassed. Wilson marched off and returned half an hour later loaded down with alcohol.

Meantime, a suit Tina had bought as a gift for Wilson arrived and was delivered straight to Tina's dressing room. She had planned to give it to him as a thankyou at the end of taping. I studied the suit and it was fabulous, a black well-tailored number with a £2,000 price tag on it. I turned it around a few times and whistled with approval. Tina paced back and forth, annoyed with Wilson's attitude. She said his behaviour reminded her of the low-rent people that were always around during her days with Ike. Those days had long since passed and Wilson's demeanour was beneath her. When he came to the stage for soundcheck, he carried with him a nasty attitude and the stench of alcohol. As soon as he opened his mouth to speak, it was clear that he was drunk. Tina simply said, 'Excuse me.' Then she ran offstage and grabbed Roger for a quick meeting.

Tina said, 'I will pay Wilson the $10,000, he can stay in the hotel tonight but I won't cover the hotel beyond that. He has a return ticket which he can keep. I won't perform with a person who has been drinking. I want him to leave immediately.'

And that was that.

I worked my butt off helping Tina prepare for the show, making wigs and carrying out all the normal duties associated with her performances. Later that night, as I unloaded Tina's bags from the car to take them into the St. James, Roger turned to me and said, 'Thanks for all the work you did over the past few days. Tina and I really appreciate it.'

I nearly bit his head off, snapping, 'I didn't do a damn thing for you. I did it for Tina.' Roger was taken back by my reaction.

When I got to Tina's suite, she softly said, 'Ed, I know you and Roger didn't always see eye to eye but he is trying. What he said to you was his way of trying to make peace.'

'Tina, I don't give a fuck what Roger thinks of me.'

Tina defended him, saying, 'You're being bitter. You fell on hard times and now you're angry. You should accept when people want to make peace.'

I argued, 'You're my friend and I've always been there for you. I'm not here for anyone else.'

Tina smiled and said, 'Thank you Ed. I appreciate that. I see every little thing you do for me and I appreciate it. Now I have something for you.' Tina handed me the £2,000 suit she had originally bought for Wilson Pickett. As she handed it to me, she said, 'I want you to have it out of love and as a thankyou for all the things you've done for me.' I still have the suit today.

It was the latter part of 1984 when Tina returned to London to rehearse her *Break Every Rule* tour before going on the road. Needless to say, she had me carrying out my normal routine of running errands and making wigs. Her 46th birthday was looming and Roger decided to throw a lavish party for her at a club on the King's Road. While she was dressing for the occasion, I quizzed her about how things were going with Erwin Bach, Tina replied, 'It wasn't easy, Ed. We started seeing each other but he didn't really commit himself to me and started dating some other girl. Well honey, I put a stop to that. We got past that bumpy patch and now, I can say, that yes, today, on my birthday, Erwin Bach is mine.'

He was invited to Tina's party and I was dying to see and meet him. Tina warned me, 'Erwin's bosses at EMI don't know we're seeing each other so we have to play it cool tonight. We really have to keep a distance because it's against the rules for employees to mix with the artists.

Roger was aware of Tina's love for all things Egyptian, and had the restaurant designed and decorated with an Egyptian theme. Tina walked along, saying how lovely everything was and it was clear Roger had spent a great deal on the gold pillars, gods, goddesses, pyramids and all the items that made people feel they had just entered an Egyptian temple. She continued smiling, telling everyone how beautifully she thought the place had been decorated, grateful that everyone had gone to so much trouble.

Tina pointed Erwin out to me then casually worked her way around the room until she reached him, treating him very professionally in front of the EMI executives. I chatted for a while with Erwin and thought he was a very nice guy. The party buzzed with beautifully dressed people drinking and dancing until it was time to sit down for meal. A table, loaded with gifts for Tina, started spilling over with stunningly wrapped gifts, causing another little pile below. Tina's gloves and handbag were placed amongst the gifts and when the packages shifted, her bag fell and emptied onto the floor. I found myself on my hands and knees, crawling through people's legs to fetch lipstick and other items that were unconsciously being kicked around by those who were dancing. Finally, after dinner, Tina and Mark Knopfler hit the dance floor and Tina, with a beaming smile on her face, twirled while flirtatiously throwing her head back.

Back at her suite at the St. James, Erwin, Tina, Judy Cheeks and I decided to have a few more drinks. Judy, who had just got a recording deal in London, had known Tina since the 1970s so the two girls had no fear of letting their hair down in front of each other. Tina and I always had our private jokes, many of which Judy would understand. We were in one of our naughty moods, making in jokes with each other that would often go over other people's heads. We kept laughing over things that Erwin didn't understand, and he didn't find it amusing, thinking we were making fun of him behind his back. Stern faced, Erwin said in his strong German accent, 'I will go. You and your friends have catching up to do.'

Tina tried to explain to Erwin that she, Judy and myself went back a long time, and that we were like the three musketeers. With that, he calmed down and stayed but kept staring at me with great suspicion and I could read the look on his face. Erwin was disturbed that Tina and I were so close and I knew that he wondered for a moment if we were more than friends. I leaned in to Judy and whispered, 'If Tina was a guy, we would be!' Then Judy and I burst into giggles which only served to make him feel more uncomfortable.

Noticing it had gone three in the morning, I hastily tidied Tina's suite, leaving all the dirty glasses and other items outside the door, wanting everything to be fresh and romantic for Erwin and Tina.

At the door, Tina and I hugged and I whispered, 'I love you.'

Tina softly said, 'I know, Ed...' Then we gazed deeply into each other's eyes, almost the way lovers would, then suddenly burst into a fit of uncontrollable laughter. Erwin's mouth tightened and it was clear he was not amused.

The next morning, the phone rang. 'Hi, Ed, it's me, Tina. Ed, wake up. Hurry. Get in a taxi and we'll have breakfast together.'

I groggily replied, 'Okay, see you in an hour.'

I snapped to full alertness when Tina excitedly said, 'No, Ed! Come now!'

Freshly showered and shaved, I reached Tina's suite within thirty minutes. Breakfast was waiting and Tina, dressed in an elegant negligée, swanned over and started pouring coffee.

As she did so, she started to laugh and said, 'Erwin got jealous over you! He says you're in love with me. He noticed how you look after me, crawling across the floor to gather all my things without me even asking. I told him you were pursuing your own career and that as much as I love you, I can't rob you of your freedom.'

I replied, 'Oh Teeenaaa, that's so sweeeeet!'

Tina added, 'Well you always look after me, more than a person who is in love.'

'Speaking of love, what's up with you and Erwin?'

'Well just wait 'til I tell you. After you left, me and Erwin were drinking champagne in the bedroom. Next thing I know, he's running his hand up and down my silk stocking until he reached the garter. Well that did the trick. Next thing I know, we were making love!'

Confused, I said, 'You mean you weren't lovers yet?'

'We only ever kissed and played around. What I'm telling you, Ed, is that making love for the first time with Erwin last night was the best birthday present I ever had! Oh yeah, speaking of best birthday presents, those earrings you got me are horrible! Return them to the shop and get something that'll go with my clothes. I mean really, Ed, dangling balls with spikes on them! I haven't got any clothes that'll go with earrings like that. I'm not a punk rocker, you know!'

We laughed, then Tina told me about her future plans, excitedly saying, 'Erwin and I decided I'll spend my weekends in Germany so we can develop a relationship away from the press and Roger Davies! I'll go to Germany between rehearsals. I'm going to work strictly five days a week, leave for Germany on Friday nights and come back on Monday mornings.'

For once, Tina travelled without an assistant on the weekends when she flew to Germany. Erwin had given her a set of keys to his modest apartment and she rearranged his flat so it was more convenient for her – including helping herself to part of his closet space. This made Erwin somewhat uncomfortable. She decided to surprise him by cooking, but couldn't work out how to go out to a butcher or supermarket to buy food because she hadn't done it in so long. In a total flap, she phoned and said, 'Ed, I had to have EMI send an office girl over to assist me and do my food shopping. I'll have to make some changes to Erwin's apartment. It's just not up to my standard. I'll need you to do some shopping for me when I get back on Monday.'

Upon returning to London, she gave me her American Express Gold Card which I used to shop for all the things Tina thought Erwin could use in his apartment. She instructed me to buy masculine items so he wouldn't feel too invaded. Ploughing through the shopping list Tina gave me, I purchased a towel rack, soap dispenser and a double-sided mirror that pulled out on an arm, each item in matching chrome. I bought sheets, towels and a rug, and a few creature comforts for Tina herself. Along with the practical gifts, Tina sent me to purchase something extra special – cigars from the specialist house, Davidoff. I nipped to Fortnum & Mason to load up on special cheeses and caviar which Tina would carry to Germany.

She flew to Germany that weekend and by the end of the first day, with all the new household items that had been shipped over, Tina had Erwin's apartment looking like a mini version of the St. James Club. She said, 'I have to do it gradually so Erwin won't notice too much.' Tina's energy is such that her idea of gradual was to totally revamp the whole apartment within 48 hours!

When she returned, she told me, 'Erwin took me to a romantic dinner and insisted on paying. We held hands the whole time. Then we got to his apartment and we were having a real good time, laughing and stuff. He opened a bottle of champagne and I told him I had a surprise for him. I pulled out a Cartier box, gave him a big kiss and handed it to him. He saw the box was from Cartier and said, "Tina, you needn't". He opened the box and saw one of a matching pair of slave bracelets that I'd bought in London. Then he noticed the other one on my wrist. You know how romantic these bracelets are, the ritual of taking the little screwdriver and attaching the bracelet to your lover's wrist. I explained the romantic meaning of the gift. He didn't even take it out of the box and told me he couldn't accept it.'

Tina's voice became emotional as she continued, 'He got so mad and yelled at me, saying I was rushing things, saying "Why are you doing this? You haven't stopped since you've been coming here. You go through my things, organise my closet, I don't even recognise my own home anymore." He just backed away from me saying this isn't what he wants. So I took the bracelet and threw it out the window. I didn't think it important enough to spoil the relationship. I felt horrible. It was just a nice gesture, the bracelet, you know, so he knows how much he really means to me, and I don't know why he got so mad.

'The next day, without me realising it, Erwin found the bracelet in the hedges. He kept it and came to my birthday party with it in his top pocket.' Tina told me later that when Erwin felt he was ready for commitment, he wore the bracelet.

'How were things left? Are you going to see him again?'

'Yeh, I'm going back this weekend. It really hurts that he's such a bachelor. He doesn't seem interested in commitment. But give it time, Ed. I just have to be careful not to move so fast. I'm going to do this real slow and I'll get him around to my way of thinking.'

Tina couldn't think about anything else but Erwin, sometimes forgetting lyrics during rehearsals and going through the motions of getting things done just so she could leave to see him. She dreaded being apart from him. For the first time ever in a relationship, she carefully paced herself knowing that if she handled things gently, Erwin would eventually be hers. Tina was honest with him about everything, not wanting him ever to hear something about her former lovers from anyone else.

Their relationship deepened, and we all sensed it would last a very long time. Erwin wasn't the type of man Tina was usually attracted to, and I asked her why she fell in love with him. She told me, 'I believe Erwin will be honest and loyal to me. I don't think, once he commits himself, that he will ever sleep with another woman and embarrass or hurt me.'

Christmas was looming, and she wanted to make it the most special one Erwin had ever known. It would certainly be memorable for all concerned, but not for the reasons Tina envisaged. As things turned out, it would be Tina's first Christmas with Erwin Bach, and the very last she would ever spend with me.

31

This particular Christmas and New Year, which would see in 1985, Tina spared no expense. Money was never an object when it came to the man she loved, and she went all out, renting a fabulous chalet up a snow-covered hill in the playground of the rich and famous, Gstaad, Switzerland. Tina enthusiastically suggested, 'Ed, Let's have a holiday together. I've never had a proper holiday with you. And now I've got the money to do whatever I want. Besides, most of the people I've invited to Gstaad are new in my life. I want to have someone there I can have fun with.'

We wrapped up rehearsals for the *Break Every Rule* tour and meanwhile, Tina's book was released, becoming an instant success which Tina celebrated by spending money like crazy. While Tina pored over her guest list, she said, 'Ed, we've got a lot of catching up to do and I want to tell you what's been going on with the family back in LA. We'll take some time on our own in Gstaad. Do you ski?'

'No, I've never had the chance.'

'Well, Ed, this Christmas, you'll ski. I'm going to do it, too. I'll pay for all your equipment and lessons. Erwin is a great skier. He's been at it for years.'

I gave Tina the latest news on Helena Springs.

I told her, 'Helena came to London and we stayed together for a while. She auditioned for Elton John's tour and got hired as a backing singer. And as if that wasn't exciting enough, she even got a record deal! Tina, what do you think she did with the money? She used the lot to buy a beautiful flat in Ladbroke Grove just near where you were living in that house in Notting Hill.'

'Some people are so lucky. Things just fall in their laps.'

I added, 'She has a girlfriend named Shirley Lewis and they met these hunky twins to die for called Matt and Luke Goss. Helena is dating Matt and Shirley's dating Luke. Apparently Matt and Luke are waiting to get signed to a label. I don't know what they sound like but they have the looks to become real pop heart-throbs.' Matt and Luke Goss later went on to get a record deal and become known as Bros, one of Britain's top pop successes of that era.

Tina replied, 'Well, I'm not worried about relationships now that I've got Erwin... or now that I've nearly got him. I'm going to make this Christmas so special that he'll just fall madly in love with me!' Then she looked as if something crossed her mind before exclaiming, 'Christmas! Oh, Ed. His presents. I made a list. Take my gold Amex and do me a big favour. I know how much you love shopping so would you mind going out and buying all the things on this list for Erwin? You've got really good taste and you know what he looks like so I know you'll choose all the right stuff.'

'I'd love to! You know I don't care who's money I'm spending as long as I'm spending! That's something we'll always have in common!' We both burst out laughing.

Tina added, 'Oh yeah, pick out something nice for yourself Ed, but don't go too crazy.'

My first stop was Armani, Bond Street, choosing a stunning tuxedo, a couple of suits, shirts, gloves and accessories for Erwin. He needed a good wardrobe if he was going to be hanging around Tina.

I popped into Browns on South Molton Street and bought a few more items before choosing a fabulous suit for myself. Armani delivered the goods I purchased to the St. James Club where Tina inspected the items before I packed them to be sent ahead of us to Gstaad.

Tina departed ahead of me, leaving an open return air ticket for my flight. She phoned from Gstaad saying, 'Ed, I have an idea. Stay on for a while after everyone leaves. This *Break Every Rule* tour is going to be huge and this will be my last chance to have some fun. I really want to spend some time alone with you.' I agreed as Tina added, 'We won't have to lift a finger. I've even got us a full time chef!'

I put the phone down and became lost in thought. The wonder of it all! There I was, the little boy from Seattle who fell in love with Tina's image on the television and now, more than twenty years on, I would be spending Christmas in the swishest resort in the world with my best friend, Tina Turner. I flew into Zurich where Tina had a car waiting to take me on the two hour journey to Gstaad. As the car drove into the legendary town, my heart nearly stopped from the beauty of it all. The architecture was astonishing, almost every building made up of ornate, carved wood. The streets were as clean as the mountain air and everyone walking on the pavements, men and women alike, were draped in expensive furs and sparkling jewels. I took a deep breath and thought that if I were to die, this is the place where it should happen because Gstaad was the closest you could get to heaven on earth. Everything and everyone smacked of elegance and splendour. The Christmas spirit along with the charm of Gstaad and its residents swept me away.

Having arrived at Tina's chalet, a young man raced out to help me with my bags. Everyone was in their rooms resting so I went straight to mine and had nice, long bath before wandering around the vast property. The ground floor had a lounge, kitchen and Tina's bedroom. The second level had the family room and a dining area with a large balcony where you could stand and view the rooftops of the other chalets dotted on the hill. Up a couple of stairs was my room with a view of snow capped trees and mountains. I was standing with my nose pressed against the window, watching snowflakes drop like diamonds, when the chef lightly tapped on my door and asked if I cared for a refreshment or snack. I wasn't ready to eat so he asked me, 'Can I get you anything at all, sir?'

I quipped, 'Yes, as a matter of fact. You can get me Tina!'

He smiled warmly and said, 'Miss Turner is awake now and waiting for you downstairs.'

I flew to the ground level and swept Tina into my arms while squealing, 'This is fantastic!'

She flicked her hair while laughing wildly as I gently lowered her tiny feet back onto the ground, then beamed while replying, 'It is, isn't it? Ed, I have a surprise for you.'

I gasped, 'Oooohhh God. What?'

She turned toward the stairway where two people were quietly standing and when I looked, I yelped, 'My God! Chris Kontos!' I raced over to shake his hand while saying, 'How are you, Chris?'

He was arm in arm with a heavily pregnant, utterly beautiful woman and I gently took her hand in mine as Chris introduced her. She was his wife and they were expecting their first child. Tina would later become the baby's godmother.

The chef came in with tea for everyone while, one by one, Tina's other guests emerged from their respective bedrooms and soon we had a party in full swing. An hour later, everyone fell silent except Tina and I who were huddled on the couch laughing like a couple of school children. Noticing the sudden silence, we stopped and looked up to see Erwin Bach glaring at us with disapproval. I jumped to my feet to shake his hand but he seemed cold and somewhat formal. He had the air of a cautious man, serious and slightly suspicious of everyone.

With the party mood broken, Chris said he was going into town to do a little shopping with his wife. Erwin stared at Tina and in his strong, German accent, solemnly stated, 'I'm going for a walk.'

Tina happily said, 'I'll go with you, darling.'

Erwin snapped, 'I wish to be on my own.'

Everyone squirmed in discomfort. I could see that Erwin was ill at ease and I remembered what Tina had said about him being uncomfortable around flamboyant people. His uneasiness reflected that of a person trapped, and I mulled over a conversation Tina and I had had about Erwin feeling their relationship was moving too fast. He was a bachelor who was finding it hard to adjust to a commitment and I realised there had been some sort of problem brewing before I had arrived. My presence only made matters worse. He seemed out of place surrounded by Tina's friends, and I thought he might have been happier if some of his own friends were there, too.

Erwin bundled up and walked off into the clean, downy snow while Tina and I raced to the privacy of her bedroom for a chat and to catch up on things. Now I think about it, Tina did most of the talking. We went for it as if we hadn't seen each other in years. 'I booked you for skiing lessons tomorrow, but I won't be joining you because I haven't insured my legs yet.'

'Well hell, Tina. I better not do either because I haven't insured mine! I do have performances booked on my return to London, you know.'

Tina put her hands on her hips and said, 'Excuse me. I'm the star here.' Then we both fell into each other's arms laughing.

Before I left the room, Tina informed me, 'We dress formally for dinner here, Ed. Have a rest and I'll see you at eight.'

Tina was a chicken and fish lover who largely favoured spicy Thai dishes. Erwin was a red meat man who hated spiced food and loathed Thai cookery. The menu was changed to suit Erwin and, it saddened me to see how Tina fawned over him, going as far as to eat foods she didn't even enjoy. The thing that bothered me was the more Tina went out of her way to make him feel comfortable, the more resentful he seemed. After dinner, we all gathered to view the first edit of Tina's *Break Every Rule* video. Tina and I got thoroughly wild, screeching with excitement over the tape. We lay down on oversized cushions, looking at the massive television screen, clapping and humming along to her video. I revelled in her blistering performance, saying, 'Go Miss Tina! Girl, you are hot!'

Thrilled by the tape, Tina cheered along with me while she roused, 'Saaaang, girl. Yeeehhhh!' I could see Tina couldn't believe it was her on the tape. For the first time ever, she finally saw what everyone else had been seeing for years.

At that very same moment, Erwin snapped at us, objecting to our noisy behaviour. Tina and I fell silent, like two children chastised by a headmaster. One very long minute later, she leaned in and whispered, 'We have to be careful, Ed. You know, a lot of little things we do... we don't want to offend Erwin. We're just going to have to have our own little time together.'

With my eyes still trained on the telly, I pointed at the screen with one hand and gripped Tina's wrist with the other, suddenly enthusing, 'Look, me!' I was pointing at my name listed at the end of the video credits, 'Personal Assistant, Wardrobe. Eddy Hampton Armani'. Seeing my name, Tina patted me on the back and gave me a little squeeze while saying, 'See, Ed. I didn't forget to add your name this time!'

The following day, after lunch, everyone retired to their rooms except Tina and I who retreated to the loft to have a good old chinwag. Tina confided, 'My relationship is getting better with Erwin. Like he's taking down some sort of barrier and letting him give himself. You know me, Ed. When I fall in love, I want the ideal situation yesterday. But it's interesting ... this taking it slow stuff ... it's nice. It's like building a bond. It's different, Ed. I never done this before ... and I like it. It feels real good. It feels ... right.'

'I've known you a long time, girl. I've never seen you like this. The thing that amazes me is... as loving and romantic as Erwin is in private, why is he so damn cold when you two aren't alone?'

Defending Erwin, Tina replied, 'You know I don't like people hanging all over me.'

Erwin heard us laughing and talking and, because we were making so much noise, we failed to hear him coming up the stairs. I don't know how long Erwin was standing in the doorway before he noticed us, but it sent Tina into a panic – she had been chatting intimately about her relationship with him. He walked in, glared at Tina, his face a mask of thunder as he abruptly said, 'I am going out. I can see you and Eddy have a lot to discuss.'

Tina leapt to her feet, offering, 'Erwin, darling, I'll go with you!'

He snapped, 'No. You can just sit here and discuss our relationship. What else do you tell him?'

Tina, realising we had been heard, told it as it was. 'Erwin, darling, It's not like that. Me and Ed are old friends. We talk about everything...'

'But there are some things that are off limits to all friends.' He stormed out.

I realised I would have to tread very carefully around Erwin in the same way that I used to have to tread around Roger Davies. He still saw me as some sort of threat or rival. And now, he realised Tina had been sharing her intimate secrets with me. I just hoped he would understand that Tina and I were simply good friends that had a lot of history together. We went to our rooms for a nap, and two hours later I woke, washed and dressed totally chic — of course! Just before leaving my room, I sprayed a little Opium cologne on, a new bottle that Tina had given me. She adored the scent and always wanted me to wear it. I went to her room and saw she was busy talking to her mother on the phone. When she spotted me, she waved me in while saying, 'Muh! I've got a surprise for you. Say hello to an old friend. Hang on...'

Tina handed me the phone and I said, 'Merry Christmas, Happy holidays, Muh!'

'Is that you, Eddy?'

'Uh huh!'

Muh laughed and stated, 'Ah shudda known Ann would have you all the way there in Switzerland with her, Eddy. Na' tell me, boy. Howz Ann? Is that girl in love again?'

'Muh, don't you worry about Tina. She looks great. She's happy. She's in love and glowing. You know what Tina's like when she's with her dream man. So don't go fretting. As long as I'm here, she'll be well looked after. You know that.'

'Na' Eddy. I know yo' can't talk na' but I just gotta know what this man Erwin is like. He dunn stole Ann's heart!'

'Muh. Don't worry.'

'Awwrat, Eddy. Na' you take good care of mah Ann. Now listen, Alline, Jackie and Craig is here and they all wanna say hello to Ann.'

'Okay, Muh. Give my love to everyone and I'll put Tina back on the phone.'

As Tina took the phone, she suddenly cupped it and whispered, 'Would you be a sweetheart and go downstairs and get us a bottle of champagne and two fresh glasses?'

I went to the kitchen and asked chef where the champagne was. He showed me and as I reached for a bottle which was freezing cold to the touch, Erwin, who had been cooking, snapped, 'It is too early for champagne. And it's not the right temperature yet.'

I explained that Tina wanted it and he snapped, 'You can tell her it is too early for that!'

Not wanting to upset him, I didn't argue and quietly turned to exit. Referring to me, Erwin loudly asked the chef, 'What is that disgusting smell in the kitchen?'

'Are you referring to me?' I retorted.

Erwin boldly said, 'Yes I am. You stink like a whore or something.'

I raised my eyebrow and calmly stated, 'I have no doubt you know all too well what a whore smells like.'

I got to Tina's room and she asked 'Ed, where's the champagne?'

I told her that Erwin felt it was to early for bubbly and that it should be colder. I didn't tell her about the exchange we had over her favourite scent that I was wearing. Tina fumed, snapping, 'Damn it. Wait a minute now, the last time I checked, I pay the bills around here. I don't care if the champagne is hot or cold, I want some now. Ed, just get it and ignore Erwin.'

I skipped back to the kitchen and stated that Tina wanted the champagne, regardless. I will admit, I was a bit messy over my tactics. I was there as Tina's guest and I was sick of Erwin trying to lock horns with me. Still stinging over his insult concerning the cologne I was wearing, I treated him dismissively upon my return to the kitchen. Chef got me two glasses and a bottle of Crystal and as he opened it, he said, 'Leave it on the ledge. The crisp weather will bring it to its perfect temperature. I thanked him warmly and as I left, I stuck my nose in the air as I passed Erwin.

I headed through the lounge, and Chris Kontos said, 'Oh! Crystal! Pour me one, Ed.'

I noticed Erwin glaring from the kitchen doorway so I loudly said, 'Sorry, Chris. I can't because Erwin Bach says it's not cold enough. I wouldn't want to insult your palate.'

'Let me taste that.' He took a sip and said, 'Ed, I was raised on this stuff. It's actually the perfect temperature. Perhaps Erwin doesn't realise that.' I happily poured Chris a glass, knowing Erwin heard every word.

Tina and I got through a glass each before people started filtering to her room. We poured everyone a glass and when Tina decided it was time to get dressed, I suggested we all go to the lounge where I would put some music on, affording Tina her privacy. Once in the lounge, I put on some tapes I'd brought with me. Finally, all Tina's guests had drifted upstairs, sitting comfortably while drinking and making conversation. With everyone settled, I picked up a copy of *Vogue* magazine and sat by a window while thumbing through the pages. Erwin passed through with the chef and after putting a few items on the table, he came up to me and loudly complained, 'You just sit, drink champagne and do nothing. There is so much to do. You can set the table.'

I was there on holiday as Tina's guest. I wasn't there to work as a servant to Erwin. The last thing I expected was to be bossed around by her jealous lover. Part of me was pleased that Erwin was jealous. It indicated that Tina was, in fact, winning his affections. Another part of me was saying I was far too long in the tooth to be pushed around by Erwin. I had pacified him to a degree but my level of tolerance had become very short over the years. I was a man and simply refused to be insulted. I coldly glared at Erwin and firmly stated, 'I am not here working. I am Tina's guest.'

Erwin argued, 'You should do something instead of doing nothing!'

By this point, everyone had gone silent and was watching our astonishing exchange. In my head, I counted to ten to quell my mounting anger then I smiled sweetly while calmly replying, 'Erwin, there is a difference between asking something of a person and ordering them. If you are gentleman enough to ask me to assist you, I will. If you order me to assist you, you'll find yourself setting the table alone. Do I make myself clear?'

'Well! I have had enough!' He ran to Tina's room to complain. Erwin returned with Tina and he and I launched into a childish slanging match, bickering like two kids.

Tina discreetly took me to the side, quietly asking, 'Ed, did Erwin ask you to help him and you refuse?'

'Tina, he didn't ask. He barked out an order. He made a demand while criticising me over lounging around reading and drinking champagne. I didn't want to start an argument so I requested he should ask rather than order. I did not refuse. I simply want to be treated with respect. Tina, you do have servants here. I am not one of them.'

'Ed, remember. Erwin is German and you may have misread his firm style of speech. Maybe Erwin misunderstood your attitude and took offence.'

After Tina's diplomatic pep talk, I went to the kitchen and asked chef if there was anything I could do for him. He didn't have a chance to open his mouth when Erwin barked, 'Yes, the cutlery and dinner service is there. Set the table.'

I went to Tina's room to see if she was ready, and after chatting for a couple of minutes, we took our seats at the enormous round table. Erwin had cooked a great meal. I sat on one side of Tina and he sat on the other. We laughed, talked and everyone was in high spirits and thankfully, the dark mood between Erwin and me seemed to pass. Then, while talking with Tina, I absent-mindedly started pouring champagne into my glass when I caught myself, apologised for my bad manners and asked if anyone wanted a topping up. Suddenly, Erwin stood, banged his hands on the table making the dishes, cutlery and glasses jump, then explosively stated, 'I have had enough!'

He stormed off with Tina in hot pursuit and they did not return until we had almost finished our meal. Five seconds after taking a seat, Erwin suddenly stood up and blurted, 'I can't sit at the same table with this man.'

Tina said, 'Oh, darling, it's okay. Ed didn't mean it. All the champagne is on the table behind us. We're all meant to be helping ourselves, aren't we?'

Erwin cut her off by saying to me, 'Who are you? What are you?' He kept antagonising me and putting me down.

I yelled at Erwin, 'Excuse me, muthafucka. I don't owe you any explanations. How dare you? How fucking dare you?'

Completely crazed with anger, Erwin challenged me to step outside and sort the matter with our fists. Tina stood up and led me away by the hand and once in my room, she said, 'Oh Ed, don't confront him. Don't feed the fire... Please, for me, Ed.'

Tina departed to have words with Erwin and thirty minutes later, Jenny came to my room and said, 'Ed, I have to find you a place to stay. Erwin insists that if you don't leave immediately, he will.

'Fine, Jenny. Would you please find a hotel for me.'

Jenny rang around to find no vacancies whatsoever in Gstaad's two hotels. With no place for me to stay, she tried to calm Erwin down but he wasn't having it. He didn't care if I had to stay on the streets as long as I was nowhere near the chalet. I thought he was conducting himself like a petulant child so I offered to be the man and apologise – I didn't want Tina's dream holiday ruined. Jenny told Erwin I offered to make peace with him but he just shouted, 'I won't be in the same room with him!'

Tina came to the large lounge and told all the guests she was retiring to her room and wouldn't be coming out on the town that evening as originally planned. We fired up a large joint, puffed away and unanimously decided that if Erwin and Tina weren't going out, we would anyway.

Early next morning, Jenny woke me, and, through my splitting headache, I heard her saying, 'Ed, I'm terribly sorry. Tina has asked me to wake you. We made arrangements for a car to collect you shortly to take you to the airport. You're going home. Tina said she'll make it up to you later.'

Seriously hungover, I threw my clothes into my luggage and didn't have enough time to get upset. Chef helped me take my belongings to the waiting car, telling me, 'I can't believe this is happening!'

Chris Kontos walked out with me, saying, 'I wish I booked my flight already because my wife and I are desperate to leave'. I told Jenny I was skint – I thought I could use my credit cards, but Gstaad only dealt in cash. Everyone had a whip round, and they raised around £10 between them. I said goodbye to all of Tina's guests and just as I was about to step out the doorway, Tina herself raced over and hugged me, saying, 'I'm so sorry Ed. I have no choice.'

My body went limp in Tina's arms and I couldn't believe she was sending me away because Erwin saw me as a menacing rival for her attention. I loved her. She was my best friend and I felt I shouldn't have to justify that to anyone. As Tina held me, I knew something had changed. I could smell her soft skin as she held me and I thought of how I had slept on her floors, dodged bullets, looked after her children, cared for her home and rubbed her feet when she was tired. I had devoted my life to Tina. She never made me do that. I did it because I wanted to. Over the years, my idol and I had become soulmates and suddenly everything we had been through together didn't count for anything. I couldn't comprehend why Tina didn't stand up for me. I wondered why she didn't remind Erwin that we were both her guests and that we should both behave. I couldn't understand why she wanted Erwin so desperately that she would go as far as letting him dictate who her friends should be. Her own sister later said to me, 'Ah told you, Ed. Ah told you what Ann's like...'

As I got into the car, I heard Tina shout, 'Ed, call me when you get home and let me know you got there safely.'

It was too late for that.

I remembered when Tina told me how she looked at Ike to make sure he was asleep before she left his life forever. At that moment, I knew what she meant. There she was, asleep to reality. Tina didn't know how to love. Friends were dispensable. But I knew she could never give what she never had, even as a child. I understood, and I knew I would love her forever.

Epilogue

One and a half years later, I moved back to LA. I had hit rock bottom and felt so low that I was on the verge of a nervous breakdown. All I wanted was my family. When I saw my sister in the distance at LAX airport, I broke down and cried.

My mother greeted me on her front porch, holding me like a parent there for her child. After years of distance, she held me as a mother should. My family rallied round and over the next few months, we finally got to know each other.

Six months after my arrival in LA, I found an apartment and set up home. I phoned Tina to see if I could collect the items I had left at her house years before. Ann Cain made the necessary arrangements, and we agreed a time for me to collect my goods.

Arriving 10 a.m. sharp the following morning, Ann took me on a tour of the ground floor of the house. It had changed beyond recognition, totally redecorated and refurnished at great cost, reflecting Tina's millionairess status. Half an hour later, while loading my car, I heard a familiar, hearty laugh. 'Who's there? Is it Eddy Hampton, or Eddy Armani?'

Like butter over fire, I melted in Tina's arms and we laughed and talked as if we had never been parted. It had been two long years. Suddenly she suggested, 'Ed, don't go. Stay for lunch.' I wanted to be strong and politely decline but as always, I could never refuse Tina.

We settled into a lovely lunch, enjoying a bottle of champagne. Although two years had passed since the parting in Gstaad, we easily slipped into our old friendship, having a riot of a good time, laughing, chatting and catching up on each other's lives. Tina asked, 'What's happening? What are you doing now?'

'I joined the rest of the world. I'm living a normal life, you know, away from the music business. I'm a normal person with a normal job. I'm a waiter in a swish restaurant and honey, I am raking in the coins – enough to pay for my apartment and bills.'

All of sudden, there she was again, lecturing me with authority. Tina straightened her back and flicked her hair while sternly pontificating, 'Ed, you have to do what you have to do. We all have to hit rock bottom and start again...'

I looked at my watch and said, 'Tina, I have to go. I have commitments today.'

She girlishly pleaded, 'Oh Ed. Don't go. Please stay. Stay the night.'

Instantly weakening at the sound of her soft voice, I quietly answered, 'Okay.' We were once again intoxicated by each other's company and it concerned me. Somewhere, in the recesses of my mind, I couldn't escape the fact that on more than a few occasions, our protective love for one another had only led to pain. That night, we did all the things we loved doing in the past, examining the pages of fashion magazines, listening to tapes and pawing through Tina's vast wardrobe. We dined, drank champagne and chatted until nearly four in the morning.

Tina told me, 'Ed, I'm selling the house. Erwin and I made a commitment. I want to move to Germany but Roger wants me to move to London.'

'Do what's really right for you. Don't let anyone dictate where you should live.'

'I only ever do what's right for me these days, Ed.'

'Haven't you always?!'

Tina laughed and said, 'I know returning to so-called normal society won't last long for you. Once you got this business under your skin, you can never let it go. You should stick with it, Ed. The biggest mistake you made was not signing over the rights to that great song you wrote, 'Pain'. If you signed the rights to us when Roger said you should, I would have recorded it and you would have ended up one of the best-known songwriters in the business. You blew it. I told you at the time that you were making a big mistake. You always have to sacrifice your first song in this business.'

'Yeah, I know that now, Tina. I didn't know it then.'

'There will be more opportunities for you, Ed. Don't make any silly mistakes next time you get your chance.'

Lying on Tina's bed, I stretched like a lazy cat before enquiring, 'What's happening with the family? What's going on with the kids? You see much of them? Come on girl, gimme the dirt.'

Tina shook her head as if totally fed up, rolled her eyes to the heavens and said, 'Ed, the kids are going through a hard time. They are beginning to search for their roots, and that's never easy for anyone.'

I lit a cigarette then settled back on oversized fluffy pillows, patting them into shape before positioning an ashtray close by. I watched Tina as she searched her thoughts. She looked everywhere and then nowhere before staring at her hands, then at me. The seconds seemed to pass like hours before she finally said, 'I'm a grandmother.'

'What? Tina sexy Turner a granny?' I was amazed.

Tina sat erect and repeated, 'I'm a grandmother. Ronnie. Ronnie went to Texas and met a local girl. She showered him with love. He loved her dearly.

They have a baby. And... and he splits his time being like me, then being like Ike.... then he goes back to her. He told Alline first. Then he told Muh. Then between Ronnie, Alline and Muh, well... they all chose the right time to tell me I was a grandmother. Well... my son and his wife have a baby. It's his and hers.'

Tina paused, then barked, 'I'm so fed up with them that if they want to talk to me, they call Rhonda or Muh. They seem to think that I'm the Valley bank! I simply cut them off, and keep up with them by speaking to Alline and Muh.'

Remembering the life-like doll Tina adored, I gingerly asked, 'How's the baby?'

Tina laughed for a moment and replied, 'Ed, at an after-show party that pop star Marilyn came up to me gushing that he wanted to see my baby. When he realised it was a doll, he screamed like a woman... well hell... I knew Baby had to be put away.'

It was nearing four in the morning when Tina and I began losing our battle against sleep. I tucked her in and before bidding her goodnight, I asked, 'Tina, I always wondered. I know you said it wasn't that sort of book but still, why... I mean after all our years together and after all we been through... why didn't you mention me in your book? Kenny Moore was shocked. So were Lejeune and Alline.'

Tina gazed through her sleepy eyes and repeated what she had told me a long time ago, 'Ed, forget about it. It wasn't that sort of book ...'

I instinctively went to my room and was surprised to find it the only room that hadn't been redesigned or redecorated. Everything was exactly as it was left many years before. The next morning I woke to the sound of familiar footsteps. It was Tina. 'Ed, throw a dressing gown on. Let's have breakfast on the patio.

Despite the fact that I was nursing a ferocious hangover, we drank fine coffee, shared a wholesome meal and laughed until my head throbbed. But throughout that magical morning, one thing hovered in the back of my mind. Somehow, I knew Tina was the feeling it, too. We were both enjoying something so much that it actually hurt. It was a key moment in both our lives. We both silently realised that enjoying each other always seemed to lead to some sort of pain. There she sat, in a dressing gown with the sun dancing through her hair and she was so breathtakingly beautiful. My heart contracted because I knew I had never loved anyone so much.

I suddenly said, 'Tina, it was great. I ... uh ... I have to go.'

She touched my hand and said, 'Ed, you'll find some things in your room that I want to give you.'

I squeezed her hand and ran off before she could see the tears forming in my eyes. In my room were an assortment of shirts, a few jackets, belts — all items perfectly suited to me and my tastes. It was just like old days. Tina had always done that in the past. I loaded my car while something gnawed away at my soul. I started feeling worried. It was almost like being in love.

When in love, people go back and get hurt time and time again until they realise it's finally time to stop. I jumped in the driver's seat of my car and switched on the engine, looking up to see Tina racing over. She breathlessly said, 'Ed, phone me.'

The look in her eyes told me what I already knew. While asking me to phone her, her eyes were pleading, 'please be strong and don't call.' I touched her fingertips and enjoyed the beautiful exchange of energy before lying, 'I will.'

As I drove away, the flash in Tina's eyes reflected my own feelings and fears. Something, somewhere, somehow, would always come between us. Slipping back into our cosy routine after years had passed was so damned easy that it was dangerous. We both knew what we had to do. Someone had to be strong and end it. Just as two people who were always one, we performed the last act ever as a single unit.

There was many a night I picked up the phone to call Tina but didn't. I wonder how many times she did the same.

Tina and I never saw or spoke to each other again.

IKE AND TINA TURNER REVUE

FAN CLUB NEWSLETTER

The Ike and Tina Turner Revue is certainly one
of the hottest acts in the world. This international
entertainment troupe is headlining in Japan and
will be covering the United States shortly there-
after. In addition to the Turners, the Revue
features The Ikettes and Family Vibes, the gifted
back-up musicians for Ike and Tina.

On the weekends, The Turners are busy performing
on the road. During the week, they are usually
at their new Bolic Sound recording studio - Ike
always at work at the console or the mikes, and
Tina doing her heavy songwriting, like "Feel Good"
and "Outrageous", the two sides of their new
United Artists 45. The Ike and Tina Turner Revue
is running hot via some new LPs such as "Blues Roots"
from Ike himself; Family Vibes' fantastic "Strange
Fruit" and "Feel Good", just released from Ike
and Tina.

And watch out this fall for a lot of Ike and Tina
on TV. They get it all together!!

Ike and Tina have four sons, Craig, Ike Jr.,
Michael, and Ronnie. While their parents are on
the road, the housekeeper takes care of the boys
who take after their folks when it comes to their
love and talent for music.

Ike and Tina have been thinking about doing a movie - maybe the
story of famous blues singer, Bessie Smith, which they could
really make go. Their record label is United Artists and this
is where they think they'll stay.

                                        continued.....

FAN CLUB NEWSLETTER
PRESIDENT: EDDIE HAMPTON
1310 NORTH LABREA AVENUE INGLEWOOD, CA. 90302 (213) 678-2632

Page Two

The Turners have been very successful in music.
Ike writes his own groovy hits. Tina takes care
of The Ikettes and their outasight steps. Ike
supervises the fantastic band. Together, Ike and
Tina are into their gold singles like "Proud Mary",
"A Fool In Love" and "Take You Higher". Tina's
voice burns the air and her body gyrates in space,
helping the world understand how energy became
atomic. In an hour's performance, Tina uses up at
least 350 calories. Off stage, her great energy
demands almost as much. Tina's the original
female powerhouse, and she'll never have a weight
problem and will always be slim and sexy.

Tina loves good food and loves to cook, so if you
have a favorite recipe, feel free to send it to
Ike and Tina.

Love and Peace!!

                    Written June 30, 1792
          by   EDDIE E. HAMPTON
                    FAN CLUB PRESIDENT

Index